Adolescent Development
and School Science

Adolescent Development and School Science

Based on the proceedings of an international seminar held at King's College Centre for Educational Studies, London in September 1987

Edited by
Philip Adey
with
Joan Bliss, John Head and Michael Shayer

The Falmer Press
(A member of the Taylor & Francis Group)
New York • Philadelphia • London

UK The Falmer Press, Falmer House, Barcombe, Lewes, East Sussex, BN8 5DL

USA The Falmer Press, Taylor & Francis Inc., 242 Cherry Street, Philadelphia, PA 19106-1906

First published 1989

British Library Cataloguing in Publication Data

Adolescent development and school science.
  1. Great Britain. Secondary schools. Mixed ability groups. Curriculum subjects: Science. Teaching. Implications of assessments of cognitive developments of students.
  1. Adey, Philip
  507'.1241
  ISBN 1-85000-428-5
  ISBN 1-85000-429-3 (pbk.)

Library of Congress Cataloging-in-Publication Data

Adolescent development and school science: based on the proceedings of an international seminar held at King's College Centre for Educational Studies, London, in September 1988 / edited by Philip Adey, with Joan Bliss, John Head and Michael Shayer.
    p. cm.
  Includes bibliographies and index.
  ISBN 1-85000-428-5 — ISBN 1-85000-429-3 (pbk.)
  1. Science—Study and teaching—Congresses. 2. Adolescent psychology—Congresses. 3. Adolescence—Congresses. I. Adey, Philip. II. King's College (University of London). Centre for Educational Studies.
  Q181.A1A36   1989
  507'.12—dc 19   88-32456

Typeset in 10/12 Caledonia by
Imago Publishing Ltd, Thame, Oxon

Jacket design by Caroline Archer

Printed in Great Britain by Taylor & Francis (Printers) Ltd, Basingstoke

Contents

Contents

Preface

Adolescent Development and School Science was the name of a seminar held at the Centre for Educational Studies (CES) of King's College, University of London, in September 1987. The seminar was attended by a small group of researchers concerned with the impact of cognitive and social development on the teaching of science in secondary schools, and with possible ways in which the science curriculum could be a context in which adolescents' development could be positively influenced.

Six plenary papers were given and these, together with a response to each, form the bases of chapters 3–8 of this volume. Working papers have been arranged in groups of three-five. Each group, with a general introduction, forms one of the chapters 9–14. The grouping of working papers into chapters was to some extent arbitrary, and too much should not be read into the chapter titles. An introduction by Paul Black, Director of CES and an overview by Ann Howe and Poul Thompsen form the first two chapters of the book. (At the seminar the overview was presented as a summary by the two 'Roving rapporteurs', but it forms an excellent advance organizer for some of the main themes in the papers.)

In order to keep the book within a manageable size and cost, all papers have been edited, some severely. Although the editors believe that all essential data and arguments have been retained, for the full texts of the papers as given at the seminar the reader is referred to the original authors. The names and addresses of seminar participants are given as an appendix. Notes were taken of discussions which followed most of the papers, and interpretations of these notes by the editors are given after each paper. Given this rather uncertain link between the discussions as they actually occurred, and as they appear in this volume, statements or opinions attributed to speakers in the discussions should be treated with caution.

Every person who attended the conference was active in some way, giving papers, chairing, reporting, or discussing (often all four at different times). Insofar as this volume is useful, it is thanks to every one of them. If you like the contents, praise the participants. If you do not like the presentation, blame me.

Philip Adey
King's College, London
May 1988.

1   Introduction

Paul Black

A central concern of this seminar must be with a theory of learners and learning which might be adequate to interpret and guide research, and even a vague perception of this should have methodological implications. Whilst these two issues are dealt with below, first I would like to draw attention to two related features which arise in several of the contributions. They concern respectively models of scientific knowledge and the importance of the context and purposes of people's knowledge.

Science — The Object of the Knowledge

The notion that there is a problem arising from a gap between how science is understood and how it ought to be understood, ought not to have received as much attention as it has without more discussion of the beliefs that are held about how it ought to be understood. The nature of any gap will depend in part on the nature of the science topic involved; dyeing, nutrition, energy, relativity each present a very different cognitive challenge, so there is a spectrum of problems.

One could talk in this way even if one took the nature of science for granted. Even if educational aims were only directed towards a scientist's science, a philosophy of science might still be needed as a guide for discerning its essentials. However, the problem becomes more subtle if we accept that the proper object of education in science has to be constructed by a transformation of scientist's knowledge and methods in the light of the aims of that education.

Such considerations affect the orientation of research in two ways. First, the choice of research topics and instruments is bound to be influenced by the view of the field of knowledge used in research: to take an extreme case, some test items discussed in the published literature seem to show that the researcher did not fully understand the topic of the research being investigated. Secondly, a programme aimed at understanding how mini-theories could be more effective would be rather different from one aimed at obliteration or coalition of them in order to establish the powerful macro-theories of high science: any theory to guide this field of research will have to be constructed in the context of a foreseen purpose and the different purposes quoted here would steer rather different theoretical developments, if successfully pursued.

Contexts and Purposes

Many have pointed out that pupils' alternative frameworks arise from the culture, including particularly the language, of their everyday lives but at least one significant question remains unanswered. Are we working with a constructivist child-as-scientist whose theories have been fashioned by encounters with reality, or with a socialized product of the culture, imbued with received wisdom? The answer may vary with age, and 'treatment' and prognosis could differ accordingly.

However, a different perspective is possible. Everyday learning and everyday theories are not just different, perhaps poor, forms of cognition. They are embedded in the contexts and purposes for which they have been developed and probably frequently modified. They have to serve the individual's need to take decisions, often of (literally) vital importance. Here, decisions about whether to rely on magic, or inscrutable authority, or on one's own capacity to understand or generate rational arguments, set limits and roles for cognition. These limits and roles must fashion its structures. They also have to conform to social exigencies. Children want a happy compromise of views, to the detriment of any objective aim of deciding who is right. In passing, it can be noted that outside of his or her laboratory, the scientist is as limited as anyone else, and has to buy houses, or decide about marriage, or vote in elections in the modes of knowing that others may have to adapt on scientific issues.

In summary, everyday contexts are profoundly different from the research or the teaching laboratory, and yet are both the origin of what pupils bring to education and the destination for what they take away. Concerns with effects of 'context' and 'motivation' are essential, but treatment of them as marginal trivializes a central issue. The aims to which research is directed, the scope of what might be demanded if any theory or model is to be adequate, and the methodological requirements (for example, on what counts as appropriate evaluation of effects of teaching) are all altered if the aim of learning is to help a mother decide about her family's needs rather than to help her children pass written examinations.

Models and Theory

Continued accumulation of data on pupils' ideas without an explicit model of learning can only be justified by faith in Baconian education. Few would think such faith justified. Collection of data needs to be informed by explicit assumptions and by sharply directed purposes, whilst the gap between any data and a working hypothesis or guide for teaching can only be crossed by way of a theory, albeit, but preferably not, an implicit one. Constructivism is the theoretical basis of much of recent work, but provides only the general conditions for a theory. For example, Piaget is certainly at home in the constructivist camp — but shares it with critics who reject any stage theory.

No model or theory is likely to emerge ready made from this seminar. If it were to do so, it would certainly be a complex specimen. It would have to deal with learning in relation to such issues as context dependence, transfer and/or context aggregation, range of applicability, level of abstraction, meta-cognition, dynamics of renewal and change, concept-process interactions, parallel processing, effects of motive, and perceptions of adequacy and of the role of outside authority.

The way in which inconsistencies may sometimes be accepted and at other times be reasons for reconstruction is an important puzzle which leads more generally to an interest in the dynamics of change. However, change under pressure from new inputs may only be a flux whereby the details change but the overall pattern persists. For progression in learning, particularly towards generalizations and abstractions which would represent qualitative improvement, radical reconstructions, perhaps at a meta-level, seem necessary. That such changes may take time and may actually lower capability whilst in progress, shows how subtle the issues might become. Piaget's equilibriation and accommodation will return to haunt us here — not surprisingly because he was committed in general to produce the sort of model that the current state of research now needs.

A system, whether or not it works with mini-theories combined with levels of operation able to reconstruct them, should have some form of structure. Most of the chapters, either implicitly or explicitly, look for or assume some guiding structure for cognition which determines the form, and potential for change, of particular aspects. Only in terms of such a model of overall structure can the many aspects of performance of any person, and their potential to change, be reconciled and understood. This need is perhaps concealed by research in which any one individual is explored on only one topic and on only one occasion.

Whilst much has been made in the past of the content-process dichotomy, the chapters in this book stress the relationship and similarity of these two. They must interact to describe any particular piece of learning, they may be inextricably packaged together in particular context binds, and they have to be remembered.

Finally, any theory should have something to say about the significance of any means of collecting evidence. Research enquiry with children is not to be construed as a dipstick or snapshot capturing a fixed state of the system. It is better seen as a piece of learning and as a conversation between researcher and pupil. Notions about dynamics of change and about the effect of perceptions, about the intent and authority of the enquirer, all apply: any theory has to collect and interpret its evidence within its own model. The 'collection' phase of research in this field may well, in retrospect, be seen to be gravely limited by the assumptions hidden inside its methodology.

Methodology

The issues of context and purpose indicate that understanding may develop through exploration of a wider range of topics and situations than those of school science, if only so that the latter can be both calibrated and put in context. Other school disciplines, or problems of understanding and decision which lie outside school contexts, may be helpful.

The breadth of issues explored in research may now need attention. There is little attention in published work to the interrelation of pupils' work across different tasks and problems. Most issues of consistency and structure require such work. Study of development and progression further requires patient cohort studies, requiring commitment by researchers (and pupils!) to testing over several years: without such study hypotheses about dynamics of structures cannot be tested. There is also a case for replacing the rather open-ended 'fishing expeditions' of much of the published research with studies designed and analyzed to explore ideas about structure.

Conclusion

Overall the message may be quite simple. This field of research has to be more clear about the object of its research and about the purposes which it is meant to serve. In the light of these, it needs to move to a more ambitious level in which theory, however naive, guides research design and interpretation, and takes critical charge of the methodology. Such general nostrums do not need a collection of chapters to justify them, but their bare bones may gain in attraction when clothed with the flesh that these chapters provide.

2   Overview of the Seminar

Ann C. Howe and Poul Thompsen

The two 'roving rapporteurs' at the seminar decided to divide up their duties: Ann Howe started the session, pointing to issues that had been raised on which there were rather obvious differences of viewpoint and opinion. Poul Thompson followed, focussing on areas in which there is broad and general agreement.

Issues and Differences

Of course it is impossible to do justice to the seminar in a short summary, particularly when our heads are still buzzing with ideas and impressions that will take a long time to sort out. It is our hope that we can be helpful in articulating some of the issues and sharpening the focus on positions that have been taken by the various speakers and participants. To articulate, to clarify, to sharpen issues — these are surely some of the main functions of seminars and conferences.

Many of the issues that became important during the seminar were raised by Paul Black in his opening remarks. He spoke particularly of the need for theory to drive and direct our work. I thought of that on Tuesday afternoon when I went down to Oxford Street to do a bit of shopping. I had thought I would remember from previous visits to London where certain shops were located, but when I got there I didn't remember a thing and muddled about for half-an-hour before I found a place to buy a map. It is tempting to draw an analogy between that experience and the situation of someone trying to do research without a theory to guide the effort.

Paul raised other points that prefigured the shape of the conference but I turn now to consider what I saw as the main issues of the seminar.

The Uses of Theory

The question is not the desirability of having a theory — everyone, I think, agrees on that — but whether theories now available are useful for understand-

5

ing and improving science education. And if one finds that available theories are not useful, how does one proceed? How does one decide what to observe, what data to collect, what to do with the data, how to interpret them?

Methodological Issues

No conference today can escape the question of empirical or quantitative versus ethnographic and qualitative methods. Questions of sampling, experimental design, and data analysis are involved. The issue here is how best to capture and represent the real-world complexities we encounter, both of the individual learner and those of the classroom. Are empirical, numerical data always necessary or will reports, observations, and impressions suffice? For what purposes and under what circumstances are different methods most appropriate?

Teaching Method

At issue here is whether we can devise or discover a general teaching method that will be effective for all science teaching. That is, should we look for one general method or should we take a more pluralistic approach?

Closely related to this is the issue of the desirability of using cognitive conflict in the classroom. The strong differences in regard to this issue were to me one of the surprises of the conference. In part this may be an issue of semantics. The word 'conflict' is troubling to some, perhaps because it is interpreted as open or overt conflict in the classroom. Another term might defuse the issue somewhat, but other questions would remain. One of these is whether cognitive conflict might lead some pupils down a path with a dead end, as some people who have thought about this believe. Another question that is of concern to some is whether cognitive conflict will lead to a contentious classroom, with the possibility of injured feelings and personal insult. And there are others who believe that cognitive conflict is a necessary condition for conceptual change.

Influence of Social Forces

The classroom is not isolated from social forces both within and without its four walls. Outside influences include the differential socialization of boys and girls, differences in social class and income, and the fact that pupils have their own individual lives and concerns. Inside the classroom there are differences of motivation, interest and intelligence and there is always the variety and complexity of interpersonal interactions. We all know that these exist, but the questions we have asked are *how* these realities should be taken into account and *how much* they should be taken into account in developing a theory of instruction, or even in planning and carrying out the instruction from day to day. To what extent can teaching be isolated from these influences? Some teachers see the classroom as a refuge from these influences; they try to provide an environment that is isolated from the outside world (which for some children has a lot of unpleasant aspects). But then there are others who see the outside world as always impinging on the classroom, and believe that the interactions between social pressures, such as the differential socialization of girls and boys, and transactions within the classroom cannot be ignored.

These then are issues that we all have to grapple with — the Piagetians, the Constructivists, and those who are neither. The seminar has brought forth new issues and reminded us of some old ones. A point that has been made by several participants is the need to respect children's views about phenomena and to establish an atmosphere where children feel free to risk their opinions and conclusions. The same applies to us. We too need to be able to risk our opinions and convictons in the knowledge that all points of view will receive the respect, if not the assent, of our colleagues. I believe that this seminar has been characterized by that spirit.

Common Ground

Where we have agreement and consensus, we can build common theories. Accordingly, I have tried to identify areas (apart from the agreement that we disagree!) where there seems to be some consensus:

1 Learning science is worthwhile — a tacit assumption which we have not even discussed. Why we *do* believe this could be the subject of another conference.

2 The content of the science curriculum has also not been a topic for debate. There do seem to be three components to present trends worldwide:
   — a movement away from the science that we are used to, towards a more human-centred form of science;
   — a change in pedagogy, from didactic teaching methods to more interactive modes;
   — a move away from content-centred, towards process-centred curricula.

   Maybe we all agree that these are the ways that the curriculum should go.

3 We do agree that there are problems that really need research even if we do not agree which are the problems that are the most important or which should take priority for funding.

4 Whether we come from a Piagetian, from a Constructivist, or from any other perspective that we may imagine, we do agree that conceptual

changes can be induced in children. Of course, the specific methodology of conceptual change depends on what you see as the root of the problem, but the idea that something can be done is common.

5 We do agree that conceptual change occurs by some sort of active construction on the part of the pupil. Rosalind Driver contrasts the 'traditional' approach where you just fill knowledge into the heads of the pupil with the Constructivist approach where you help pupils with active construction, but I think that no matter what school you belong to, you agree that conceptual changes do happen via active construction in the pupil's mind, and what the teacher needs to do is to help pupils to make these constructions.

6 Motivation has not really been discussed very much here. What is interesting for the pupils to begin with? There are papers concerned with boys' and girls' interest in science, and with interest deteriorating over time. It is well known that the amount of interest in science is more or less inversely related to the time for which children have been subjected to science teaching. Some years ago the idea of taking motivational psychology seriously was abandoned, but perhaps it is an important aspect of 'starting from where the child is'. I do not know whether or not we agree about that.

7 We do agree about the importance of metacognition. Either explicitly or implicitly it comes into almost all of the papers in this seminar. We believe that learning gets better, more effective, if the pupils know that they are learning and if they know what they are doing when they are learning. I have seen this from the Constructivist viewpoint, from the Piagetian viewpoint and from somewhere in-between.

8 We also agree that learning theories must be put into practice. Whatever one's theory of learning or of personal development, because we believe that learning science is worthwhile, our task is to put these theories into concrete contexts in the classroom. In that way, theories *will* guide practice. Just how these theories can be put into practice, I do not know. We have seen examples from the CLIS project and from the CASE project. We have also seen examples of something that looks like *no* theory leading to practice.

9 The last point I have is that we all agree about the crucial role of the teacher. We can have nice theories, we can devise smart teaching sequences, we can try these teaching sequences out and rely on the Hawthorne effect to get gains. The crucial point is whether you can go from this experimental situation to an all-population situation; whether you can make teachers follow the teaching sequence, not exactly as you have defined it, but in a way that is in accordance with their construction of how the teaching should be, so that it is not rote learning by the teachers (after all we do not want rote learning by pupils) but is really an internalization of the pedagogy of the scheme. We also know that the teacher can play a crucial role for good or for

bad. A bad teacher can really spoil anything, and a good teacher can make almost any teaching scheme good.

The story of a man looking under a lamp-post for a coin he has dropped is well known. A second man asks him "Are you sure you dropped the coin here?" 'No of course I didn't, I dropped it over there', the first man says, 'I'm looking here because this is where the light is.' I feel that this may say something about researchers in science education, working under different lamp-posts. One is standing here trying to make the light a bit brighter, widening the cone of light, while another over there is working under his lamp-post illuminating a different part of science education. One lamp may stand in the personal part of science education, another in the social part, and others in cognitive parts.

In conclusion I would like to draw attention to one lamp-post that I have missed at this conference — that of artificial intelligence. At the moment there is lot of work going on about how the brain works, physiological brain reasearch about perception and processing within the brain. My friends who work in this area tell me that when you are exposed to some new phenomenon, the first thing that happens is that in the deep part of your brain you give a preliminary value to it: 'is it interesting or not?' If it is not, you don't give it any more attention at all. (That is where motivation comes in). If it *is* interesting then after about 10 seconds or so it enters the right hemishphere, which tries to make some holistic sense of the event: 'what's all this about?' If this succeeds, processing then goes across to the left hemisphere where the brain tries to deal with it analytically. If this picture represents, more or less, the way that we attend to the world, then it has important implications for the methodology of science education.

Finally, to return to my lamp-post analogy: Paul Black says that we need a theory. I believe that we need more than one theory. We need lamp-posts here and there, and we need to work out from each of these lamp-posts. If the lamp-posts are good enough, they will shine brighter and their light will spread further. If a lamp-post is inadequate it's light will just whither away under the brightness of the others. We may hope that in the end we will have the whole thing illuminated.

DISCUSSION: These are some of the points made from the floor following Howe and Thompsen's presentation. They relate to different participants' views of the seminar as a whole, rather than to the presentation itself.

A distinction needs to be made between those who think they know what to tell teachers, to improve practice in whatever direction is deemed desirable, and those who would give the responsibility of improving practice to the teachers themselves. We have perhaps seen too much of the former in this seminar.

Teachers do not necessarily trust the feelings of other teachers, and may not like to see the curriculum driven by teachers without significant input from researchers and other academics who have more time and wider experience.

During the last twenty years educators have followed the major swing in psychology away from a study of rats and pigeons towards what might be termed 'group grope' or 'feels good' psychology. Although a strand of the seminar has shown something of reaction to this swing, there is still little which could be described as a scientific approach to learning.

The seminar has had too much on school science, and not enough on adolescent development.

We should be able to go forward with the notion that we are all interested in the curriculum tasks that will assist in leading a child from a state A to a (more desirable) state B. Apart from agreeing on what constitutes 'more desirable', the questions around the 'curriculum tasks' are whether they are most usefully informed by the nature of the science concepts, by the children's prior conceptions, or by the psychological factors which mediate learning.

There has been a remarkable meeting of minds here, a preparedness to listen to other people's points of view and, through better understanding, to seek common ground.

3 Research on Advanced Reasoning, Concept Acquisition and a Theory of Science Instruction

Anton E. Lawson

Introduction

The purpose of this chapter is to present a general theory of science instruction which has as its aim the enhancement of students' ability to successfully apply advanced reasoning patterns and their acquisition of scientifically acceptable conceptual systems. I will first review a series of studies conducted by myself and some of my colleagues during the past ten years which have investigated the use of advanced reasoning patterns in students grades six through college and the interaction of these patterns and students' ability to acquire appropriate scientific concepts. This review will provide the empirical background for the introduction of the instructional theory. I will conclude with a few examples of how the theory can be put into practice and tested in the classroom.

Use of Advanced Reasoning Patterns Across Adolescence

Lawson, Karplus and Adi (1978) reported the results of a survey of reasoning patterns used by a sample of students ages 11.5 to 20.0 years from the San Francisco Bay Area in the United States. Students were tested on their ability to use proportional, probabilistic, and correlational reasoning as well as rules of propositional logic. Problems included the Pouring Water Task requiring use of proportional reasoning (see figure 3.1), the Mice Puzzle requiring use of correlational reasoning (see figure 3.2) and the Four Card Task (from Wason and Johnson-Laird, 1972) requiring use of rules of propositional logic (see figure 3.3).

Results of that survey are shown in figure 3.4 which compares percentage of correct responses given on the seven problems with grade in school. The Pouring Water Task is shown as item 1. Item 3 is the Mice Puzzle and item 7 is the Four Card Task. As can be seen, with the exception of the two propositional

Anton E. Lawson

Figure 3.1   Pouring Water

Water is poured into a wide cylinder
up to the 4th mark. (see A).

This water rises to the 6th mark when
poured into a narrow cylinder. (see B).

Water is now poured into the *wide*
cylinder up to the 6th mark.

Question: How high would this water
rise if it were poured into the narrow
cylinder?

Answer: _____

Please show how you found your
answer.

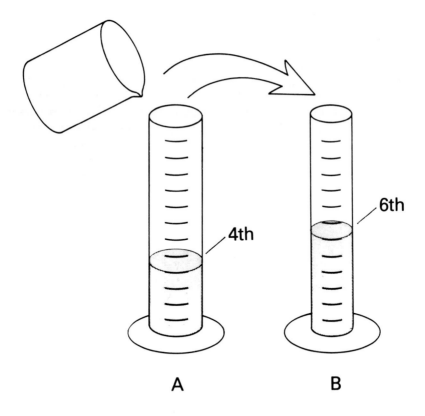

A   B

Figure 3.2   The Mice Puzzle

Farmer Brown was observing the mice that live in his field. He discovered that all of them were either fat or thin. Also, all of them had either black tails or white tails. This made him wonder if there might be a relation between the size of the mice and the color of their tails. So he captured all of the mice in one part of his field and observed them. Below are the mice that he captured. Do you think there is a relation between the size of the mice and the color of their tails?

YES   NO   (circle one)

Please explain your choice.

Anton E. Lawson
Figure 3.3   The Four Cards

Below are pictures of four cards.

You know that each of these cards has a letter on one of its sides and a number on its other side. Read the following rule:

If a card has a vowel on one side, then
it has an even number on the other side.

You want to find out whether this rule is true or false. In the spaces below name those cards, and only those cards, that <u>need</u> to be turned over to find this out.

| Would you <u>need</u> to know what is on the other side of this card?

Why? _____
_____
_____ | **E** | Would you <u>need</u> to know what is on the other side of this card?

Why? _____
_____
_____ | **4** |
| Would you <u>need</u> to know what is on the other side of this card?

Why? _____
_____ | **K** | Would you <u>need</u> to know what is on the other side of this card?

Why? _____
_____ | **7** |

logic items, student performance improved considerably with age/grade. The sixth graders were generally unsuccessful while the college students were generally successful. Further improvements with age were generally linear.

I view these results as extremely important for two reasons. First they indicate that the use of advanced reasoning patterns does, in fact, improve with age during adolescence and second they indicate that the improvements do not arise directly as a consequence of instruction. This is clear on at least two counts. First proportions are typically taught in grades 6, 7 and 8 yet sixth, seventh and eighth graders typically did not use proportions while the improvement in use of proportions continued through grades 10 to 13–14. Second, correlations are not taught at all in grades 6 through 13–14 yet steady improvement on the correlational reasoning items was found from grade to grade. Two important questions are raised. If schooling is not responsible for improved use of advanced reasoning patterns, then what is? Further, why do some students at any particular grade successfully use the reasoning patterns while others do not?

The relatively poor performance on the propositional logic items is of interest as well. These items involved familiar materials (for example, cards, letters, and numbers) and required use of the most basic of rules of propositional logic yet were failed by the majority of students at all grade levels including students who were successful on the other items. Why were these items so difficult?

The student responses were subjected to a principal components analysis

Figure 3.4   Graphical presentation of percentage of subjects responding correctly to each of the test items at each grade level

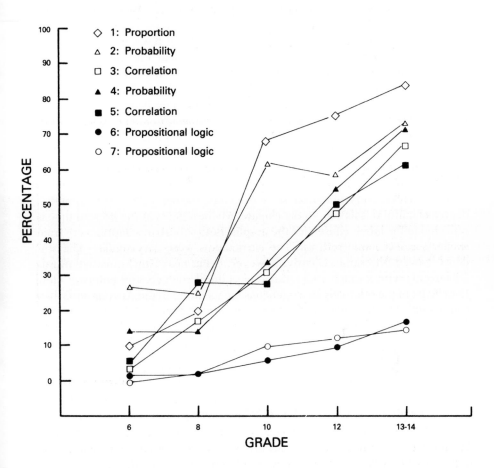

to determine the number of psychological 'factors' which presumably account for successful performance. The analysis showed two factors with items 1–5 clustering near factor 1 and items 6 and 7 clustering near factor 2. This result indicates that the seven items are most likely measuring only two psychological factors. Items 1–5 require use of one of them while items 6 and 7 require use of the other. Thus it would then appear that whatever 'develops' across age and causes the improved performance on items 1–5 is not a series of separate developments but is instead a single development. Of course this is precisely what Piagetian theory predicts. Further its relationship to propositional logic is at best unclear and at worst, none at all and this is precisely what Piagetian theory does *not* predict.

Use of Advanced Reasoning Patterns in Different Populations

Lawson and Bealer (1984) administered the Pour Water Task and the Mice Puzzle to sixth, eighth, tenth and twelfth grade students from two school districts in Arizona. One district was in a rural small town in South-eastern Arizona. The other was in a suburban community near Phoenix. Figures 3.5 and 3.6 compare performance across age for the two Arizona districts on the two problems with each other and with the San Francisco Bay Area sample. The San Francisco sample is labelled suburban heterogeneous while the Phoenix, Arizona sample is labelled suburban homogeneous. The South-eastern Arizona sample is labelled rural. The graphs show clear improvement with age for all three samples but also show clear superiority for the suburban heterogeneous sample. The obvious question is, what causes the superiority? Clearly there is no easy answer to this question and numerous previous studies have implicated everything from the curriculum, socioeconomic level, genetics, degree of cultural isolation, to the climate. My best guess at the present time is reflected in the labels chosen for the graphs. Both suburban samples were from similar socioeconomic settings. The curriculums were very similar. The students 'looked' the same. Clearly, however, living near San Francisco affords adolescents with a much wider range of cultural contacts and points of view than living in the relatively homogeneous monoculture in the Arizona suburban community. My view is that whatever is acquired during adolescence needed for successful performance on these tasks requires the confrontation with opposing points of view for its emergence. Isolated rural communities or suburban monocultures presumably do not provide these confrontations.

Relationship with Academic Achievement

What relationship, if any, does performance on these tasks have with academic achievement? A large number of studies have sought to answer this question with the general finding similar to that shown in table 3.1 (from Lawson, 1982). The table reports correlation coefficients among two Piagetian Tasks (Bending Rods and Balance Beam), my Classroom Test of Formal Reasoning (Lawson, 1978), and school achievement in a sample of seventy two ninth grade students (mean age 15.1 years) as measured by the *Iowa Tests of Educational Development* (Science Research Associates, 1970). Note that the coefficients comparing task performance and achievement are all positive and substantial. Note also that they are *not* higher for science and mathematics achievement than for reading and social studies achievement. These results support the hypothesis that whatever reasoning patterns or unified set of reasoning patterns the tasks measure it is not used solely in science and mathematics but rather appears to be of general importance. Thus it would appear to be of considerable importance for educators to not only identify what this unity is but

Figure 3.5   Percentage of correct responses on the Pouring Water problem requiring proportional reasoning.

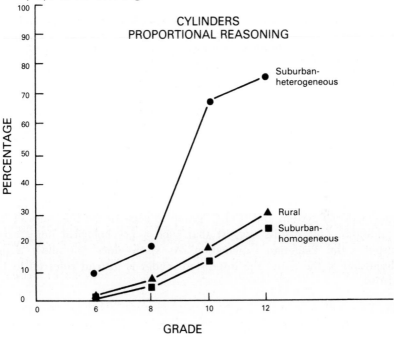

Figure 3.6   Percentage of correct responses on the Mice Tails problem requiring correlational reasoning.

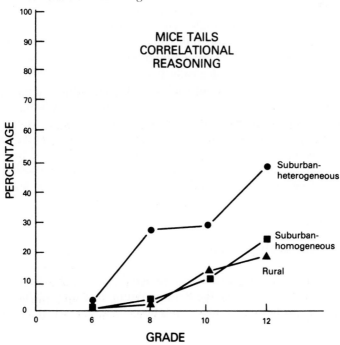

Table 3.1   Pearson Product-Moment Correlation Coefficients Among Piagetian Measures of Formal Reasoning and Achievement Measures

	Achievement					
Piagetian Measures	Reading	Language arts	Mathematics	Composite score	Social studies	Science
Bending rods task	.66	.51	.55	.61	.69	.68
Balance beam task	.61	.42	.53	.56	.58	.58
Summed task score	.67	.48	.55	.62	.65	.57
Classroom test total	.69	.60	.70	.73	.72	.69

to develop and implement instruction to ensure that a greater percentage of students aquire it (cf. Shayer and Adey, 1981).

It should be pointed out that Piagetian theory postulates the existence of a combinatorial system and 'INRC' group to account for the unity of 'formal' operations. Our results suggest that such a psychological unity exists but disputes the Piagetian explanation. As space does not allow a detailed discussion of the issue, the interested reader is instead referred to Lawson (1979).

The Central Question

The central question which follows from the preceding discussion is simply this: What is the nature of the psychological unity required to solve tasks such as the Pouring Water Task and Mice Puzzle? To simplify matters further in hopes of making an answer possible yet hopefully still general and useful, let us limit our discussion to one task — the Pouring Water Task. This seems a reasonable choice as it seems to be psychologically tied to other important tasks yet is relatively straightforward and yields only a few types of student responses. Thus our central question becomes, what general reasoning pattern is required to solve the Pouring Water Task? Or said another way, why do some students correctly choose a proportions strategy and predict that the water will rise to 9 while other students incorrectly choose an additive strategy and predict the water will rise to 8? Keep in mind that it has already been clearly shown that 'knowing' how to solve a problem such as $4/6 = 6/x$ for x in no way assures that the student will respond with a 9 to the Pouring Water Task.

The General Hypothesis

An answer to the preceding question is expected to reveal the key reasoning pattern that enables one to solve the Pouring Water Task and related tasks. As Piagetian theory has held a prominent position in the psychology of reasoning for many years it should be of considerable interest to consider Piaget's early position regarding the acquisition of advanced reasoning. Piaget (1928) had this to say:

> The development of logical reasoning occurs as a consequence of 'the shock of our thoughts coming into contact with others', which produces doubt and the desire to prove ...
>
> The social need to share the thought of others and to communicate our own with success is at the root of our need for verification. Proof is the outcome of *argument* ...
>
> Argument is therefore, the backbone of verification. *Logical reasoning is an argument which we have with ourselves,* and produces internally the features of a real argument. (p 204)

In other words, Piaget seems to be saying that reasoning follows patterns of external verbal arguments, i.e., is the internalized pattern of verbal arguments.

Also consider Vygotsky's (1962) position concerning the internalization of patterns of verbal discourse. Vygotsky views speech as social in origin and only with time does it come to have *self-directive* properties that eventually result in internalized, verbalized thought.

Finally, consider Luria's (1961) proposed four steps in the differentiation of language to regulate behavior:

1 The child learns the meaning of words.
2 Language can activate behavior but not limit it.
3 Language can activate or inhibit behavior via communication from an external source.
4 The internalization of language can serve a self-regulating function through instructions to oneself.

The preceding quotations suggest the following general hypothesis regarding the nature and origin of advanced reasoning. Advanced reasoning consists of the regulation of behavior via an internalized language driven process used to evaluate the correctness of alternative imagined behaviors. More specifically the pattern of this internalized verbal thought follows patterns of external logical argumentation made in social contexts. Thus advanced reasoning is social in origin.

The Specific Hypothesis

More specifically still I am advancing the hypothesis that the key internalized pattern of discourse is isomorphic with the scientific falsification strategy where alternative hypotheses are *imagined* and advanced to answer a causal question. Reasoning proceeds as follows: *If* the hypothesis is correct *and* some sort of manipulation is performed, *then* specific logically deducible consequences should occur (predictions). If these logical consequences do not occur (i.e., a result other than that predicted occurs), one can, *therefore*, conclude that the hypothesis is probably wrong (i.e., has been falsified) and an alternative hypothesis needs to be considered. Logicians refer to such a reasoning pattern as reductio ad absurdum (for example, Ambrose and Lazarowitz, 1948).

Although it is not assumed that the specifics of each students' reasoning on the Pouring Water Task is identical, in general it is assumed that three general scenarios exist. In the first scenario the student focuses on the fact that the water rose *two more* units from 4 to 6 hence the notion of addition 'pops' into his/her head. Once this notion 'pops' into the head it is simply applied to solve the task $4 + 2 = 6$, therefore, $6 + 2 = 8$.

In the second scenario the student also focusses on the rise of water *two more* units from 4 to 6 and likewise the notion of addition 'pops' into his/her head yet he/she pauses to consider the consequences of this 'hypothesis' in other cases, for example, what would happen if there were only one unit in the wide cylinder? Does it seem reasonable that one unit would rise to $1 + 2 = 3$ units if poured into the narrow cylinder? Or would two units in the narrow cylinder disappear if poured into the wide cylinder $2 - 2 = 0$? Obviously not, as water cannot disappear simply by pouring it from one container to another! Thus this type of reasoning involves generating predictions and comparing them with other known facts (results) and allows the student to falsify the addition hypothesis. Thus the second scenario student eliminates the additive strategy but fails to consider the correct proportions strategy and ends up guessing (for example, $7\frac{1}{2}$, 14, 10, etc.).

The third scenario is similar to the second except that the student quickly eliminates the incorrect additive hypothesis and hypothesizes the proportions strategy and correctly solves the problem.

Thus I am hypothesizing that solution of the Pouring Water Task requires use of an internalized language driven falsification process to eliminate use of the developmentally earlier more salient additive hypothesis prior to adopting the less salient but more appropriate proportions hypothesis. Hence the task is an indirect measure of the extent to which this hypothetico-deductive linguistic falsification pattern has been internalized. The quantitative answers of 8 vs. $7\frac{1}{2}$, 10, 14 vs. 9 reflect qualitatively different stages in the internalization of this pattern.

Testing the Hypothesis: The Four Cards

To test this hypothesis a more direct measure of this linguistic pattern is needed. But what can be used as a direct measure? The Wason Four Card Task appears to require use of a hypothetico-deductive pattern which can lead to the falsification of hypotheses [i.e., If a card has a vowel (p) on one side, then it has an even number on the other side (q), given a card with a 7 on one side (q̄), the card must be turned out to see if it has a vowel (p) on the other side because if it

Table 3.2   Immediate and Delayed Four-Card Post-test Performance with Developmental Level (n = 100)

| | Immediate Post-test | | | Delayed Post-test | |
	Incorrect	*Correct*		*Incorrect*	*Correct*
Concrete	28	17	Concrete	36	9
Formal	11	44	Formal	16	39
	$x^2 = 16.82$, $p < .001$			$x^2 = 23.72$, $p. < .001$	

does, then you have $p \cdot \bar{q}$ which falsifies $p \supset q$]. Yet as we have seen, almost no-one solves the Four Card Task correctly upon initial testing and it appears not to be psychologically related to the Pouring Water Task (for example, Lawson, Karplus, and Adi, 1978; Wason and Johnson-Laird, 1972).

An alternative hypothesis can be advanced however. That hypothesis is simply that the Four Card Task is in fact a good measure of this pattern of advanced reasoning — however, initial confrontation with the Four Card Task yields confusion and erroneous responses bacause the problem is cast in the absolute terms of the logician not the probabilistic terms of the 'real' world in which causal hypotheses are generated and tested and in which the reasoning patterns develop in the first place. Accordingly the prediction follows that once hypothetico-deductive reasoners are briefly told what is expected of them (using a verbal argument which embodies the pattern of hypothetico-deductive reasoning) they will immediately assimilate the instructions and be able to apply the correct reasoning to novel yet logically isomorphic problems. Conversely people who have not yet internalized the necessary hypothetico-deductive linguistic pattern will not be able to assimilate the brief verbal instruction, will not be able to apply the correct reasoning, and will fail the logically isomorphic transfer task.

To test this prediction a sample of 100 high school students ages 14.9 years to 19.1 years, mean age = 16.4 years who were administered the Pouring Water Task and responded with an 8 or a 9 were also administered the Four Card Task in individual interviews. Only two of the 100 Ss (both responded with a 9 to the Pouring Water Task) correctly selected the E and 7 cards upon initial testing. Immediately following the initial testing, Ss were informed of their mistakes. Instruction was direct and amounted to telling Ss which cards they should have turned over and why.

Immediately following this direct minimal instruction another set of four cards showing a triangle, a square, green dots and red dots was placed in front of the S with another rule as follows: If a card has a triangle on one side, then it has green dots on the other side. The s was then asked which cards should be turned over to test the rule. Results are shown in table 3.2. The table shows that of the forty-five additive Ss only 17 (38 per cent) gave correct responses on the transfer problem while 44 of the 55 proportional Ss (80 per cent) did so. The χ^2 value of 16.82 indicates a highly significant relationship (p < 0.001) between performance on the Pouring Water Task and performance on the logic problem thus providing support for the study's major hypothesis.

To determine whether or not this significant difference in performance would last, an additional logic problem was administered one month later. This delayed post-test logic problem involved a new rule (If there is a fish on one side, then there is an odd number on the other side) and four new cards (fish, dog, odd number, even number.) Results of the delayed post-test problem, also shown in table 3.2, were generally similar to those for the immediate post-test. Only 9 of the 45 additive Ss (20 per cent) gave correct responses while 39 of the 55 proportional Ss (71 per cent) did so. The χ^2 value of 23.72 again showed a highly significant (p < 0.001) relationship between Pour Water Task performance and logic problem performance indicating that, for the most part, additive Ss did not assimilate the brief verbal instruction while proportional Ss did and that they retained those instructions for one month (details can be found in Lawson, 1987).

Additional support for the hypothesis that the Pouring Water Task requires use of an internalized pattern of hypothetico-deductive reasoning of the form just described was obtained by Lawson and Bealer, (1984).

A New Research Tradition

Thus far I have argued that advanced reasoning depends upon the internalization of social discourse of the hypothetico-deductive form if . . . and . . . then . . . therefore utilized to argue the merits and demerits of alternative propositions (hypotheses). Once the child or adolescent has internalized this verbal pattern of discourse to the extent that he/she can use it to guide his own thinking (internal discourse) he/she has acquired a new and powerful device for guiding behavior. He/she no longer must depend upon others to make decisions regarding the truth or falsity of competing explanations. He/she can internally weigh the evidence for him/herself.

It seems to me that this view of the development of advanced reasoning and its emphasis on alternative conceptions or misconceptions leads quite naturally to a theory of science instruction which quite happily has the potential to unite two previously competing research traditions in science education-namely the Piagetian tradition with its emphasis on reasoning and 'hands on' discovery learning and the Ausubelian tradition with its emphasis on concept acquisition and verbal learning.

Importantly over the past few years a new research tradition has emerged which owes its existence in part to Piagetian theory and in part to Ausubelian theory. That research tradition, which focusses on students' alternative conceptions and misconceptions (for example, Driver, 1981; Clement, 1986; Posner, Strike, Hewson and Gertzog, 1982; Anderson and Smith, 1986;

Halloun and Hestenes, 1985) provides an opportunity to synthesize the best of the Piagetian and Ausubelian traditions into a view of the learner and the learning process which fills a gap created by these two traditions and leads directly to a theory of instruction, which if implemented should produce learners not only with adequate understanding of domain specific scientific concepts, but with truly general reasoning skills of the sort classified as 'formal operational' by Piaget.

The primary purpose of the remainder of this chapter is to attempt to substantiate that claim through explication and extension of a model of classroom instruction known as the learning cycle (cf., Atkin and Karplus, 1962; Karplus *et al*, 1976). The learning cycle, as originally conceived, is too simplistic and limited to serve as a general guide to instructional practice which has both the teaching of domain specific science concepts and the development of general reasoning patterns as primary aims. Nevertheless it is proposed that extension and differentiation of the original learning cycle into three types of learning cycles referred to as (i) descriptive, (ii) empirical-inductive; and (iii) hypothetical-deductive, can form the basis of a theoretically satisfactory and educationally practical model of instruction to accomplish these aims.

Misconceptions and Reasoning Patterns: A Possible Link

What, if any, relationship exists between student misconceptions and reasoning ability? Parmenedes, the ancient Greek philosopher stated that 'the senses deceive us'. Personal experience provides the basis for knowledge that is at times inaccurate (for example, optical illusions, Piagetian non-conservation responses). Leading naturalists of the past advocated ideas such as spontaneous generation, special creation, and the inheritance of acquired characteristics. These ideas have their roots in personal experience. Maggots appear to be spontaneously generated from rotting flesh; people create objects so living objects must also be created by 'people' (with special God-like properties); children look like their parents so changes in the appearance of the parent will cause changes in the appearance of an as-yet-to-be-born child.

The rejection of these ideas during the past required the generation of alternative hypotheses and their test through hypothetico-deductive reasoning, experimentation, data collection and considerable argumentation. Open-minded scientists who became aware of these alternative ideas (for example, evolution, natural selection, genetics), the available evidence, and were able to follow the lines of reasoning used to argue the cases, were generally convinced and were able to overcome prior 'misconceptions' in favor of the more scientifically accurate conceptions.

By analogy, it can be hypothesized that the same thing can happen in the science classroom. For students to modify prior conceptions they must become aware of the scientific conceptions, as well as their own alternative conception(s), and they must become aware of the evidence *and* reasoning which bears on the validity of the alternative conceptions. In other words, they must be able logically to 'see' how the evidence supports the scientific conceptions and contradicts the prior alternative(s) (cf., Posner, Strike, Hewson and Gertzog, 1982). Logically 'seeing' this, however, requires the use of hypothetico-deductive reasoning.

Because hypothetico-deductive reasoning is precisely that used to evaluate alternative conceptions in a logical manner, students who have failed to internalize this reasoning pattern would be expected to hold more misconceptions than their hypothetico-deductive peers. A recent study by Lawson and Thompson (1987) found this to be precisely the case. On a test following instruction on concepts of evolution and genetics, a sample of empirico-inductive seventh grade students revealed an average of 1.67 misconceptions per student while their hypothetico-deductive classmates held only 0.43 misconceptions per student. The conclusion is simply this: students who have internalized the hypothetico-deductive reasoning pattern hold fewer misconceptions because this pattern is necessary to overcome prior misconceptions.

The Process of Conceptual Change — Equilibration

We can, therefore, conclude that teaching scientific concepts requires much more than simply verbally introducing students to those concepts. Rather, students must occasionally unlearn their own misconceptions. Anderson and Smith (1986) refer to teaching procedures which attempt to induce students to discard misconceptions in favor of scientifically valid conceptions as 'conceptual change teaching' and as we have seen, success depends in part on the reasoning patterns of the students.

Assuming that students are capable, how are misconceptions modified or discarded during the learning process? This is a difficult question to answer primarily because the process takes place inside students' heads often at a subconscious level, thus it is not only hidden from the researcher but is sometimes hidden from the subject himself! To get a handle on this problem Howard Gruber (Gruber and Barrett, 1974) analyzed the thinking of Charles Darwin during the time period from 1832 to 1838 when he underwent a conceptual change from a creationist perspective of the world (a misconception) to that of an evolutionist (a currently valid scientific conception). Fortunately for Gruber and for us, Darwin left a record of his thinking during that time period in copious diaries. Figure 3.7 highlights the major changes in his thinking during that time.

In Piagetian terms figure 3.7(a) represents a state of conceptual equilibrium as Darwin's creationist concepts are internally consistent and can be adequately used to assimilate environmental input. From the point of view of modern science, however, his ideas represent a number of scientific misconceptions. Figure 3.7(b) represents cognitive disequilibrium because a contradiction is implied by realization that the physical world actually changes while the

Figure 3.7 Charles Darwin's changing world view from 1832 to 1838 as an example of mental equilibration (after Gruber and Barrett, 1974).

(a) 1832 and before: The Creator (C) made an organic world (O) and a physical world (P): O was perfectly adapted to P. Mental equilibrium exists.

(b) 1832–1834: The physical world undergoes continuous change, governed by natural forces as summarized in Lyell's *Principles of Geology*. A logical contradiction is implied which induces a state of disequilibrium.

(c) 1835: Activities of organisms contribute to changes in the physical world (e.g., coral reefs). Disequilibrium persists.

(d) 1836–1837: Changes in the physical world imply changes in the organic world if adaptation is to be maintained; the direct action of the physical environment "induces" organic adaptations. Equilibrium is partially restored.

(e) 1838 and after: The physical and organic worlds continuously interact and induce reciprocal changes to maintain adaptations. The role of the creator is unclear. He may have set the system into existence yet stands outside. Mental equilibrium is restored at a higher, more complex plane.

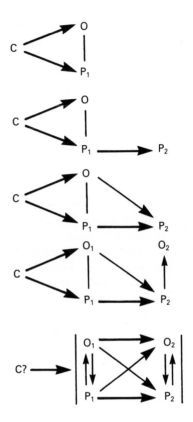

organic world does not, yet the organic world must somehow remain perfectly adapted to the changing physical world. Since this is clearly not possible without the organic world also changing (which, of course, would contradict the initial creationist doctrine) a cognitive conflict, i.e., state of disequilibrium, exists. Notice that this state of disequilibrium in Darwin's mind existed for more than four years in spite of the fact that it could be easily resolved merely by imagining that the organic world also changes!

The fact that disequilibrium persisted for such a long time in spite of the fact that the necessary modification in thinking is logically trivial, illustrates just how tenacious prior misconceptions can be. Figure 3.7(c) represents the beginning of mental accommodation with the realization that the organic world can cause changes in the physical world while Figure 3.7(d) finally recognizes that the organic world must also change in response to changes in the physical world. Figure 3.7(e) represents the final accommodation and restoration of equilibrium with a more complex and accurate model of organic and physical world interactions. It should be noted, however, that the role of the creator is not entirely clear, therefore, it seems safe to assume that Darwin's new plane of equilibrium, although able to assimilate more experiential data, is not as conceptually 'stable' as his initial naive equilibrium.

In summary, the process of testing alternative conceptions and the selection of a scientifically valid conception appears to involve the process of equilibration as described by Piaget. According to Piagetian theory, reasoning patterns are internalized during the process of equilibration, yet Darwin was most assuredly an accomplished thinker at the outset. Further, Darwin most certainly was not engaged in this activity for the purpose of acquiring new reasoning patterns. Rather Darwin was motivated by a desire conceptually to understand nature. Nevertheless, if we continue to accept the Piagetian hypothesis that the process of equilibration can lead to the internalization of reasoning patterns we must ask how? The answer previously proposed is simply this. Adequate evaluation of evidence and arguments to support or refute alternative causal hypotheses requires the use of the hypothetico-deductive reasoning pattern, therefore, when one engages in this enterprise, that reasoning pattern is exercised (if already internalized) or becomes internalized as one becomes aware of the patterns of verbal discourse used by others.

The Learning Cycle

The central thesis of the present chapter is that the research tradition into student alternative conceptions and that into student reasoning patterns both imply the same method of instruction because examining the adequacy of prior conceptions forces people to argue about and reflect on the *reasons* for those conceptions which in turn provides the opportunity to abstract the forms of argumentation (patterns of reasoning) from the external arguments that arise when people with opposing conceptions come face to face. *The central instructional hypothesis is that correct use of the learning cycle provides the opportunity for students to reveal their prior conceptions/misconceptions and the opportunity to debate and test them which can result not only in the improvement of students' conceptual knowledge but also in an increased awareness of and ability to use the reasoning patterns involved in the generation and test of that conceptual knowledge.*

Although there are the three types of learning cycles (not all equally effective at producing argument, disequilibrium, and improved reasoning) they all follow the general three-phase sequence of exploration, term introduction, and concept application. During EXPLORATION, the students learn through their own actions and reactions in a new situation. In this phase they explore new materials with minimal guidance. The new experience should raise questions or complexities that they cannot resolve with their present conceptions or accustomed patterns of reasoning. In other words, it provides the opportunity for students to voice potentially conflicting and at least partially inadequate ideas (misconceptions) that can spark debate and an analysis of the *reasons* for their ideas. Exploration also leads to the identification of a pattern of regularity in the phenomenon explored such as the straight line which occurs on a graph when volume is plotted against mass of brass objects of varying sizes and shapes.

The second phase, TERM INTRODUCTION, starts with the introduction of a new term or terms, such as density, that is used to label the pattern discovered during EXPLORATION. The term(s) may be introduced by the teacher, the textbook, a film, or another medium. This step always follows EXPLORATION and relates directly to the pattern discovered during the EXPLORATION activity. Students should be encouraged to identify as much of a new pattern as possible before it is revealed to the class, but expecting students to discover all of the complex patterns of modern science is unrealistic.

In the last phase of the learning cycle, CONCEPT APPLICATION, students apply the new term and/or reasoning pattern to additional examples. The CONCEPT APPLICATION phase is necessary for some students to recognize the pattern and separate it from its specific contexts and/or to generalize it to other contexts. Thus, without a number and variety of applications, the pattern may not be recognized or its generality may remain restricted to the context used during its definition.

Note that the last phase is referred to as CONCEPT APPLICATION while the previous phase was labeled TERM INTRODUCTION. I am defining a concept as a mental pattern (i.e., a pattern in one's mind) that is accessed by a verbal or written symbol (i.e., a term). Thus a concept is the recognized pattern plus the term. A person can have the pattern *or* the term but he does not have the *concept* until he has both. Teachers can introduce terms to students but students must recognize the pattern themselves. EXPLORATION provides the opportunity for students to discover the pattern. TERM INTRODUCTION provides the teacher with the opportunity to introduce the term which refers to the pattern and it provides students an initial opportunity to link the pattern with the term, thus acquire the concept. Finally, CONCEPT APPLICATION allows students repeated opportunities to recognize the pattern and/or to discover applications of the new concept in new contexts.

Three Types of Learning Cycles

Learning cycles can be classified as one of three types — descriptive, empirical-inductive, and hypothetical-deductive. The essential difference among the three types of learning cycles is the degree to which students either gather data in a purely descriptive fashion (not guided by explicit hypotheses they wish to test) or initially set out to test hypotheses in a controlled fashion. The three types of learning cycles, therefore, represent three points along a continuum from descriptive to experimental science. They obviously place differing demands on student initiative, knowledge, and reasoning ability. In terms of student reasoning ability, descriptive learning cycles generally require only descriptive reasoning patterns while hypothetical-deductive learning cycles demand use of hypothetico-deductive reasoning patterns. Empirical-inductive learning cycles are intermediate and generally involve reasoning that can best be termed transitional.

In descriptive learning cycles students discover and describe an empirical pattern within a specific context (exploration); the teacher gives it a name (term introduction); and the pattern is then identified in additional contexts (concept application). This type of learning cycle is called descriptive because the students and teacher are merely describing, seriating, classifying, etc. what they observe without attempting to generate hypotheses to explain their observations. Descriptive learning cycles answer the question, What?, but do not raise the causal question, Why?

In empirical-inductive learning cycles students again discover and describe an empirical pattern in a specific context (exploration); but they go further by generating possible causes of that pattern. This requires the use of analogical reasoning (abduction is the term used by Hansen, 1958) to transfer terms/concepts learned in other contexts to this new context (term introduction). The terms may be introduced by students, the teacher, or both. With the teacher's guidance, the students then sift through the data gathered during the exploration phase to see if the hypothesized causes are consistent with those data and other known phenomena (concept application). In other words, observations are made in a descriptive fashion, but this type of learning cycle goes further to generate and initially test a cause(s), hence the name empirical-inductive.

The third type of learning cycle, hypothetical-deductive, is initiated with the statement of a causal question to which students are asked to generate possible answers (hypotheses). Student time is then devoted to deducing the logical consequences of these hypotheses and explicitly designing and conducting experiments to test them (exploration). The analysis of experimental results allows for some hypotheses to be rejected, others retained, and terms to be introduced (term introduction). Finally the relevant concepts and reasoning patterns that are involved and discussed may be applied in other situations at a later time (concept application). The explicit generation and test of hypotheses through a comparison of logical deductions with empirical results is required in this type of learning cycle hence the name, hypothetical-deductive.

Descriptive Learning Cycles

Descriptive learning cycles are designed to have students observe a small part of the world, discover a pattern of regularity, name it and look for the pattern elsewhere. Little or no disequilibrium may result as students will most likely have few, if any, misconceptions. Graphing a frequency distribution of the length of a sample of a species of sea shells will allow you to introduce the terms *normal distribution* but will not provide much argumentation among your students. A descriptive learning cycle into skull structure/function allows the teacher to introduce the terms herbivore, omnivore, and carnivore and also allows for some student argumentation as they put forth and compare ideas about skull structure and possible diets. Yet seldom are possible cause-effect relationships hotly debated and hard evidence is not sought in descriptive learning cycles.

Empirical-Inductive Learning Cycles

On the other hand, consider the following empirical-inductive (EI) learning cycle which involves the concept of air pressure. It, like other EI learning cycles, requires students to do more than describe a phenomenon. An explanation is required. Explanation opens the door to a multitude of misconceptions, suction in this case, and the resulting arguments and analysis of evidence and reasoning represent a near perfect example of how EI learning cycles can be used to promote disequilibrium and the development of conceptual knowledge *and* reasoning patterns.

To start, students invert a cylinder over a candle burning in a pan of water. They observe that the flame soon goes out and water rises into the cylinder. Two causal questions are posed. Why did the flame go out? Why did the water rise? The typical explanation students generate to answer these questions is that the flame used up the oxygen in the cylinder and left a partial vacuum which 'sucked' the water in from below. This explanation reveals two misconceptions: (i) flames destroy matter thus produce a partial vacuum; and (ii) water rises due to a non-existent force called suction. Testing of these ideas requires use of the hypothetico-deductive pattern of reasoning utilizing the isolation and control of variables (see figure 3.8).

Hypothetical-Deductive Learning Cycles

Like EI learning cycles, hypothetical-deductive (HD) learning cycles require explanation of some phenomenon, thus open up the possibility for the generation of alternative conceptions/misconceptions and the resulting argumentation, disequilibrium, and analysis of data to resolve conflict. Unlike EI cycles, however, HD cycles call for the immediate and explicit statement of alternative hypotheses to explain a phenomenon. In brief, a causal question is raised and students must explicitly generate alternative hypotheses, which in turn must be tested through the deduction of predicted consequences and experimentation. This places a heavy burden on student initiative and reasoning ability.

Figure 3.8   The box on the left represents the key question raised. In this case,
Why did the water rise? The subsequent hypotheses, experiments,
predictions, results, and conclusions follow the hypothetico-deductive if
... and ... then ... therefore ... pattern of reasoning and require
students to isolate and control independent variables in comparison of
water rise with one and four candles. As shown, the initial hypothesis
leads to a false prediction, thus must be rejected (reasoning to a
contradiction). Students must now generate an alternative hypothesis or
hypotheses and start over again until they have a hypothesis that is
consistent with the data (i.e., not falsified).

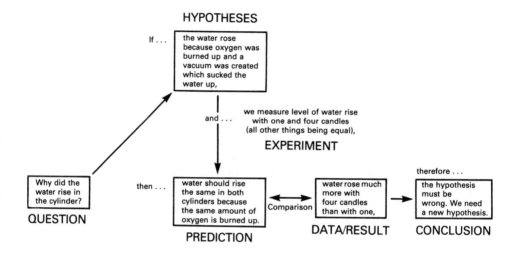

Consider, for example, the question of water rise in plants. Objects are
attracted toward the center of the earth by a force called gravity, yet water
rises in tall trees to the uppermost leaves to allow photosynthesis to take place.
What causes the water to rise in spite of the downward gravitational force?
The following alternative hypotheses (alternative conceptions/misconceptions)
were generated in a recent biology lab at Arizona State University: (a) water
evaporates from the leaves to create a vacuum which sucks water up; (b) roots
squeeze to push water up through one-way valves in the stem tubes; (c)
capillary action of water pulls it up like water soaking up a paper towel, and (d)
osmosis pulls water up.

Of course, equipment limitations keep some ideas from being tested but
the 'leaf evaporation' hypothesis can be tested by comparing water rise in

plants with and without leaves. This requires the reasoning patterns of the isolation and control of variables. The 'root squeeze' hypothesis can be tested by comparing water rise in plants with and without roots; and the 'one-way valve' hypothesis can be tested by comparing water rise in right-side-up and upside-down stems. Results allow rejection of some of the hypotheses and not others. The survivors are considered 'correct', for the time being, at least, just as is the case in doing 'real' science, which of course is precisely what the students are doing. Following the experimentation, terms such as transpiration can be introduced and applied elsewhere as is the case for all types of learning cycles.

The water rise in plants question may involve misconceptions but few students would feel strongly committed to any one point of view as these points of view are not likely to be tied to others which do have strong intellectual and/or emotional commitments. But consider the case of evolution and special creation. Here commitments often run very deep, thus a hypothetical-deductive learning cycle into the question — Where did present-day life forms come from? — can stir up considerable controversy, argumentation and reflective thought.

A look back at figure 3.8 will serve to summarize the major differences among the three types of learning cycles described. Descriptive learning cycles start with explorations which tell us what happens under specific circumstances in specific contexts. They represent descriptive science. In the context of the candle burning experiment they allow us to answer questions such as, how high and how fast will the water rise under varying conditions? But they stop before the question, what causes the water to rise? is raised. Empirical-inductive learning cycles include the previous but go further and call for causal hypotheses. Thus, they include both the question and hypotheses box of figure 3.8 and may even go further to include some or all of the subsequent boxes. Hypothetical-deductive learning cycles generally start with a statement of the causal question and proceed directly to hypotheses and their test, thus represent the classic view of experimental science.

Clearly there is some overlap among the three types of learning cycles as they represent various phases of the generally continuous and cyclic process of doing science. As is the case with any classification system, some learning cycles will be difficult to classify as they will have characteristics of more than one type of learning cycle. Nevertheless, it is my hope that the system will prove to be helpful in curriculum design and instruction. For the sake of clarity the major postulates of the theory of science instruction presented in the chapter are listed in table 3.3.

Table 3.3   *Postulates of A Theory of Instruction for Concept Acquisition and Reasoning Development*

1	Students often hold alternative conceptions (misconceptions), i.e., knowledge derived from personal experience and/or classroom experience which is incompatible with established scientific theory.
2	Misconceptions may be instruction resistant impediments to the acquisition of scientifically valid conceptions.
3	The overthrow of misconceptions requires students to move through a phase in which a mismatch exists between the misconception and the scientific conception and provokes a 'cognitive conflict' or state of mental 'disequilibrium'.
4	The improvement of reasoning skills arises from situations in which students are engaged in exchanges of contradictory conceptions where arguments are advanced and evidence is sought to resolve the contradiction.
5	Argumentation provides experiences from which particular forms of argumentation (i.e., patterns of reasoning) may be abstracted.
6	The learning cycle is a method of instruction which consists of three phases called exploration, term introduction, and concept application.
7	Use of the learning cycle provides the opportunity for students to reveal prior conceptions/misconceptions and the opportunity to argue and test them, thus become 'disequilibrated' and develop more adequate conceptions and reasoning patterns.
8	There are three types of learning cycles (descriptive, empirical-inductive, hypothetical-deductive) which are not equally effective at producing disequilibrium and improved reasoning.
9	The essential difference among the three types of learning cycles is the degree to which students either gather data in a purely descriptive fashion or initially set out to explicitly test alternative conceptions (hypotheses).
10	Descriptive learning cycles are designed to have students observe a small part of the world, discover a pattern, name it and seek the pattern elsewhere. Normally only concrete operational reasoning is required and little or no disequilibrium occurs.
11	Empirical-inductive learning cycles require students to describe *and* explain a phenomenon thus allow for misconceptions, argumentation disequilibrium and the development of formal reasoning patterns.
12	Hypothetical-deductive learning cycles require the immediate and explicit statement of alternative conceptions/hypotheses to explain a phenomenon and require formal reasoning patterns in the test of the alternatives.

References

Ambrose, A. and Lazerowitz, M. (1948) *Fundamentals of Symbolic Logic*, New York, Rinehart, Inc.

Anderson, C.W. and Smith, E.L. (1986) 'Teaching science', in Koehler V. (Ed.), *The Educator's Handbook: A Research Perspective*, New York, Longman Inc.

Atkin, J.M. and Karplus, R. (1962) 'Discovery or invention?', *Science Teacher*, 29, 5, p 45.

Clement, J. (1986) 'Misconceptions in high school physics', *Cognitive Processes Research Group Newsletter*, 1, 2, pp 2–3.

Driver, R. (1981) 'Pupils' alternative frameworks in science', *European Journal of Science Education*, 3, 1, pp 93–101.

GRUBER, H.E. and BARRETT, P.H. (1974) *Darwin On Man*, New York, E.P. Dutton & Co. Inc.

HALLOUN, I.A. and HESTENES, D. (1985) 'The initial knowledge state of college physics students', *The American Journal of Physics*, 53, 11, pp 43–55.

HANSON, N.R. (1958) *Patterns of Discovery*, Cambridge, Cambridge University Press.

INHELDER, B. and PIAGET, J. (1958) *The Growth of Logical Thinking From Childhood to Adolescence*, New York, Basic Books.

KARPLUS, R., LAWSON, A.E., WOLLMAN, W., APPEL, M., BERNOFF, R., HOWE, A., RUSCH, J.J. and SULLIVAN, F. (1976) *Science Teaching and the Development Reasoning: A Workshop*, Berkeley, CA, Regents of the University of California.

LAWSON, A.E. (1978) 'The development and validation of a classroom test of formal reasoning', *Journal of Research in Science Teaching*, 15, 1, pp 11–24.

LAWSON, A.E. (1979) 'The developmental learning paradigm', *Journal of Research in Science Teaching*, 16, 6, pp 501–15.

LAWSON, A.E. (1982) 'Formal reasoning, achievement, and intelligence: An issue of importance', *Science Education*, 66, 1, pp 77–83.

LAWSON, A.E. (1987) 'The four-card problem resolved? Formal operational reasoning and reasoning to a contradiction', *Journal of Research in Science Teaching*, 24, 7, pp 611–28.

LAWSON, A.E. and BEALER, J.M. (1984) 'Cultural diversity and differences in formal reasoning ability', *Journal of Research in Science Teaching*, 21, 7, pp 735–43.

LAWSON, A.E., KARPLUS, R. and ADI, H. (1978) 'The acquisition of propositional logic and formal operational schemata during the secondary school years', *Journal of Research in Science Teaching*, 15, 6, pp 465–78.

LAWSON, A.E. and THOMPSON, L. (1987) 'Relationships among biological misconceptions, reasoning ability, mental capacity, verbal I.Q., and cognitive style', paper presented at the Annual Meeting of the National Association for Research Teaching, April.

LURIA, A.R. (1961) 'The role of speech in the regulation of normal and abnormal behavior', in Tizard, J. (Ed), Oxford, Pergamon.

PIAGET, J. (1928) *Judgment and Reasoning in the Child*, Paterson, N.J., Littlefield, Adams & Co. (1964 edition).

POSNER, G.J., STRIKE, K.A., HEWSON, P.W. and GERTZOG, W.A. (1982) 'Accommodation of a scientific conception: Toward a theory of conceptual change', *Science Education*, 66, 2, pp 211–27.

Science Research Associates Inc (1970) *Iowa Tests of Educational Development*, Grades 9–12, form X5, Chicago, Science Resource Associates Inc.

SHAYER, M. and ADEY, P. (1981) *Towards a Science of Science Teaching*, London, Heinemann Educational Books.

VYGOTSKY, L.S. (1962) *Thought and Language*, Cambridge, MA, MIT Press.

WASON, P.C. and JOHNSON-LAIRD, P.N. (1972) *Psychology of Reasoning and Structure and Content*, Cambridge, MA, Harvard University Press.

Respondent: Mary Simpson

Professor Lawson has done a signal service in collating and presenting with admirable cogency the results of his many studies of formal reasoning. The thesis which underlies the generalized theory of science instruction he advances, is that formal reasoning is an internalized pattern of hypothetico deductive argument which is social in origin and conveniently measurable by the 'Pouring Water' task.

I have certain reservations about both the thesis and its applications. Firstly, it is extremely difficult to know what tests of formal reasoning actually measure. Do they genuinely distinguish subjects by their *capacities* to reason in a hypothetico deductive mode? Or are the apparent differences in reasoning merely the outward signs of differences in, for example, modelling, working memory, or the extent to which subjects have been able to automatize elements of the task (all of which are a reflection of the subjects prior knowledge and experience)? The point is crucial since the various answers direct us to quite dissimilar educational strategies.

The correlations reported by Lawson are intriguing. Taken at their face value, they do *not* indicate that formal reasoning is related in any direct way with skill in the hypothetico-deductive process. Performance on the 'Pouring Water' task does *not* correlate with performance on the 'four-card' test, which unarguably requires hypothetico deductive reasoning but it *does* correlate with the capacity to profit from direct formal instruction in that task, *ie* to apply the taught reasoning when that task is re-presented, and to identify the linguistic labels which should be attached to the components of such reasoning; no evidence is offered that proportional reasoners, after such instruction, will use the hypothetico deductive strategy in a wholly new context. However, I am cautious in attaching much significance to these data since there is no information on the extent to which the variances are attributable to the admitted covariable, the subjects' academic attainment.

However, even setting these strictures aside, one must query the appropriateness of the instruction from which proportional reasoners appeared to profit while additive reasoners did not. Instruction on the four-card test appears to have been deficient since it left subjects to derive for themselves the crucial information that since one *cannot* prove a theory to be true (but merely add to its probability) the strategy must be to determine only which cards should be examined to prove it false.

This last criticism is an example of my main reservations about this chapter — that it pays too little attention to the quality of instruction. Thus, for example, Lawson's strategy for dealing with misconceptions ignores the fact that many — perhaps most — misconceptions have their origins in classroom instruction and are the result of pupils' attempts to construct meaning from defective messages. The underlying problem is that teachers cannot see the gaps and anomalies in the information they present to pupils because of the high level of unconscious inference which is implicit in the discourse of every subject expert. As a result, typical school science instruction is characterized by (i) a failure to define what prerequisite knowledge must be available to pupils starting a new course; (ii) the use of simplified models which do not adequately account for the phenomena they purport to describe and/or which cannot support more advanced understanding; (iii) ambiguities and sources of interference in texts and experiments; (iv) practicals in which key features are salient only to the knowledgeable and hidden to the novice by 'noise' (Simpson and Arnold, 1983). The appropriate strategy for dealing with misconceptions of this type is not 'cure by argument' but prevention, and at a stage long before genuinely logical argument is deemed to be possible by Piagetian theory.

My final concern is that the practical expression of Lawson's thesis within the classroom is not only inappropriate but is potentially damaging. His procedures for dealing with deeply rooted misconceptions imply that these have to be 'unlearned' and 'overthrown' by experiment and logical argument, and are reminiscent of the views of Posner *et al* (1982) who stress the importance of the teacher creating 'cognitive conflict', 'confronting students with problems', identifying 'defensive moves' and 'ruthlessly demanding consistency in beliefs'. Unfortunately, however, there is no evidence that remediation by confrontation actually works, and much to suggest that it does not. Crisis is not enough.

Evidence from the neurosciences suggests that information encoded in long term memory can not be 'unlearned' as if it were data erased from a magnetic tape. The only strategy which is available to us as educators is the modest one of attempting to increase the probabilities that pupils will use the approved concepts we teach in preference to their own naive schemata.

Pupils will treat the scientific paradigm as being true, not because it is shown to be logical but because they find it to be meaningful and useful. This will not happen until teaching practices are so much better informed by accurate perceptions of what pupils need to know and actually *do* know, that what is taught is *capable* of being meaningfully understood. When a pupil does misunderstand a topic it is often for reasons so remote from the topic area as to be unrecognised as being relevant by both teach and pupil; difficulties in understanding osmosis, for example, have been traced to misunderstandings derived from instruction in digestion! Such sources cannot be recognised if the mode of instruction is logical/confrontational. They can best be elucidated, and responded to in a diagnostic/therapeutic mode.

In summary, the danger which is inherent in Lawson's approach is that it appears to offer support to an all too widely used 'pupil deficit' model to explain learning failure. Teachers can now serve pupils with four indictments, each of which have been given respectability by educational research. Firstly, pupils have not got the 'intelligence' to understand the material offered in class. Secondly, they have not got the 'formal reasoning' necessary to understand the material. Thirdly, since learning is cognitive change and since cognitive change requires effort, they clearly have not put in enough effort. And, now, number four — their heads are full of misconceptions brought into the classroom from outside. We can not be so readily absolved. Until we are prepared to be considerably more critical of what we teach and how we teach it, we will, alas, continue to fail the pupils.

References

POSNER, G.J., STRIKE, K.A., HEWSON, P.W. and GERTGOG, W.A. (1982) 'Accomodation of a scientific conception: Toward a theory of conceptual change', *Science Education* 66, pp 211–27.
SIMPSON, M. and ARNOLD, B. (1983) 'Diagnostic tests and criterion referenced assessment: Their contribution to the resolution of pupil learning difficulties', *Programmed Learning and Educational Technology*, 20, pp 36–42.

Discussion (Reporter: Joan Solomon)

Lawson was asked whether any correction had been made in the data presented for students who had 'dropped out'. He explained that the data in figures 3.4–3.6 was not longitiudinal, but based on different samples from each grade. There was little drop-out between the grades concerned.

It was suggested that the term 'private models' would be preferable to 'misconceptions'. The speaker denied that the use of one term implied a particular method of teaching or attitude on the part of the teacher. In a lesson on photosynthesis, for example, students were asked for their views. The 'alternative hypotheses' offered were not labelled as wrong, but the students were required to justify them and to devise experimental tests for them.

A questioner described how he had found that children could be more successful with Wason's four-card trick if the context was more familiar, and asked whether the speaker knew of cases where it had been used in reverse order. Lawson replied that better results within more familiar contexts was not due to better logical reasoning, but to other causes altogether.

4   Hewers of Wood and Drawers of Water? or Populations in Change?

Michael Shayer

Hewers of Wood and Drawers of Water

My title comes from the following fantasy — purely hypothetical of course — that a far from benevolent Empress has taken over the country. She has found, let us say, some apparent sanction in the Biblical notion of the importance of having enough hewers and enough drawers to provide wood and water for the elite in their highly valuable task of playing with and exchanging cowrie shells. She tells her Education Secretary to make sure that not too many elite are reproduced in the next generation, and that the hewers and drawers, as in Huxley's *Brave New World*, get trained to like the place in society to which they have been allotted. He in his turn — more hypothetical than ever — has his aids look up the research literature. They discover that a certain Swiss psychologist has produced an interesting account of the development of the epistemic cowrie-shell player. Further, they find that a British research team (Shayer, Küchemann and Wylam, 1976; Shayer & Wylam 1978), some twelve years previously, had actually carried out a representative survey on opinion — poll size samples of 10-year-olds, 11-year-olds, etc. up to and including the year containing pupils in the last year of compulsory schooling (15/16-year-olds) of the genesis of cowrie-shell players in the population. Arise, Sir Kenneth, she says, as he presents what his aids had gleaned.

They produced figure 4.1 first.

But while the present proportion of those with access to cowrie-playing skills was a little under 30 per cent, and those with advanced competence by the age of 16 was a satisfactory average 12 per cent with a very satisfying sex differential, a disturbing picture emerged as they dug further into the data (see figure 4.2).

Although the top curve was that of the development of the hewers, the other was very worrying. The original British team hadn't noticed it at the time, and to elucidate its significance it was necessary to bring back from banishment a certain Danish statistician who had earlier been thrown out to further the career of a native Academic. While the Dane's appropriate probabilistic model

Figure 4.1   *Development of formal operational thinking in representative British sample*

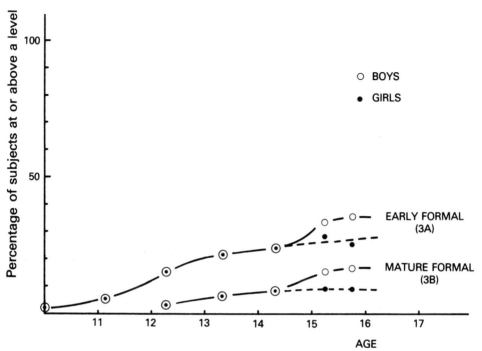

Source: Shayer and Wylam (1978).

(Rasch, 1980; Wright and Masters, 1982) showed that those following up the line of the concrete generalisation curve had an 80 per cent probability or more of competence on any task requiring concrete modelling, it also showed that they had a 28 per cent probability of success on early cowrie-shell playing tasks, and there was, moreover, no differential between the sexes on this curve.

When the physiologists were asked what was the meaning of the two growth spurts showing on the bottom curve around 11 and 15, they said (John, 1977; Eichorn and Bayley 1962) that there are brain-growth spurts at these two ages, and it rather looks as though they are genetically programmed to assist further development. The education experts were then asked, What can we do to make sure that this development is not realized so that too many elite are not produced? Their answer was this: you must suppress the phenotype, and this is how you can do it. Notice how, in looking at figure 4.2, that although about 40

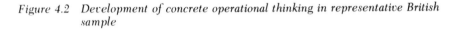

Figure 4.2   *Development of concrete operational thinking in representative British sample*

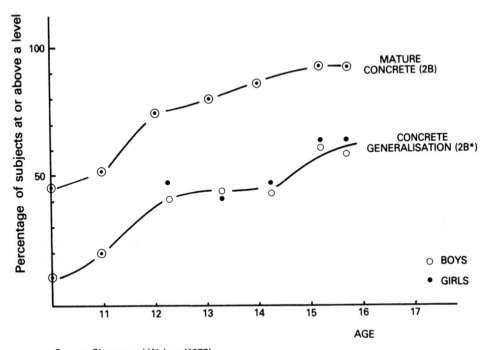

Source: Shayer and Wylam (1978).

per cent seem to have been pre-prepared by nature to develop into the elite during adolescence with even a second chance for some 20 per cent more at 15, in fact our society, perhaps walking in its sleep, has succeeded in only selecting a small proportion of these for phenotypic expression, as shown in the curves in figure 4.1. What you have to do is structure the curriculum so that it just suits the developmental profile of those who will be the top 10 per cent by the end of adolescence. Make sure the learning experiences are exclusively in the style of the top curve in figure 4.1 from the age of 12 to 14, and then raise them to the level of the bottom curve from 14 to 17. In this way phenotypal expression will be limited to the desired proportions, there will be enough second-tier elite produced to keep the cowrie-shell enterprise fully manned, and the hewers and drawers will hardly be able to wait to escape from schooling.

Lest our transatlantic friends feel too amused by this, let me say my fantasy has an aged Emperor friend across the waters who also summoned his advisers (Renner and Lawson, 1975; Sayre and Ball, 1975; Hautamaki, 1987) who came out with a different solution producing the same result. They said, It rather looks as though the genetic programme is so strong that 10 per cent will get through by the end of adolescence whatever happens. So the thing to do is produce schooling that gives no stimulation whatsover, and keep the elite learning programmes until the students are in the 16 to 18 range. By this time the weaker phenotype will have been suppressed by removal of its appropriate environment, and you can recruit from the desired proportion.

If consultants seem to figure rather predominantly in my fantasies it may be for a more melancholy reason than appears, and rather from a sense of incipient guilt. The story is told that when Hitler obtained power in 1928 he summoned the famous historian, Oswald Spengler, and asked him what advice he could offer him in light of his learning. Perhaps his answer, Make strong your Praetorian Guard, was a joke, but he must have lived to regret it.

Now follows a linking passage to the main theme of my talk, which is populations in change? I hope it is needless to say that my fantasies were directed only at the past. What fun we might have with the Great Education Bill with its phase 2 schemes for driving all future cowrie-shell players into private schools, for making all the 'good' state schools into private schools, and using the apparatus of state to condition the hewers and drawers and their teachers with mandatory tests at 7, 11, 14, etc.! But we mustn't. I have been digging with some gratitude into the work of the alternative misconceptions movement, and one reason for the gratitude is that it contains by implication all the grounds of indictment which are necessary to bring against the tradition of science teaching as we have known it. It has been shown that university students have such a tenuous ability to relate to reality the theories whose 'mastery' they demonstrate on their exam papers that many of their preconceptions coexist with, and are untouched by, orthodox models they have been taught. It has been shown that this university experience is prefigured by correlative (or is it causative?) learning experiences in secondary or high school where the individual's ability to relate his or her own thinking and experiences to the tightly framed world within which scientific theories have their application is not addressed. There isn't time. And there are two lines of argument here: for example, Joan Solomon's that traditional science teaching leads to an almost absolute barrier between pupil's life-world experience and their science learning. (This I interpret as the *generalist* objection: that science as so taught isn't the element of everyone's general education it should be); and the pure scientist's argument that the experience of science mediated through the teaching is a false one likely to produce uncritical and unimaginative scientists.

Yet to my surprise despite massive cumulative multifaceted arguments marshalled by, for example, Driver and Erickson (1983); Osborne and Wittrock (1985) and policy documents from our own DES in this country (*Science 5–16*) nobody actually comes out with the blunt three letter word which by implication is describing the science teaching tradition they wish to replace. They chip away and chip away with an effect which I shall describe with a borrowed metaphor as rather like being nibbled to death by geese. (When their fire has mistakenly come in my direction I have sometimes felt like this myself). So let me say it, the tradition is BAD. In my judgment it is BAD for two reasons over and above the ones given above. Firstly, it isn't good for the very able students: not for the future very able science student because it simply puts off until his or her own first experience of post-PhD research work their personal experience of what science is about. Not for the very able arts student because he or she never begins to have the access to the intellectual world of science which I would claim every educated citizen should have. Second because, depending on how strict a criterion one uses, between 90 per cent and 70 per cent of the population are excluded, for reasons I gave earlier, from participating in science at all.

This brings me back to the CSMS developmental survey evidence. My strong claim from this is that hitherto science education research has addressed itself at the most to about 30 per cent of the secondary student population. The basis of the argument is a simple one: the agenda of the science learning to which research has been addressed requires early formal modelling at least for its comprehension. If you base the actual learning structure of a science course on concepts requiring formal modelling (as distinguished from intermittently using formal process skills in some of the investigations the course incorporates), then inevitably it acts as a two-edged sword, admitting some to Paradise and excluding the rest. We applied a strong pass criterion to the Piagetian measures we used — that of a 67 per cent success rate on items for assessment at a certain level — because we wanted to concentrate on their predictive validity, their power to predict potential performance on science learning on courses as we knew them. The Piagetian tasks we used were structured to be more *competence* estimators than *performance* estimators, and I still believe we made the right decisions as applied researchers, even though the real story is more complex. My hope is that this evidence will now be used on both sides of the Atlantic in the realization that there are two major segments of the population whose learning problems in science have not been explicitly addressed (although I would both claim and acknowledge that they are implicitly addressed in the applied curriculum development research deriving from a constructivist basis). There are those between the 70th percentile and the 40th percentile (see figure 4.2) who perhaps should have developed generalised formal thinking and did not, and there are those below the 40th percentile whose experience of schooling is generally unsatisfactory, and whose problems will not get addressed without an adequate and positive model which (a) distinguishes their qualitative difference from the previous segment; and (b) takes their further learning as certain and valuable as that of the other two segments.

Michael Shayer

Populations in Change?

Let me begin by quoting from Jerome Bruners's recent book, since many of the positions he has adopted and worked within underly the assumptions maybe of most people at this conference. In *Actual Minds, Possible Worlds* (1986) he looks back at intellectual sources on which a psychologist with a major interest in education has found it possible or at least plausible to draw. Amongst other things, he examines the work of Freud, Piaget and Vygotsky, and finds them all wanting, but in different and complementary ways. Freud he credits with having extended the individual's awareness of personal drama, caught as in Greek tragedy by determining forces produced by family figures acting when the patient was in their absolute power, and inasmuch as he has led to patients partial freedom from being determined by their actual or imagined past, it is through their more conscious awareness of themselves rather than by a more active reconstruction of themselves. Bruner faults Freud in not drawing enough on the resources of language and culture for the present development of the individual.

Piaget he describes rather paradoxically, although I do agree that the paradox is present in the work of Piaget and is not contributed by Bruner. 'To learn is to invent', Bruner quotes from him approvingly, in the sense that although the person structures reality through the logical schemata he has available, this is no passive or inevitable processing as one can or cannot expect, as the case may be, from selecting the key on ones wordprocessor. The individual still has to be challenged to *use* his possible programmes to create an active learning against a natural sloth (Piaget's form of original sin?) which finds it more congenial to select the processing which requires least effort in minimum time. Yet if one looks at the bulk of the Genevan work what one has is a static structuralist description of successive and more complex levels of development, with only 'natural growth' to 'explain' the transition through the series. And as I have argued elsewhere (Shayer, 1987), quoting I think from Hume, 'You can't get an "ought" from an "is"'. Thus Piaget's own main lifework seems to offer no model for actualizing the learning he recommends.

Vygotsky was predominantly the psychologist of development itself, but his theory of the 'Zone of Proximal Development' was applied as much to social change as to children's development. It is an idea much used by the Israeli psychologist Feuerstein, whose work I will discuss later. Bruner quotes from Vygotsky '... the only "good learning" is that which is in advance of development'. The only way for this to take place is by adults or more competent practitioners to frame various inputs to the learner and offer various challenges and hints in such a way that the gap between the processing the learner would produce spontaneously, and the present limits of his zone of proximal development (ZPD) is utilized so as to extend his competence. Such a system of 'support' can also in principle be used to extend the political consciousness of backward adults, and Bruner picks on the fact that on this model '... the learner begins without a proper basis for criticizing what is being 'fed' to him by ones whose consciousness exceeds his own'. Bruner also raises the issue, probably his own more than Vygotsky's, of whether the approach is too tinged with 'twentieth-century liberalism', and says ' . . . his (Vygotsky's) is a view of the nurturing of mind that fits, say, the Oxford tutorial system or the discussion methods of the elite academy far better than it fits the ordinary common school'. And this issue I will also come back to.

To continue the Vygotskian theme. I want to begin by citing work that I and others have done which in principle is concerned with the development of the bottom 30 per cent of the population of adolescents. I am proceeding in this order because it does help to clarify some of the issues of intervention theory, ZPD, and the relation between effect of an intervention and improved learning ability. Reuven Feuerstein has an extensive intervention programme, Instrumental Enrichment, used usually on early adolescents. Instrumental Enrichment is a two to three-year curriculum ideally taught for one hour a day, but still quite effective at the rate of three sessions a week.

Not only is the subject matter of the course not taken from the field of science, it avoids almost completely successfully the agenda of any recognizable school subject. The reason for this is to avoid association with previous failure in school. The major aim of the course is ' . . . to increase the capacity of the human organism to become modified through direct exposure to stimuli and experiences provided by the encounters with life events and with formal and informal learning opportunities,' with a related sub-goal, among others ' . . . to arouse the learner from his role as passive recipient and reproducer of information and turn him into an active generator of new information'. There is no necessary reason, we can see, for these aims to be associated with the lower end of the school population. But my evidence happens to be taken from there.

As of about four years ago there was a scatter of research evidence both from Israel and from North America about the possible effect of IE on pupils. Unfortunately, although the IE project is a wonderful exemplar — perhaps the *only* one — of formative evaluation, and revision and development of the theory and practise in light of feedback gained over ten years, the research on its effect has tended to suffer from over-ambitious programmes of training too many teachers, and there was so much noise in the data that one couldn't honestly estimate its potential. I therefore set out to try to replicate the research on the effects of IE under optimum conditions. I didn't totally succeed in my attempt, because I only got 3 lessons a week out of the school rather than the desired five. But in other respects the attempt was successful.

The work was undertaken in a school for moderately educationally subnormal pupils. The intake of such a school is defined as the bottom 5 per cent of the school performance range, but excluding those with severe organic defects or with learning problems so severe that they appear ineducable. In terms of their performance on standardised tests of reading, writing and mathematics, the pupils really were in the bottom 5 percentile range. I was trained in IE and also his method of clinical testing, Learning Potential Assessment (LPA) by Feuerstein himself, and I was able not only to take a small practise class of six 'difficult cases' myself, but was able both to train the teacher concerned with the study, and assist her with her group for two lessons a week until I was confident that she had internalized the underlying model.

The experimental and control groups were obtained by random selection of ten pupils each from a single class of twenty 12-year-old pupils who were taught for the rest of the week by their own class teacher. The IE class was withdrawn for three one-hour IE sessions a week, and while this was going on the control group was given 'Think-Tank' — that is a set of learning experiences drawn from various publications which had been tried in the school before. We tested the effects in some detail which I have reported elsewhere (Shayer and Beasley, 1987). But of interest here are two of the modes of testing: an individual interview battery of twelve Piagetian tasks which I used myself, and the Learning Potential Assessment which Frances Beasley developed for her PhD study, and was also used as pre- and post test. Both IE and LPA are based directly on Vygotsky's ZPD, through Feuerstein's model of Mediated Learning Experience (MLE). The LPA results are interesting, because Beasley was able to make the ZPD estimates quantitative. They were of the order of eighteen to twenty-two months in mental age terms. And during the twenty months of the intervention, the experimental group moved up to what had been the forward limit of their ZPD, while the control hardly moved at all. Moreover, the experimental group's ZPD had now moved forward correspondingly so as still to be a further twenty months in advance.

The results on the Piagetian test battery are best viewed against a general developmental diagram, and I have chosen Tanner's curves for displaying the results. You will see that the control group has not moved at all — a result which will not surprise those who have worked in special schools — whereas the experimental group have moved up either at a rate comparable to the adolescent at the 50th, percentile, or faster.

Because I did the Piagetian testing I was also able to add two of the Piagetian formal tasks (Pendulum and Equilibrium in the Balance) to the individual interview battery to check if at post-test any of the pupils were showing formal operational thinking. They did not.

To sum up, during the intervention we were able to show that, compared with the controls the experimental group put on about two years more development, and in Piagetian terms were at mature concrete or concrete generalization level by the time they were 14. Since concrete generalization is the level of processing required by most skilled labour we can see that in principle, provided teachers can change their professional skills to utilize this change in general intelligence (fluid intelligence) it is not so idiotic as it might at first have seemed to suggest that those at the 5th percentile might be brought up to the present level of the average pupil. Another aspect of these results may have struck some of you. In terms of the pre-test, the pupils I tested were between the 25th and the 65th percentile, in Piagetian terms. When I turned up the pupils' psychologist's reports, similar figures were found recorded in terms of their Wechsler test results. Children find their way into special schools

Table 4.1 Zones of Proximal Development estimatial during LPA testing, using Ravin's Matrices

Experimental				Control			
May 1983		May 1984		May 1983		May 1984	
Unassisted	Post Mediation	Unassisted	Post Mediation	Unassisted	Post Mediation	Unassisted	Post Mediation
7.7 (0.65)	9.5 (1.8)	9.6 (2.4)	11.2 (2.2)	8.3 (0.43)	10.5 (2.1)	9.3 (2.0)	10.7 (2.2)
Mean age 13/0		14/0		13/1		14/1	

Figure 4.3 'Tanner' — development curves for Piagetian measures

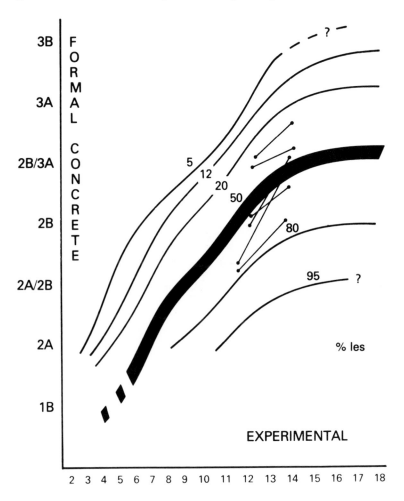

because they can't read or write and don't seem to have numeracy. The corrolary of this is that there must be many pupils who in general developmental terms are in the bottom five percentiles who are in ordinary high or comprehensive schools because they *can* read and write. Indeed one of my own pupils in the ESN (M) school who had been the most retarded in the school had been saved by her mother from an ESN (S) school because on advice her mother used every effort to get her to read and write.

Moving up to the part of the adolescent population between the 30th and the 70th percentile, we can see the background rationale of the CASE project. Here we were endeavouring to intervene in the development of those for whom it would not have been a reasonable expectation that they would have developed substantial competence even in early formal operational thinking by

Figure 4.4 *'Tanner' — development curves for Piagetian measures*

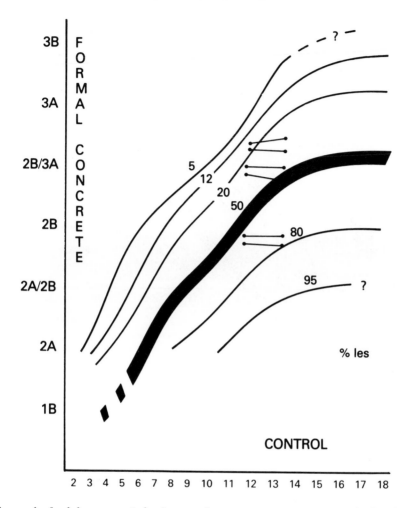

the end of adolescence. I don't want here to anticipate too much the details which you will here from Philip Adey, but the principle we adopted was to train not on one or two, but on all the formal operational schemata described by Piaget, and learning from the Feuerstein research we deduced that a two-year period was needed if the effects were to be substantial and permanent. And unlike the IE intervention which was independent of school subjects, our CASE intervention was within the context of ordinary science lessons. I suppose we also borrowed in part from Feuerstein the notion of Mediated Learning, where the role of the teacher is to assist the pupil become more aware or his or her own resources for thinking rather than to teach them algorithms. This notion of metacognition is probably what links the IE research and the CASE research using formal operational schemata: in both cases the idea is to put the control of

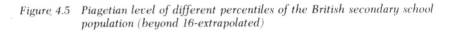

Figure 4.5   Piagetian level of different percentiles of the British secondary school
population (beyond 16-extrapolated)

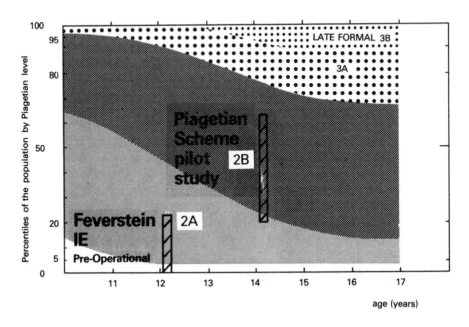

the means of gathering and processing information into the hands of the pupils.
Now what can we say about the effects of CASE?

These are the results obtained from our laboratory school, where both
Philip Adey and Carolyn Yates had experimental classes, and there were also
two control groups. The measures used were Piagetian group tests, and '7' on
the scale corresponds to 3A, early formal, in Piagetian terms. You will see that
we had chosen deliberately to work with a near-average population, somewhat
creamed of the top 20 per cent. You can see that the experimental group had
been moved up to the level of the controls by the post-test, and during the
fifteen months after the intervention had ceased the experimental group's
developmental line had joined and stayed with that of the controls. Note also
the developmental plateaux both for experimental and control in the range 13
to 14 years of age. I obtained a similar effect-size myself about five years ago in
a feasibility study on a class of 14 to 15-year-olds.

Figure 4.6   CASE study: Laboratory school

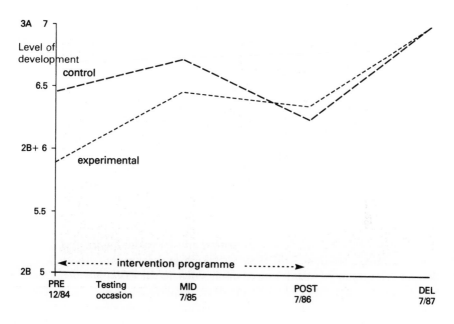

Table 4.2   CASE Pilot Study

| | Experimental | | Control | |
	Pre	Post	Pre	Post
Period of Training: 10 weeks. Pre- and Post-test: Flexible Rods.				
3B	2	4	8	8
3A	9	17	13	13
2B/3A	4	1	7	7
2	8	1	1	1

I think I would attach less weight to my own results, because the tests used to measure the effects were related to the schemata trained.

This is the kind of evidence which lay behind the things I said in fantasy at the beginning of my talk. What I have found from direct experience of the Feuerstein work, which is entirely due to his virtue and none of mine, is that it is possible not only to keep a class of so-called retarded adolescents at full intellectual stretch for a whole hour at a time, but to be kept oneself at full intellectual stretch at the same time perhaps more so than in teaching an advanced science lesson. There is so much professional expertise we have to learn if we are to be worthy of teaching this category of pupil. From the CASE work I think that I draw the conclusion that if we based our teaching on developing the pupil rather than merely utilizing what he or she seems to have developed using his own resources, we might substantially transform the life — expectations of getting on for half of our school population.

Before passing on to discuss the problems raised by this evidence, I would like to comment on Bruner's opinion about Vygotsky's approach. Before watching Feuerstein myself at Yale I would have probably have assented to Bruner's opinion. But I saw him given a black boy from the remedial department of a school in Connecticut and within two days in front of forty psychologists from all over the world the boy was coming in like a king and talking through how he solved tasks which they themselves had already declined to attempt publicly. I would describe this as out-Socrating Socrates, in that Socrates only got his boy to answer, yes, or no. IE depends essentially on the teacher's success in mediating the meta-cognitive ideas to the pupils so that it is they who use them in class discussion and individual work and it is they who exchange experiences of their successes and failures so that the effort becomes communal. Oxford tutorial discussions may occasionally be as good as this, I wouldn't deny, but I know from direct experience of my own and others I have watched, that the mediated learning principle stemming from the Vygotskian interpretation of the potential for growth does not depend for its successful application that its recipients have access to high-level thinking ability or sophisticated verbal skills. Bruner himself reported (p.75 and 76) its use by a gifted teacher on 3 to 5-year-olds. But a case can be made that the onset of adolescence, for social reasons, gives people fresh motivation to achieve.

I have been speaking here as though the teaching programmes for the changes I have been pre-figuring are already present for our decision to use. This is far from being the case. Let me say first that in none of the interventions which I have reported has any increase in academic achievement been reported at post-test. Inasmuch as we are able to measure general intelligence, then on a variety of measures I would claim that substantial changes in what Cattell (1971) called fluid intelligence — the ability to process fresh data and problems here-and-now — have been demonstrated. Why have these not been translated into school achievement? There are two different reasons for this. For the first I can't do better than quote directly from Shayer and Beasley (1987):

> If one considers both achievement tests and tests of crystallized intelligence, and asks the question, When did the pupils develop the skills which show on the test-items? The answer has to be, some of them before the intervention even begun, and many during the period of the intervention itself. If one postulates some kind of exponential learning curve still on the rise at the end of an intervention, then only

towards the end of an intervention will its overall effect be sufficiently large substantially to modify the path and content of pupils' school learning. Its potential effect, then, will be heavily diluted by pupil experience unaffected by the intervention if the post test is given at the immediate end of the intervention. *The right way to test the effect of an intervention programme such as IE is on fresh learning experienced both by the experimental and control groups after the intervention has finished, rather than on standardised tests of achievement.* If this interpretation is correct, it makes one grieve for the studies which have in part been lost, including the one presented in this chapter for lack of understanding of this point.

It will not surprise you to hear that three research proposals based on this understanding have failed to penetrate the consciousness of the referees involved. Until such a test has been carried out I believe it best to treat this as a type 2 error: that a non-effect has been concluded because of inadequately powerful tests of the effect expected.

The second reason would remain valid even if the first were remedied. It is related to my description earlier of the secondary science we have still with us. This was that if a style of curriculum adapted to the cognitive development of selected students (selected, that is, on the basis of parental income, social standing and stringent entrance exams; or electively by criteria rather comparable) is produced, then it will produce another social effect: that of exclusion of the rest of the student population. This will produce an effect on the teachers of which they will be unconscious: their teaching style will be conditioned so as to sort the sheep from the goats. This will be defended in terms of maintenance of academic standards. I would maintain, on the basis of the two different intervention projects with which I have been associated, that the professional expertise which is needed to *change* the development of pupils is so radically different from that required to teach them knowledge and skills on the basis of their *present* understanding that if the potential of early adolescents is eventually to be realized teachers will have to relearn their craft. In Feuerstein's IE this transformation of the craft is called 'Bridging', and is, I believe, the weakest link in the Feuerstein methodology. Each and every lesson, pupils are encouraged themselves to relate the successful strategies they have used on the task in hand to quite other contexts, in and out of school, where the strategies would be useful and relevant. Please note that I am not criticizing the idea or the practice. What I am saying is that it is left entirely to personal inspiration. And a few can do it. Likewise the teachers, when they take ordinary lessons with their pupils, are encouraged to relate the meta-cognitive ideas of the IE lessons and their memory of the particular IE contexts where their pupils utilized them successfully, to the learning problems of the subject lessons. Had they done this I believe that their students' school achievement would have been transformed also. But our Schools Council project (Weller and Craft, 1983) reported bridging to be that aspect of IE least mastered and practised by the teachers involved. Likewise, during the CASE project in our in-service sessions we also stressed 'bridging' by the teachers from the intervention lessons featuring schemata of proportion, compensation, control of variables, correlation, probability, etc. to the actual subject matter of the other five science lessons in each fortnight. But I think Philip will not have much success to report to you on this aspect of our research. If the teachers could internalize the underlying model of the intervention successfully, then perhaps they could afford to dispense with the special intervention lessons. I think I am suggesting that the process of 'bridging' needs just as much further research on how it might be used to transform the style of science teaching, and how to train teachers to practice it, as did the specialized intervention lessons I have mentioned both from IE and in the CASE Project.

Lest this sound too speculative, let me cite some evidence. About five years ago a South African, Mervyn Mehl, and I got together for about a couple of months to see what could be made of the intervention literature. At the time I had been discussing with Feuerstein whether his underlying intervention principles and theory could be embodied in the context of a school subject. He had favoured the idea, but said that none of his own team knew how to do it. Mehl teaches physics at the University of the Western Cape. This is a University with a coloured student intake and staff. I gathered from Mehl that the high schools for coloured South Africans are resourced more comparably with schools in the rest of black Africa than with those for white South Africans. The usual drop-out rate in the first year in University physics is 50 per cent, on the basis of exam performance at the end of the year. Mehl tried first teaching IE directly to his students, but they didn't seem easily able to relate it to the learning of their physics. He then embarked on the more difficult task of analysing the specific learning problems in physics and the faulty strategies of his first year students in terms of the IE list of deficient cognitive functions.

In IE these aspects of information gathering, problem-solving and solution-communicating are shared with students as part of the meta-cognitive approach. Mehl then restructured the classes of his students so that the relevant cognitive functions were highlighted in context — for example in Newton's Laws and Dynamics — and led, by collaborative discussion, to the students developing strategies for success in problem solving. The net result was that at the end of the year all the students passed the first year exams and continued on successfully into the second year. The control group were an equal number of Afrikaans speakers who showed the same 50 per cent failure rate as in previous years the English-speaking group had also shown. Now how Mehl teaches other University teachers how to do likewise I don't know. But I did put a Master's student onto this approach this year, and for her dissertation she reconstructed about three weeks third-year chemistry learning using the same principles. Her control group was a class being taught exactly the same syllabus content by the head of department, who was a chemist. On the basis of a pre-test achievement post-test comparison her class outperformed the control

Table 4.3   Instrumental Enrichment Cognitive Functions

I   Gathering all the information we need (Input)
1   Using our senses (listening, seeing, smelling, tasting, touching, feeling) to gather clear and complete information (clear perception).
2   Using a system or plan so that we do not skip or miss something important or repeat ourselves (systematic exploration).
3   Giving the thing we gather through our senses and our experience a name so that we can remember it more clearly and talk about it (labeling).
4   Describing things and events in terms of where and when they occur (temporal and spatial referents).
5   Deciding on the characteristics of a thing or event that always stay the same, even when changes take place (conservation, constancy, and object permanence).
6   Organizing the information we gather by considering more than one thing at a time (using two sources of information).
7   Being precise and accurate when it matters (need for precision).
II   Using the information we have gathered (Elaboration)
1   Defining what the problem is, what we are being asked to do, and what we must figure out (analyzing disequilibrium).
2   Using only that part of the information we have gathered that is relevant, that is, that applies, to the problem and ignoring the rest (relevance).
3   Having a good picture in our mind of what we are looking for, or what we must do (interiorization).
4   Making a plan that will include the steps we need to take to reach our goal (planning behavior).
5   Remembering and keeping in mind the various pieces of information we need (broadening our mental field).
6   Looking for the relationship by which separate objects, events, and experiences can be tied together (projecting relationships).
7   Comparing objects and experiences to others to see what is similar and what is different (comparative behavior).
8   Finding the class or set to which the new object or experience belongs (categorization).
9   Thinking about different possibilities and figuring out what would happen if you were to choose one or another (hypothetical thinking).
10   Using logic to prove things and to defend your opinion (logical evidence).
III   Expressing the solution to a problem (Output)
1   Being clear and precise in your language to be sure that there is no question as to what your answer is. Put yourself into the "shoes" of the listener to be sure that your answer will be understood (overcoming egocentric communication).
2   Think things through before you answer instead of immediately trying to answer and making a mistake, and then trying again (overcoming trial-and-error).
3   Count to ten (at least) so that you don't say or do something you will be sorry for later (restraining impulsive behavior).
4   If you can't answer a question for some reason even though you "know" the answer, don't fret or panic. Leave the question for a little while and then, when you return to it, use a strategy to help you find the answer (overcoming blocking).

by a mean difference of more than 0.6 standard deviation on the test of the chemical objectives covered in the three weeks (Froufe, 1987).

Finally, I want to return to the politics of change. I am afraid I wrote my abstract in a flush of enthusiasm engendered by an evening with Luis Machado, but I haven't succeeded in catching up with him since and therefore cannot deliver as I had hoped. But in 1979 the Christian Democrats were elected into power in Venezuela, and Machado was appointed Minister for the Development of Intelligence. He first set about getting the trainers trained, which was where I first heard of him as some of them were on Feuerstein's course where I was trained myself. I only hope that his 'cascade' model worked better in practise than our own DES scheme for training teachers for GCSE. But in 1981/82 the programme involved training 200 trainers who would then be responsible for giving in-service training to 100,000 teachers. Among the methods used were Feuerstein's IE, and the DeBono training scheme. It is rather nice to see the equivalent of one of our government White Papers from 1982 with the title *The Democratization of Intelligence* with contents free alike from the smell of Marxism and the similarly repulsive doctrinaire thinking that we have to suffer almost daily from our politicians in this country. I would dearly like to lay my hands on the result of all this. It is curious to see how very very much more pessimistic Bruner is on this issue within only two years of this Venezuelan paper. He says (p 148): 'We are . . . in deep malaise. It is difficult for any theory of human development to gain a hold on the 'cultural imagination' of those who dread [because of the danger of our annhilating ourselves with unthinkably powerful weapons] that there may be no future.'

But why do we have to be so defensive about 'twentieth-century liberalism'?

This is, of course, a rhetorical question. The Christian Democrats are now out of power in Venezuela, and even if Machado claimed 'In Venezuela the development of intelligence has not been tarnished by party rivalry' it does appear to me that there is a connection between the specifics of the details of teaching and education and politics in a deeper sense. Kenneth Baker, with the Centre for Policy Studies behind him, have not only realized this, but are actively beavering away at the specifics of how to change schools so as to reinstitutionalize privilege. Not only I but many of the constructivists here have been into applied research and related curriculum development with the same implicit universalist assumptions as Machado used. Have we all faced the political reasons which governed the development of our educational practices which we all seem to be trying to change? It seems to me that if the intervention programmes that I have discussed were wholeheartedly put into practice then we need to anticipate the effects of the gradual transformation of the spectrum of pupil achievement, and the gradual transformation of the professional expertise of the teacher which would accompany it. You cannot expect to change the scope of the pupil without at the same time altering the scope of the teacher. And you must anticipate political reaction to the whole process. If I were at the beginning of my career I hope I would have the sense to realize that working on the means is not enough: unless you have a working theory of ends and how they interact with means, you are not likely to get the chance to implement the means. I hope I would have chosen not to be so politically innocent.

References

BRUNER, J. (1986) *Actual Minds, Possible Worlds*, Harvard, Harvard University Press.

DRIVER, R. and ERICKSON, G. (1983) 'Theories-in-action', *Studies in Science Education*, 10, pp 37–60.

FEUERSTEIN, R. in collaboration with RAND, Y. and HOFFMAN, M.B. (1979) *The Dynamic Assessment of Retarded Performers: The Learning Potential Device*, Baltimore, MD, University Park Press.

FEUERSTEIN, R. in collaboration with RAND, Y., HOFFMAN, M. and MILLER, R. (1980) *Instrumental Enrichment*, Baltimore, MD, University Park Press.

FROUFE, J. (1987) 'Feuerstein's theory applied to the school science curriculum', MA dissertation, King's College, University of London.

HAUTAMAKI, J. (1987) 'The measurement and distribution of Piagetian stage of thinking in Finnish comprehensive school', *Publications of Social Sciences 1*, University of Joensu.

JOHN, E.R. (1977) *Functional Neuroscience* (Volume II), Hillsdale, N.J. Lawrence Erlbaum Associates, pp 248–9.

MEHL, M.C. (1985) 'The cognitive difficulties of first year physics students at the University of the Western Cape and various compensatory programmes', PhD, University of Cape Town, S. Africa.

OSBORNE, R. and WITTROCK, M. (1985) 'The generative learning model and its implications for science education', *Studies in Science Education*, 12, pp 59–87.

SAYRE, S. and BALL, D.W. (1975) 'Piagetian cognitive development and achievement in science,' *Journal of Research in Science Education*, 12, 2, pp 165–74.

SHAYER, M. (1987) 'Neo-Piagetian theories and educational practice', *International Journal of Psychology*.

SHAYER, M. and BEASLEY, F. (1987) 'Does instrumental enrichment work?', *British Educational Research Journal*, 13, 2, pp 101–19.

WELLER, K. and CRAFT, A. (1983) *Making up our Minds: An Exploratory Study of Instrumental Enrichment*, London, Schools Council.

Respondent: Pinchas Tamir

The main message that emerges from Shayer's chapter is to the teachers: it is that we can change our schools and we can change our students. It is possible to teach our students much more than we are currently achieving in schools. It is interesting to note that from a completely different psychological starting point, Bloom used a model of individual tutoring and mastery learning, and apparently showed that it was possible to raise achievement levels by about one standard deviation. Much as one would like to believe in such possibilities, one must be very careful in drawing conclusions from small-scale studies.

I am not very clear about the implications for teaching of the 'brain-growth spurts' to which Shayer has referred. The existence of such brain-growth spurts does not, in itself, say much about the possibilities of learning during brain growth spurt periods.

Returning to the teachers, there is a question raised about the most effective way of transmitting our 'new' methodologies to teachers. Is it possible to *train* teachers in the techniques, in a rather mechanistic way? Or should we rather work together with the teachers as they teach science, to learn from them as much as we introduce some new ideas.

There is the question also of what we see as the content of the science curriculum. If we only want to teach reasoning skills, we could as well teach this through the Talmud, but our aim in science education is not only to develop reasoning skills but also to lead students to a better understanding of science concepts. What we need, it seems to me, is pedagogical understanding which is subject-specific. Teachers need to be inducted both into scientific understanding and into the pedagogy of teaching science. People who understand both pedagogy and science are the ones who are in a position to develop a specific pedagogy of science teaching. The study of misconceptions is a good example of the development of such a specific understanding related to the learning of science.

A rather disturbing aspect of the work reported by Shayer is the apparent absence of any effect on science achievement tests. This may be something to do with the type of achievement tests used, and perhaps a further investigation using tests composed of items of the multiple-choice plus justification type would yield richer data. Improvement in reasoning ability should be reflected in improvement in the quality of the justifications given.

Discussion (Reporter Piet Lÿnse)

Shayer agreed almost entirely with the points made by Tamir — the point about brain-growth is that although, in itself, it does not tell us much, it is age-related, differently for boys and girls, and seems to be a variable that we should at least recognize as having the possibility of bearing on learning and cognitive development.

A questionner wondered why Shayer concentrated on such narrow issues as the development of specific reasoning patterns. She was more concerned with the application of general scientific principles to the phenomena of everyday life, such as sunset and sunrise. This involves the shift of pupils' conceptualization from naive to more sophisticated forms, related to the real world as they know it. Did any of Shayer's work relate to the transfer of reasoning skills from one concept to another?

Shayer responded that this was an important task, so far bigger than they had tackled specifically, although the methods he had described did include a requirement to 'bridge' concepts and thinking skills from the immediate context to other contexts that were familiar to pupils from everyday life or from other science lessons.

One participant said that he was not surprised that no gains had been apparent in achievement tests. To expect there to be such gains would suppose the type of link between 'intelligence' and achievement implied the psychometrics of Cyril Burt. The Piagetian notion of cognitive development is not so directly linked to achievement.

In order to gain a deeper insight into what is happening in the teaching process, the idea of a diary to be kept by pupils and by teachers was proposed. This technique allows for reflection on teaching and learning practice, and so promotes metacognition.

Finally, the point was made of the need for teachers to internalise the new methodologies that we are promoting. It is not sufficient to *tell* teachers. Rather, it is necessary to work with them. Teacher education is not simply a matter of replacing one set of skills with another.

5 Theory in Practice: How to Assist Science Teachers to Teach Constructively

Peter J. Fensham

The purpose of this chapter is to explore how research in science education can inform and influence the practice of science education through the pre- and in-service education of teachers. To this end, past, present, and developing styles of research are considered in order to demonstrate the links between some currently popular approaches to research and earlier investigations of science learning.

This sort of reflection on previous work inevitably should involve an elaboration of the personal epistemologies of those responsible. Consequently the discussion deliberately draws heavily on the evolution of the research in science education at Monash University over the last two decades (Gunstone, White and Fensham, 1988). This leads to a consideration of present research in terms of the relations between research and practice, and of the implications these have had for the education of science teachers.

Past Research — Focus on Treatments

In the late 1960s educational research was dominated by experiments featuring multivariate statistical analyses in which the main concern was to see whether one treatment of teaching/learning was better than another, rather than to consider how or why individuals differ. Research in the learning of science was no exception, but by the later 1970s a different research perspective had emerged in which the beliefs of individuals were important and the comparison of treatments was given much less attention. This general description of progression in science education research is mirrored among the group at Monash University so that presenting it as a detailed case study helps to identify reasons behind this change in focus.

The beginning of science education research at Monash University about 1970 was naturally influenced by the characteristics of the people involved. All of the then researchers had had strong background studies in science and recent science teaching experience at secondary or tertiary level. Hence, either because of explicit experience of the sorts of empirical investigations in common use in the physical sciences or because of a natural familiarity with them through their extended learning of these sciences, they had an easy and natural affinity with the sorts of experimental designs for educational research that had been described so cogently by Campbell and Stanley (1963).

Accordingly, a number of the early studies at Monash (for example, White, 1974; Linke, 1974; Gardner, 1974; West and Fensham, 1976) are marked not only by their adherence to a manipulative or experimental method, but by the contributions they made to extend the modes of analysis for the data of such research (for example, Gardner, 1970; White and Clark, 1973; McArthur and West, 1974).

Complex designs and sophisticated mathematical analyses were thus, as it happened, easier ways for these ex-science teachers to enter research into the teaching and learning of science than was a more contemplative approach to the teaching and learning situation itself. In hindsight, we all accepted uncritically some primitive and over-simple models of learning which ignored most of the context of the learner and of the teaching situation, and which even gave little acknowledgement to the nature of the scientific knowledge being learnt. Hence we ignored important factors such as the nature of the content to be learned, the motives of the learners, their reactions to our experiment, and whether they perceived any conflict between the experiment and the educational context to which they were accustomed. The effect of these factors in producing variation between students' scores within each experimental group was seen as a nuisance. That variation was labelled 'error', and deplored because of its tendency to mask group differences. It was, however, in the long run the consideration of these 'errors' that led to questions which spurred much of our subsequent research.

Two of the apparently simple learning models which had a complementary attractiveness for us were those of Gagné and Ausubel. Gagné's (1968) stress on the hierarchical nature of cognitive learning was naturally attractive to the learning of the sciences which we had so often been told were sequential in the nature of their knowledge relationships. White (1974), Thomas (1975) and Beeson (1977) all used these sorts of hierarchies for research into topics in secondary school physics and chemistry, but this simple approach to what was to be learnt was challenged when university level teachers of the sciences found the task of spelling out hierarchies far from easy and tended to want to define multiple routes and much more complex interactions between the concepts and skills. Among the questions which were raised by subsequent reflection on the results of this series of studies were: why did some students learn faster or better than others who received the same treatment? And why did some remember the subject matter longer?

These questions were important in that they encouraged us to consider both the nature of memory for science knowledge, and the strategies that people use in learning (Gagné and White, 1978), issues that have become prominent in our subsequent research.

The studies based on Ausubel's theory (for example, West and Fensham, 1976), intensified our interest in both these issues. Ausubel's concern for the process of learning and, in particular, for how the existing knowledge of a learner interacts with new information presented for learning, seemed to fill a gap between the levels of the hierarchies (West and Fensham, 1974), but again, despite a sophisticated design and analysis, the authors were conscious that their research had not really lifted the veil from the learning process.

The fascination of what lay beyond the idea of hierarchy in science learning and how to organise new learning was hinted at by several other studies. Fensham (1972) had found that certain knowledge the students had successfully acquired in physics and chemistry was responsible for unhelpful and erroneous assumptions many of them made about other topics they were subsequently required to learn. Heffernan (1980) investigated what he called a 'hierarchy of understanding'. In studies that involved three fields of science knowledge, he found discrepancies between what the teachers and their senior students saw as the higher level of understanding. The teachers saw problem solving that involved the application of algorithms embodying relations between concepts as the ultimate level, whereas the students tended to regard stating the nature of the relations themselves as more difficult.

A few minor studies did replicate Piagetian procedures for interacting with individual students (Phillips, 1972; Phillips, 1977) but the great bulk of our interactions with learners were via paper and pencil instructions or tests under controlled conditions of administration. Nevertheless these few studies and the active debates in Australia in the early 1970s about the appropriateness of Piagetian theory as a basis for the science curriculum and teaching (for example, Australian Science Education Project, 1974; Blake, 1973 and 1978; Dale, 1970; Nixon, 1978; Tisher, 1967) and the possibilities of group versus individual tests of Piagetian stages (Henry and Hanna, 1978; Moritz, 1972; Tisher, 1971) did serve to keep us aware of alternative data collection procedures that were to become our dominant mode after 1980.

Other Formative Influences

Research experience was not the only influence on the Monash group. The active involvement of various members in decisive roles for the curriculum content of school science (such as external examiners, designers of curriculum materials, and pre- and in-service educators of science teachers) encouraged the group to reflect on the powerful contextual constraints that operate to maintain certain definitions of what science is, how it should be taught, and what is recognized as learning of worth (for example, Fensham 1976 and 1980). Significant for the group's directions was its growing acceptance of all of these pointers to the complexity of what had initially been seen as a relatively simple sort of learning.

Table 5.1 Stages in a strand of research studies based on conceptions of scientific concepts and natural phenomena

Stages in Science Conceptions Studies
1   Student conceptions of natural phenomena
2   Teachers conceptions of natural phenomena
3   Conceptual change in students and teachers
4   Teaching involving methods of conceptions research
5   Action research with teachers in schools informed by conceptions research

Convergence to Two-lanes

By the middle of the 1970s the several rather separate approaches described above needed to converge. A common focus in the questions explored by the separate strands of Monash work was the learner. However, it took us quite a time to recognize this, possibly because it required us to switch from a stance which essentially was a teacher perspective (socialized by our own and their success in science) to one that reflected much more the view that learners (unsocialized by such success) have of science and science teaching. At this point it also became apparent that the experimental paradigm for research, with its inherent feature of 'treatment' is consistent with a teacher perspective but certainly is not consistent with a learner's stance. This shift of focus and its accompanying search for new research methods were gropingly explored in several papers as the 1970s became the 1980s (Fensham, 1983; Gilbert, Osborne and Fensham, 1982; White, 1982).

In taking the learner seriously we also had to take the science content more seriously. It was no longer good enough to assume that science content is established with a meaning that is provided by public (i.e. contemporary scientists) or textbook science. It was the meaning, that learners attached to it and its phenomena that we had to explore, if we were to have any hope of knowing how and why learners relate to the real world of natural phenomena and hence to what happens in their science classes.

Two major strands then began to develop in our research which are evident precursors to what we are now doing in the education of science teachers — both initial and inservice. Each of these has logically developed over the last decade, although one strand preceded the other by several years, perhaps inevitably, given our original backgrounds in science rather than in psychology.

Conceptions Research

The first strand is indicated in table 5.1 and can be entitled Science Conceptions Studies. The second strand is presented in table 5.2 and is suitably described as Metacognitive Studies.

Our initial work on science conceptions occurred in physics (Gunstone and White, 1980) and chemistry (West, Fensham and Garrard, 1982). Visits to and from Roger Osborne (University of Waikato, New Zealand), Audrey Champagne (University of Pittsburgh) and Joe Novak (Cornell University) enabled us to explore with confidence a range of techniques for eliciting data. Hence, we gained experience of Interviews about Instances and Events, DOE, and Concept Mapping and V-diagrams. We had already tried word association procedures in some earlier studies (for example, Gunstone, 1980).

As our appreciation of the strengths and weaknesses of these research tools grew, we began to consider and try some of them as teaching/learning procedures. This was an obvious stage (the fourth in table 5.1) since in our data collection for these research studies we often experienced the sense of 'ah-ha' from the student respondents as well as the 'ha-ha's' that made this new more intimate style of research such good fun.

In 1979 Margaret Brumby joined the group, adding biological conceptions to our range of studies, and equally importantly familiarity with Gilbert's group at Surrey and the interests and ideas of Pask (1976) and Marton (1981). The association with Marton has grown steadily since then and has been a spur to link these research findings to teacher education.

Our interests in the historical development of concepts in science meant that we, like many other research groups in the conception's field, recognized similarities between the explanations children gave to us and those that were orthodoxy in the earlier development of the sciences when the scientists of those times also built and invented theories on empirical evidence that was much more restricted than that that provides the current scientific descriptions and views.

The next stage in this conceptions strand was to explore in several studies the conceptions that science teachers hold of the sorts of concepts and phenomena we had been studying in young learners. Some isolated studies (Fensham, 1984; Garrard and Brumby, 1984) led on to a major longitudinal study (Arzi, White and Fensham, 1987) that is still proceeding. It quickly became clear that teachers can hold a range of conceptions about science phenomena that include, and differ from, the contemporary scientific one, and which are sometimes similar to those alternative frameworks that our studies of learners had revealed. This was particularly (although not exclusively) so for concepts and phenomena that are mainly associated with sciences that were other than those formally studied by our teacher respondents. This is important in Australia where science is taught in an integrated way till at least grade 10 or 11 so that most science teachers are teaching topics they have not formally studied. We have also observed in the science field in which the teacher has been fully trained, a tendency for 'teacher conceptions' of some phenomena or concepts. These conceptions seem to be a consequence of the pedagogical situation that science teachers are in, where for example, the distinction between an observable fact and its associated concepts or explanation easily get blurred.

Table 5.2 *Stages in a strand of research studies based on awareness of learning processes*

Stages in Metacognitive Studies

---

1 Differences in learning styles
2 Bad habits in learning
3 Teaching students about learning and changing learning habits
4 Action research with teachers in schools focussed on student learning

---

We have been conscious from the early days of this strand of our research that one could go on studying children's conceptions of one science concept (or phenomenon) after another for a long time in a 'stamp collecting way'. A visit (again two-way) by Merle Wittrock (University of California, Los Angeles) helped us to relate more substantially to a constructivist view of learning. His generative learning theory (see Osborne and Wittrock, 1985) was one that made sense with our findings. We needed a theory of learning that accepted that quite young learners could relate their prior knowledge and experience in logical ways to the sorts of problems our research probes presented. The restrictions that the developmental bases of Piagetian reasoning placed on young learners was not consonant with our findings and our use, in our research reports and practices, of the term 'children's science' was largely to emphasize the way limited empirical experiences were logically built on by our respondents (Gunstone, 1988).

The third stage of this strand was to study how these science conceptions could be changed, and several studies with both students (Gunstone, Champagne and Klopfer, 1981; Mitchell and Gunstone, 1984), and with teachers (Baird, 1986; Champagne, Gunstone and Klopfer, 1985) were undertaken. Through the many opportunities we had to share with teachers our findings about their students' conceptions at science teacher conferences and in-service events, we also learnt the hard way that teachers also need to construct for themselves new conceptions about science and about their students' ideas about science. About this time the importance of 'context' as a key aspect for research on teaching/learning began to get formal recognition (White, 1985).

The fourth stage in table 5.1 was accelerated through the involvement of teachers who were undertaking postgraduate studies for research degrees in education, and by the voluntary return to the science classroom for a year of Gunstone and Northfield — two of the Monash researchers. These studies (Northfield and Gunstone, 1985; Gotts, 1982; Fensham, Garrard and West, 1981) enabled us to identify some research practices, (see 1, 2, 3 in table 5.3) from conceptions studies that were adaptable for use in the normal teaching of science in classrooms.

The fifth stage in table 5.1 coincides with the last stage in table 5.2, so its description will be delayed until our first forays into meta-cognition have been described.

Metacognitive Research

The second strand of research studies is presented in table 5.2.

It began when Baird and White (1982a), in an intensive case study of how a few adult learners learnt a new topic in genetics, identified two contrasting learning styles, one of which seemed to be more likely to lead to deeper understanding. It was characterized by reflection by the learner on the meaning of the information being presented, and by a drive, again from the learner herself, to relate it to subjects outside the topic itself such as literature, history and personal experience. The other learning style was limited to dealing with the information in its own boundaries and in the directions the teacher presented.

The second stage in table 5.2 resulted from another case study by Baird and White (1982b) in which a group of tertiary students were probed about their learning styles and the effects these had on their effective learning in biology. Seven bad habits were identified that can be generally described as geared to superficiality, premature closure and lack of reflection on the meaning of new information and how it relates to existing beliefs. Little success was reported in this study in the efforts over six weeks that were made to improve the learning styles.

In a now classic study, Baird and White (1984) then spent six months in one school working with a teacher and three of his biology classes to promote purposeful and reflective learning. This third stage study (table 5.2) involved many different forms of observation and measurement — videotaped lessons, audio-taped conversations with the teacher and the students, concept maps, the keeping of a learning diary that emphasised the rating of learning styles and self-ratings of each student's approach to learning. This study had moderate success with the students, little effect on the teacher, and was constrained by being confined to only one of the students' interactions with teaching and learning, namely, their biology classes (Baird, 1986).

As a consequence, a more substantial project emerged that is the first of the studies now underway entitled Action Research with Teachers (stage 5 in table 5.1 and stage 4 in table 5.2). The project now well known by its acronym PEEL was a Programme to Enhance Effective Learning. Mitchell — a Monash researcher — was also a teacher half-time in a hitherto rather undistinguished suburban high school in Melbourne, and Baird and White, as university-based consultants or 'friends', obtained the willingness of nine other teachers of various subjects at the lower levels of secondary education to commit themselves to work together *to improve the quality of learning among their students* over a period of two years.

Initially the teachers were aware of little more than the aim just stated, although it was suggested that this would involve various procedures for increasing students' knowledge of what learning is, and how it happens. As time passed each teacher both explored some of the possibilities suggested by Mitchell or the 'friends' and suggested others themselves.

As weeks became months the teachers increasingly controlled the project, making more suggestions, determining its pace, and reflecting on and accepting responsibility for its outcomes in their students. They were, through all of these processes and in their collaboration with the 'friends', changing as persons in the way they viewed their task as teachers, their students as learners, and their subject as content to be taught. The progress of the project is, to my mind, constructivism in practice. White (1988) has analyzed the interplay of theory and practice in this project and indicated how practice informed theory as well as theory informing practice. He also points to the need for researchers in this sort of collaborative action to prepare themselves for practices they may not envisage.

During its second year the teachers and the 'friends' felt the need and had the interest to describe for others the project and their experiences in it. The result was the book *Improving the Quality of Teaching and Learning: An Australian Case Study — The Peel Project* (Baird and Mitchell, 1986). This remarkable achievement and outcome of the project would have been unimaginable by these high school teachers at the beginning of their tentative adventure together fifteen months earlier.

Three reviews of the PEEL project have recently been reported and their contrasting assessments of the usefulness of its findings for teacher education are striking. Northfield, one of the key figures in the research-based approach to science teacher education at Monash, found the report from the project of the experience of the teacher and the outcomes in the classroom for students, a very positive set of findings to transfer into the programme of a year of teacher training for science graduates that is common in Britain (PGCE), and in Australia (DipEd.) (Baird, Mitchell and Northfield, 1987). He dismisses the obvious suggestion that the project and its findings are idiosyncratic reflections of the personalities of this particular group of teachers because he finds the conditions for change, the broad outcomes and the effects on the teachers, to be consistent with those found and recorded by others who have studied effective change in teachers (for example, Posner, Strike, Hewson and Gertzog, 1982; Hewson and Hewson, 1983).

West (1988), on the other hand, reaches a much gloomier conclusion about the usefulness of the PEEL project, although he too does not simply dismiss its findings on idiosyncratic grounds.

More careful examination of the reactions by these two teacher educators and a knowledge of the conditions under which they work enables sense to be made of these otherwise rather conflicting appraisals. Northfield is involved in teacher training programmes where the critical features of PEEL, namely ongoing professional and peer support, extended time for reflection on conceptions and understanding of the content being taught, and repeated opportunities for critical self-appraisal are all possibilities in the year available for these programmes.

West, on the other hand, is involved in teacher education much more marginally. He is part of a higher education research and advisory group, part

Table 5.3 Data collecting and other procedures from conceptions and metacognitive research studies that have been adaptable for teaching/learning use in classrooms

Teaching/Learning Practices from Research
1   Word and other associations with content for learning
2   Concept mapping
3   Interpretive discussion of alternative frameworks
4   Categorising knowledge
5   Keeping Learning diaries
6(a) Asking types of questions
6(b) Answering types of questions
7(a) Identifying my errors in learning
7(b) Correcting my errors in learning

of the responsibilities of which is to improve teaching and learning in the university across the whole spectrum of faculties. He is involved in short one or two session workshops just prior to the start of each academic year on 'teaching' (or more specifically on 'lecturing' or 'running small group tutorials') and in giving advice to individual staff who, on a voluntary basis, may seek help during the year with an aspect of their teaching. The critical variables of PEEL are not available to him as he seeks to offer tips on better communication to university style lecturers.

The third review is by Barnes (1987), who visited Monash from Leeds in 1986 while the book was being finalized. Barnes was able to spend time in the school on a number of occasions, so had first hand experience of the project as well as the book to review. He was struck by the fact that 'perfectly normal teachers are thinking analytically about teaching on the basis of principle, and that the project has generated a powerful current of purpose and mutual support that would benefit any school'.

Adapting Research and Theory to Classrooms

In table 5.3, a number of teaching practices or learning activities are given that have, through our own and others research, proved to be adaptable from research studies (such as those in tables 5.1 and 5.2) to classroom practice.

As our teaching responsibilities at the University relate to the education of teachers, an obvious task was to try to incorporate what we were learning from research into our teacher education programmes.

None of the practices in table 5.3 were significantly used in our initial teacher education programme for science teachers or in our in-service work with practising teachers before the later 1970s. It is the gradual incorporation of these over the last few years into the Monash teacher training programme and into in-service work that justifies in part our claim to be putting theory into

Table 5.4   Conditions and activities that are included in initial teacher education as a result of research findings

1   Sharing findings from conceptions research
2   Activities that engage student teachers in the construction of their own conceptions of scientific topics.
3   Providing skills that enable student teachers to explore collaboratively adolescent students conceptions of scientific topics.
4   Activities that help student teachers to construct conceptions of how adolescents and they themselves learn and are taught science.
5   Interpersonal support for engaging in 2, 3 and 4.
6   Time to share experiences and their outcomes.
7   Personal and group reflection on the learning and teaching in the teacher training course — diary keeping and sharing.

practice. The rest of the claim depends upon other changes to the programme and to the style of in-service which make these activities in it, not simply more tricks for teachers to master for use when they get to classrooms, but means whereby these persons are enabled to construct new conceptions of the science they are going to teach, new views of the learning processes they themselves are undergoing and of the teaching/learning experiences that make up the life of school classrooms.

The research studies, and particularly the way they have evolved in each of the two strands, have also provided us with a confidence in our generally constructivist theory or view of learning, so that we ourselves are better able to understand and to cope with what can happen when it takes on a practical form like teacher education.

Table 5.4 lists some of the features of the current initial teacher education programme at Monash that are direct consequences of our research.

Needless to say it has been necessary to drop a number of other traditionally present parts of year-long programmes for science teacher education.

Elsewhere several more detailed accounts of these features and the programme are now available (Northfield and Gunstone, 1983; Gunstone and Northfield, 1987; Baird *et al*, 1987). The last of these references also outlines the first stage of an evaluation of this programme which will follow a group of these student teachers through their first two years in the classroom.

In like manner, but less systematically, the findings of our research are appearing in the way we participate in in-service education. Because of the format of the events that constitute opportunities for in-service education of teachers, the consistent application of key features of our findings are often impossible. The single session at a conference or even a two or three-hour workshop are hardly conducive to the reconstruction and reflection processes we have found to be essential features of both adolescent and teacher learning.

Accordingly, we have moved towards the establishment of networks of science teachers. The single session or workshop at an in-service event is used not in a pretence of affecting change, but to advertise and recruit teachers for subsequent networking. These networks are groups of teachers who agree to work together on common classroom related tasks, to share experiences gained in such tasks, and to support each other in various ways. In this way important conditions such as 'time' and 'support' in table 5.4 and its other constructivist activities can be elements of teacher in-service education.

A group of teachers meets monthly at Monash after school with a focus they describe as children's science. Another network has been trying to use short essays by Australian scientists with their classes. Baird is currently working with the science staff of two suburban schools. In each case our central intention is to facilitate the teachers becoming active constructors of their own lives as science teachers of adolescent learners in the contexts that schooling recognises and allows.

Acknowledgements

I am indebted to many colleagues at Monash, a number of whom are referred to in this paper. In particular I would like to thank Dick Gunstone and Dick White, friends and collaborators over many years, who rehearsed with me the first attempts to provide a case history that has, we hope, meaning beyond ourselves.

References

ARZI, A., WHITE, R.T. and FENSHAM, P.J. (1987) 'Teachers' knowledge of science: Early results from a longitudinal study', paper given at the annual meeting of the American Educational Reaseach Association, Washington, D.C., April

Australian Science Education Project (1974) *A Guide to ASEP*, Melbourne, Victorian Government Printer, pp 59–71.

BAIRD, J.R. (1986) 'Improving learning through enhanced metacognition: A classroom study', *European Journal of Science Education*, 8, pp 263–82.

BAIRD, J.R., GUNSTONE, R.F., WHITE, R.T. and FENSHAM, P.J. (1987) *Research in Science Education*, 17, pp 182–91.

BAIRD, J.R. and MITCHELL, I.J. (1986) *Improving the Quality of Teaching and Learning: An Australian Case Study — The Peel Project*, Melbourne, Monash University Printery.

BAIRD, J.R., MITCHELL, I.J. and NORTHFIELD, J.R. (1987) 'Teachers as researchers — the rationale and the reality', *Research in Science Education*, 17, pp 129–38.

BAIRD, J.R. and WHITE, R.T. (1982a) 'A case study of learning styles in biology', *European Journal of Science Education*, 4, pp 323–37.

BAIRD, J.R. and WHITE, R.T. (1982b) 'Promoting self-control of learning', *Instructional Science*, 11, pp 227–47.

BAIRD, J.R. and WHITE, R.T. (1984) 'Improving learning through enhanced metacognition: A classroom study', paper given at the annual meeting of the American Educational Research Association, New Orleans, April.

BARNES, D. (1987) 'Helping pupils to be better learners, A review of the PEEL Project', *Journal of Curriculum Studies*, 19, 6, pp 566–7.

BEESON, G.W. (1977) 'Hierarchical learning in electrical science,' *Journal of Research in Science Teaching*, 14, pp 117–27.

BLAKE, A. (1973) 'Psychological theory and science teaching practice', *Australian Science Teachers Journal*, 19, 4, pp 73–9.

BLAKE, A. (1978) 'The logical capabilities of students in science: Implications for curriculum development', *Australian Science Teachers Journal*, 24, 3, pp 5–14.

CAMPBELL, D.T. and STANLEY, J.C. (1963) 'Experimental and quasi-experimental designs for research on teaching' in Gage N.C. (Ed.), *Handbook of Research on Teaching*, Chicago, IL, Rand McNally.

CHAMPAGNE, A.B., GUNSTONE, R.F. and KLOPFER, LE. (1985) 'Effecting changes in cognitive structures among physics students' in WEST, L.H.T. and PINES, A.L. (Eds) *Cognitive Structure and Conceptual Change*, Academic Press.

DALE, L.G. (1970) 'The growth of systematic thinking replication and analysis of Piaget's first chemical experiment', *Australian Journal of Psychology*, 22, 3, pp 277–86.

FENSHAM, P.J. (1972) 'Prior knowledge — A source of negative factors for subsequent learning', *Research 1972* (Aust. Sci. Ed. Res. Assoc.) pp 50–7.

FENSHAM, P.J. (1976) 'Social content in chemistry courses', *Chemistry in Britain*, 12, pp 148–51.

FENSHAM, P.J. (1980) 'Constraint and autonomy in Australian secondary education', *Journal of Curriculum Studies*, 12, pp 189–206.

FENSHAM, P.J. (1983) 'A research base for new objectives of science teaching', *Science Education*, 67, pp 3–12.

FENSHAM, P.J. (1984) 'Selective cueing among chemistry teachers', *Research in Science Education*, 14, pp 146–56.

FENSHAM, P.J., GARRARD, J.E. and WEST, L.H.T. (1981) 'The use of cognitive mapping in teaching and learning strategies', *Research in Science Education*, 11, pp 121–9.

FENSHAM, P.J., GARRARD, J. and WEST, L. (1982) 'A comparative critique of several methods of collecting data for cognitive mapping', *Research in Science Education*, 12, pp 9–16.

GAGNÉ, R.M. (1968) 'Learning hierarchies', *Educational Psychologist*, 6, pp 1–9.

GAGNÉ, R.M., and WHITE, R.T. (1978) 'Memory structures and learning outcomes', *Review of Educational Research*, 48, pp 187–222.

GARDNER, P.L. (1970) 'Test length and the standard error of measurement', *Journal of Educational Measurement*, 7, pp 271–3.

GARDNER, P.L. (1974) 'Deterioration of high school students' attitudes to physics', *Nature*, 250, pp 465–6.

GARRARD, J. and BRUMBY, M. (1984) 'Students' perceptions of health', *Research in Science Education*, 14, pp 1–13.

GILBERT, J.K., OSBORNE, R.J. and FENSHAM, P.J. (1982) 'Children's science and its consequences for teaching', *Science Education*, 66, pp 623–33.

GOTTS, D.R. (1982) 'Concept mapping — its use in the school context', MEd thesis, Monash University.

GUNSTONE, R.F. (1980) 'Word association and the description of cognitive structure', *Research in Science Education*, 10, pp 45–53.

GUNSTONE, R.F. (1988) 'Learners in science education' in Fensham, P.J. (Ed) *Developments and Dilemmas in Science Education*, Lewes, Falmer Press, Chapter 4.

GUNSTONE, R.F., CHAMPAGNE, A.B. and KLOPFER, L.E. (1981) 'Instruction for understanding: A case study', *Australian Science Teachers Journal*, 27, 3, pp 27–32.

GUNSTONE, R.F. and NORTHFIELD, J.R. (1987) '*Constructivist views of teacher education*', paper given at the meeting of the South Pacific Association of Teacher Education, Ballarat, Victoria, July.

GUNSTONE, R.F. and WHITE, R.T. (1980) 'A matter of gravity', *Research in Science Education*, 10, pp 35–44.

GUNSTONE, R.F., WHITE, R.T. and FENSHAM, P.J. (1988) 'Developments in style and purpose of research on the learning of science', *Education, Science*, 65.

HEFFERNAN, M.W. (1980) *'The measurement of understanding'*, unpublished MEd thesis, Monash University.

HENRY, J.A. and HANNA, P.J. (1978) 'An analysis of a group test for distinguishing formal from concrete thinkers', *Australian Science Teachers Journal*, 24, 2, pp 85–91.

HEWSON, M.G.A.B. and HEWSON, P. W. (1983) 'The effect of instruction using students' prior knowledge and conceptual change strategies', *Journal of Research in Science Teaching*, 20, pp 731–42.

LINKE, R.D. (1974) 'Influence of cultural background on hierarchical learning', *Journal of Educational Psychology*, 66, pp 911–8.

McARTHUR, J.T. and WEST, L.H.T. (1974) 'Multiple regression as a general data analysis technique', *Research in Science Education*, 4, pp 185–92.

McDERMOTT, L.C. (1984) 'Research on conceptual understanding in mechanics', *Physics Today*, July, 37, 7, pp 24–32.

MARTON, F. (1981) 'Phenomenography', *Instructional Science*, 10, pp 177–200.

MITCHELL, I.J. and GUNSTONE, R.F. (1984) 'Some student conceptions brought to the study of stoichiometry', *Research in Science Education*, 14, pp 78–88.

MORITZ, K. (1972) 'Some suggestions for research related to ASEP', *Research 1972*.

NIXON, M. (1978) 'The nature of the learner: A point of view and implications for curricula', *Australian Science Teachers Journal*, 24, 3, pp 15–22.

NORTHFIELD, J.R. and GUNSTONE, R.F. (1983) 'Research on alternative frameworks: Implications for science teacher educators', *Research in Science Education*, 13, pp 71–7.

NORTHFIELD, J.R. and GUNSTONE, R.F. (1985) 'Understanding learning at the classroom level', *Research in Science Education*, 15, pp 18–27.

OSBORNE, R. and WITTROCK, M. (1985) 'The generative learning model and its implications for science education', *Studies in Science Education*, 12, pp 59–87.

PASK, G. (1976) 'Styles and strategies of learning', *British Journal of Educational Psychology*, 46, pp 128–48.

PHILLIPS, A.H. (1972) *'Children's understanding of causality of some natural phenomena'*, unpublished MEd thesis, Monash University.

PHILLIPS, J.C. (1977) *'Science and language'*, unpublished MEd thesis, Monash University.

POSNER, G.J., STRIKE, K.A., HEWSON, P.W. and GERTZOG, W.A. (1982) 'Accommodation of a scientific conception: Toward a theory of conceptual change', *Science Education*, 66 pp 211–27.

THOMAS, I.D. (1975) *'Mathematical skills in electrostatics'*, unpublished MEd thesis, Monash University.

TISHER, R.P. (1967) 'My father told me: Children's explanations of some natural phenomena', *Australian Journal of Education*, 11, 3, pp 204–11.

TISHER, R.P. (1971) 'The Piaget questionnaire applied to pupils in secondary schools'. *Child Development*, pp 1633–6.

WEST, L.H.T. (1988) 'Implication of recent research for improving senior science learning' in Ramsden, P. (Ed.) *Improving Learning: New Perspectives*, Kogan Page, Chapter 3.

WEST, L.H.T. and FENSHAM, P.J. (1974) 'Prior knowledge and the learning of science: A review of Ausubel's theory of this process', *Studies in Science Education*, 1, pp 61–81.

WEST, L.H.T. and FENSHAM, P.J. (1976) 'Prior knowledge or advance organizers as effective variables in chemical learning', *Journal of Research in Science Teaching*, 13, pp 297–306.

WEST, L.H.T., FENSHAM, P.J. and GARRARD, J. (1982) *Describing the Cognitive Structure of Undergraduate Chemistry Students*, Report to E.R.D.C., Clayton, Victoria,

HEARU, Monash University.

WEST, L.H.T., GARRARD, J, and FENSHAM, P.J. (1982) 'Intended cognitions in science teaching', *Australian Science Teachers Journal*, 28, 1, pp 5–12.

WHITE, R.T. (1974) 'The validation of a learning hierarchy', *American Educational Research Journal*, 11, pp 121–36.

WHITE, R.T. (1982) 'Changes in theories, paradigms, methods and questions', *Australian Educational Research*, 10, 1, pp 5–14.

WHITE, R.G. (1985) 'The importance of context in educational research', *Research in Science Education*, 15, pp 92–102.

WHITE, R.T. (1988) 'Theory into practice' in FENSHAM, P.J. (Ed) *Developments and Dilemmas in Science Education*, Lewes, Falmer Press, Chapter 6.

WHITE, R.T. and CLARKE, R.M. (1973) 'A test of inclusion which allows for errors of measurement', *Psychometrika*, 38, pp 77–86.

Respondent: Ann C Howe

Fensham has given us a very interesting account of the evolution of science education research at Monash and a thoughtful assessment of where they are now and how they got to this point.

The period covered in his chapter corresponds to the period of my own involvement in science education and his review of the changes in interests and enthusiasms that have occurred during that time certainly apply to science education in the United States in the past two decades.

Research in science education in the United States in the 60s and 70s was partly driven by a need for academic respectability. Many of those involved had been trained in one of the sciences and felt that they had to prove themselves, and make science education respectable, by the rigor of their research. I think this is one reason why there was such enthusiasm for complex statistics, Campbell and Stanley, comparison of treatments and all the other efforts to reduce a complex reality to a set of small numbers. Michael Polanyi, the physicist turned philosopher, remarked that psychology had imitated science in its research methods but that the science the psychologists imitated was not good science. I think science education for a time was imitating psychology imitating science and now, looking back, we can see that our efforts were not as productive as we hoped they would be. I had an opportunity several years ago to talk with Don Campbell (the Campbell of Campbell and Stanley fame) about the almost slavish adherence in science education in the United States to their research designs and he said, as we would expect, that that was much too narrow a range of possibilities to be adopted for research in any field and particularly in education.

All of this is to say that the description of science education given in the chapter seems very familiar to me and, I expect, to others of us who were working in the United States during that time.

For me the most exciting thing in the chapter we have just read is the effort to get teachers — and ourselves — to examine their own — and our own — conceptions, not about physics or chemistry or biology, but about teaching, about how pupils learn, and about how change is brought about. Unlike some of my colleagues, I do not think that teaching can ever be scientific in the sense that we will be able to predict with certainty that a given action will always produce a given result, but we can hope to establish some general principles by working with teachers in the context of their classrooms. If we have been atheoretical, as we have often been accused of being, it may have been because there were so few useful theories and, if that is indeed the case, it may be more productive now to develop theory grounded in the reality of the classroom than to search for and apply a ready-made theory that ignores much of the reality that we know.

I must say that I am glad that I have lived long enough to see a return to the recognition of the central place of the teacher and the demise of the teacher-proof curriculum. For those of you who are not familiar with that term

— if there is anyone — it referred to a curriculum that could not be affected in any way by the teacher; just as a rust-proof automobile cannot be attacked by rust. The teacher was to be a technician soon to be replaced, in the minds of some, by a television screen. The child-proof curriculum was also in vogue at one time in the form of such things as individually prescribed instruction, a curriculum that took all children through the same small steps in the same sequence, usually without benefit of interaction with the teacher or other children.

Now we are seeing a general movement in educational research, and not only science education research, in which the focus is on the teacher and the pupils in the classroom. Coming from different perspectives and different disciplines, researchers are studying what teachers are thinking, how they teach, what pupils are thinking and how they learn, not in isolation but in the classroom.

This, it seems to me, is the kind of research that the Monash group is now engaged in. It is noteworthy that in moving away from their previous concerns and research questions they have also moved away from theory-driven research to research that is atheoretical and more intuitive. In my view what Fensham has given us is not an account of putting theory into practice, as the title of his talk suggests, but, rather, an account of studying practice without benefit of theory. Thus he has raised one of the central issues in educational research at the moment; that is, whether we need an alternative to the old model of research based on theory and, if so, what guidelines are available for an atheoretical research agenda.

Discussion (Reporter: Trevor Bond)

Fensham's historical review of the development of educational research in Monash University struck a responsive chord in many colleagues who had similarly been involved in this type of enterprise over an extended period. His reflection on earlier work as having been done strictly within a psychometric paradigm seemed to imply that the quest for academic respectibility was of considerable, if not prime, importance. Apparently, a successful research program only goes part of the way to answering the original pedagogical questions — more often, it refocusses those questions or raises altogether new questions about science, those who teach it and those who learn. The consequent inappropriateness of the psychometric tradition to these new questions had led researchers to new paradigms based on action research.

Discussion indicated considerable support for Fensham's claim that educational research needed to be deemed by teachers as worthwhile and that this type of relevant research was more likely to come about where academics work with teachers to solve questions and problems about learning and learners that are raised by the teachers in schools. This change in emphasis was seen to be paralleled by changes in other aspects of development in education — where the supposedly teacher-proof/child-proof curricula have given way to content and methods which involve the close cooperation by all those party to the educational process.

It was suggested however that a need existed for empirical evidence to support the claims made for these cooperative ventures. While it was conceded that changes in classroom variables are quite often induced/produced, there was still a necessity to demonstrate the effect of these changes, in terms of some empirical assessment of improvement in selected learning outcomes.

6 Changing Conceptions

Rosalind Driver

Children's Conceptions and School Science

This chapter will consider the implications of research on children's conceptions in science and current perspectives on the processes of conceptual change for the teaching of science in schools.

An extensive literature has been built up in recent years which indicates that children develop ideas about natural phenomena before they are taught science in school (Pfundt and Duit, 1985; Jung *et al*, 1982; Helm and Novak, 1983; Gentner and Stevens, 1983; Driver, Guesne and Tiberghien, 1985). In some instances these ideas (variously described as preconceptions, misconceptions, intuitions, alternative conceptions, alternative frameworks, naive theories) are in keeping with the science which is taught. In many cases, however, there are significant differences between children's notions and school science.

Surveys undertaken in various countries have identified commonalities in children's ideas and developmental studies are giving helpful insights into the characteristic ways in which these ideas progress during the childhood years (Carey, 1985; Strauss with Stavy 1982). In-depth investigations have indicated that such ideas are to be seen as more than simply pieces of misinformation; children have ways of construing events and phenomena which are coherent within their domains of experience yet which may differ substantially from the scientific view. Studies also indicate that these notions may persist into adulthood despite formal teaching (Viennot, 1979).

Cognitive ethnographies undertaken in classroom settings indicate that students' prior ideas are an important factor in their understanding of school science. Students make observations and inferences about phenomena which differ from those intended because of their different interpretive schemes. Observations are selected or rejected on the basis of their 'fit' with expectations (Rowell and Dawson, 1983). Children's conceptual schemes also influence their investigations, the questions they ask, the variables they consider as influential or non-influential and the way results are interpreted (Driver 1983).

Furthermore, children's schemes also influence their understanding of science texts (Bell and Freyberg, 1985); children construct meaning by relating what they read to what they already know and may therefore construct meanings other than those intended by the writer.

Possible outcomes of the interaction between students' conceptions and science instruction have been suggested by Gilbert, Osborne and Fensham (1982). Solomon (1983) has suggested that rather than trying to relate what is taught to their prior ideas, students may maintain them as separate domains, the 'life world' and the 'science world' each relevant to its own range of contexts.

The recognition of the existence of students' conceptions prior to teaching and their influence on learning outcomes has prompted a reappraisal of the assumptions underlying the processes of teaching and learning in science and in particular has led to the reconceptualisation of learning as conceptual change (West and Pines, 1985).

If it is accepted that learning in science involves the restructuring of students' conceptions, then not only do educators need to appreciate the ideas that children bring to the learning situation, but they need to understand the processes by which conceptual change occurs in order that this can be taken into account in the design of learning programmes.

This issue, of interest to both primary and secondary science, is currently setting the agenda for a number of research groups in various countries including the work of the Children's Learning in Science Project at Leeds. This chapter will give an account of the rationale and research programme of this project and discuss it in relation to other theoretical and empirical studies in the field.

Theoretical Bases for the Research Programme

Constructivist Epistemology

The Children's Learning in Science Project has addressed the issue of promoting conceptual change in classroom settings within the general perspective of constructivist epistemology (Driver, 1988). The central premise of this perspective is that knowledge, whether personal or public, is a human construction. It is also claimed that the way a situation is construed depends not only on the features of the situation but on the interpretive schemes brought to bear on it; observations are theory laden whether made by scientists within the social matrix of science or by individuals in the common round of life. Furthermore, since it is argued that there is no way in which a model can be checked against an independently existing reality, constructivism makes an important claim about the status of knowledge. The only check on the validity of human knowledge constructions is the extent to which they 'fit' with experience; experience can indicate that a particular construction does not 'fit' — in this sense knowledge constructions can be falsified. However, there may be many constructions which do fit with experience and in this respect knowledge can be seen to be valid if it is useful in interpreting experience. There is thus no ultimate check that a particular construction is 'right' insofar as it is isomorphic with an externally existing reality.

Contemporary developments in a number of fields can be seen to reflect this perspective; cognitive psychologists studying individual thinking and learning use the notion of mental representations or mental models constructed by individuals to interpret their experience (Gentner and Stevens, 1983; Johnson-Laird, 1983); the role that language plays in the negotiation and shaping of knowledge within social groups including classrooms indicates that the process of knowledge construction has a social dimension (Edwards and Mercer, 1987); furthermore, contemporary philosophy of science supports the view that science as public knowledge is constructed by a community of scientists.

Although these perspectives are by no means new, they have quite radical implications for science education which have as yet to be worked through in terms of curriculum and pedagogy.

Implications for Science Teaching

The view that knowledge is personally and socially constructed has various implications for science classrooms and the activities that take place in them.

(a) *Learners* from this perspective are not viewed as passive recipients of an instructional programme but are seen as purposive and ultimately responsible for their own learning. They will have developed, through previous experiences, in school and out, conceptions about the natural world which in many cases may be well adapted to the situations they have encountered.

(b) *Learning* is seen as involving a change in the learner's conceptions. This process of change requires the active construction of meaning by the learner. This construction of meaning may take place during interaction with phenomena, with text, through interpersonal negotiation, or through internal reflection.

(c) *Personal knowledge* is not 'objective' but is personally and socially constructed. Its status is provisional and it is evaluated by learners in terms of the extent to which it 'fits' with their experience, is useful in giving them control over situations, and is coherent with other aspects of their knowledge.

(d) *Science as public knowledge* is also a product of human corporate endeavours. If it is one of the goals of school science that children come to understand the way science itself is carried out then this may need to be reflected in the knowledge construction process undertaken in the classroom. Furthermore, since scientific ideas are products of a social enterprise in this sense they are conventions; students will not discover them through 'asking nature'. There needs to be an input, therefore, from the teacher or other authorities to shape students' thinking if they are to see the world through scientists' eyes.

(e) *Teaching* is not the 'transmission' of knowledge but the negotiation of meanings. It involves the organization of situations in the classroom and the control of tasks in a way which promotes intended learning outcomes.

(f) *Curriculum* is not that which is to be learned, but a programme of learning tasks, materials and resources which enable students to reconstruct their models of the world to be closer to those of school science.

An important point to make here is that the curriculum is not something that can be planned in an 'a priori' way but is necessarily the subject of empirical enquiry. As Posner (1982) points out:

> ... if we want to understand a student's experience, the process of learning, and the reasons why some learning outcomes are occurring and not others, we must understand the tasks in which students are engaging and not just the tasks the teachers think they are 'giving' to students. (p 343)

Further we need to determine the extent to which the tasks students do engage in are effective in promoting the intended conceptual change. The learner comes to the lessons with prior ideas which need to be taken into account since they influence the meanings that are constructed in the learning situations. During a learning sequence a path has to be traversed by the learners from their present to some future knowledge state. The curricular question is what are the *learning activities* which enable this to happen effectively?

This question can be answered in part by analysing the domain of knowledge itself. However, since what is learnt from a situation depends both on the situation and on what the learner brings to it in terms of purposes and schemes, the design and selection of learning experiences must ultimately involve empirical investigations of classroom learning.

The teacher's role in such a scenario becomes much more complex than a manager of a 'delivery system'. As a mediator between scientists' knowledge and children's understandings the teacher is required to act as a diagnostician of children's thinking and at the same time to carry a map of the conceptual domain which enables appropriate activities to be suggested and meanings negotiated.

Curriculum Development as Action Research

What might such an approach look like in practice? And how might it be implemented? In considering these questions, two strategic decisions were made which shaped the working of the project. The first was to involve teachers as collaborators. This was seen to be important since teachers are involved in such a fundamental way in the successful implementation of a curriculum. As Malcolm Skilbeck comments 'the best place for designing the curriculum is where learners and teachers meet'. At a simple level it was hoped that by involving teachers in this way then the classroom approaches developed would be workable; furthermore the project could obtain feedback from a range of classrooms and schools. At a more fundamental level it was considered to be important to involve teachers not in an instrumental way as 'users' of materials but as collaborators who understood the rationale for the work and who could contribute responsively in both its development and later dissemination.

The second, strategic decision was to focus on teaching and learning within a limited number of science topic areas commonly taught in secondary schools. By focussing on specific topics it was hoped to develop a generalized map of students' conceptual paths in learning in the topics in question. Such a 'route map', if it could be produced, would be useful then to other teachers. The project had already undertaken research into children's alternative conceptions in selected areas in science and just as it was apparent from these studies that there are commonly occuring notions among children, so it was hypothesized that there may be general patterns that can be identified in the paths that learners take in their thinking as they are involved in conceptual change. Checking this out and identifying what such paths might be was an important feature of the programme. The topic areas selected for attention, energy, the structure of matter and plant nutrition, were among those which the project had already identified as presenting conceptual problems.

In order to implement this work, secondary science teachers from schools within travelling distance of the University of Leeds were invited to take part in an initial two-year project and over thirty teachers undertook the commitment. The purpose of the project was outlined as involving the development of teaching approaches in three topic areas. The teaching approaches were to take account of students' prior ideas and to promote conceptual change. Although the premises on which the project is based were outlined to the participating teachers, these were initially construed in various ways by those involved. It is not only the students' prior knowledge which is of concern, teachers also have prior ideas about teaching and learning which influences their practice. This has meant that the project has in effect had two parallel agenda (a) the development of teaching schemes which promote conceptual change in secondary school students; and (b) the implementation of a way of working as a project which promotes the conceptual development of participating members. Three working groups of about ten teachers, each with a researcher, were set up, one for each topic area. The programme of work for the two years for each group is represented in figure 6.1. The first task each group undertook was to study the learning of the topic in question by students in their own classes (in the age range 12–15 years). All participants taught the selected topic in their normal way (this involved a sequence of lessons over six to eight weeks).

Figure 6.1   The programme of working groups

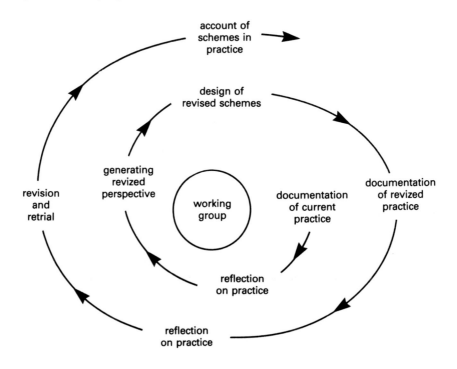

Students' learning was studied using a number of approaches. Teachers gave their class a diagnostic test before and after teaching the topic and kept a diary while the lessons were progressing. The researcher from the group visited some teachers and kept a more detailed account of the lessons by audiotaping them and interviewing students and the teacher.

The documents which were produced (Bell and Brook, 1985; Brook and Driver, 1986; Wightman, et al, 1986) were used as a basis for reflection on current practice by the group. Students' particular conceptual problems were documented and pedagogical concerns were also identified. At this stage, the groups were attempting to make explicit their views on the scientific ideas to be taught and to share their developing perspectives on the teaching and learning processes.

Towards the end of the first year each group worked together for a week to devise a revised teaching scheme for their topic, drawing on the insights gained over the year and further reading of the research literature. All the schemes were designed to take account of students' prior ideas in the topic and to provide learning activities and a learning environment aimed at promoting conceptual change. (General features of the strategies adopted are given in the next section.)

The revised schemes were implemented in the second year of work and the learning taking place in the classrooms was monitored again in the same way. Towards the end of the second year, the groups reviewed the findings from the first trial of the schemes. Undoubtedly these first trials led to a greater understanding of some of the students' conceptual problems and provided information on the paths in their thinking. It also gave insight into reactions by teachers in implementing a much more open approach in their classrooms. As a result of this phase, revisions were made to the schemes which were retrialled prior to publication.

Factors Which Were Taken Into Account in the Design of the Schemes

The factors which were taken into account by the working groups in the initial design of the teaching scheme are shown in figure 6.2.

Learning Goals

An analysis was undertaken of the intended learning outcomes. This, of course, is a traditional feature in curriculum planning. However, an issue which now needs to be addressed in addition to an analysis of the knowledge domain itself is whose goals are being considered? If the goals are those of the teacher how are they to be adopted by the learner? How might learners' interests and purposes be considered?

Students' Prior Conceptions

In science there are now many domains of knowledge in which children's prior conceptions have been documented. It is generally recognized that there are 'commonalities in the ways in which people who belong to the same culture account for a phenomenon' (Johansson, Marton and Svensson, 1985, p.236).

Although the conceptions that individual children may use tend to depend on the context, it is possible to obtain a probabilistic picture of the conceptions available within a class for a particular domain of knowledge (Engel Clough and Driver, 1986). Information concerning these domain-specific conceptions is

*Figure 6.2   Factors which were taken into account in the design of the teaching
schemes*

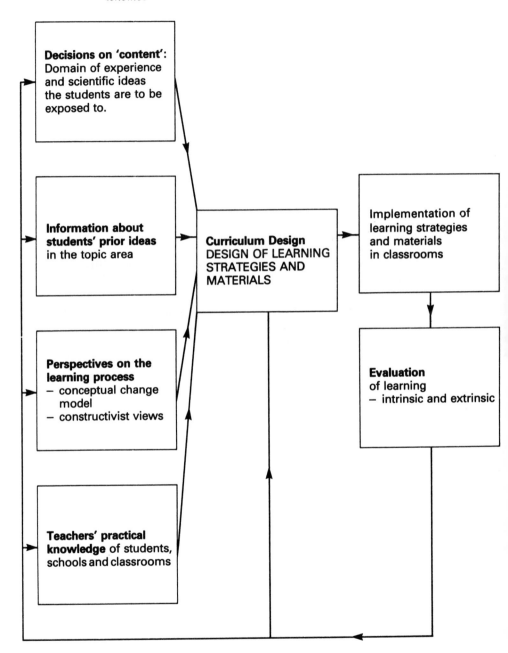

necessary in order to decide the types of tasks to include in the teaching. Tasks may be chosen, for example, which extend the range of applicability of a conception or to provide disconfirming instances.

It should be noted that an analysis of students' conceptions is needed not only prior to teaching but continually during teaching and although some 'a priori' information can be provided to help teachers to anticipate aspects of children's thinking, the teacher's role as diagnostician in the classroom is essentially an ongoing one.

It is also important to recognize that students' prior conceptions may differ from scientific conceptions not just in substance but in more fundamental ways. For example, students may have context specific conceptions which may conflict with each other, yet which serve their purposes in specific contexts; the need for internal coherence may not be recognized by students. Students' notions about what constitutes an explanation may also differ from the scientific perspective. Students tend to see explanations in terms of linear causal sequences, whereas the scientific explanations provided within school science are often formal or analogical models of classes of phenomena (Driver, Guesne and Tiberghien, 1985).

Prior information about students' conceptions at both a general and particular level has been used in planning materials and activities in advance and in sensitising teachers and researchers to the ideas and ways of thinking that may occur in classes. In the actual classrooms, students' ideas have also been elicited as part of the process of promoting change in their thinking.

A View of Learning

Information about students' conceptions is important but it does not by itself give an indication of how these may change or develop. In its planning, the project adopted a conceptual change view of learning (Hewson and Hewson, 1983) designing sequences which start by taking account of the students' ideas and then offering opportunities for these to be progressively restructured (see figure 6.3 for a general outline of a teaching sequence).

Opportunities were given for students to construct and reconstruct their understandings during the teaching sequence. Reflection on the earlier documentation of current classroom practice as well as reference to the literature suggested a number of features which were seen to facilitate this.

Metacognition
A number of research groups interested in promoting conceptual change are underlining the importance of helping students become more aware of their own learning processes and to take responsibility for them (Baird and Mitchell, 1986). Students tend to think of learning science as 'taking in' discrete facts. Strategies which encourage students to reflect on their own learning helps them appreciate that a process of conceptual change is involved, also that their

Figure 6.3   General structure to teaching sequence

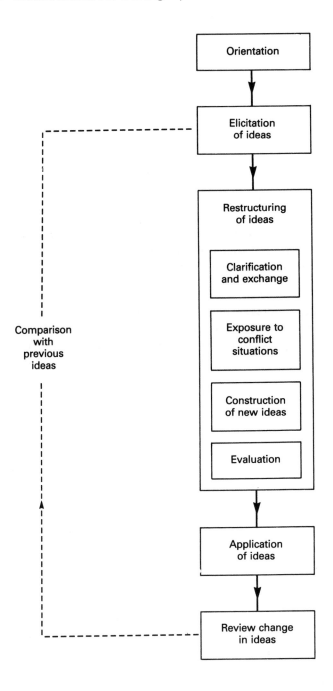

knowledge is structured and interrelated. Techniques which have been used to encourage this process include students comparing their ideas at the beginning and end of a learning sequence also keeping personal learning logs (small notebooks in which they record their reactions to lessons, notes on what they think, things that puzzle them, things they find difficult etc.).

Non-threatening learning environment
A learning environment which requires students to make their ideas explicit and to test out new ways of thinking could be very threatening. If students' efforts are evaluated too early by the teacher or by other students then they will tend not to be willing to be exploratory but will want to be told and thus possibly short-circuit the necessary process of knowledge construction.

Such environments have been set up in classes through the use of cooperative group methods. This has required teachers in many cases to change their class management strategies. Teachers' questioning routines have also had to be modified so as to avoid closed questions, to encourage a range of contributions from the class and to give opportunities for students to reflect on and evaluate each others' suggestions.

Small group work
The importance of talk in enabling learners to represent their ideas to themselves has been recognised for years (Barnes, 1976). Small groups of about four students form the structural unit around which the scheme of activities takes place. Group activities include discussing and representing theories or ideas on a topic, devising experiments to test ideas, developing more complex models to represent experiences, undertaking practical construction tasks in which students' apply their ideas.

The context of learning tasks
As far as possible the learning tasks were chosen to be set in contexts which were meaningful to students (for example, some of the work on energy was set in domestic contexts and involved reading meters, using fuel bills). Since knowledge tends to be contextually embedded, the contexts provided for learning may be important in maintaining attention, facilitating later applicability of the conceptions and hence breaking down the possible divide between school science and everyday knowledge.

Knowledge of Classrooms and Schools

It is only realistic to recognize that there are constraints operating in classrooms and schools which need to be taken into account in planning. In addition to the obvious physical constraints of teaching time available, the limitations on teaching space and equipment, there are also more subtle constraints due to teachers' and learners' expectations about knowledge, science, schools and classrooms and their roles in them.

An Example of a Scheme in Action

One of the schemes is described here in order to illustrate the types of approaches used and the way the schemes are responsive to students' ideas. The scheme relates to the teaching of the structure of matter. It has been developed for use with 12-14-year-old students and takes about ten-twelve teaching hours. The scheme aims to introduce students to the idea that matter is particulate in nature and gives students opportunities to consider features of the particulate model. Perhaps of greatest importance is the opportunity the scheme offers to help students appreciate the nature of models in science and their relationship with evidence.

A number of features of students' conceptions in this topic area were identified from previous studies and these are addressed during the teaching of the scheme. (An outline of the scheme is given in figure 6.4).

The unit starts with a series of demonstrations designed to capture students' interest in thinking about the varied properties of matter. Students are then asked to describe and explain a wide range of phenomena set out around the class. (These phenomena include feeling syringes with solids, liquids and gases in them, observing blocks of equal size but of different mass, noticing what happens when the top is taken off an air freshener.) Students initially describe what they notice and consider their explanations in pairs. They are then asked to join in fours to prepare a poster which explains one of the presented phenomena. At this stage, it is quite common for the posters to represent only macroscopic properties of matter, although some may introduce particle explanations. Students take turns to explain their posters which are then left displayed on the classroom wall.

The next sequence of work is designed to help students to reflect on the nature of theory making and its place in science through a number of simulation games. (It is not just the content of students' ideas but general features of their thinking, such as what constitutes an explanation or a theory, which needs to be addressed.)

Students are then given the task of classifying a wide range of substances as a basis for reflecting on and generating a list of general properties of solids, liquids and gases. This is an important preliminary activity for the next crucial part of the sequence, in which students are asked to generate their own theories of what ice, water and steam are like 'inside'. This theory generation is done in groups and students are asked to prepare a large poster which is presented and discussed by the rest of the class.

At this point it is found that students invariably use particle ideas in their explanations. There are, however, a number of characteristic features of the students' particle models which have been identified in all the classrooms studied. Students attribute macroscopic properties to microscopic particles (particles are seen to melt or be squashy); the question of what is between the particles (air?) is problematic as are the issues of particle motion (what keeps them moving?) and bonding.

Figure 6.4   The teaching scheme on the structure of matter

ORIENTATION

Teacher demonstrations of some eye-catching and thought provoking properties of substances.

ELICITATION OF IDEAS

Circus.   Students work in pairs studying a range of phenomena and explaining them on their own terms. for example, how smell reaches you, air in syringe is squashy, loaded wire stretches.
Feedback.   The pairs join in fours to produce a poster giving explanation. Posters are displayed, presented and discussed.

RESTRUCTURING
Theory making

Group work.   Students are involved in some simulations of theory making and testing including including the solution of a murder mystery.
Class review.   The processes involved are reviewed in order to consider how evidence is used, how solutions are generated and checked.

Patterns of properties

Circus.   Students work in pairs reviewing the properties of a wide range of solids, liquids and gases.
Class review.   A consensus pattern of properties of solids, liquids and gases is produced.

Theory generation

Group work.   Students discuss what ice, water and steam might be like inside. Posters are produced which are displayed, presented and discussed.

Theory shaping

Issues emerging from the students' models are focussed on in a responsive way by the teacher using demonstrations, group work and discussion, working towards a consensus view.
Emerging issues:
(a)   Particles are invariably the basis of student models.
(b)   Properties of the particles are used to account for properties of substance e.g. air — squashy molecules.
(c)   What is between the particles? Notion of continuity of substance maintained by suggesting air is between particles.
(d)   What keeps particles moving?
(e)   What holds particles together?

APPLICATION

Circus.   Students given opportunities to try out their particle model in order to explain some new situations.

REVIEW

Group work and class review.   Students revisit earlier posters and comment on the changes in their explanations.

Experience in a range of classrooms has indicated that it can be anticipated that these issues will emerge from a discussion of students' models. A series of demonstrations and discussions are then undertaken to help students explore each of these factors in turn and to promote a development in their models through a consideration of evidence and alternative models. In the case of bonding, for example, it is typical for students to argue that solids are *solid* and hold their shape because they cannot be pushed any closer. This notion of solidity accounts for the behaviour of solids under compression. Building models of a solid using polystyrene spheres indicates to students that an explanation of holding a shape requires more than the notion of close packing.

Once the notion of 'something' holding the particles together is introduced this then needs to be thought through in terms of what happens during a change in state. The following transcript illustrates the conceptual problems which are typical and also the progress that one or two students made in thinking through the problem to the point where they realize that bonding does not 'disappear' during a change in state, but that the particles have enough energy to 'overcome' it. The discussion occurred when 14-year-old students were asked to explain the differences between ice, water and steam.

(S — student; I — participant observer)

S2 — we are more or less clear how things go from solids to liquids to gases, but not from gases to liquids to solids.

S1 The point is in the gas the bonding has totally gone.

S2 So how does it happen that bonding comes back?

This issue of the reversibility of the process continues to exercise the group and a number of hypotheses are raised.

S1 I suppose it works vice versa, when it's heated it destroys the bonding, when it's cold it, you know, remakes it.

S3 — but how does it remake it? What does it — remake it out of, though?

S2 If atoms are bonded an atom can't change into a bond to hold the other atoms together, can it?

I How do you imagine bonding?

S4 Sort of like a string between the atoms sort of holding it all together.

S1 No, it isn't. He explained to us about magnetic, magnetism. Some sort of force.

S4 Static, static electricity or something like that.

S2 Yeah. That kept them together. And I suppose if it was hot, then it wasn't magnetized as much or something, and then when it was cold it — magnetizes more.

S4 When they are hot they vibrate more, so that the static isn't as strong.

S2 Yeah, I know, but they vibrate more and break the bonding and then they finally get to a gas and that's as far as they to ... but *how does it get the bonding back?*

S4   When it starts to cool down, they don't vibrate as much.

S1   Ah, yeah — when they cool down, the bonding will be increased so they won't be able to move around as much. That fits in, doesn't it?

S2   Yeah, but the point is how do we get the bonding back?

S4   Slow down the vibrating —

The question of *how the bonding comes back* continues to be considered until one student suggests:

S4   I suppose it's ever present there but — yeah it hasn't got a chance to like grip, grip them, you know, and keep them together. Well where it slows down, you know, it might get to grips with the —

S3   A bit easier to keep slower things together.

This transcript illustrates the progress made by a group of students in their understanding of quite a subtle issue through group discussion. Similar progress has been made in considering the other problematic features of the model, though students will vary in the extent to which their thinking progresses.

In the final sequence in the unit a discussion is held on the features of the model about which there is a consensus and the school science view is presented. The students are then asked to use the developed model to explain a range of everyday phenomena including some of the phenomena which were studied at the beginning of the unit. In this way students revisit their earlier ideas represented on posters and consider the way their models have changed.

Outcomes and Results

The project has a number of different kinds of outcome. This section will review the products in terms of teaching schemes, their influence on classroom environment and the attitudes of participants.

The Schemes of Work

Schemes of work, all incorporating strategies which encourage active learning on the part of students, have been produced in three topic areas (Children's Learning in Science Project, 1987). At the basic level of practicability we know the schemes do work in classroom settings and with students of a wide range of ability. At a deeper level, because of the reflexive way in which they have taken account of the sense students were making of the teaching tasks, we see the schemes as *adapted* to students' thinking.

After the first trial of the scheme on the structure of matter, a participating teacher commented:

What is beyond doubt is that the series of lessons did 'go well' — pupils, teacher and researcher all agreed upon this ... novel teaching

strategies had to be adopted. What had been a problematic area ...
was transformed into an attractive series of lessons involving practical
work, whole class discussion, small group work and so on. (Scott and
Wightman, 1985, p 4)

In preparing the schemes for use by others it was considered important not only
to include the usual type of information (the aims of the scheme, the activities,
apparatus required, organizational suggestions etc.), but also to provide
information about the conceptual ecology of the classroom — the ideas students
may tend to use at different points and how these might change. In this way,
the schemes are illustrative of a more diagnostic approach to teaching and also
provide suggestions as to possible lines of action. It is hoped that this type of
information will help others to anticipate issues which may emerge when they
use the materials so they are not too daunted by the task of responding
appropriately to the range of students' ideas.

A further point about the schemes which teachers have valued is that they
are based on a coherent overall perspective on learning. Teachers comment
that the perspective on learning and the strategy for teaching 'makes sense', it
is not just a set of 'things to do' or 'tips for teachers'.

Finally it should be said that the schemes are not seen as the only way to
treat each of the topics in question nor necessarily the best way. Indeed in
teaching in a reflective and diagnostic way, individual teachers will need to
adapt the suggestions to the needs of their own classes. What is claimed,
however, is that whatever teaching programme is adopted in a particular topic
area, students are likely to be confronted with a similar set of conceptual issues
to think through; in other words, the evidence from a range of classrooms
supports the view that a map of students' conceptual paths in learning a topic
can be produced and that this may be generalizable.

Evaluating Activities in the Classroom

The detailed ethnographic documentation of the same teacher's classroom
during current practice and when using the revised schemes has given clear
evidence of the greater amount of active participation in lessons by students
using the revised schemes.

Some pilot studies have been undertaken in which the same teacher has
taught the same topic to parallel classes; in one case using the school's scheme
and in the other using the project's scheme. An observation schedule based on
that used by Rennie and Parker (1985) was devised to record the time spent in
class on differrent types of activity. A comparison of profiles is shown in
table 6.1.

The differences in the distribution of time spent on different activities is
apparent in two main categories. The CLIS class spent about a quarter of the
time on planning and discussion compared with nearly zero for the other class.

Table 6.1 Profiles for time on different activities for classes following CLIS and normal school science.

	% Time on activity			
	CLIS SCHEME		CURRENT PRACTICE	
	B	G	B	G
ACTIVITY	n = 13	n = 15	n = 11	n = 15
Watch/listen	12	9	27	26
Read/write	24	28	47	51
Manipulate apparatus	23	22	12	13
Planning/discussion	24	29	3	4
Other on task	2	2	0	1
Off task	9	5	9	4
Teacher contact	6	5	2	1
TOTAL:	100	100	100	100

The activity of each student was recorded in a sweep round the class every 120 seconds. Data collected over four double periods for each class.
Total observations = 2978 CLIS scheme
= 1735 Current practice

Half the time in the current practice class was spent on individual reading or writing compared with a quarter of the time in the CLIS class. This, of course, by itself says nothing about the quality of the activities. However, it does indicate that opportunities existed in the CLIS lessons for more active participation by students in the control of their own learning.

The ethnographic accounts and the systematic observation studies indicated a greater participation of girls in class discussion in CLIS classes. In addition it was found that there were considerably more topic related student initiated questions in the CLIS classes than for current practice.

Teachers' Reactions to the Schemes

In general, teachers have been positive about the teaching approach proposed. There are differences, however, in the ways different teachers interpret and implement the approach in practice (Johnston, 1987). As a result of the classroom work and feedback from teachers over the last few years there are a number of features in teachers' changing ideas and practice which have been identified.

Eliciting children's ideas
The value of eliciting children's ideas is quickly appreciated and techniques for doing this are employed effectively. Teachers see the value to themselves and

to the members of the class of giving students opportunities to explore their own ideas.

> I became acutely aware of the very large range and variety of ideas which the pupils were carrying and which were creating difficulties in their understanding of particulate theory. Some pupils could not conceive of there being 'nothing' between gas atoms; others could not see why atoms in all three phases should *continue* to move of their own accord ... and so on. My previous teaching ... never gave the opportunity for these kinds of difficulties to come to light ... (it) did not even provoke the pupils into considering that they might have conceptual difficulties. (Wightman *et al*, 1986)

Responsive teaching
Initially teachers expresses concern (and even a sense of panic), when they considered how to deal with the notions raised by students in their classes.

> — the strategy of encouraging pupil contributions meant that a lot of unusual ideas were put forward — the 'removal of the lid from a can of worms'. Dealing with each contribution sympathetically *and* trying to channel ideas in the right direction demanded quick thinking. (Scott and Wightman, 1985, p 4)

The shift in perspective away from the security of the scientist's knowledge frame to the shifting sands of students' understandings seems initially to be very threatening to secondary school science teachers. It was noted, however, that the second time teachers used one of the schemes they reported feeling much more comfortable since they could anticipate the issues that would arise. Teachers also found it interesting and reassuring in meetings to find similar issues emerging across classes in different schools.

Group discussion
Initially teachers were somewhat hesitant about the use of small group discussion in science classes. Concern was expressed about how to organize it effectively. There was also some lack of confidence that the students would make progress by themselves without teacher intervention.

We found that tape recording group discussions provided reassurance that, given a reasonably clear task, students' discussions would be on task and useful.

> I was exceedingly *pleased* when what seemed to me to be relatively ordinary children ... went from nothing, throwing around un-connected ideas, to ... sorting out the theory ... in a discussion they will have a sense of achievement doing that.

Other teachers have commented:

> I feel happier about using (discussion work) now I understand more clearly the processes that take place in discussion groups and the time it takes.

Obtaining closure

Science teachers seem to feel a strong and understandable pressure to get to the 'scientific answer' within a lesson. This means that open ended exploration of ideas and experimentation by students, which may go in some apparently strange directions, may be dismissed as 'a waste of time' or 'rubbish'. Furthermore, attempts by groups or a whole class to explain phenomena and reach a consensus may be frustrating to a teacher because of what appears to be lack of convergence. This can lead teachers initially to resort to exposition and to 'short circuit' the thinking process that students have to go through to make sense of ideas. The temptation to be directive is very strong in the face of what initially appears to be a confusion of ideas.

What seems to be important in dealing with this is again experience. Once teachers have been through a teaching sequence, they gain a confidence that the ideas will 'come together' — though it may take several lessons for a new consensus to be developed.

The growth in awareness of students' ideas seems to be accompanied with a patience and a realization by teachers that it is not what they teach that matters, it is what students learn.

> I think what you have to hope is that you get them interested, ... and
> *they* will then do the learning. It's got to be something that comes from
> them, not from me. It doesn't matter what *I* do really — it's what *they*
> do that counts. (Wightman *et al*, 1986)

Time constraints

Time constraints are a real dilemma for science teachers. As they begin to appreciate the issues involved in learning a topic from the students' point of view they see the need to spend more time on it. However, the realities of school teaching schemes and examination syllabuses militate against adopting a more relaxed schedule. Some project teachers are suggesting that taking more time in teaching in this way with younger children could lay better foundations for later learning. At this stage this must remain an open question.

Harder work

Teachers do acknowledge that it is harder work to teach in a more responsive way. The amount of thinking on ones feet during the lessons coupled with the flexibility which is needed in the planning between lessons can be stressful. However, despite this there is general agreement that it is also more rewarding.

Students' Reactions

In general we have found that students have responded well to the more open learning environment. They were very enthusiastic about being given control over the design of an experiment or being allowed to make choices about activities. Though they are often hesitant and self-conscious to begin with about presenting their arguments or experimental results to the rest of the class, this was appreciated as an important learning activity. As one student commented:

> it is not often in science class that someone says something and nobody laughs.

Acknowledgements

The project has been supported with grants from the Department of Education and Science, the School Curriculum Development Committee through the Secondary Science Curriculum Review and the Manpower Services Commission.

References

BAIRD, J.R. and MITCHELL, I.J. (1986) *Improving the Quality of Teaching and Learning*, Melbourne, Victoria, Monash University Printery.

BARNES, D. (1976) *From Communication to Curriculum*, Harmondsworth, Penguin.

BELL, B.F. and BROOK, A. (1985) *The Construction of Meaning and Conceptual Change in Classroom Settings: Case Studies on Plant Nutrition*, Children's Learning in Science Project, Centre for Studies in Science and Mathematics Education, University of Leeds.

BELL, B. and FREYBERG, P. (1985) 'Language in the science classroom' in OSBORNE, R. and FREYBERG, P. (Eds) *Learning in Science*, London, Heinemann.

BROOK, A. and DRIVER, R. (1986) *The Construction of Meaning and Conceptual Change in Classroom Settings: Case Studies on Energy*, Children's Learning in Science Project, Centre for Studies in Science and Mathematics Education, University of Leeds.

CAREY, S. (1985) *Conceptual Change in Childhood*, Harvard, MA, MIT Press.

CHILDREN'S LEARNING IN SCIENCE (1987) *CLIS in the Classroom: Approaches to Teaching*, Centre for Studies in Science and Mathematics Education, University of Leeds.

DRIVER, R. (1983) *The Pupil as Scientist?*, Milton Keynes, Open University Press.

DRIVER, R. (1988) 'Theory into practice: A constructivist approach to curriculum development' in FENSHAM, P. (Ed.) *Developments and Dilemmas in Science Education*, Lewes, Falmer Press.

DRIVER, R., GUESNE, E. and TIBERGHIEN, A. (1985) *Children's Ideas in Science*, Milton Keynes, Open University Press.

DRIVER, R. and OLDHAM, V. (1986) 'A constructivist approach to curriculum development in science', *Studies in Science Education*, 13, pp 105–22.

EDWARDS, D. and MERCER, N. (1987) *Common Knowledge*, London, Methuen.

ENGEL CLOUGH, E. and DRIVER, R. (1986) 'Consistency in the use of students' conceptual frameworks across different task contexts', *Science Education*, 70, 4, pp 473–96.

GENTNER, D. and STEVENS, A. (1983) *Mental Models*, New York, Lawrence Erlbaum Associates.

GILBERT, J.K., OSBORNE, J. and FENSHAM, P.J. (1982) 'Children's science and its consequences for teaching', *Science Education*, 66, 4, pp 623–33.

HEWSON, M.G. and HEWSON, P.W. (1983) 'The effect of instruction using students' prior knowledge and conceptual change strategies on science learning', *Journal of Research in Science Teaching*, 20, 2, pp 731–43.

HELM, H. and NOVAK, J. (1983) *Proceedings of the International Seminar: Misconceptions in Science and Mathematics*, Ithaca, Cornell University.

JOHANSSON, B., MARTON, F. and SVENSSON, L. (1985) 'An approach to describing learning as change between qualitatively different conceptions' in WEST, L.H.T. and PINES, A.L. (Eds) *Cognitive Structure and Conceptual Change*, Orlando, Florida Academic Press.

JOHNSON-LAIRD, P.N. (1983) *Mental Models*, Cambridge, Cambridge University Press.

JOHNSTON, K. (1987) 'Changing teachers' conceptions of teaching and learning', paper presented at the British Conference on Teachers', Educational Research Association Professional Learnings, University of Lancaster, July.

JUNG, W., PFUNDT, H. and RHONECK, C. (1982) *Problems Concerning Students' Representation of Physics and Chemistry Knowledge*, Ludwigsburg, Selbstuerlag, Pedagogische Hochschule.

PFUNDT, H. and DUIT, R. (1985) *Bibliography Students' Alternative Frameworks and Science Education*, Kiel, IPN.

POSNER, G. (1982) 'A cognitive science conception of curriculum and instruction', *Journal of Curriculum Studies*, 14, 4, pp 343–51.

RENNIE, L.J., PARKER, L.H. and HUTCHINSON, P.E. (1985) *The Effect of Inservice Training on Teacher Attitudes and Primary School Science Classroom Climates*, Research Report No. 12, measurement and statistics laboratory, Department of Education, University of Western Australia.

ROWELL, J. and DAWSON, C. (1981) 'Volume, conservation and instruction: A classroom based Solomon Four group study of conflict', *Journal of Research in Science Teaching*, 18, 6, pp 533–46.

SCOTT, P. and WIGHTMAN, T. (1985) 'Teaching the particulate theory of matter — a constructivist approach', paper presented at annual meeting of the British Educational Research Association, Sheffield.

SOLOMON, J. (1983) 'Learning about energy: How pupils think in two domains', *European Journal of Science Education*. 5, 1, pp 49–59.

STRAUSS, S. (Ed.) with STAVY, R. (1982) *U-shaped behavioural growth*, New York, Academic Press.

VIENNOT, L. (1979) 'Spontaneous reasoning in elementary dynamics', *European Journal of Science Education*, 1, 2, pp 205–222.

WEST, L. and PINES, A (Eds) (1985) *Cognitive Structure and Conceptual Change*, Orlando, Florida Academic Press.

WIGHTMAN, T. *et al.* (1986) *The Construction of Meaning and Conceptual Change in Classroom Settings: Case Studies on the Particulate Theory of Matter*, Children's Learning in Science Project, Centre for Studies in Science and Mathematics Education, University of Leeds.

Respondent: Joan Solomon

I want to make some points under three general headings which I hope will be useful for guiding our discussion:

First I want to talk about the notion of constructivism as it applies to the learner, to the scientist, and to the classroom.

Secondly I want to redirect your attention to the twin notions of 'restructuring' thought, and 'conceptual change or conflict'.

Thirdly, and to a much smaller extent, I would like to look at the work of CLISP with reference to the norms of action research.

1   I am sure that Driver would agree that to say human knowledge is a human construction verges on the trite. To claim that learning is an active constructive process on the part of the learner goes only a little way further. Indeed I have been trying to think of any kind of learning which might **not** be an active construction, and came up only with learning prayers in a foreign language at one's mother's knee. Even here I remember that some of these incomprehensible sounds were built up into childish mental ikons, half sound and half sense. Years later when my own children went to primary school and, in the educational fashion of the times, began to learn French orally in class, we found out later they had reconstructed what they so frequently heard as 'Isabel' — 'il s'appelle John, il s'appelle David'! The urge to construct and make sense of what we hear is a universal human trait which needs no great polemic.

On the trail of how children construct their prior notions about scientific matters Rosalind has quoted liberally from educational sources, almost too liberally perhaps, for she is driven to conclude that

> it is likely that individuals' prior conceptions derive from experience
> with the environment, their existing ideas which are used to model
> new situations, and from cultural transmission through language.

Most of this attempt runs a serious risk of being recursive. Since we no longer believe that experience is the sum of the neutral sense-data received but that it is constructed in the light of theories, metaphors, or idiosyncratic notions there is little mileage to be got from affirming that prior conceptions are derived from the environment. In one sense they obviously are, and yet the possibilities are in no way reduced by such a statement.

How is it that fairly stable notions, which are consensual enough to be used in general conversation with others, can be derived from experiences? This is the sort of question that Vygotsky might have asked and this reformulation certainly makes it a little easier to answer. It must be that the prior notions are either derived, or shaped, or reinforced by the process of speaking about them to other people — parents in the first case, and peers in later life. This is social constructivism about which Driver merely remarked that I had said it occurred 'for reasons of social conformity'. Of course I did not say that, but anyhow I would strongly recommend reading Mead, or Schutz — not Solomon! I find it curious that someone whose action research is so very strongly social — with extensive use of small group discussion — should make so little use of sociological theory.

Let us treat ourselves here not to the reach-me-down views of education-alists like me, but to the words of the masters themselves. First, G.H. Mead:

> The social process of communication is responsible for the appearance of new objects in the field of experience, an object whose meaning is not intrinsic to that object, but arises from how the group are prepared to act towards it ... (*Mind, Self and Society*, p 133)

And now for Schutz

> ... The natural attitude is characterised by the assumption that the life-world accepted by me is also accepted by my fellow men.... I can always test the adequacy of my interpretative schemata by referring to objects in our common surrounding world. It is thus in the 'we relation' that the intersubjectivity of the life-world is continually confirmed. It is not my private world, nor your private world, nor yours and mine added together, but rather it is the world of our common experience. (*Structures of the Life World*, p 68)

Driver is, of course, perfectly right when she asserts that scientific knowledge is also a social construct, but it is quite different to the social construct that is life world knowledge because the social group which constructs scientific know-ledge is so totally different. The highly socialized community of scientists decide through the medium of publication, peer review, citation, and education not just what theories they will accept as consensual scientific knowledge, they also decide upon the consensual types of questions to be asked, on the consensual methods to be used, on the consensual style of debate, and even on the consensual goals of the whole process. This is all set out in detail and with the greatest clarity by John Ziman in *Reliable Knowledge*

> The goal of science is to achieve the maximum degree of consensuality. Ideally the general body of scientific knowledge should consist of facts and principles that are firmly established and accepted without serious doubt ... The consensuality of such systems is tested by such strategies as the attempted confirmation of predictions or by the discovery of marginal phenomena that might prove inconsisitent with accepted theories. It is important to realize that much of the research literature of science is intended **rhetorically** — to persuade other scientists of the validity of a new hypothesis or to shatter received opinion. (p 7)

These descriptions of two such different socially constructed knowledge systems point up the difficulty of the social arena in between the two, that in which our pupils will try to learn science by reconstructing its theories by experiment, discussion or rhetoric. Few have thought seriously about the sociology of the learning laboratory, and I found much of what Driver had to say about this, under 'Implications for science teaching', very valuable. I particularly liked her encapsulation of teaching as

> not the transmission of knowledge but the negotiation of meanings. It involves the organization of situations in the classroom and the control of tasks in a way which promotes the intended learning outcomes.

2 This brings me to my second area. Driver in common with other forward-looking science educators, has adopted an explicitly metacognitive strategy in which the pupils become aware of their own learning and the direction in which it is taking them. That is excellent. But it is also essential that the teacher directs this somewhat introspective journey with as much cognitive respect and gentleness as possible. When I look at the pattern of teaching that is provided in figure 6.2 I become a little worried.

I may be wrong but I reconstruct the Driver model of constructivist teaching in the following way:

— the pupils arrive with a range of incomplete prior notions,
— these are made explicit,
— they are then restructured to make them more robust **even though they are not scientifically correct!**
— cognitive **conflict** is then arranged,
— the children adopt new scientific ideas
— they see how they have changed by reference to 'paper memories'.

I do understand that the difficulty of trying to challange or change a loose and fluid life-world meaning is that, as Steven Pepper said, it tends to be illusive and 'cognitively irritable' under the pressure of a logical argument. Nevertheless it seems to be expensive of both time and spirit to try so hard to bolster up ideas by clarification and exchange only to knock them down by arranging subsequent conflict situations. I should hasten to add that I find nothing so cognitively 'brutal' if I may be allowed such a word in any of the accounts that Driver has given us today. On the contrary they are full of care for the children's ideas. I have, however, heard much rougher talk from some of the CLISP teachers, and it troubles me.

There is an alternative approach using a more generative or evolutionary model of cognitive change such as that developed by Miles Barker in LISP. Here every effort is made to incorporate those parts of children's notions which are at all valuable and head-on conflict is avoided wherever possible. As I have argued consensual and socially useful ideas are unlikely to die so it is doubly important that we use them.

And that brings me very nicely to my third and final point about action research.

3 It would be boring to discuss the results of action research under the heading of 'How to avoid the Hawthorne Effect'. The effect is there and in one very superficial way it always ensures that you cannot win, however good your

results. But the reason behind the effect, that you have enthused good science teachers to teach even better also ensures that you cannot have lost. That argument is thus closed and trivial.

But it means that all action research must fully incorporate the teachers since in a very real sense, it is theirs and not ours. It is they who are shocked into seeing the urgent need for action. It is they who go out into their own classrooms, naked and bereft of their usual professional beliefs and strategies to teach in a new way. It is they who observe tacitly or explicitly the differences their action makes both to themselves and to their pupils. They are not the tools or implements of research, as some researchers have tried to make them, nor are they transmuted into non-participant researchers who can pretend that their activity is at a far remove from themselves. The 'invisible research' always was a suspect concept; for action research it is not a viable fiction even for a moment. The action research is **done by the teacher and on the teacher** just as much as it is **done on the class**. This means that not only should action research be written up in the first person singular, as Jack Whitehead argues, it should not and cannot be judged by the research norms of universality and repeatability. What it rests upon is its strong links with theory, and its recognition by insiders, by those who also took part in it and hung their own action and reputation on the line by so doing.

In this case we know that Driver like Shayer and Adey, put her academic reputation into the leaky crucible of classroom action research and has reported it to us in person. This makes her account credible and important, but most of all it becomes a tribute to high scholarly courage.

Discussion (Reporter: Valda Kirkwood)

It was the opinion of the first speaker from the floor that the idea of cognitive conflict was not at all threatening, but extremely attractive. He wondered what Driver found agreeable and disagreeable about cognitive conflict? She replied that she did not reject the place of cognitive conflict in promoting conceptual change, but did not believe that it was anything like the whole story.

Joan Solomon doubted whether cognitive conflict played any significant role in conceptual change. We are all able to hold at once many views of a situation, and to move fluidly from one to another without conflict between different views leading to change in either. The first questioner disagreed, believing that cognitive conflict was a necessary, if not sufficient, condition for conceputal change. Another participant quoted from multicultural research: the use of a conflict model for prejudice reduction seems to lead to a hardening of currently held concepts, rather than to their revision. Is there a risk of the same thing happening in science concept formation? Another participant felt that prejudice conflict was completely differrent from cognitive conflict, since the former is in the affective domain. Doubt was expressed whether everyone was using the term cognitive conflict in the same way. If we cannot agree amongst ourselves about the nature of cognitive conflict, how can we use the notion in the education of teachers?

Some questioners pursued the nature of reality. One asked, if reality can be constructed, what is the nature of the reality of the constructors? Another felt that the notion of reality as a construction of the mind was dangerous when applied to science education. One group were working on the nature of relationships between concepts, rather than relationships in classrooms, and it was suggested that this might help us to choose more wisely the range of experiences to provide in the classroom.

Driver was asked whether the methods proposed empowered students to become more successful adults. She replied that students were being enabled to take responsibility for their own learning and through that to make better sense of their world, but that more investigation into the possibilities of transfer were required.

7   Physics Education and Students' Development

Marie-Geneviève Séré
Annick Weil-Barais

We shall first expose the different directions of research developed at LIRESPT in the last years, related to development. We shall then give our contribution to this question: In what way does the teaching of physics contribute to students' cognitive development? This will be done with reference to results obtained about the construction of physical dimensions by students from 10 to 15 years.

The Main Directions of Research at LIRESPT

LIRESPT is a laboratory which studies problems that come up within the teaching of physics, chemistry and technology. The first work that was done in the laboratory was aimed at finding reasonable propositions for teaching physics to children between 11 and 15 years in junior high school. This has particularly led to the setting up of textbooks for students and teachers for the four classes of the junior high school. The analysis of possible links between teaching and child or adolescent development is not therefore the centre of the laboratory's preoccupation. Nevertheless studies have never been carried out without a certain number of hypotheses concerning the development of children and adolescents.

With the foundation of the laboratory, researchers were principally using Piaget's theory. These are some of the uses which have been made of it:

(a)   Taking into account the stage which the student is in: The behaviours of the students are situated with respect to the stage of development that they are in. The characteristics of the stages (concrete/formal operations) are used as a basis to interpretate students' behaviour.

(b)   Respect of developmental rhythms: The collection of textbooks is called: *Libre parcours* ('Free route'). This means that there are several possible lesson planning and developmental transitions. The teachers are invited to choose those which take into account the development of the students in their class. The accent is put on the process of reasoning, rather than on a production of correct answers. The activities which are proposed try to question the child and to make him begin a possible personal research towards the construction of his knowledge.

(c) Taking into account the child's and the student's way of thinking: This research has tried to list and analyze the conceptions or private models which students have of different phenomena within the courses (electrical phenomena, light, mechanics, chemistry, states and transformations of matter), and of some physical dimensions introduced at this level (temperature, pressure, force, energy).

(d) Trying to place the students in situations where they are able to be active and to change their fashion of thinking: In reference to Piaget's analysis of evolutionary processes of thinking: assimilation, accommodation, equilibration.

Thus, the Piagetian theory has had a triple use:

(a) It leads to the development of the analysis begun by Piaget of children's conceptions of the physical world. Examples are the works on students' conceptions:
*   Electrical circuits (Ben Hamida, Delacote, Tiberghien)
*   Light (Guesne)
*   Temperature, heat (Tiberghien)
*   Combustion, chemical reactions (Meheut)
*   Gaseous state, pressure (Séré)
*   Force (Kraïbani, Lemeignan)
*   Energy (Lemeignan)
    Let us note that the conceptions of the students are studied in situations which are used in class. In this way the teachers become informed of the students' way of thinking before teaching and thus are aware of the obstacles that the students are going to meet.

(b) It is a basis for the interpretation of the behaviour of the children (the egocentrism of child's thought, the centering on objects and not on relations between objects, etc ...). At the same time, it contributes to define what is possible on a psychological level.

(c) It allows us to think of new ways of didactic intervention, with an accent put on the manipulation of objects and the resolution of problems. (Not so much counting on oral speeches and experimental demonstrations).

Along with this psychological framework, the researchers in the laboratory felt very early that there was a need to initiate an analysis of the content of teaching and to think over this content in relation to the school level of the students and the objectives to be attained. J.L. Martinand especially contributed to the development of an applied epistemology of teaching. He has also shown interest in taking into account different social practices in order to define the objectives of scientific education.

New orientations of the laboratory have contributed to change the relations between psychology and didactics. Researches are now centered on learning, especially on the study of conditions which permit the acquisition of scientific models at the different levels of the courses. Psychology not being able at this time to propose a general model of learning, reseachers in didactics have been obliged to elaborate psychological knowledge related to the topics to be taught. This has favoured the emergence of new collaborations between didacticians and psychologists. What we are going to talk about today is an illustration of such a collaboration.

The studies were done at different school levels, and consequently for different educational end points:

— Primary school (students 7–11 years old). This is basic, fundamental teaching. (Martinand, Séré, Tiberghien, Weil-Barais).
— Junior high school (students 11–15 years old) (Guesne, Méheut, Séré, Tiberghien, Weil-Barais).
— High school (students 15–18 years old) (Brénasin, Caillot, Carré, Durey, Journeaux, Larcher, Lemeignan, Weil-Barais).
— University (Durey, Journeaux)

The themes which were studied for the teaching of physics are the following:

— problem solving: conception of problems, elaboration of categories of analysis of the answers, elaboration of instructional aids in solving (Carré, Caillot, Lemeignan, Weil-Barais).
— conception of computer aided instruction (Caillot).
— use of microcomputers (Durey, Journeaux).
— elaboration of contents for teaching (Larcher, Lemeignan, Martinand, Meheut).
— conception of didactical sequences (Lemeignan, Meheut, Séré, Weil-Barais).

To different degrees, the researchers have tried to define:

— models which could be the object of teaching at a given level.
— possible objectives.
— the empirical range to be explored, and the 'situations — problems' available for students.
— didactic aids (computer aided instruction, guides).
— possible ways of evaluation.
— an analysis of students' intellectual behaviour and a study of development which can be reasonably hoped for, in a teaching situation.

Marie-Geneviève Séré and Annick Weil-Barais

The Construction of Physical Dimensions by Students

Now let us talk about some of the works of the laboratory to which we have contributed. These works have had to do with the construction of physical dimensions. The studies we shall speak about have to do with the quantity of matter and momentum. These two dimensions are introduced in teaching at very different school levels, which enables us to question the relation between acquisition of scientific knowledge and intellectual development.

The Quantity of Matter (the end of primary school and the beginning of junior high school)

The quantity of matter is defined in physics by the number of moles. The use of such a dimension necessitates a particulate representation of matter. This representation is introduced relatively late in teaching. However before the introduction of such a model, the students are brought to use the concept of quantity of matter. This is defined in practice in an operational manner during primary school education, by the practice of weighing. The students arrive at junior high school when they are 11, knowing that an object is characterized by its mass, often called incorrectly 'weight' (by identification with the name of the objects used for weighing). The mass of an object is recognized as invariable. This idea of the conservation of mass has to be confirmed by the teachers when the children arrive in the first year of junior high school. They often use the Piagetian tests of conservation of solids and liquids. The conservation of mass is then generally enlarged to the conservation of quantity of matter without any specific mention being made of the development. This is done regardless of the state of matter. Thus, the teachers present a certain number of experiments to the junior high school students, which can only be interpreted correctly if the students are aware of the conservation of quantity of matter. Let us take the example of an experiment showing the expandability of gas. A glass flask containing air is heated. The membrane over the flask rounds out. If heated more, the membrane explodes. The expandability of air is interpreted at this school level as the idea that the volume of air has increased. This can only be understood if the students realize that something does not change, which is the quantity of matter in the flask.

However the data we have collected concerning gaseous state show that the realization of the invariability of a quantity of gas depends very much on the experimental context, as will be shown below.

The Data of a Transverse Study

We gave a written test concerning conservation of air in various situations, to 280 children aged 11 to 14. The results are given in table 7.1.

Table 7.1 *Percentages of Correct Answers to the Tests of Conservation for the Different Grades*

	6th grade (11+ years)	5th grade (12+ year)	4th grade (13+ year)
Inflating a football	83	89	94
Inflating a balloon	96	90	99
Decanting air from a container into another one of a different shape	31	41	58
Decanting air from a container into three other ones	37	44	50
Heating in the sun. V ↗	57	51	72
Heating with a flame V ≡	54	61	75
Heating with a flame V ↗	19	49	65
Chilling V ≡	78	74	93
Chilling V ↘	37	61	66
Compressing V ↘	35	57	63
Expanding V ↗	41	55	64
Total number	93	115	72

Experimental Situations

The experiments consisted of various transformations of air. Among them, two were situations of non-conservation:

* Inflating an elastic balloon or a football (considered as rigid). These two experiments were proposed to see if the students were able to dissociate quantity and volume. The other experiments were all situations of conservation:

* Decanting air from a container to another of a different shape and to three other smaller containers.

* Heating air. Two ways of heating: the sun and a flame. In this last case there were two different experiments: the containers were closed with a rigid cork, or an elastic membrane.

* Chilling air with ice-cubes. Two experiments with a rigid cork, or an elastic membrane.

* Compressing/expanding air. This was done by moving the piston of a syringe containing a tiny balloon. According to the direction of the displacement, this small balloon swelled or shrunk.

The Sample

* The first level was the '6th grade' which is the first in the French junior high school. It is at this level that children study physics for the first time, and particularly physical properties of gas. Questioned at the beginning of the year, they had not yet received this teaching. These children were aged from 11 to 14 years.
* The second level was the '5th grade'. When questioned, these children had already had lessons about air and gas (the concepts of mass, volume, pressure) less than one year ago. These children were aged from 11 to 16.
* The third level was the '4th grade'. These children had been informed the previous year about the effects of changing temperature of gases (rigid or elastic containers are heated in different ways, for instance). Either the volume, or the pressure is maintained constant.

Results

About the two situations of non-conservation, it can be said that most of the children, at any level, recognize that there is more air when a balloon or a football is inflated. Eleven per cent in 6th grade, 8 per cent in 5th grade, 6 per cent in 4th grade did however confuse quantity and volume, by answering that there is 'as much air' when the volume is constant (the drawings before/after were identical).

Concerning the situations of conservation it can be said that the percentages differ widely from one grade to another.

These differences cannot be interpreted only by confusion of quantity and volume, for the percentages are neither different nor better when volume is constant. The only group for which this happens is the 6th grade for the situations of heating. When the volume increases (elastic membrane), 81 per cent give an inadequate answer.

The development is sometimes significant from 6th grade to 4th grade. It is so for the heating by a flame. It is not so, for the two situations of decanting. In spite of this development, it appears that even for students having been taught about air and gas, there are a lot of answers indicating non-conservation.

The arguments of logical order (identity, compensation, reversibility) are rarely brought out. In fact the students very often interpret the experimental operations as operations modifying the 'content', the matter itself. This is the case with the operations of heating by flame or cooling down by contact with ice.

The argument of compensation only appears later on among those students who have had some teaching on pressure. The argument of reversibility appears in the 'syringe-balloon' situations where they can more easily link states and transformations.

In a general manner, the students focus on the transformations which are thought as being irreversible. Successive states which are analyzed, are then thought as being different situations.

Being able to take into account the state of a gas, in a given container, necessitates a quite complex analysis where numerous dimensions come into account (temperature, pressure, number of moles, the volume of the container, its resistance and so on). Obviously, children sampled in our study have no mastery of these dimensions, except for volume for which they can evaluate changes by looking at it. *A fortiori*, they have no mastery of the relations between the dimensions. Knowing that the operations of weighing a gas are very difficult and not convincing, it appears that recognizing the conservation of a quantity of gas can only be a presupposition. It is linked to the possibility of describing the changes intervening in the experiments, in terms of the variation of physical dimensions. (This sort of reading of an experiment allows the children to reason by means of co-variations and contravariations).

A didactic sequence about gas
We have observed and studied a teaching situation, involving twenty-one students of a class in the last year of primary school. This didactic sequence was conceived in relation to the analysis which we have made of the experiments which need a knowledge of conservation of the quantity of matter. We aimed at a description of states and transformations in terms of physical dimensions. The problem was thus to find situations which lead the students to consider pertinent physical dimensions: mass, volume, temperature and pressure. At this school level, it was not a question of defining the totality of these dimensions and their relations. It was merely a question of giving the idea of their existence, and the links between them by examining covariations and con-travariations. The existence of dimensions was pointed out by the nature of the characteristics which vary (colour, resistance of the object on the body), or by the nature of an operation of measurement (weighing on scales).

Our principal objective being that the students arrive at recognizing the invariability of quantities of gas, we proposed the experiments detailed below. They concern the experimental field that students explore during the following years in junior high school (where quantity of matter is a prerequisite): decanting air from one container to another, gathering air in a container, compressing/expanding air, and raising up/lowering temperature. The containers can be flexible, rigid, or partially elastic. They can be open or closed.

This last characteristic permits us to extend the limit of the system beyond the container, taking into account other systems, such as the atmosphere. The children are brought to question the entry of gas to the container and its exit, and thus to realize that matter in a gaseous state does not disappear. Such questioning leads the children towards the understanding of what will be later considered as the 'interactions' and 'systems'.

Description of the experiments made by the students
The sequence was essentially experimental, and the experiments carried out by the children themselves. The rule, made explicit to the children, was to construct interpretations taking into account the totality of the experiments,

even though these were carried out one by one over a period of five sessions of about ninety minutes. The role of the teacher was to propose the experiments and the questions about them, to help each group of children to carry them out, to direct the collecting and coding of data, highlighting some of them, and to propose comparisons of results to allow for a comparison of the students' predictions inferred from their representations, and the observed effects, eventually pointing out contradictions.

The experiments were the following:

* preparation of a coloured gas (nitrogen dioxide). Compression and expansion of it in a syringe.
* preparation of carbon dioxide from an Alka-Seltzer tablet and water, in two different ways. First, in a container closed by an elastic membrane (the gas fills the volume and inflates the membrane), then in an open container on the plate of a scale. (The equilibrium of the scale is broken).
* Air is weighed approximatively by putting a neon light tube (which contains a very small amount of gas) on scales, balancing the scales, then breaking one of the tips of the tube. This experiment is completed by breaking a similar fluorescent tube in water.
* simulation of the take off of a hot air balloon (with a large plastic bag and a bunsen burner as a source of heat). The same experiment is carried out with the same plastic bag and a bunsen burner, without lighting it.
* putting two squashed ping pong balls into boiling water. One was smashed but not pierced, the other had a small hole. The first one recovered its spherical shape, the other gave off bubbles, without changing its shape.
* inflating a tire with a pump.

Results

The results of the tests (the same as in the previous study) prior to and after teaching (in brackets) are given in table 7.2.

Prior to teaching, the results are rather bad and quite similar to those obtained previously in a 6th grade. After teaching, sixteen out of twenty-one students improved their performance (five of whom succeeded for all questions). The confusion between quantity and volume remains but is less frequent. From a Hierarchical Automatical Classification, experimental operations are classified from the easiest to the most difficult, as follows: decanting, compressing/expanding, chilling, heating.

The most important improvements concern decanting. They probably come from the fact that the teaching helped the children to realize that air is matter.

The distance between chilling and heating shows that all children do not conceive these operations as contraries, which is confirmed by some of the

Table 7.2   Answers of the students to the tests of conservation of quantities of air, prior to teaching and after teaching (in brackets) (N = 21)

	More air	Less air	As much air	I don't know
Inflating a football	20(19) ⎫ 20(16)	0(1)	1(1)	
Inflating a balloon	21(18) ⎭	0(0)	0(3)	
Decanting air from a container into another one of a different shape	15(2)	3(0)	1(18) ⎫ 1(17)	2(1)
Decanting air from a container into three other ones	15(2)	2(1)	3(18) ⎭	1(0)
Heating in the sun. V ↗	4(4)	3(2)	4(12) ⎫	10(3)
Heating with a flame V ≡	3(9)	1(1)	4(11) ⎬ 2(7)	13(2)
Heating with a flame V ↗	16(9)	0(0)	5(10) ⎭	0(0)
Chilling V ≡	0(2)	2(2)	14(16) ⎫ 3(10)	5(1)
Chilling V ↘	0(0)	18(6)	3(11) ⎭	0(2)
Compressing V ↘	2(0)	13(9)	1(12) ⎫ 1(12)	5(0)
Expanding V ↗	12(8)	4(0)	1(13) ⎭	4(0)

The number on the right of a brace shows the number of students who correctly answered both questions.

commentaries during teaching. Moreover these two operations are not thought by children as reversible.

Most of the students have been led to give up some of their spontaneous interpretations, generally directed by the events: 'the hot air balloon rises up' ... 'the pierced ball makes bubbles' ... Some are able to realize that such events are two different modalities of a changing of temperature. This showed them the usefulness of a same dimension to describe different experiments.

As to pressure, one can also note improvements due to new explanations like: 'there is as much air but it is tight, or compressed ...', good answers coming from interpretations acquired during the teaching.

On the whole, it can be said that the main objectives of the teaching have been attained.

Finally this study has highlighted the importance of 'local knowledge', which is specific to each situation, in the judgments of conservation of children. It has shown in an evident way that these experiments and this questioning have contributed to the construction of an invariant reputedly 'precocious', according to the works of Piaget. Consequently we can say that the analysis of the knowledge necessary to treat situations concerning matter in a gaseous state, makes it possible to conceive teaching which is appropriate. This teaching was uniquely based on the analysis of experimental situations easy to put into operation, but which make the students question. Predictions which they make are often in contradiction with the results obtained.

In fact, the work on the physical dimensions is extremely limited. This is only a first approach. The dimensions are not really defined, they have been able to be influenced by the effect of perceptual clues, which covary with the dimension (for instance, when the gas becomes darker, pressure increases). All this work on the study of covariations and contravariations of clues (for instance, for the small balloon, smaller means harder), can be the beginning of work on the relations between dimensions, as will be shown below.

Momentum (first year of high school)

The students who arrive at high school are already familiar with some physical dimensions. Let us say that they have at least worked with them under the form of a verbal 'label' to designate the variations of a measurement that they have made. In high school, they must go beyond such an approach. The properties of dimensions must be known as well as the relations which exist between them. The understanding must be such that the students can bring numeric and literal solutions to experimental problems which are given to them.

It is from this viewpoint that we have undertaken a study concerning the teaching of mechanics in order to define a progression taking into account the constitution of physical dimensions. Our epistemological analysis concerning the three fundamental dimensions in mechanics ($\vec{p}$, $\vec{F}$, E) has led us to choose the momentum $\vec{p}$ as the first dimension to be introduced. $\vec{p}$ in fact does not necessitate previous construction of the representation of objects. It can be constructed starting from two dimensions that the students know, m and $\vec{v}$. The teaching project that we have conceived involves the 'construction' of $\vec{p}$ by the students, using the same processes as a researcher elaborating a model. Thus the determination of $\vec{p}$ and its properties is the final point of a whole set of previous work:

* Carrying out experiments, in order to look for dimensions which have an effect on the studied phenomena. The experiments concern collisions and the breaking-up of two mobiles which are small wagons on horizontal rails. The wagons are sometimes moving and sometimes at rest, before they hit into each other. The students can load them in order to modify their movement.
* Gathering and treating measurements with a view to finding the functional relations which take into account variations of the dimensions used (speed and mass). When gathering these measurements, conflicts may come up between what is predicted and what is actually obtained.

* The search for a common form in a set of relationships and the search for the properties of that form. We chose this point to start constructing a physical dimension which is 'mv'. It appears to be able to describe the mobile, to 'belong' to it, and the possibility of being transferred, added, conserved is under question.

The model built up is then used to create hypotheses for treating new experimental situations (with or without friction, colinear or uncolinear speeds, for example). The students are thus brought, little by little, to elaborate the experimental field and to define the domain of validity of the model.

The didactic sequence set up on the basis of an epistemological analysis of the domain, and from the determination of a certain number of objectives (education to scientific thought). The aim of this study was to state precisely under what conditions such a progression was feasible for students in first year of high school.

The study of the feasibility of such a sequence leads us to specify the following:

* the experimental field which is explored with the students (that was fixed at first concerning the movement of the two mobiles in one direction only).
* symbolic representations and the treatment of the symbols which can be used. We firstly chose arithmetic relations, then algebric relations. Vectors were only introduced when there were experiments which needed to take into account several directions.
* The problems and the succession of problems which were proposed to the students. (Thus the first problems concern an experimental study of the experiments, seeking functional relations between dimensions. The last problems were meant to help the students use the new dimension constructed, $\vec{p}$).
* The knowledge that the students can induce by themselves.
* The guidance which was able to help the students' progress in resolving problems. Setting up these aids was based on the analysis of procedures 'invented' by the students (they are considered as 'developmental precursors' in the terms of Case, 1985) and on an analysis of expert behaviour. This allowed the setting up of the generation of the 'new' to be learnt by the 'already known'.

The results that we obtained show that in the school level considered, certain problems do not offer any special difficulties. This is the case for:

* looking for a dimension which has an effect on the studied phenomena. The students very rapidly are able to identify the mass of each of the mobiles and the speed of the mobiles before collision. They are able to eliminate a certain number of factors which come into play initially in

their explanations, for instance the length of the wagons, the width of the wheels.
* planning of the gathering of measurements, with a view to looking for the relations between the dimensions mass and speed. (The procedure which consists in systematically varying each of the dimensions and keeping the others constant is something which is available very early, as we have shown in other studies Cauzinille-Marmèche, Mathieu and Weil-Barais, 1983.)

Other problems can only be resolved with specific training. This is the case of the procedure of seeking out a functional relationship. The analysis of those intellectual activities which must go to work in order to help the research progress, was the object of particular care in this study (Lemeignan and Weil-Barais, 1987).

We have noticed a certain number of procedures which are used in the elaboration and the use of the dimension momentum. We shall call these 'operational invariants', because they are also present for other physical dimensions. These are:

* The selection of events.
* The division in time (before and after the collision).
* Regrouping objects in a system and characterizing the states of the system by a set of values of the dimensions.
* The use of a principle of conservation.

The first 'invariants' concern the construction of a representation of a given empirical situation. The last one concerns the study of experimental conditions which allow the use of a model.

The hypothesis which we have proposed is that the acquisition of such 'operational invariants' is a *sine qua non* condition of the ability to use processes of modelling. Thus we can say that these processes constitute a way of thinking which is quite elaborated, and permits the growth of the possibility of interaction between the subject and his surroundings.

The difficulty in mastering these invariants related to model acquirement, is important. Even if we leave aside affective and motivational aspects, the cognitive skills which these invariants require are complex. Let us remember that school is the specific place for learning such skills, which do not take place in everyday life. Students' failure in science probably means that their teaching presently does not sufficiently take into account the formation of such difficult cognitive skills. It is thus necessary, so it seems to us, to study in detail intellectual activities which are required in order to assimilate scientific knowledge. Such an analysis may lead to teaching better adapted to the actual possibilities of students.

We have shown that it is possible to link an epistemological analysis in the area of knowledge, to an analysis of expert practices, a psychological analysis of students' behaviour and cognitive skills, and educational activities.

To conclude, we wish to emphasize the value of considering and studying the teaching of science in a developmental context. The acquisition of scientific knowledge is a long-term matter, due to the number and the complexity of the operational invariants involved. All of these invariants cannot be acquired at once. Some of them are prerequisites for more complex approaches: for instance, the setting of functional relations pre-supposes the mastery of causal analysis. We have already mentioned that these invariants can be taught by taking advantage of a first approach to some physical dimensions, based upon the study of covariations and contravariations of perceptual clues. However, mastering physical dimensions can only occur when the students have acquired the whole set of the related operational invariants. This can only occur late. From such a viewpoint a new organization of teaching becomes necessary. Presently it remains too focused on the exposition of concepts and theories of little practical value for the students, because it is missing any training about operational invariants related to them.

References

Caillot, M. (1985) 'Problem representation and problem-solving procedures in electricity' in Duit R., Jung W. and von Rhöneck C. (Eds) *Aspects of Understanding Electricity, 139–51, IPN-Arbeitsberichte*, Kiel, RFA.

Caillot, M. (in press) 'Modelling the students' errors in the ELECTRE tutor' in Self, J. (Ed.), *Intelligent Computer-Aided Instruction*, London Chapman and Hall.

Caillot, M. and Dumas-Carre, A. (1985) 'Activités et connaissances nécessaires à la résolution de problèmes: un exemple an physique', *Cognitiva 85*, PARIS CESTA, pp 81–6.

Caillot, M. and Dumas-Carre, A. (1987) 'PROPHY: Un enseignement d'une méthodologie de résolution de problémes de physique, Rapport final de la R.C.P. INRP', *Résolution de problémes en mathématique et en physique*, p 45.

Case, R. (1985) *Intellectual Development: Birth to adulthood*, New York, Academic Press.

Cauzinille-Marmeche, E., Mathieu, J. and Weil-Barais, A. (1982) 'Le raisonnement expérimental des pré-adolescents: stratégies de test d'hypotèses', *Enfance*, 1–2, pp 23–38.

Cauzinille-Marmeche, E., Mathieu, J. and Weil-Barais, A. (1985) *Les Savants en Herbe*, (2nd edn) Berne, Peter Lang.

Cauzinille-Marmeche, E., Meheut, M., Sere, M.G. and Weil-Barais, A. (1985) 'The influence of a-priori ideas on the experimental approach', *Science Education*, 69, 2.

Delacote, G. and Tiberghien, A. (Eds) (1984) Recherche en didactique de la physique, La Londe les Maures, Paris, Editions du CNRS, 660p.

Driver, R., Guesne, E. and Tiberghien, A. (1985a) 'Children's ideas and the learning of science' in Driver, R., Guesne, E. and Tiberghien, A. (Eds), *Children's Ideas in Science*, Milton Keynes, Open University Press, pp 1–9.

Driver, R., Guesne, E. and Tiberghien, A. (1985b) 'Some features of children's ideas and their implications for teaching' in Driver, R., Guesne, E. and Tiberghien, A. (Eds), *Children's Ideas in Science*, Milton Keynes, Open University Press, pp 193–201.

Dumas-Carre, A. (1987) 'La résolution de problème en physique au lycée; Le procédural: appretissage et évaluation', *THESE d'Etat ès Sciences*, Université Paris 7.

DUMAS-CARRE, A. and LARCHER, C. (1987) 'The stepping stones of learning and evaluation', *International Journal of Science Education*, 9, 1, pp 93–104.

DUREY, A. (1987) 'Vers des activités didactiques de mise au point de modèles de physique avec des micro-ordinateurs. Exemples: trajectoires, frappés et rebonds de balle en rotation', *THESE d'Etat ès Sciences*, Université Paris 7.

DUREY, A. and JOURNEAUX, R. (1987) 'Expérience d'Elihu-Thomson, un exemple de modélisation par étapes', *European Journal of Physics*, 8, 18.

GUESNE, E. (1985) 'Light' in DRIVER, R., GUESNE, E. and TIBERGHIEN, A. (Eds), *Children's Ideas in Science*, Milton Keynes, Open University Press, pp 10–32.

KHRAIBANI, S. (1984) 'Registres d'interprétation des élèves et des professeurs de collège dans le domaine de la mécanique, *Thèse de 3ème Cycle*, Université PARIS 7.

LARCHER, C., MEHEUT, M., CHOMAT, A. and BARBOUX, M. (1987) 'Modèles particulaires et activités de modélisation au collège', *GRECO Didactique et Acquisition des Connaissances Scientifiques*, 13p.

LEMEIGNAN, G. and WEIL-BARAIS, A. (1987a) 'Etude de quelques activités de modélisation; la recherche de relations fonctionnelles entre grandeurs physiques', *GRECO Didactique et Acquisition des Connaissances Scientifiques*, 17p.

LEMEIGNAN, G. and WEIL-BARAIS, A. (1987b) Construction inductive d'un modèle en mécanique et résolution de problèmes, rapport de fin de contrat: R.C.P., INRP, 'Résolution de problèmes en mathématiques et en physique', 53p.

MARTINARD, J.L. (1986a) 'Connaître et transformer la matière; Des objectifs pour l'initiation aux sciences et techniques', Peter Lang (Ed.), BERNE, 155p.

MARTINARD, J.L. (1986b) 'Sur la caractérisation des objectifs de l'initiation aux sciences physiques', *ASTER, Recherches en didactique des sciences expérimentales n°1*, INRP, p 141.

MARTINARD, J.L. (1986c) 'La recherche française en didactique des sciences physiques', *E.P.S. Contenus et Didactique*, SNEP, pp 287–91.

MEHEUT, M., LARCHER, C., CHOMAT, A. and BARBOUX, M. (1986) 'Structure de la matière, modèles particulaires', *Rapport de recherche n° 1–09–84–87 INRP DP1*, Juin 86.

MEHEUT, M., SALTIEL, E. and TIBERGHIEN, A., (1985) 'Students conceptions about combustion (11–12 years old)', *European Journal of Science Education*, 7, 1, p 83–93.

PALIÈS, O., CAILLOT, M., CAUZINILLE-MARMECHE, E., LAURIERE, J.L. and MATHIEU, J. (1986) 'Student modelling by a knowledge-based system', *Computational Intelligence*, 2, pp 99–107.

SÉRÉ, M.G. (1985) 'Analyse des conceptions de l'état gazeux qu'ont les enfants de 11 à 13 ans, en liaison avec les notions de pression et propositions de stratégies pédagogiques pour en faciliter l'évolution', *Thèse d'Etat ès sciences*, Université PARIS VI, 364 p.

SÉRÉ, M.G. (1986) 'Children's conceptions of the gaseous state, prior to teaching', *European Journal of Science Education*, 8, 4, pp 413–456.

SÉRÉ, M.G. and WEIL-BARAIS, A., 'Nouvelle approche de la conservation des grandeurs physiques. Etude transversale de la conservation de la quantité de gaz auprès d'élèves de 11 à 15 ans', Enfance.

TIBERGHIEN, A. (1985) 'Heat and temperature, the development of ideas with teaching', in DRIVER, R., GUESNE, E. and TIBERGHIEN, A. (Eds), *Children's Ideas in Science*, Milton Keynes, Open University Press.

TIBERGHIEN A. (1986a) 'Difficulties in concept formation' in LAYTON, D. (Ed.) *Innovations in Science and Technology Education*, Paris, UNESCO.

TIBERGHIEN, A. (1986b) 'Research in physics education and teaching materials' in Shimoda and Ryu (Eds), *Proceeding of an International Conference on Trends in Physics Education*, Tokyo, Physics Education Society of Japan.

VAUTREY, ALEMANI, L. and MARTINARD, J.L. (1987) 'Horizontalité et verticalité à l'école primaire', *Bulletin de l'Union des Physiciens*, 690, pp 81–109.

WEIL-BARAIS, A., SERE, M.G. and LANDIER J.C. (1986), 'Evolution of expectations of constancy of quantity of air by 10–11 years old students', *European Journal of Psychology of Education*, 1, 3, pp 9–30.

WEIL-BARAIS, A. and SERE, M.G. (forthcoming), *Conceptual Change Position About the Development of Physical Constancies by Students aged 10 to 16.*

Respondent: Jon Ogborn

I shall use this occasion to make a few general remarks, stimulated by this chapter, but also relating it to others presented here and to some issues I think are of importance to us.

We should first of all note, and pay due honour to the fact that workers at LIRESPT were amongst the very first to see that curriculum development ought to be done in relation to finding out about children's ideas. They were doing the work we are all now taking for granted, before most of us saw any importance in it at all. This I think has been the main influence of Piaget on their work — the idea of taking the child's thinking and ideas seriously, to be looked at *sui generis*, not as a deformed version of adult or of some other thinking. They can also teach some of us a lesson in not confusing respect for the child and for the child's ideas, with having something to teach in terms of which there are, whatever some say, right answers, and so having that other respect for the child which obliges one to say that his or her ideas are in error.

I think that in a few years we will also discover that they anticipated us in another way, in an analysis of what is involved in the creation of a teaching material. I suspect that we will all soon speak of *transposition didactique* and of *pratique de reference*, perhaps coming to think that we thought of them ourselves.

The particular work reported here seems to me to be important in being a collaboration between science educators and psychologists. I have been distressed too often by the arrogance of scientists thinking that understanding psychology is easy, who have grossly misunderstood and misused the work of several, notably that of Piaget.

One benefit of the collaboration, I suspect, is that the work here is both severely practical — studies of learning in science classrooms — and yet is framed in terms of relatively fundamental questions. Research in the Anglo-Saxon tradition rather rarely speaks of making an epistemological analysis, or looks into the acquiring of fundamental elements of the epistemological basis of looking at the world in terms of physical quantities. I happen also to think that this kind of perspective on the difficulties of science is essential to us; that we have to concern ourselves with metaphysical issues as well as with scientific concepts and children's concepts. I mean that the difference between child and scientist is often at the level of a whole way of looking at the world, whether as particles in empty space, or as having nothingness filling space. In fact the study of gases here may be seen as a step in finding out how to change an ontology, to give what seems to children non-real the status of matter on an equal level with other more tangible stuff. How easy it is to forget the metaphysical leap involved in imagining the earth surrounded by a cloak of air.

Other papers at the conference have raised the same issue. I note particularly that by Ruth Stavy on conceptions of matter. I think also that the children Rosalind Driver showed on videotape were engaged in doing *metaphysical* work. They discussed what could be, how things could work, reasoning qualitatively from categories one might apply. This is deciding how to look at the world, rather than the detailed finding out about the world which follows later and cannot be done — and more important to us — cannot be understood, if one doesn't know or understand the world view which makes that finding out sensible and relevant.

I have no doubt exaggerated the extent to which one can see all this in the specific studies presented here; indeed I would like to have seen this theme emphasized more strongly. But certainly this work goes some way along the path I have indicated. It leads to the description of learning progress, not in terms of test scores, but in terms of profiles of basic ideas changed. This is the kind of map I would count as indicating success in teaching.

Discussion (Reporter: Mary Simpson)

A questioner commented that while in the first study it seemed that pupils were merely being asked to use competencies which they had previously acquired to interpret new experiments, the second involved the development of a two variable model. In this case one would expect to have to increase the competency of pupils if they are to improve their performance.

The authors replied that often we are so used to the experiments, that we suppose children can do the things that we can do. The model that the teacher would have of temperature scales and relationships would be something like:

dry ice — ice — hands — boiling water — flame — sun

Pupils do not have such a scale to refer to. They have only dissociated events.

The questioner said that this was the very point: children have the competency to use scales, they just have not yet generated performance in these particular events. The authors disagreed, saying that the pupils' frame of reference does need to be changed, since previously their attention was on the change of state, now it is to be on the change of scales. In the second study, the key issue is the acquisition of the ability to recognize new functional invariants.

A query was raised about the level of motivation and interest generated, especially by the second study: this seemed to be very demanding, requiring students to understand the physical phenomena and at the same time construct the logical operations required to model them. It was imagined that in England the approach would have set the conceptual work in some relevant context, to justify the expenditure of time. The authors replied that although this had worried them initially, in fact the students were very well motivated, and so were the teachers. 'But what exactly did the pupils get out of it?' It was explained that in this presentation it was not possible to show the range and variety of methods actually used in the classroom, which included computers, simulations, and other techniques which proved motivating.

One questioner asked about the conceptual framework within which the work on momentum was set, since research shows that the concept of momentum requires a general framework to guide its development — something along the lines of an advanced organizer. Séré and Weil-Barais replied that pupils already knew about mass and velocity, and then partly inductively the idea of momentum was introduced, and then force, and energy. The non-inductive part involves the interpolation of the model within the evidence that they establish. Each part of the scheme is introduced by the teacher with an overview, and followed by a summary, leading on to an overview of the next part, and so on.

Another participant asked about the characteristics of the sample of pupils. To what extent could results be generalized to other pupils, other teachers, other schools? The authors replied that there was nothing special about the sample. They were a mixed group from a variety of socioeconomic backgrounds. 'But if the pupils and the teachers were ordinary, in what respect did their experiences differ from normal?' It was very different. Normally the topic would have been dealt with in one lesson, with a traditional approach, the teacher writing on the board, perhaps followed by a demonstration and questions by the teacher to the pupils.

8   Science Teaching from a Developmental Perspective: The Importance of Central Conceptual Skills

Robbie Case

Introduction

During the past eighty years, an interesting progression has taken place in the field of intellectual development. From the turn of the century until about the 1960s, the view of intellectual development which dominated was that children's minds grew in a very general and orderly fashion. Children were seen as passing through very general stages, in which the form of intellectual operations that they possessed (and therefore the knowledge of the world they were capable of acquiring) changed dramatically as a function of general experiential and/or maturational factors. The major psychologists whose names were associated with this view were James Mark Baldwin and Jean Piaget.

As Piaget's theory became known in North America during the 1960s and 70s, however, and was subject to careful empirical scrutiny, a reaction set in against it. Evidence from a variety of sources suggested that the supposedly general stages which Piaget had described did not actually exist, and that children's intellectual operations changed in a domain-specific fashion as a function of the particular experience to which they were exposed, and the particular constraints to which each domain was subject. The way in which the field grew during this period was by building detailed models of children's intellectual operations and knowledge in a wide variety of particular domains (see, for example, the work of John Flavell, Rochel Gelman, David Klahr, Ann Brown, and Frank Keil).

This view is still the dominant one. However, during the past five or six years, a compromise position has been proposed by a number of different theorists, each working quite independently. This position holds that the development of children's intelligence involves both general and domain specific components. While individual intellectual operations and knowledge structures are indeed acquired in a domain specific fashion, it is proposed that a common structural sequence can nevertheless be discerned across domains.

Moreover, a common general ceiling appears to be reached at any age, due to general organismic constraints, in any situation in which sufficient domain-specific experience is provided. The theories of Kurt Fischer in America, Graeme Halford in Australia, and Andreas Demetriou in Greece all exemplify this latter position.

My own theory (Case, 1985) also falls into this same general category, and has been developed in response to the same historical factors. Thus, what I shall do in the first part of my presentation is to offer a general overview of the theory and then illustrate its central postulates with examples from a familar scientific reasoning task.

Summary of Model

In summary, the present neo-Piagetian theory may be thought of as having been generated by the dilemmas posed by the 'process' analyses of the 1970s, and as offering one potential solution to these problems. Whereas the roots of the theory are in the rationalist tradition, it may be seen to have been strongly influenced by developments in the empiricist and historico-cultural traditions as well. The general structure of the theory may be summarized by means of the following postulates.

Models of Children's Early Intellectual Capabilities

1   At the most elementary level, children's mental processes may be divided into two categories: (a) those which represent recurrent patterns of stimulation; and (b) those which represent ways in which these patterns can be transformed. The former may be labelled *figurative schemes*, or *state representations*. The latter may be labelled *operative schemes* or *operations*.

2   From the age of birth, if not earlier, the activation of any scheme or set of schemes is experienced as having a particular affective character: either positive, negative, or neutral.

3   From the age of birth, if not earlier, children are capable of exercising some degree of voluntary control over their own cognitive and affective experience.

4   The structures which permit this executive control consist of temporally organized sequences of figurative and operative schemes, which may be parsed into three components: (a) schemes representing some particular state in which the child recurrently finds itself; (b) schemes representing some other state that has a higher affective value; and (c) schemes representing the sequence of operations that will take the child from one of these states to the other. These three components may be labelled *problem representations, objectives,* and *strategies* respectively.

Structural Model of Development

1 Although each executive control structure represents a device for dealing with a different specific problem situation, all executive control structures undergo a similar set of transformations with time, and pass through a general and universal sequence of stages en route to assuming their adult form.

2 Four major stages of executive development may be identified between the ages of 4 months and 19 years, namely the stages of sensorimotor, relational, dimensional, and vectorial operations. What differentiates these stages is the level of relationships that the child must represent and manipulate.

3 Within each major stage a universal sequence of three substages may also be identified, namely the substages of *unifocal*, *bifocal*, and *elaborated* coordination. What differentiates these substages is the number of elements that they represent, and the way in which these elements are organized.

4 Under normal rearing conditions, each stage and substage of development is traversed during a characteristic time period, across a broad range of content domains. The particular ages that are associated with each stage and substage are given in figure 8.1.

5 The transition from one stage to the next in any given problem domain is brought about by the *hierarchical integration* of executive structures that were assembled during the previous stage, but whose form and function were considerably differrent from each other.

6 The transition from one substage to the next in any domain also occurs by a process of integration. However, this integration need not be hierarchical, and the elements that are involved need not be different from each other.

Process Model of Development

1 Four elementary information processes on which structural development depends are schematic search, evaluation, retagging, and consolidation.

2 These processes form a part of most of children's day-to-day activities, both those that are independent and those that are socially directed. They form a particularly important part of children's exploration, problem solving, imitation, and mutual regulation.

3 An important form of mutual regulation, and one which plays an increasingly significant role in children's thinking at each successive stage of their development, is instruction.

4 Children's capability for hierarchical integration is constrained by the size of their short term storage space. The amount of space that is available at each stage and substage is also shown in Figure 8.1.

Robbie Case

Figure 8.1 *Overall sequence of stages and substages postulated in theory*
Source: *Case, 1985.*

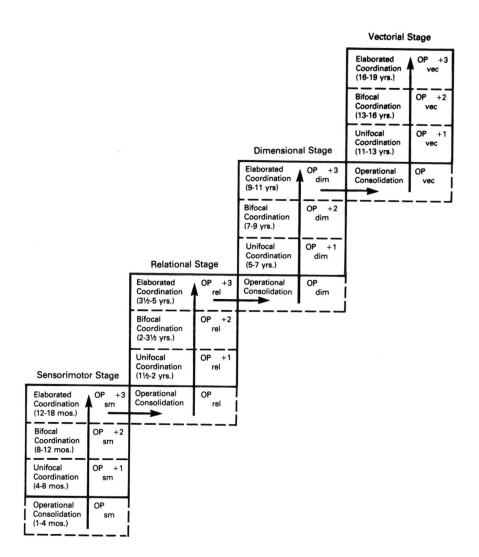

5   The growth of short term storage within each stage is brought about by an increase in operational efficiency.

6   Increases in operational efficiency are to a considerable extent dependent on maturational factors such as neurological myelinization. However, a certain amount of practice is necessary as well.

The Development of Dimensional Control Structures of Middle Childhood

In accordance with the focus of this seminar I shall describe in more detail only the dimensional and vectorial stages, illustrating their characters with examples from a balance beam problem.

The Dimensional Stage

Substage 1: Operational Coordination (5–7 Years)

Although preschoolers can focus on weight or number in situations where only one of these dimensions is of importance, they cannot focus on both dimensions, or use one as a means of drawing a conclusion about the other. Such a capability does emerge, however, between the ages of 5 and 7 years. The balance beam task that highlights this shift is the one designed by Siegler (1976), which is illustrated in figure 8.2.

Figure 8.2   Balance beam designed to investigate school-age children's control structures.
Source: Siegler, 1976.

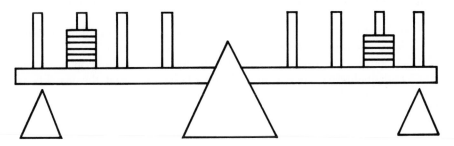

On the surface, the question children are asked in Siegler's problems is an easy one: which side of the balance beam will go down, when the supports are removed. If there is a gross perceptual difference between the stacks of weights, or if children know in advance which stack is heavier, they can answer this question at the age of $3\frac{1}{2}$ to 5 years. In the form that is illustrated, however, the only way they can answer the question is by coordinating their focus on the dimension of weight with a focus on the dimension of number.

I have adopted the following abbreviated notation for representing the control structures on which this achievement depends.

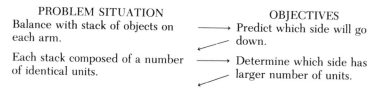

    PROBLEM SITUATION   OBJECTIVES
Balance with stack of objects on   ⟶ Predict which side will go
each arm.   down.

Each stack composed of a number   ⟶ Determine which side has
of identical units.   larger number of units.

                    STRATEGY
    1   Count each set of units; note
        which side has the bigger
        number.
    2   Pick side with bigger number as
        the one which will weigh more
        (and therefore go down).

There are several things to note about the preceding structure.

1   It has been assembled out of two qualitatively distinct precursor structures, each of which was already available, but each of which previously served a different function.
2   The integration that has taken place involves the subordination of one structure to another, in a means-end fashion.
3   In the course of or prior to this integration, a number of subtle changes have taken place in the components of each structure.
4   Accompanying this sort of differentiation and coordination is a large and qualitative change in children's behaviour, and the insights of which they are capable.

Substage 2: Biofocal Coordination (7–9 Years)

Although children can focus on a variety of quantitative dimensions by the age of 5 to 7 years, they can only focus on one such dimension at a time. During the second substage of the period, they begin to focus on a second quantitative dimension as well. On the balance beam, this may be seen in the situation where an equal number of weights is placed on each side of the balance. By the age of 7 or 8 years children no longer predict that the beam will balance. Instead, they *decenter*, and compute the distance from the fulcrum of each weight. They then predict that the weight that is at a greater distance from the fulcrum will go down. The executive control structure for arriving at this conclusion may be represented as follows:

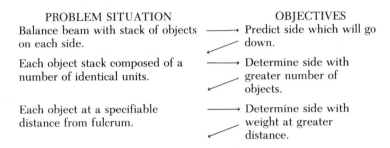

PROBLEM SITUATION | OBJECTIVES

Balance beam with stack of objects on each side. ⟶ Predict side which will go down.

Each object stack composed of a number of identical units. ⟶ Determine side with greater number of objects.

Each object at a specifiable distance from fulcrum. ⟶ Determine side with weight at greater distance.

STRATEGY

1   Count each set of weights; note which side has greater number.
2   Repeat 1 for distance of pegs.
3   If the weights are about equal, predict that the side with the greater distance will do down. Otherwise predict that the side with greater weight will go down.

This structure contains one more feature in its problem situation than did its predecessor. It also contains one additional subgoal in its list of objectives. Finally, it contains one additional subroutine in the strategy, an iteration of step 1 for distance instead of weight.

Substage 3: Elaborated Coordination (9–11 Years)

Although the strategy of substage 2 is more powerful than that of substage 1, it does not always lead to success because weight and distance are never related to each other directly. On problems where there is a difference both in weight and in distance from the fulcrum, children must choose between the two. What they do is simply to fall back on weight as the basis for prediction (Siegler, 1976). This leads to failure on a great many trials.

At the third substage, children become aware of this problem, and no longer base their decisions entirely on weight when the two are in conflict. On the other hand, because they cannot yet compute torque, they have to make a more intuitive compensation between the action of the two variables. Inhelder and Piaget (1958) have suggested that addition and subtraction strategies are common during this range. Moreover, Karplus and Peterson, (1970), Karplus, Karplus, and Wollman (1973), Furman (1981), and Marini (1984) have all obtained data which show that the majority of children in this age range do apply one of these two strategies to the task.

The addition strategy is quite simple. Children merely add the number of weight and distance units on each side, and pick the one with the greater total value as the one which will go down. The subtraction strategy is more complicated, but follows the same basic logic. Children first compute the difference between the two weights, and the difference between the two distances. They then base their decision on the dimension with the greater difference. For example, if the weights are 2 and 8, and the distances are 4 and 3, they pick the side with the greater weight to go down, because the difference along this dimension is greater than that along the distance dimension. The executive control structure for executing this sort of strategy may be presented as follows:

PROBLEM SITUATION	OBJECTIVES
Balance beam with stack of weights at various distances.	⟶ Predict which side will go down.
Action of weight and distance in opposite directions.	⟶ Determine whether weight or distance has a greater effect.
Each weight stack composed of equal amounts.	⟶ Determine relative number of weights on each side.
Each distance composed of a number of equal units.	⟶ Determine relative distance on each side.

STRATEGY

1   Count each distance; note size as well as direction of difference.
2   Repeat step 1 for weight.
3   Compare the magnitude of the results in steps 1 and 2. Notice which is bigger.
4   Focus on dimension of greater difference. Pick side with higher value as one which will go down.

The above compensation strategy marks the pinnacle of what Piaget labelled 'concrete operational thought', and what I am calling 'dimensional thought'. Marini (1984) has reported the percentages of children who function at each level. These are given in table 8.1.

The Vectorial Stage

Substage 0: Operational Consolidation (9–11 Years)

Children who compare the magnitude of one quantitative dimension with that of a second may be said to be executing a second-order or abstract dimensional operation. They are no longer comparing quantities that are calculable by

Table 8.1 Percentage of Children at Each Substage of Dimensional Stage, During the Period from $3\frac{1}{2}$ to 10 Years of Age

Theoretical age range (mean age of sample)	Level 0: Perceptual assessment of weight (%)	Level 1: Assessment of weight by counting (%)	Level 2: Assessment of distance by counting when weight equal (%)	Level 3: Weight and distance compensation via addition or subtraction (%)
$3\frac{1}{2}$-5 yr (4 yr, 5 mo)	75	25	0	0
5–7 yr (6 yr, 10 mo)	100	95	5	0
7–9 yr (9 yr)	100	100	65	15
9–11 yr (10 yr, 10 mo)	100	100	95	55

Source: Marini, 1984.

enumerating the objects in front of them. Rather, they are comparing quantities that must be calculated by executing a second operation on the product of each of these primary ones (i.e., subtraction). I shall represent the particular vectorial operations underlying 10-year-old performance on the balance beam in abbreviated form as follows:

PROBLEM SOLVING   OBJECTIVE
Weight and distance in   ⟶ Determine relative
opposition.   magnitude.

STRATEGY
1   Compare weight difference to
distance difference. Pick larger as
more potent.

Ratio plays an extremely important role in the development of abstract thought in science and mathematics. Like counting in the development of concrete thought, ratio is used to bring a quantitative precision to relationships that were previously perceived in only a rough, qualitative fashion. Ratio is an abstract or second-order dimensional operation that is similar in complexity to that of variable-compensation, but which has a different function, and a different internal form. The earliest problems children can solve with this operation (about grades 3 or 4) are as follows: 'For two dollars you get eight francs. How many francs will you get for one dollar' The control structure on which successful solution depends may be represented in abbreviated form as follows:

PROBLEM SOLVING   OBJECTIVE
2 dollars = 8 francs.   ⟶ Determine number of
1 dollar = ?   francs for one dollar.

STRATEGY
1   Divide up the number of francs (8)
among the dollars (2). Note how
much each one gets (4).

Substage 1: Operational Coordination (11–13 Years)

Although children can execute isolated vectorial operations by the age of 9 or 10 years, they cannot coordinate two such operations. As a consequence, they cannot assemble abstract *structures*, and their thought does not yet appear to be qualitatively different from that which is observed at younger ages. By about the age of 11 to 13 years, however, such a qualitative shift is observed. Children are now reported as showing their first glimmerings of abstract reasoning, or scientific thought. For example, faced with a problem where two weights on the left are opposed by one weight on the right, while two distance pegs on the left are opposed by four distance pegs on the right, they note that there are twice as many weights on the left or 'two for one', and that there are twice as many distance pegs on the right as well. They therefore conclude that the two sides will balance. This sort of reasoning does not appear if the subjects have no experience with the balance beam, that is, if they have no feedback that the reasoning of the previous stage is inadequate. Presumably it would also not appear if they had no experience in thinking in terms of ratios. Given that these two conditions are met, however, the reasoning does appear to emerge with considerable regularity and the control structure underlying it may be represented as follows:

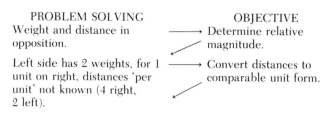

PROBLEM SOLVING   OBJECTIVE
Weight and distance in   ⟶ Determine relative
opposition.   magnitude.

Left side has 2 weights, for 1   ⟶ Convert distances to
unit on right, distances 'per   comparable unit form.
unit' not known (4 right,
2 left).

STRATEGY
1   Divide up the distance pegs on
     the right, to see how many each
     distance peg on the left 'will
     get' (2).
2   Compare the two resulting unit
     ratios. If equal, predict that the
     beam will balance; otherwise pick
     the stronger as more potent.

Note that, as was the case at the previous stage-transition points, the above structure involves two operations which were available at the previous stage as components. Further, these operations previously served quite different functions, and were used in very different contexts (i.e., science or causality problems versus math or sharing problems). One of the two operations has been subordinated to the other, in the sense that its end state now serves as a means to resolving a dilemma which the application of the other structure presents. In all these respects the nature of the transition that takes place at 11 years is similar to the one which took place at 5 years, (or earlier still at $1\frac{1}{2}$ years or at 4 months).

Substage 2: Bifocal Coordination (13–15 Years)

Although 11-13-year-olds can utilize some notion of ratio or 'dividing things up' when reasoning about two opposing dimensions, they can do so only when this operation has a single and very simple focus. By the age of 13 to 15 years, however, they are capable of taking a second division operation into account as well. One of the problems that they can solve as a consequence is one where the distances on the two sides are five and two and the weights are one and two. The behaviour that emerges is that children take the quantity which is 'left over' after two is divided into five (i.e., one) and divide it up as well. They end up comparing the unit ratio of the weights which is given (2:1), with the unit ratio in the distances which they have computed ($2\frac{1}{2}$:1). The control structure for doing so might be represented as follows:

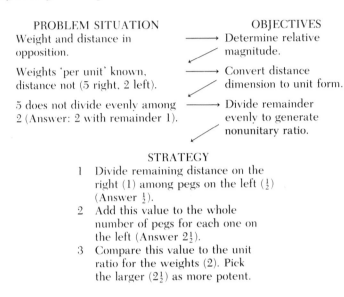

PROBLEM SITUATION   OBJECTIVES
Weight and distance in   ⟶ Determine relative
opposition.   magnitude.

Weights 'per unit' known,   ⟶ Convert distance
distance not (5 right, 2 left).   dimension to unit form.

5 does not divide evenly among ⟶ Divide remainder
2 (Answer: 2 with remainder 1).   evenly to generate
            nonunitary ratio.

STRATEGY
1   Divide remaining distance on the
   right (1) among pegs on the left ($\frac{1}{2}$)
   (Answer $\frac{1}{2}$).
2   Add this value to the whole
   number of pegs for each one on
   the left (Answer $2\frac{1}{2}$).
3   Compare this value to the unit
   ratio for the weights (2). Pick
   the larger ($2\frac{1}{2}$) as more potent.

An important characteristic of this approach is that it requires that a greater number of elements be represented, and a greater number of subgoals be established, than at the previous substage.

Substage 3: Elaborated Coordination (15–18 Years)

The elaboration that is introduced at the final substage is that the particular set of operations that were used to adjust one of the dimensions into a new ratio at the previous substage can now be executed for the second dimension as well. The subject can therefore deal with a problem in which neither quantity is stated in unit form, and in which neither set of quantities can be transformed in any fashion into a ratio that is directly comparable to the other. What the subjects do to solve this problem is to convert both ratios into a new form. For a problem involving seven weights and three weights, at distances of two units and five units, they may therefore reason that two distance pegs and five distance pegs is the same as 1 for $2\frac{1}{2}$, while three weights and seven weights is the same as 1 for $2\frac{1}{3}$. Thus, the distance factor should predominate, and the balance beam should tilt in the direction of the greater distance. This thinking has a truly abstract quality, because neither of the entities that the children end up comparing has any direct visual counterpart in the physical world, yet one of these entities can be pitted against or seen as reversing the effect of the other. One control structure for executing this sort of thinking might be represented as follows:

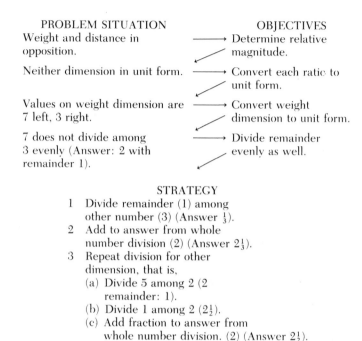

PROBLEM SITUATION	OBJECTIVES
Weight and distance in opposition.	→ Determine relative magnitude.
Neither dimension in unit form.	→ Convert each ratio to unit form.
Values on weight dimension are 7 left, 3 right.	→ Convert weight dimension to unit form.
7 does not divide among 3 evenly (Answer: 2 with remainder 1).	→ Divide remainder evenly as well.

STRATEGY

1 Divide remainder (1) among other number (3) (Answer $\frac{1}{3}$).
2 Add to answer from whole number division (2) (Answer $2\frac{1}{3}$).
3 Repeat division for other dimension, that is,
   (a) Divide 5 among 2 (2 remainder: 1).
   (b) Divide 1 among 2 ($2\frac{1}{2}$).
   (c) Add fraction to answer from whole number division. (2) (Answer $2\frac{1}{2}$).
4 Compare results from 2 divisions, pick large ratio ($2\frac{1}{2}$) as more potent.

The sort of thought that is observed on the problems of this substage represents the pinnacle of what Piaget termed formal operational thought and what is here termed abstract-dimensional or vectorial thought. The percentage of children at each age level who were functioning at each substage in Marini's study is indicated in table 8.2. As may be seen, the majority of children did reach the higher levels of the stage. In this respect, the results are unlike those in many other studies. However, it must be remembered that the children were presented the problems in a sequence of ascending complexity, and that they were shown how the beam really reacted for the first few problems at every level. The percentages thus represent estimates of the complexity of the control structures that adolescents can assemble at each age level, when they have access to all the facts about a given domain which are relevant. In effect, they present an estimate of the sort of knowledge adolescents are capable of creating under optimal conditions, not the sort of knowledge they bring to the task spontaneously.

Table 8.2 Percentage of Children Capable of Functioning at Each Level of Vectorial Stage during the Period from 9 to 18 Years

Theoretical age range (mean age of sample)	Level 0: Comparison via addition or subtraction (%)	Level 1: Comparison of unit ratio with simple multiple of it (%)	Level 2: Comparison of unit ratio with nonintegral ratio via two-step reduction (%)	Level 3: Comparison of two nonintegral ratios, with reduction of both (%)
9–11 yr (10 yr, 10 mo)	85	10	5	0
11–13 yr (13 yr, 2 mo)	100	80	30	5
13–15½ yr (15 yr, 8 mo)	100	95	75	25
15½–18½ yr (18 yr, 5 mo)	100	100	95	65

Source: Marini, 1984.

Implications for Education

Let us see now how this model of cognitive development may be applied to education.

The Transfer Problem

Of all the various problems with which contemporary instructional psychologists have struggled, probably none has proved as fundamental or as recalcitrant as the problem of transfer. Two basic approaches have been tried. The first has been to teach children very specific strategies for solving specific types of tasks. Although early results suggested that this sort of training produced little transfer (Brown, 1974), more recent work suggests that, as long as there is some variety in the original training materials, and the training includes a specific generalization component which stresses the underlying goal for which the strategy in question is useful, then students may show a reasonable degree of transfer, within the specific problem class (Bransford, 1986; Brown and Campione, 1984; Cristafi and Brown, 1986).

The second approach has been to train general heuristics or strategies, of the sort that humans are supposed to apply across a wide range of problem classes (DeBono, 1969; Feurstein, 1980). Here the original findings also indicated a rather low degree of transfer. Moreover no strategies for circumventing these problems have as yet been discovered (Chipman, Segal and Glaser, 1984). What the general pattern of data adds up to is that the most one can hope to achieve with current instructional methods is a very modest degree of transfer, within a relatively narrow problem class.

On the basis of the model outlined already, we have a framework in which the development of central conceptual skills could be promoted. Our operational hypotheses are as follows:

1   Certain quantitative skills which children acquire during one stage of cognitive development, via culturally facilitated processes such as imitation, interactive role-play, etc., can at the next stage of cognitive development become tools for independent scientific and logical thought.

2   Although these skills may not be completely general, in the sense that they can be applied to problems in all possible domains, they may have extremely wide utility within the domain of logico-mathematical reasoning. They may thus occupy a central status in that domain.

3   In order to acquire the higher-order capabilities which are characteristic of logico-mathematical reasoning, the central quantitative skills on which these insights depend may not only have to be mastered, they may also have to be automated.

4   Once these skills have been mastered and automated, progress through the structural levels of the next stage may come relatively easily, given

Table 8.3   Percentage of subjects passing various logico-mathematical tests

Items	Trained (N = 12)		Control (N = 15)		Significance Level-Fischer Exact Test
	Pretest	Post-test	Pretest	Post-test	
(a) **NEAR TRANSFER** More/less problems, with money	0%	66% (100%)*	0%	8%	p < .05
(b) **INTERMEDIATE TRANSFER** Balance Beam Test	0%	33% (57%)*	0%	0%	p < .05
Birthday Party (Social) Test	16%	75% (100%)*	0%	0%	p < .001
(c) **REMOTE TRANSFER** Money: Misleading Comparison $5 vs. $1 + $1	0%	92% (100%)*	0%	13%	p < .05
Time Telling (which of these two times is longer)	0%	50% (86%)*	0%	0%	p < .01

* Figures in brackets indicate percentages for those subjects for whom the quantification training clearly 'took': i.e. who were able to quantify and compare the magnitude of two sets of objects, when this was set as separate task.

Source: Case, Sandieson and Dennis (1986).

exposure to appropriate domain-specific experience, and motivation to make the most of that experience.

In order to check on the above set of hypotheses, we initially carried out a study with young children in which we manipulated the efficiency of a basic skill with a group of children who were on the threshold of a stage transition, and then determined whether there was a 'ripple' effect in areas which on the surface were relatively remote from this skill, and which required a level of insight normally associated with higher level functioning. Since the higher-level measures that we had available all entailed counting as a basic prerequisite, we chose this skill as our focus. What we did was to train a group of low SES 3½-year old children in a number of quantification activities, using a developmental approach. We then examined the consequences of this training for their performance in areas such as scientific reasoning, social reasoning, time telling, money handling, and so on. To control for the passage of time and exposure to stimulating curriculum materials, we also exposed a similar group of children to a comparable period of intellectual games on a computer, without directly involving them in any quantification activities.

As indicated in table 8.3, the results were extremely suggestive. Although none of the $4\frac{1}{2}$-year-olds in the control group showed any evidence of acquiring higher level insights, about half the $4\frac{1}{2}$-year-olds (Those whose quantification improved) started passing most of the tests of scientific and practical reasoning we administered, with responses that were indistinguishable from those of normal 6-year-olds. Although the data are still rather tenuous, since they are based on a small number of subjects, we believe that this finding has considerable importance for theories of cognitive development. It is the consequences for education, however, and particularly for curriculum design, which I would like to explore for the balance of the present chapter.

Curriculum Design

For the present purpose, it is probably best simply to provide an example of curriculum design at the secondary level. Consider, therefore, the problem of how to improve the teaching of *ratio* to normal children who are just making the transition to the vectorial stage. Five phases may be identified.

Phase 1: Specification of Goals

Ratio problems are of considerable importance in the everyday world outside the classroom, as well as in certain classroom subjects that are taught in secondary school such as physics and chemistry. They are also an important subset of the tasks that are usually designated formal or vectorial. A method of solution is normally taught around the age 11 or 12 years.

The general form of the problems to which children are exposed is as follows: a verbal description of some situation is provided, in which two equivalent ratios are operative, but in which one of the quantities in one of the ratios is not known. The students' task is to represent the situation mathematically, and to determine the missing quantity. This is a typical example:

> John purchased 24 loaves of bread to sell in his grocery store last week,
> at a total price of 26 dollars. If he wishes to buy 30 loaves next week,
> how much will he have to spend?

Tests indicate that the majority of children do not master such problems, even by grade 8. In fact, the success rate reaches a value no higher than 50-60 per cent, even in adulthood (Karplus and Peterson 1970). Given these statistics, it seemed likely to us that the procedure for solving these problems might require a higher level of intellectual functioning than many 11- and 12-year-olds are capable of, at least under current methods of instruction. It also seemed that the task of teaching students to solve these problems would serve as a good test case with which to assess the utility of our developmental approach.

Accordingly, Alan Gold and I established the task of teaching children how to solve these problems as our goal.

Phase 2: Analysis of Adult Control Structures

The above sort of problems may be solved by setting up an equation such as this:

$$\frac{24 \text{ loaves}}{26 \text{ dollars}} = \frac{30 \text{ loaves}}{D \text{ dollars}}$$

The equation may then be simplified and solved as follows:

$$24 \times D = 26 \times 30$$

$$D = \frac{30}{24} \times 26 \text{ (dollars)}$$

The answer is that John will have to pay $32.50 for the bread.

Although this seems straightforward, and although children can be instructed in the various steps that it entails with relative ease, their poor performance on transfer and retention tests suggests that they do not fully understand it. Accordingly, it becomes of interest to know how they do understand the problems, and what sorts of structures they assemble spontaneously for dealing with them. In short, it becomes of interest to know what the natural developmental precursors of this procedure are.

Phase 3: Analysis of Developmental Precursors

Three different sorts of children must be studied, in order to determine the developmental precursors of the adult structure: (i) those who show no success on the problem, (ii) those who show complete success, and (iii) those who show some sort of intermediate level of performance.

1 *Early control structures that lead to failure.* It turns out that the most frequent incorrect structure is one which involves addition or subtraction. Children reason that because John paid $2.00 extra for the bread the first time, he will have to pay $2.00 extra the second time as well. The answer they give is then $32.00 (Inhedler and Piaget, 1958; Gold, 1978; Dennis, 1981).

2 *Analysis of early structures that lead to success.* Although the successful adult strategy is one which involves setting up a formal equation and solving it via simplification or cross-multiplication, this method is rarely used by successful 11- or 12-year-olds, even if it is explicitly taught via a carefully constructed learning heirarchy (Gold, 1978). The strategy that children use instead might best be called the *for every* strategy, or — somewhat more formally — the *unit method*. Children realize that the person in the problem has to pay a particular amount for every loaf of bread. Their first

step is therefore to determine what this amount per unit is. Having determined this amount, they then determine what the total amount would be, if several units were purchased instead of one:

> If John paid $26.00 for 24 loaves, this means that he must have been paying a little over $1.00 for every loaf. The exact amount is 26 divided by 24, or 1.083.
>
> If John wants to buy 30 loaves next week, that means he will have to pay 30 times 1.083, or $32.50.

In accordance with our general developmental approach, it was this strategy for solving the problems, not the adult strategy, which we set out to teach the children.

3   *Analysis of intermediate structures.* Interestingly enough, and in accordance with the trend that was described for the balance beam during this age range, even children who successfully apply the unit method often seem transitional, in the sense they use the method on some problems but not on others, falling back on the subtraction method instead. Although it is hard to say for sure, they appear to fall back in this fashion when they cannot see their way through the various semantic complexities that a problem entails. The easiest problems for them to solve are ones where one ratio is stated in unit form, and the other ratio is a simple multiple of it. Slightly harder problems are ones where the unit ratio must first be determined. And the hardest problems of all are ones where the unit ratio is not an even one, as in the example above.

Arranging these tasks in order of increasing complexity, a developmental hierarchy may be suggested and then the educational task becomes one of designing a set of activities appropriate for children who are functioning at lower levels (levels which are typical for normal 11- and 12-year-olds) but which will enable them to move on to the simplest or easiest level at which all forms of the task may be solved.

Phase 4: Design of Curriculum

The job of designing such as instructional sequence involved three basic steps.

Our first step was to create a developmentally appropriate instructional paradigm (i.e., one where the goal of the paradigm would be clear to all students, and where all students would also be able to achieve some degree of success at their current developmental level). An additional concern was that the task be one where students could determine the adequacy of their current approach on their own. The rationale here was to ensure that children would genuinely understand the reason for any change in their spontaneous procedure which they introduced and that, as a result, this change would be a permanent one with a broad range of applicability — not an isolated piece of rote knowledge.

The task that we devised was introduced as follows (figure 8.3): The package on the left has two pieces of bubble gum in it. If the packages on the

Figure 8.3   Materials for introducing the bubble-gum problem (level 0)

right are the same, how many pieces of gum will we have on that side?
This example does not require any but the simplest of arithmetic operations
(i.e., addition), and uses very small numbers. The task draws on cultural
knowledge available to American children, in combination with a clear visual
display, to make it clear just how this operation is to be applied. Given the
nature of the array, it would be very unlikely that any child would apply
the level O strategy, and suggest that three pieces of gum were necessary on
the right. Note that, because concrete props are provided, children actually
have the option of checking their answers to see if they are right. The children
do not have to rely on the instructor to make this determination for them.

Our next step was to design a sequence of problems that would become
progressively more complex, and that would give students the opportunity to
elaborate their original insight in a fashion that would ultimately lead them to
the creation of a higher order control structure. The basic problems that we
created to bridge this gap were as shown in figures 8.4–8.7.

*Figure 8.4   Materials for the first instructional problem in the bubble-gum sequence
(level 1a)*

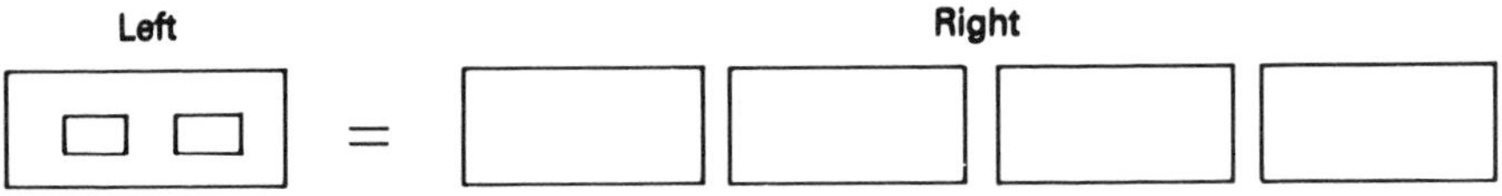

Left   **Right**

The only feature that has changed is the number of gum boxes on the right, to give the students a reason for using multiplication rather than successive addition.

The new feature in figure 8.5 is that the number of pieces per box on the left is not given. Although the students can determine this number by visual inspection, they must nevertheless do so before they are able to apply the strategy of the previous level.

Figure 8.5   Materials for the next set of instructional problems in the bubble-gum sequence (level 1b)

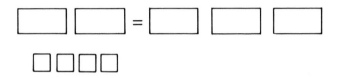

The altered feature in figure 8.6 is once again the size of the set being used. This is to encourage the students to use division rather than visual inspection as a means of determining the number of pieces of gum per box on the left.

Figure 8.6   Materials for the next set of instructional problems (level 2a)

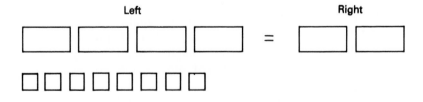

The new feature in the final example (figure 8.7) is that the number of pieces of gum do not divide evenly into the number of gum boxes. To cope with this feature children can simply add a loop for computing the remainder or a decimal into the strategy which they have already developed.

Robbie Case

Figure 8.7 *Materials for the final set of instructional problems in the bubble-gum sequence (level 2b)*

The final step in designing the minicurriculum was to create a number of practice examples at each level, in order to help students consolidate their new cognitive operations. To ensure that the new structures were generalizable, examples were also included at this point where students had to determine the number of gum boxes rather than gum pieces, and deal with situations that involved other materials entirely.

Phase Five: Implementation of the Curriculum (Gold, 1978)

In the implementation phase, two different teachers took charge of the instruction, with each teacher teaching half the students in each of two different groups. One of these groups was composed of normal 10 and 11-year-olds. The other was composed of 12 and 13-year-olds who were normal in most respects, but who seemed to have particular difficulties with math. Both groups of children appeared to be at the same level in the developmental hierarchy at the outset. On problems using large or complex numbers, they would use the lowest-level strategy, namely addition or subtraction. On problems using small numbers, and for which one ratio was unitary, they would use the level 1 approach, with a strategy that employed either multiplication or successive addition.

Because the instructional paradigm was designed for children who were functioning precisely at this level, it proved to be quite effective, with the practice examples in effect serving as diagnostic probes to identify any residual problems. Virtually all the children succeeded on the first few examples, thus gaining confidence in their own ability to understand the task, and to devise a procedure for solving it. As the instruction moved on to level 2 (i.e., to problems in which the unitary ratio first had to be computed) individual differences began to emerge. Some children understood that the problems were the same basic variety as they had just attempted, and that they simply had to calculate the number of gum pieces on the left-hand side first. Other students reverted to an addition or subtraction strategy. As specified by the general approach, the

146

Table 8.4   Percentage of children passing ratio post-test

Task population	Developmental method %	Learning-hierarchy method %	Standard school curriculum %
Normal students	100	88	33
Math-disabled students	100	22	11

Criterion: 65% of items correct.

students who reverted were encouraged to actually place the pieces of gum in boxes, and to see what was wrong with their answer; then given prompts on succeeding problems until they were responding with insight and in an error-free fashion. A verbal rule was also provided to summarize what they had learned. By contrast, the students who used the reduce-to-unit strategy immediately were permitted to continue functioning in a more independent fashion. The instruction was continued until all the students appeared at least reasonably automatic in their performance, a criterion which took about 40 minutes for average students to reach in both the normal and math-disabled groups.

A post-test was administered both one week and one month after the instruction. The test included items for which the content and numerical values were different from those used in the curriculum, but the basic problem type was the same. However, it also included ones where the type of problem and specific procedure were different as well.

The results on the post-test- using 65 per cent as a passing criterion- are presented in table 8.4. As may be seen, very few children profited from the regular approach. By contrast, the majority showed a clear benefit from the developmental approach, and an intermediate number — depending on the particular group — profited from an approach which had been based on the view of development proposed by Gagne, namely that of cumulative learning.

One further word is perhaps in order, concerning the cumulative learning results. The cumulative learning curriculum was based on a learning hierarchy approach to the teaching of ratio which had been developed and validated by Anderson (1977). The strategy which the children were taught was the adult one (i.e., the cross-multiplication strategy) and the method was to first teach all the prerequisite skills. As may be seen, the more talented students showed a clear benefit from this approach. Interestingly enough, however, when the performance of these students was examined in more detail, it was found that they were not succeeding by using the approach which they had been taught. Rather, they were succeeding by using the more natural developmental precursor of this method (i.e., the unit-method). Evidently, by breaking down the adult task into a number of subcomponents and by teaching those subcomponents which were not in the students' repertoire already, the learning heirarchy curriculum had enabled them to create their own understanding of the task, i.e., an understanding which was at their own level of development. That it did so is certainly to its credit. However, it seems clear (i) that it would have been a good deal easier for even the successful students had they been introduced to the more natural approach directly; and (ii) that it was the failure to teach this sort of natural approach which prevented the less-talented students from learning. This interpretation gains further support from a follow-up study which was conducted by Dennis (1981). What Dennis showed was that — as long as the natural strategy was taught — it did not matter whether children were given concrete props to manipulate, and it did not matter whether the examples which they were given were familiar and concrete, or unfamiliar and abstract. Because these variations are the ones that are normally of significance in instructional research, it seems clear that the procedure of adapting the type of algorithm that is taught to children's natural way of looking at a problem is an important and potentially powerful one in overcoming the trouble spots in existing curricula, and teaching high-level cognitive operations more effectively.

Conclusion

It would appear, then, that one important direction for further research would be to supplement this mini-curriculum with exercises designed to bring the skills to full mastery then administer it within the context of the same sort of experimental design. (That is, we should select a group of students who are likely to be at the stage transition to vectorial thought by the criterion of chronological age, but are unlikely to have reached that point by the criterion of environmental opportunity (due to low S.E.S.).) We should then train these students in proportional computation and comparison until these operations are fully mastered, and automated. Finally, we should posttest the children on a wide varity of scientific and logical reasoning tasks, comparing any gains that may be achieved to those made by an equivalent control group.

Should the evidence of broad transfer be borne out by such further studies, the hypothesized role of central conceptual skills in children's intellectual development would receive considerable support, as would the notion that these skills should be taught with increased precision and developmental sensitivity in our school curricula. We could then begin the task of isolating other such central skills, and constructing an experimental curriculum in which they featured more prominently, and were taught more effectively.

What might such a set of central conceptual skills look like? Since multiplicative reasoning is the logical inverse of proportional reasoning, and equally important in scientific problems, this skill would presumably have to appear on any central list. Another possible candidate, one which is perhaps less obvious, is the skill of 'rounding off' within the decimal system, and making 'closeness judgments'. This skill seems to underpin the vectorial skill of computational estimation. It may also be critical for the understanding and flexible use of such algorithms as long division and square-root computation which, although they are presently taught during the dimensional period, rarely seem to be used appropriately until considerably later. If we were to teach just these three conceptual skills more effectively, our guess is that the ramifications for children's scientific and logical development might be profound.

References

ANDERSON, L.H. (1977) 'Developmental effects in learning hierarchy structure for problems involving proportional reasoning', unpublished doctoral dissertation, Berkeley, University of California.

BRANSFORD, J. (1986) invited address, annual meeting of the American Educational Research Association, San Francisco, April.

BROWN, A.L. (1974) 'The role of strategic behaviour in retardate memory' in ELLIS N.R. (Ed.) *International Review of Research in Mental Retardation*, (Vol. 1), New York, Academic Press.

BROWN, A.L. and CAMPIONE, J.C. (1984) 'Three faces of transfer: Implications for early competence, individual differences, and instruction' in LAMB M., BROWN A. and ROGOFF B. (Eds) *Advances in Development Psychology*, 3, Hillsdale, N.J., Erlbaum, pp 143–92.

CASE, R. (1978) *Intellectual Development: Birth to Adulthood*, New York, Academic Press.

CASE, R., SANDIESON, R. and DENNIS, S. (1986) 'Two cognitive — developmental approaches to the design of remedial instruction', *Cognitive Development*, 1, pp 293–333.

CHIPMAN, S.S., SEGAL, J.W. and GLASER, R. (Eds) (1984) *Thinking and Learning Skills: Current Research and Questions*, (Vol. 2), Hillsdale, N.J., Erlbaum.

CRISTAFI, M.A. and BROWN, A.L. (1986) 'Analogical transfer in very young children: combining two separately learned solutions to reach a goal', *Child Development*, 57, pp 953–68.

DEBONO, E. (1969) *Lateral Thinking*, London, Penguin.

DENNIS, S. (1981) 'Developmentally based instructions: How low memory demand, contextual meaningfulness, and concrete objects influence the learning of proportionality', unpublished MA thesis, Ontario Institute for Studies in Education, University of Toronto.

FEURSTEIN, R. (1980) *Instrumental Enrichment: An Intervention Program for Cognitive Modifiability*, University Park Press.

FURMAN, I. (1981) 'The development of problem solving strategies: A neo-Piagetian analysis', unpublished doctoral dissertation, Berkeley, University of California.

GOLD, A.P. (1978) 'Cumulative learning versus cognitive development: A comparison of two different theoretical bases for planning remedial instruction in arithmetic', unpublished doctoral dissertation, University of California.

INHELDER, B. and PIAGET, J. (1958) *The Growth of Logical Thinking from Childhood to Adolescence*, New York, Basic Books.

KARPLUS, R. and PETERSON, R.W. (1970) *IDBES II: Ratio — A Survey*, Berkeley, CA, Lawrence Hall of Science.

KARPLUS, R., KARPLUS, E. and WOLLMAN W. (1973) *Ratio, the Influence of Cognitive Style*, Berkeley, CA, Lawrence Hall of Science.

MARINI, J.M. (1984) 'The development of social and physical cognition in childhood and adolescence', unpublished doctoral dissertation. Ontario Institute for Studies in Education, University of Toronto.

SIEGLER, R.S. (1976) 'Three aspects of cognitive development', *Cognitive Psychology*, 4, pp 481–520.

Respondent: Trevor Bond

Case's presentation reveals a laudable aim to bring together the best aspects of developmental theories available to us at present and to complement that with some direction as to how educators can help to bring about cognitive change in their students. There are apparently some inconsistencies between Case's earlier and later work, such as the role and design of the teaching cycle and the relegation to the lesser divisions of the role of M-space. That had seemed like a cornerstone in the Case/Pascual-Leone rationale for departing from the more orthodox Piagetian view of stages. It is apparent, too, that Robbie Case is his own chief revisionist.

We cognitivists have righteously lambasted behaviourists who told us how to change behaviour with procedures, but omitted any guidelines concerning how we are to select those behaviours which should or should not be changed. A crucial issue for teaching, according to Case, is the use of instructional analogies; but the lack of guidelines concerning which analogies are appropriate, or how teachers go about selecting appropriate analogies, may leave teachers in even more of a dilemma than the behaviourists did. The strength of these teaching strategies lies in the contention that instructional analogies are stripped down versions of more complex or traditional versions of the task — the crucial intellectual ability is retained while the distracting, misleading, and/or irrelevant aspects are removed. This approach has much to commend it to both teachers and researchers, but when the stripped-down version of the task (a good example in the UK is Bryant's version of the Piagetian seriation task) loses some crucial elements of the original problem, then the instructional analogy technique fails. If this contention can be maintained against such an eminent researcher as Bryant, then what practical chance does the regular classroom teacher have in constructing analogies that are properly congruent with the problem to be solved?

Finally, Case seems to tread a risky path when he ascribes ages for the levels of competence that he describes. This might be a very worthwhile outcome of the investigation, but it does need to be correlated with his claim that the acceleration of these competencies is not only possible, but are an important aim of education.

Discussion (Reporter: Les Smith)

The first question was whether formal operational schemes were the same as conceptual structures. Case answered that schemata such as proportionality, probability, and ratio were conceptual structures, but that the INRC grouping was not. He could not accept Piaget's account of the structure of formal operations.

Another participant wondered whether such an account of the development of conceptual structures, or for that matter of formal operations, could be applied to such diverse fields as sports, or music. The author pointed out that one must distinguish between, say, a description of the moves of a game, and the ability to provide an account of the causes of one move or another. There are different domains of human concern, including logico-mathematical, causal, musical, and motor/movement; each domain has its own character and concepts, and each can be characterized by the stage theory, in four main levels. However, a person may be at level 2 in one domain, and level 4 in another. Level 4 in sport is *not* a logico — mathematical or causal level.

Where did Case stand on the debate between constructivists and Piagetians? He has his own views on the development of thinking, based on the idea of *teachable* structures. The questioner returned, asking what was the role of the child's social interaction in the acquisition or use of cognitive structures? Can we use the model that Case had described to find common ground amongst the various theories which are currently informing science education? Case replied that it was perfectly possible to select tasks which were both Piagetian in nature and related to the real world. However, what constituted the important 'real world' depends on the culture. Adults can provide children with some tools, such as counting and number scales, via a mechanism of cooperative transmission, but children cannot get the uses of the tools from adults. These have to be independent inventions. The adult conception is the criterion of understanding to which the child aims, but different cultures have different criteria of understanding. Children's misconceptions have to be developed into the criterial understanding within a given culture.

9 Beyond the Cognitive

John Head

The five contributions contained in this chapter develop one common theme, that the learning of science should not just be conceptualized in terms of the cognitive. The very success of cognitive science in the past fifteen years brings its own problems, such that we can fall into the trap of talking about pupils learning science as if they were science learning machines, devoid of feelings and other demands on their attention. It was these considerations which caused the conference organizers to employ the term 'adolescent development' in the conference title, with the word adolescent acting as an invitation to debate the emotional and social factors which affect students at this time of their life.

The first three papers concentrate on the affective aspects of the individual. Claxton sees these affective qualities manifest in a series of stances which pupils can bring to bear on their learning of science, stances which will largely determine the outcomes of that learning experience. He argues that consideration of this range of stances might do more to help teachers improve the quality of learning in their classes than the findings from most empiricial studies on learning and classroom activities.

Head explores four areas related to the affective which he argues merit further study by the science education community. These four areas are gender differences, descriptions of adolescent development, attitudes to science and differences in cognitive styles. The four are not seen to be independent, indeed they clearly interact, but they provide alternative starting points for a research agenda.

The issue of gender differences is taken up in more detail in the third contribution, by Sjøberg, which reports on two major empirical studies made in Norway. These studies not only provide additional evidence for the growing corpus of gender-and-science literature but contain some novel and important insights into pocesses occuring in adolescence.

Howe's paper also picks up one of Head's four research areas, that of cognitive style, which bridges the cognitive-affective divide. In one sense she produces a negative report, that Witkin's concept of field-dependence and independence has not proved useful to her, but that finding confirmed a growing body of opinion among researchers about this model, and highlights the need for new and more effective way of studying cognitive styles to be developed.

The final paper by Kubli deals with attitudes to science, which can be seen as products of the affective concerns of a person. That topic has been extensively studied over the years, but not always effectively. Often it has been an area where fools have been too willing to tread, and poorly conceptualized models and ill-designed studies have only served to muddy the water. Kubli's work is of a different quality, marked by a careful methodology and a genuine effort to build a rigorous developmental model. Clearly attitudes are important, as precursors to choices and behaviours, and merit such serious study.

9.1 Cognition Doesn't Matter If You're Scared, Depressed or Bored

Guy Claxton

Introduction

Typically, models for thinking about the learning of school science (for example, Ausubel, 1968; Driver, 1983; Shayer and Adey, 1981) have approached the problem in purely or predominantly intellectual terms. Ausubel focusses on the integration of new knowledge into existing cognitive structure. Shayer and Adey note the disparity between the intrinsic difficulty of school science and the generalised intellectual capacity (à la Piaget) that many school pupils have attained. And even the recent bandwagon of 'constructivism' — set in motion as much by Driver as anyone, but leapt on by many — is concerned almost exclusively with the subset of 'pupils' implicit theories that are epistemological, concerned with representing a hypothesized External Reality (von Glaserfeld, 1984). The shared assumption of these approaches is that pupils' difficulties in learning school science reflect structural or functional characteristics, or more frequently limitations, of the cognitive system. Given this, it follows that appropriate remedial action must be aimed at freeing the cogs of cognition: structure teaching experiences more carefully; match them to the 'cognitive level' of the pupils; uncover and acknowledge pre-existing understandings; promote group discussions or cognitive conflict. Whilst the proponents of such views are busy arguing, elbowing and wriggling, they nevertheless are all occupants of the same cognitive bed.

The present paper, whose alternative stance is somewhat brazenly announced by its title, seeks to locate the problems of school science learning within the wider context of pupils' emotional, personal and social lives. As the title of the original seminar invited, this paper puts the 'Adolescent Development' before the 'School Science', and thus adopts a viewpoint that must inevitably reflect better the pupils' own order of priorities. By reversing the order, as many of the seminar papers implicitly did, the tradition of starting from the perspectives of *teacher* priorities, values and assumptions was preserved, with the inevitable consequence of making cognition the 'figure' and turning personal and emotional considerations into mere 'ground'.

Thus my approach, based on what I shall call *stances*, starts from contrary assumptions. Pupils' achievement and demeanour in lessons can only be properly understood as the response of a 'whole person' to a complex 'whole person' predicament. The nature of the intellectual task is represented by one cluster of variables in the personal equation that determines how to *be* in a lesson. But there are many others to do with personal concerns and feelings, unresolved issues from outside the classroom, competing priorities and ambitions, assessment of personal capabilities and limitations, the social mood and structure of the class as a whole, and feelings and assumptions about the teacher. Thus pupils should more properly be viewed as tacit tacticians, architects of their own learning and authors of their classroom behaviour, than as cage-birds, imprisoned within the limitations of their cognitive systems. The stance they adopt in a lesson is the outcome of a subtle decision-making process, which in its turn influences strongly what and how they learn.

If one is to approach pupils' learning from a constructivist perspective, it is to some such position that one is inevitably led. The meaning that they (we) make of situations can only be understood as a product of the *priorities* that are created by a construct system (Kelly, 1955) and not merely of its *propositions*. To apply constructivism only within the cognitive domain is like keeping a tiger to catch mice: it does the job but it is likely also to turn round and start mauling the owner's carefully constructed framework.

Stances

Pupils' main priority in lessons is to construct a repertoire of stances that they can deploy to maximize goals and minimize threats. Because the range of concurrent goals and threats are as much social and emotional as they are intellectual, so a selected stance sets the parameters both of academic accomplishment and of classroom 'presence'. To illustrate the approach here I shall make the simplifying assumption that pupils already possess a relatively stable repertoire of stances, and that their problem therefore is to select between them rather than to create or customise them. Clearly a full account will have to explicate these important processes as well (see Claxton, 1988). We might imagine that the stances a pupil possesses are like a library of floppy disks that can run on a personal computer. When 'loaded', each stance makes available to a learner a particular *knowledge base* on which they can then draw. (Immediately we are able to account for the lack of transfer of knowledge from lesson to lesson, or from school to 'real-life' that is of such perennial concern to teachers and employers. If knowledge is not recorded on the disk currently running, it is functionally inaccessible). Given a particular base, with its idiosyncratic format and structure, the parameters of *salience* and *significance* are set: the learner's attention is directed towards certain kinds of event and away from others. In addition a stance may comprise its own cluster of *learning strategies*, so that, for example, a learner may be set to learn by rote, to seek for deep intellectual understanding, to aim for practical skills, or to explore the personal significance of what is going on. Thus the stance determines *additions* to the knowledge base: the kind as well as the amount of what is learnt. Finally, as part of the package-deal, an orientation towards classroom *demeanour* is prescribed — quiet, keen, sociable, jokey or disruptive, for example.

Each learner's set of stances will be idiosyncratic, depending on their hopes, fears and histories. But some tend to recur, and are familiar to teachers (Woods, 1984) and pupils (Beynon, 1985) alike. In *swot* stance, pupils are oriented towards exam passing and teacher approval. They feel safe when copying down notes they can then 'learn' (verbatim) and resist 'red herrings' if they are 'not on the syllabus' and therefore 'not proper work'. In *thinker* stance, pupils are willing to engage intellectually with what is offered and to seek for sense and meaning in it. If swots sit at the front, thinkers are only a row behind and will ask 'interesting' questions which the teacher brushes aside, or takes up (to the discomfiture of the swots). Science teachers are familiar with a variant of thinker we might call the *boffin* stance, where a pupil seeks deep understanding of particular, personally chosen topics, to the frequent exclusion of other parts of the syllabus, exasperation of teachers, and friendly contempt of peers. In *socialite* stance, pupils keep half an ear on the teacher in order to pick up fragments of information that are intrinsically interesting, unusual or funny and which make no intellectual demands. They do not seek systematic understanding and are chatty and distractible, being very sensitive to social status and dynamics. In *dreamer* stance, pupils withdraw not unhappily into the productive inner world of fantasy play and emotional work, and may be found sitting along the side walls out of the teacher's line of vision. In *rebel* stance, pupils are oriented towards the maintenance of self-esteem by seeking peer approval and creating more or less direct opportunities to challenge authority. Rebels traditionally sit at the back. While in *sinker* stance, pupils are often withdrawn but unlike the dreamers are confused, depressed, self-critical, panicky and glassy-eyed (Dweck, 1986). Their learning capacities — which in other stances may be considerable — are in disarray. The computer is 'down'.

The Cost-Benefit Analysis

Stances are selected on the basis of an intuitive, largely unconscious decision-making process that may take into account any or all of the following considerations. What is my current portfolio of *priorities* — academic, vocational, emotional and social? Which of these are compatible and which not? Which are more important or urgent and which less? What potential conflicts or sacrifices are there? What *opportunities* seem to be afforded by the situation — intellectual, social and behavioural? Is the teacher 'good'? Can she control us? What can you get away with? Does she explain things at a level I can understand? Does she make it interesting? Will I be humiliated if I say something stupid? What is my relationship with the peer group? Do they laugh at my jokes? Is there equipment (squeezy bottles, gas taps) to muck about with? What *demands* will the lesson content make on me if I try to learn it? What sort of tests will be set? And do I have the *internal resources* to meet these demands? What is my history of success? If I 'try', will it be worth it? Am I good at remembering things? At understanding them? What about *external resources*? Will the teacher explain if I don't understand? Are there friends in the class who will help me? Will I be able to get to the library? Have I got the time to go into it deeply? Is there somewhere out of earshot of the telly at home to study? And perhaps most important, what *costs* and *risks* might be entailed by adopting different stances? What will happen to my self-esteem if I try and fail? Will other people start to expect too much of me if I try and succeed? Will the socialites and rebels tease me if I decide to swot? Will Dad be angry if he finds out I am being a rebel? Do I care? Do I risk losing my 'roots' if I start to get 'too clever by half' or 'talking posh'?

Individual Differences

These questions represent just a selection of those that may be thrown, knowingly or not, into the stance-selecting melting-pot. Individual pupils will obviously differ in the *particular questions* they consider, in the *answers* they give themselves, in the *weight* that these answers carry in the computation, in the *breadth* and *subtlety* of the range of considerations that are taken into account and in the degree of *provisionality* of, or *commitment* to, a stance once selected, as well as in the range and nature of the *stances* they are selecting between. Some pupils shift stances within lessons, or from topic to topic (Furlong, 1976). Swots may become socialites or dreamers if they think the lesson has gone off track. Socialites and rebels may become thinkers when the teacher introduces some exciting, real life examples (Jones, 1987). Thinkers may become sinkers in the face of failure or frustration (Dweck, 1986). Socialites may become rebels if they think they have been treated unfairly by a teacher. And so on.

Sometimes, the most dramatic shifts of stance occur between subjects, causing teachers to say 'I don't think we can be talking about the same person'. Swots and thinkers in the high status subjects (English, maths and science) may take 'time out' to regain some peer-group status by mucking about in music or art (Measor, 1984a). While some pupils seem to lock themselves in to a once-for-all stance — whether 'good' or 'bad' — towards school as a whole.

Implications

The stance of the present paper asserts that adolescents in school should be seen as always *either* learning something that they judge to be of value *and/or* defending themselves against something they judge to be a threat. What they are 'up to' (in all senses) is the outcome of a tacit decision-making process, based only on subjective estimates of competing priorities, opportunities, demands, resources and risks, which is, in their terms, sensible or even vital. Only if the emotional/motivational factors in this decision permit or encourage intellectual learning *and* the subjective assessments are accurate, will achievement be limited by such cognitive factors as 'ability' or 'alternative conceptions'. (Dweck, 1986, for example, has shown that the proneness to switch from thinker to sinker is entirely unrelated to 'ability'). So one may not infer from pupils' progress or comportment anything about their 'ability', or even their 'motivation'. Such talk does violence to the intricacy and inscrutability of a learner's cost-benefit analysis. We might surmise that many pupils' achievement is poor not because of the lack of such crude commodities but because the decision they have made is a bad one, based on inaccurate estimates of risk, resource or demand — errors that teachers may inadvertently have overlooked or even fostered by their own pedagogical or personal style.

Conclusion

The intricate interplay of cognition and emotion has been widely recognized in the conext of girls' attitudes to school science (see the chapters by Head and Sjoberg in this volume). The predominantly masculine image of science and scientists impinges directly on a girl's developing self-image and weighs heavily in the balance of subject choice, for example. Reactions are anticipated from peers of both sexes (in mixed schools and classes) and costs, both real and imagined, must be assessed (Measor, 1984b). It is somewhat surprising, therefore, that the broader decision-making framework that such insight necessarily attributes to adolescent girls has not commonly been applied, at least not with its full power, to an analysis of the predicament faced by all pupils.

We might note here the reciprocal failure to generalize shown by the prolific ethnographic and classroom observation research of sociologists such as Beynon (1985), Hammersley and Woods (1984) and Woods (1980). This research shows in great detail the varieties of strategy used by pupils to cope with the social pressures and expectations of classrooms. But these workers seem loath to involve themselves with the specific demands of different subjects and subject-matters, and so fail to explore the interaction between intellectual and social demands. Subjective estimates of the demands of lesson content lead to social and behavioural responses, just as the forces of the social context have repercussions for the pupil's decision about whether, when, why and how to learn.

It would be healthy for researchers in science education, many of whom have recently adopted a rather parochial and constricted version of 'constructivism', to allow such areas of research to inform their thinking, so that the full power of this psychological position is revealed. If science pupils, along with the

Guy Claxton

rest of us, create their Reality, then this applies not merely to cognition but *a fortiori* to the entire intra and interpersonal sphere.

References

Ausubel, D.P. (1968) *Educational Psychology: A Cognitive View*, New York, Holt, Rinehart and Winston.

Beynon, J. (1985) *Initial Encounters in the Secondary School*, Lewes, Falmer Press.

Claxton G.L. (1988) 'Adolescent Learning', Open University Course EP 228, *Frameworks for Teaching*, Unit 4, Milton Keynes.

Driver, R. (1983) *The Pupil as Scientist*, Milton Keynes, Open University Press.

Dweck, C. (1986) 'Motivational processes affecting learning', *American Psychologist*, 41, pp 1040–8.

Furlong, V.J. (1976) 'Interaction sets in the classroom' in Hammersley, M. and Woods, P. (Eds) *The Process of Schooling*, London, Routledge and Kegan Paul.

Hammersley, M. and Woods, P. (Eds) (1984) *Life in School: The Sociology of Pupil Culture*, Milton Keynes, Open University Press.

Jones, A. (1987) '*The introduction of technology into school physics*', unpublished DPhil, Hamilton, New Zealand, University of Waikato.

Kelly, G.A. (1955) *The Psychology of Personal Constructs*, New York, Norton.

Measor, L. (1984a) 'Pupil perceptions of subject status' in Goodson I.F. and Ball S.J. (Eds) *Defining the Curriculum*, Lewes, Falmer Press.

Measor, L. (1984b) 'Gender and the sciences: Pupils' gender-based conceptions of school subjects' in Hammersley, M. and Woods, P. (Eds) *Life in School: The Sociology of Pupil Culture*, Milton Keynes, Open University Press.

Shayer, M. and Adey, P. (1981) *Toward a Science of Science Teaching*, London, Heinemann.

von Glaserfeld, E. (1984) 'Radical constructivism' in Watzlawick, P. (Ed.) *The Invented Reality*, New York, Norton.

Woods, P. (Ed.) (1980) *Pupil Strategies*, London, Croom Helm.

Woods, P. (1984) 'Negotiating the demands of schoolwork' in Hammersley, M. and Woods, P. (Eds) *Life in Schools: The Sociology of Pupil Culture*, Milton Keynes, Open University Press.

Discussion (Reporter: Michael Watts)

Three main issues were discussed: the generalizability of Claxton's stances, the qualitative nature of stances, and implications of change within and between stances. Although Claxton stressed the point that stances should not be seen in a hierarchial sequence ranging from good modes to undesirable, there was some concern about what interventions might be helpful to help the 'sinker'. Claxton argued that our understanding of mechanisms relating to self-esteem was not sufficient to indicate how a simple and direct intervention can assure success.

It was noted that Claxton's stances were not a categorization of empirical data, in fact he believed that empirical research produced little impact on educational practice. Stances are intended to serve more as templates for organizing teachers' intuitive understanding of their pupils and their learning difficulties.

9.2 The Affective Constraints on Learning Science

John Head

Introduction

We can identify three phases in our thinking during the last twenty five years about the learners of the school science curriculum.

1   Initially the learner was taken as being non-problematical, provided the material was well selected and sequenced (Bruner: 'any subject can be taught effectively in some intellectually honest form to any child at any stage of development'). Concern with the science content dominated thinking in early National Science Foundation and Nuffield schemes and curriculum development arose from scientists in a given field identifying what they saw to be the key concepts in their subject and the curriculum developers weaving these concepts in a logical sequence with a variety of practical exercises. In so far there was an implicit learning theory, it was a belief in 'discovery learning', a belief which was rarely scrutinized to explore its limitations.

2   By about 1970 it became recognized that some of these schemes, for example, the Chemical Bond Approach, were too difficult, almost unteachable in the school context. The second phase was to match curriculum content with the learner's developmental stage (Piagetian work) or with the learner's existing concepts (constructivist approach). The curriculum analysis carried out by Shayer in the early 1970s was typical of this phase and led to some changes in the selection and sequencing of topics in various curriculum schemes. For example, when the Nuffield 'O' level chemistry materials were revised in the early 1970s the treatment of the mole concept was modified to meet the criticism of Ingle and Shayer (1971) that the previous scheme had made excessive cognitive demand on the learners by introducing them to difficult concepts prematurely.

3   We can now recognize that these two earlier stages were not in themselves adequate. Often the major problem is that the pupils do not like science. It

162

is their feelings, rather than their thoughts, which we need to consider. That argument does not deny the value of the earlier initiatives. The original schemes of the 1960s contained many novel and worthwhile features. In particular, a variety of new practical exercises were generated which are of such a quality that when editing the newly published Nuffield 11 to 13 materials I found it difficult to improve on the existing bank of well tried practical exercises. Similarly, no one will deny that the content of a school science scheme has to be within the competence of the pupils and we cannot just take hold of what professional scientists perceive to be important and introduce these ideas uncritically into schools. We have to find out how the pupils work and how difficult they find each topic.

My argument is that the affective area, phase three, will prove to be crucial, in research and curriculum planning, in the next decade. There is overwhelming evidence that, despite the twenty-five years of curriculum reform, pupils are voting with their feet, away from science.

Approaches to the Affective

It is fair comment that our thinking in psychology about the affective is less certain than with the cognitive and we have yet to experience anything like the revolution which occurred in cognitive psychology in the early 1970s and the growth of cognitive science. Nevertheless, a number of promising growth points have opened up in recent years and the four outlined below provide a possible agenda for the next phase in our work.

Gender and Science

It is almost impossible to overestimate the importance of the women-and-science movement. Initially concern was just with the lack of female recruits, in the belief that it denied women access to important careers and starved the science community of talent. The initial concern was simply to redress the imbalance by removing the barriers which discouraged girls choosing careers in science. To a considerable extent that battle has been won. Publishers are now sensitive to sexist language and examples in the texts they handle and gone are the days when the illustrations all showed the boys being actively involved in the science activity while the girls stood to one side and watched. Care is being taken to provide role models of female scientists and engineers for the girls and a variety of classroom practices are being tried, for example, girls-only science and computer lessons within coeducational schools, in an attempt to reduce the sense of competing with boys in a male domain.

We can recognize two changes which have occurred since the girls-and-science movement first started in the mid-1970s. The first has been the development of a large international invisible college of researchers in this field. Alison Kelly in her introductory editorial to a recently published book (Kelly, 1987) wrote:

> Six years ago I edited a book called *The Missing Half* which looked at the question of girls and science education. At the time this was a very new area of interest. Nothing much had been published on the topic. To get articles for the book I had to write round to friends and acquaintances who I knew were interested, and ask them to put their thoughts on paper . . . This time I didn't have to write round to friends, asking them to contribute. All the papers already existed: many had been published before.

The importance of this development is that this particular invisible college now represents one of the most powerful and important pressure groups within science education.

The second change may be less widely recognized but is even more important. That is a change in the agenda. Initially science and science education were accepted as they were found and the task was seen to make them more acceptable to girls by some minor changes in presentation, what has been described as 'sugaring the pill'. But as the community of workers explored the issue their concerns widened such that they now provide some of the best critiques of science within the Western community (that of purpose and control); of science education (both selection of curriculum materials and organization of classroom practices); and of psychology, particularly that relating to adolescent development. It would now be possible to mount a challenging and worthwhile course on the nature of science, or on the future of science education, solely based on the texts from the girls-and-science movement. The literature is vast ranging from the proceedings of the Girls and Science and Technology (GASAT) international conferences to such challenging papers as that of Bentley and Watts (1987).

One line of argument has been that there exist some gender linked differences in modes of thinking, see the section on cognitive styles below, and as a consequence the introduction of more women in science will make the science community more aware of the context of science, for example ecological problems, and the responsibility of scientists to protect the delicate equilibrium of the biosphere. It has been suggested that women bring a more caring and holistic approach to research, which can help yield new insights, as shown by the work of Barbara McClintock in genetics and Lynn Margulis in developing the idea of endosymbiosis (Keller, 1986). The arrival of more women into science may not mean just more of the same but bring about qualitative changes within the science community.

Adolescent Development

As most people first experience the activities identified as 'science' during their adolescence and it is also at that stage in their life that crucial choices are made about school subject options and careers it is an obvious tactic to set these experiences and choices within the framework of adolescent development. I used Erikson's concept of identity development to make sense of the ways secondary school pupils respond to science (Head, 1985). Despite the obvious criticisms of Erikson, that he solely described Western middle-class males, the concept of identity development is becoming increasingly more widely used within research, witness its central role in the conceptualization of the current Economic and Social Research Council 16 to 19 Initiative in Britain and the findings of individual workers such as Breakwell (1986). It is likely that the concept of identity can be extended not only to explain the dynamics of choice in secondary schools but also to explore how scientists work and interact within research communities, a possibility which at last allows psychology to contribute to the debates about the social issues in science.

It might be a valid criticism that in selecting the issue of identity development as the most promising field for research related to adolescence that I have ignored alternative psychological models. Michael Shayer and I have in the past played with one such alternative, Jane Loevinger's model of ego development (Head and Shayer, 1980), and we need to be alert to developments relating to adolescence reported in the psychological literature.

Attitudes to Science

The evidence has been clear (Gardner, 1975; and Schibecci, 1984). Many pupils see science as being remote from everyday life, solely of interest and relevance to the few who become professional scientists. As a consequence many of our most intelligent and lively pupils feel alienated by science and we might suspect that some of the pupils who do opt for science do so as a retreat from the demands, particularly emotional demands, of social intercourse and careers involving a lot of social interaction. That theme is developed in Head (1985).

The obvious implication for curriculum designers in attempting to widen the appeal of science is to bring out the social and applied aspects of science and the newly-published Nuffield 11 to 13 materials sought to do just that. Perhaps we need to make a radical rethink of the purpose of school science. For too long our thinking, at least in Britain, has been dominated by the need to produce professional scientists, which in turn has led to curriculum design from the top downwards. Each phase of schooling has been planned to meet the demands of the next phase. As a consquence each phase has been planned with the needs of a minority in mind. Perhaps we ought to ask what science a boy or girl of a given age may need to know, regardless of the potential career. In that event we might go for a more extensive 'science studies' style curriculum, trying to set science within a wider context, rather than the current intensive science courses.

Now that technology is to have a central place in the British national curriculum we need to think through a set of issues, the relationship between science and technology, do adolescents perceive these areas as being similar, can the same psychological arguments, for example, of identity, be applied to make sense of their response to technology.

Cognitive Style

This topic has been poorly conceptualised and although over twenty possible styles have been identified in the literature (Messick, 1976) it is not clear how they relate to each other. Nevertheless, differences in cognitive styles seem central to many contemporary concerns in science education and therefore it is imperative that this area is sorted out. The work of Cohen (1986) may provide a lead.

Studies of cognitive style bring about a convergence of work on gender, alternative frameworks (what causes someone to resist new ideas and evidence), and personality. The suggestion that women tend to think more holistically (Gilligan, 1982) illustrates the interaction with the issue of gender, described above. If the Gilligan line of argument is right, then it has implications for the ways we assess pupils, as techniques such as multiple choice which were believed to be culture fair may in fact prove to have a gender bias. Scrutiny of examination reponses has tended to support this criticism.

Perhaps the main criticism that we can level at the constructivist school within science education is that we are given little advice on how to handle the alternative constructs once they have been identified. The presentation of dissonant evidence may make the pupil more willing to change but the problem is partly affective and dissonance may lead to confusion and resistance to the newly-taught science. The literature on dogmatism and authoritarianism might yield some useful insights. For reasons such as these the science education community will have to give some thought to the issues of cognitive style.

Summary

The time has come to pay more attention to the affective in the learning of science. The four areas outlined above, taken separately and in combination, provide a possible plan for such work.

References

BENTLEY, D. and WATTS, M. (1987) 'Courting the postive virtues: The case for feminist science' in KELLY, A. (Ed.) *Science for girls*, Milton Keynes, Open University Press.
BREAKWELL, G. (1986) *Coping With Threatened Identities*, London, Methuen.
COHEN, R. (1986) *Conceptual Styles and Social Change*, Acton, MA, Copley.

GARDNER, P.L. (1975) 'Attitudes to science: A review', *Studies in Science Education*, 2, pp 1–41.

GILLIGAN, C. (1982) *In a Different Voice*, Boston, MA, Harvard University Press.

HEAD, J.O. (1985) *The Personal Response to Science*, Cambridge, Cambridge University Press.

HEAD, J.O. and SHAYER, M. (1980) 'Loevinger's ego development measures — A new research tool', *British Educational Research Journal*, 6, pp 21–7.

INGLE, R.B. and SHAYER, M. (1971) 'Conceptual demands of Nuffield 'O' level chemistry', *Education in Chemistry*, 8, p. 182.

KELLER, E.F. (1986) 'How gender matters' in HARDING, J. (Ed.) *Perspectives on Gender and Science*, Lewes, Falmer Press.

KELLY, A. (1987) *Science for Girls*, Milton Reynes, Open University Press.

MESSICK, S.M. (1976) *Individuality and Learning*, San Francisco, CA, Jossey-Bass.

SCHIBECCI, R. (1984) 'Attitudes to science: An update', *Studies in Science Education*, 11, pp 26–59.

Discussion (Reporter: Joan Bliss)

It was generally agreed that research into gender differences had been one of the most fruitful areas in recent years although there was some uncertainty how useful this work will prove in the future, whether ideas of a feminine or a feminist science really held out a new paradigm for the science community.

The issue was raised whether we can sensibly study individual development and characteristics outside a description of the social context, as social forces are so crucial in shaping the way an individual behaves. Head argued that Erikson's model of identity development specifically recognized that point and that was why Erikson talked about psychosocial development. The individual psyche merited study, not least because individual students had to make choices in their secondary school education. In that sense the work could be located in an existential tradition in which the concept of choice was paramount.

Although it was felt that the research agenda outlined by Head would provide some challenges, not least in the development of appropriate methodologies and models, distinct progress in the study of these affective aspects has been made in recent years, and it was reasonable to assume that this progress will continue.

9.3   Gender and the Image of Science

Svein Sjøberg

Introduction: The Problem

The problem is simple and well-known: compared with boys, a low percentage of girls choose science in schools and few women are found in careers in science and technology. This is a world-wide phenomenon, although educational and employment statistics show great and interesting variations between different parts of the world. (For a survey, see Harding, 1985.)

In this chapter, we will only present a few data bearing on the problem, and will not go into any detail on a possible theoretical framework or practical consequences. A more comprehensive account is attempted in another place (Sjøberg and Imsen, 1987).

In the following, we will draw on Norwegian data from a previous project 'Girls and physics' (Lie and Sjøberg, 1984) and from a recent project, the Norwegian version of the International Association for the Evaluation of Educational Achievement–Second International Science Study (IEA-SISS) project.

The Norwegian SISS Project

The SISS study includes tests on science knowledge and questionnaires on background variables, attitudes and interests etc. Each of the about twenty-five participating countries were free to include national items, and in the Norwegian version of the study, we included items on aspects not covered in the international study. These included a range of questions on science-related out-of-school activities, future plans and job priorities and some questions bearing on the perceived image of scientists as persons. The pupils also judged their own qualities on the same attributes. The data presented here are mainly from the national items in the questionnaire.

Representative samples were drawn from three populations:

1   Pupils at the age of 11, i.e. grade 4 (N = 1386).
2   Pupils at the age of 16, i.e. grade 9 (N = 1490).

3 Pupils at the age of 19, i.e. grade 3 of upper secondary school (N = 3314).

Populations 1 and 2 include *all pupils* at that particular age.

Population 3 includes all pupils leaving *the academic branch* of upper secondary school. At this level there is considerable degree of specialization in different directions of study. The population is therefore divided in sub-populations according the choice of subject specialization.

Population 3 is divided in to the following sub-populations:

3N: Non-science students: students choosing to specialize either in the social sciences or the humanities. (N = 1212).

The rest are science specialists, with the following sub-groups:

3B Biology specialists (N = 541, 71 per cent girls).
3C Chemistry specialists (N = 635, 59 per cent girls).
3P Physics specialists (N = 926, 30 per cent girls).

(The percentages are representative for the proportion of girls in these school subjects, but the number in each sub-population is not proportional to the size of that particular sub-population).

Many pupils take more than two of the sciences up to the top level, hence some pupils may belong to more than one group.

Samples from all populations were drawn in a two-stage stratified sampling procedure, and are representative national samples

In addition, data were also collected from teachers (N = 1469) and the participating schools (N = 336). Pupil data may be linked with data from teacher and school.

A major report from the study has been published (Sjøberg, 1986), two more have been printed (Ringnes, 1987; Horsfjord and Dalin, 1987) and more are being planned.

Sex Differences in Test Scores

All pupils in population 3 were tested with a battery of multiple choice items for understanding in science. The non-science students were given a general test consisting of items from all sciences. The subject specialists were also given a test in that particular subject area.

We found a pattern that has been noted in many countries: the differences are in favour of boys, and they increase with age. For the 'science specialists' in population 3 we note that differences are rather small in biology, greater in physics and greatest in chemistry. The results for chemistry can partly be explained by the choice of *other* school subjects for this group. (Many girls have biology as the only science at highest level, hence they have a lower degree of specialization in science.) If we compare the score of girls and boys with similar background in other sciences, the differences in chemistry scores are around 10 per cent in favour of boys.

The frequency of 'no response' is higher for girls in all pupil groups, but far too small to account for the differences in test score (typically 2–3 per cent).

Although boys have higher scores than girls in most content areas, there are some areas that are typically female and typically male:

Girls score higher on questions linked with human reproduction, venereal diseases, effect of hormones, heredity etc.

Boys score (much!) higher on question concerning physics topics like electricity, mechanics, sound and light. (The last two are somewhat surprising in the light of the fact that girls express particular interests in these areas: colours, the eye, hearing, music etc [see below].

Sex Differences in Experiences

It is a pedagogical cliché that one 'should build on the experiences of the learner', and 'go from the concrete to the abstract'. These statements become more interesting and problematic when one realizes that children bring with them *different* sorts of experiences. By taking some experiences for granted and as the starting point for abstraction, one may unintentionally favour certain groups of pupils.

The SISS study for populations 1 and 2 included a survey of children's out-of-school experiences that might be of relevance for the learning of science in schools. The purpose of including the list of experiences in the investigation was manifold: the list was meant to give a background for analysis of existing curricula and for possible revisions. The results also make it possible to investigate possible connection between experience and score on knowledge items from the same 'area' — for instance electricity. Here we restrict ourselves to give an overview of the 'raw' results.

Table 9.3.1 shows only a very limited range of the results and is meant only to demonstrate the following points that emerge from the list as a whole:

1   Girls dominate strongly on all activities connected with home and household. They also dominate on activities connected with biology, gardening, nature study, health, handling and caring for animals. Activities like 'collecting stones' and 'take photographs' are also 'girls' activities'.

Boys dominate most strongly on activities connected with cars (except for 'washing a car', where boys and girls are equal). The activities include 'charging the battery', 'using the jack', 'renewing the plugs', etc. Boys dominate on activities related to electricity, strongly on activities like 'attaching a lead to a plug', smaller differences on 'changing batteries' and 'changing bulbs'. Boys also have higher activity index on the use of a variety of mechanical tools.

Svein Sjøberg

Table 9.3.1 Experiences: Differences between boys and girls

Activity	Girl-boy difference	
	11 years	16 years
Girl-dominated (positive value: higher index for girls)		
Knitted	0.37	0.51
Used a sewing machine	0.24	0.37
Made jam from wild berries	0.09	0.23
Collected flowers for a herbarium	0.18	0.21
Planted seeds and watched them grow	0.13	0.20
Collected stones	0.10	0.19
Read about how the body functions	0.00	0.12
Boy-dominated (positive value: higher index for boys)		
Used a saw	0.20	0.18
Played with a chemistry set	0.19	0.25
Changed a fuse at home	0.20	0.32
Used a gun or a shot gun	0.22	0.42
Helped with repairing a car	0.24	0.46
Used a car jack	0.36	0.52
Attached an electric lead to a plug	0.26	0.55
Renew the plugs on a motor	0.21	0.59

Source: Sjøberg (1986).

2   Most differences in experience are dramatically larger at age 16. Although the study is not a longitudinal study of the same children, it is likely that this finding can be interpreted as an increase of differences with age. And the pattern is interesting: whereas girls systematically score higher on 'male' experiences the older they get, it is often the opposite with boys: their scores become lower the older they get. Compared with 11-year-olds, boys at the age of 16 have lower index on most household activities and also on activities like:

> Watching an egg hatch,
> Raising tadpoles or butterflies,
> Planting seeds to see them grow,
> Growing vegetables in a kitchen garden,
> Study fossils,
> Make jam from wild berries,
> Collect flowers for a herbarium

So, while girls in general gradually get familiar with male experiences, the boys move even further away from the 'world of girls'.

Most of the 100 activities listed in the questionnaire have some relevance to science. They constitute possible starting points for school science, or they can be used as concrete examples in the treatment of science topics. if we compare the list of experiences sorted by sex differences, we are immediately struck by the fact that (Norwegian) school science builds on boys' experiences.

Sex Differences in Interests in Subject Matter

Differences in experiences are of course strongly linked with differences in personality. Several investigations shed light on this (for an international survey, see Lehrke *et al*, 1985). Our Norwegian results agree with most of these results. Some examples (all published in Lie and Sjøberg, 1984):

Example 1
Pupils at the age of 12 and 14 are presented with lists of topics that may possibly be covered in science lessons. They are invited to tag the subject matter that appeals to them, topics that they would like to learn more about.

Boys are strongly interested in subject matter related to cars and motors, girls are interested in subject matter related to health, nutrition and the human body. But the differences show up also in the kind of context that is implied in the description of the subject matter:

In general, girls are interested when the subject matter is placed in a context related to daily life or to society (key word: 'relevance'). Girls are also in majority on subject matter that has aesthetic ('snow crystals', 'the rainbow') or ethical aspects ('consequences of . . .').

Different key words for 'the same' 'subject matter' give widely differing results: girls are interested when key words are 'colours', 'the eye' etc. while boys are in majority on items when 'pure' physics concept 'light' or 'optics' are given. Similar for 'acoustics': girls are interested in 'music', 'instruments' and 'the ear', while boys react more positively to 'sound'.

Example 2
A representative group of university students covering different fields of study gave answers very consistent with the above results. They were invited to give their views on 'what should be given higher priority in the school physics curriculum in order to make it more interesting' by tagging topics from a long list. The topics that came out on top of the list were: 'how physics is used in society', 'the physics of daily life', 'the body and the senses'. It is interesting to note that although the female students came out much higher than male students on those topics, they were also on top of the list for male students. This shows that a science curriculum more suited to the interests of girls need not be to the disfavour of boys!

Example 3
More open approaches to the same problem area have also been undertaken. In one investigation, 14-year-old pupils were invited to write some lines, given the following guidelines: 'scientists make new things or try to understand what happens in nature and with people. If you could decide, what would you ask scientists to do?'

The results were analyzed and classified. Table 9.3.2 shows the aspects which came out on top of the list for the two sexes:

Svein Sjøberg

Table 9.3.2

Girls' research priorities	(%)	Boys' research priorities	(%)
Body, health	23	Technology	24
Anti nuclear weapon	14	Astronomy	14
Animals	14	Animals	11
History	13	Body, health	9

All differences between girls and boys are statistically significant to <0.1%.

We see that the general pattern is the same as in the investigations with closed alternatives: girls are oriented towards biology, health, the body and towards the consequences of technology.

Sex Differences in Choice of Future Jobs

In the SISS study, pupils in all populations were presented with a list of aspects of possible importance for the choice of future jobs.

The pattern remains the same for all the populations: girls score higher on aspects oriented towards care and other people, boys score higher on aspects that are ego-oriented and related to their own personal benefit. We also note that the differences increase with age.

The last group in the study, age 19 years, is particularly interesting, since it consists of 'science specialists'. A frequently heard argument is that girls who choose male-dominated fields of study have to develop the same set of values and priorities as their male competitors, maybe even more than the men do. The results for the last group show exactly the opposite of that assertion: The differences between girls and boys are larger for this group than for any other group of pupils!

In the above presentation, we have pooled all 'scientist'. Let us now take a closer look at possible differences between the various 'kinds' of scientists. Let us focus on only two of the above factors, the 'person-oriented' factors on top of the list (table 9.3.3)

The results here are in line with what other researchers have found (i.e. Collins and Smithers, 1984): scientists are in general less person-oriented than non-scientists, physicists less than biologists. Within each group, girls are more person-oriented than boys. Our data also show that the least person-oriented group of girls (physics girls) is more person-oriented than the most person-oriented group of boys.

Let us now link this index of person-orientation to the future plans of the pupils (table 9.3.4).

We see here that medicine is an attractive field of study for pupils who are oriented towards other people. Pupils choosing technology have a very small index of person-orientation. In each group, girls are more person-oriented than

Table 9.3.3   *'Person-orientation' among different sub-populations of 19-year-olds*

Student group	Girls	Boys
Non-science student	0.74	0.48
Biology students	0.73	0.48
Chemistry Students	0.69	0.43
Physics Students	0.60	0.38

Based on Ringnes (1987).
All differences between girls and boys are
statistically significant to $<0.1\%$.

Table 9.3.4   *Person-orientation and future plans*

Future plan	Girls	Boys
Technology	0.48	0.34
Medicine	0.86	0.78
Study, but not science	0.72	0.53
No studies	0.75	0.40

Based on Ringnes (1987).
All differences between girls and boys are
statistically significant to $<0.1\%$.

the boys, although the difference between the different fields of study is greater than between the sexes.

The Image of Science and the Scientist

Pupils learn about science from many different sources. During this process, they gradually develop an idea about what science is 'really' all about and how scientists are as persons. This image of science is probably more stable than the facts and laws pupils learn in their school lessons.

An image of science is projected mostly covert and implicit, as a cumulative result from various influences at school: textbooks, teachers' behaviour and personalities (including the sex of the science teacher). Images of science are also developed through out-of-school influences: cartoons, fiction books, television series, mass media news coverage etc. In many cases, the scientist is presented as an old, absent-minded professor (always male), sealed off from the rest of the world in his laboratory, where he invents strange chemicals or bombs that may blow the whole world to pieces. 'The crazy scientist' is a nearly mythological figure, kept alive even in children's science programs on TV.

Let us give two examples of empirical evidence from our own studies.

Svein Sjøberg

The Typical Physicist

University students from different faculties were presented a list of different personal traits. They were asked to indicate on a scale whether 'the typical physicist or physics student' was more or less than average on these traits (Lie and Sjøberg, 1984, p 59).

The following 'personality profile' of the physicist emerged:

THE PHYSICIST

YES: More than average for the following traits:	NO: Less than average for the following traits:
Logical	Artistic
Intelligent	Interested in people
Determined	Politically engaged
Objective	Extrovert
	Imaginative
	Responsible

When we compare this image of the physicist with the often documented self-concept of girls and with their important priorities for choice of occupation, we see that the image of the physicist is nearly the negation of what the average girls value.

The Humane Biologist and the Inhuman Physicist

In the SISS-study, pupils are presented with several pairs of words with opposite meaning (like good — evil). These dichotomous descriptors are placed on each side of a 5-point scale. The pupils are invited to place for instance 'a typical physicist' by a tag on this scale.

A range of such pairs of words were given to pupils at different ages. On the questionnaire, the order varied from 'positive' first to 'negative' first. The pupils were asked to describe two different 'sorts' of researchers in two different fields: 'physics or technology' and 'biology or medicine'. The results indicate a 'personality profile' of these categories of scientists, as perceived by pupils.

The overall picture is that girls and boys differ very little in their perception of the typical scientists. Noteworthy is also the fact that the different populations of pupils in general have the same impression: Rather young pupils in the obligatory school have the same conception of the scientist as the 19-year-old 'specialist'.

Both the biologist and the physicist are considered to be very accurate and intelligent, with the physicist a little in front. (This was particularly the case in the eyes of girls.) Both are also industrious. Both types are also rather imaginative, the biologist more than the physicist.

On the remaining qualities, the biologist came out more positive than the physicist:

The biologist as caring, the physicist as selfish;
The biologist as open, the physicist as closed;
The physicist was also considered as boring and unartistic; while the biologist was considered to be 'neutral' on these traits.

Altogether, the image of the physicist is far from flattering. For most girls (and certainly also for many boys!), it is expected that this image will be frightening: On the one hand, the cool, rational intellect; on the other hand, the lack of warmth, care and human characteristics that we have seen are part of the girls' culture.

Faced with this empirically documented image of the physicist, two possibilities exist:

1 The impression is false, physicists are not like that!
2 The impression is correct, this is exactly how physicists are!

In the first case, science educators have a problem: how can false impressions like this be developed, even among 'science specialists' at school? And how can we change this stereotyped image?

In the second case, society at large has a problem: is it not frightening that people with these personalities shall hold positions with great influence and power, so central for the shaping of the future society?

We will not try to argue for a decision between those two possibilities, but will idicate that we may have a vicious circle. That is, the image of science is likely to have a great influence on the recruitment of future scientists; and since girls are more person-oriented, it is likely that this image will have special significance on their choices. Persons who feel uncomfortable with the cold and intellectual image of physics are not likely to choose it as a career. Hence, we may recruit future scientists that correspond to this widespread stereotype; the hypothesis may be self-fulfilling.

Conclusion

In this chapter, we have pointed to differences in girls' and boys' experiences and interests in subject matter. We have suggested that expecially the physics curriculum tend to be based on boys' experiences and interests. This implies a thorough rethinking of the science curriculum both in respect to selection and organization of material. Such an analysis is not pursued here, but has influenced recent curriculum reforms in Norway.

We have documented gender differences in factors of importance for choice of future jobs. We have also shown how pupils imagine the typical

Svein Sjøberg

scientist of different areas. We have shown that the image of the typical physicist is at odds with values of importance for girls, and have given evidence that this may be an important factor in explaining why so few girls choose technologically oriented careers. Pupils tend to choose futures where they think people have similar personalities as they have themselves.

These findings suggest a deeper analysis of how the stereotypes of scientists are formed (and possibly how 'real' they are!). Girls' choices are based on how they perceive the 'cultures' of different occupations. From this perspective, the choices are rational and should not be treated as a deficiency. This perspective also suggests that many 'intervention programs' are likely to fail unless they take the underlying values in the 'cultures' of girls and boys seriously.

References

COLLINS, J. and SMITHERS, A. (1984) 'Person orientation and science choice', *European Journal of Science Education*, 6, 1, p 55–65.
GASAT I (1981) RAAT, J. *et al.* (Ed.) Contributions, GASAT — conference 1981, Eindhoven, Eindhoven University Press.
GASAT II (1983) SJOBERG, S. (Ed.) Contributions to the second GASAT Conference, Oslo, University of Oslo, Centre for Science Education.
GASAT III (1986) HARDING, J. Contributions to the Third GASAT Conference, London, King's College.
GASAT IV (1987) DANIELS, J.Z. and KAHLE, J.B. (Ed.) Contributions to the fourth GASAT Conference (Vol 1–4) Ann Arbour, MI, University of Michigan.
HARDING, J. (1985) 'Science and technology — A future for Women?', Paper prepared for the world Conference to Review and Appraise the Achievements of the United Nations Decade for Women, Nairobi, July, Paris, UNESCO.
HARDING, J. (Ed.) (1986) *Perspectives on Gender and Science*, Lewes, Falmer Press.
Horsfjord, V. and Dalin, P. (1987) *Skole — og loererrapport* (trans: Report on schools and teachers) SISS Report no 2. Oslo, Universitetsforlaget.
KAHLE, J.B. (Ed.) (1985) *Women in Science: A Report from the Field*, Lewes, Falmer Press.
KELLY, A. (Ed.) (1987) *Science for Girls?*, Milton Keynes, Open University Press.
LEHRKE, M. *et al.* (Ed.) (1985) *Interests in Science and Technology Education*, Kiel, Institut für die Pädagogik der Naturwissenschaften.
LIE, S. and SJOBERG, S. (1984) *"Myke" jenter i "harde" fag?* (transl: Soft girls in hard science?) Oslo, Universitetsforlaget.
RINGNES, V. (1987) *Naturfag i videregaende skole* (transl: Science in upper secondary schools) SISS report no 4, Oslo, Universitetsforlaget.
SJOBERG, S. (1986) Naturfag og norsk skole. Elever og loerere sier sin mening (transl: Science and Norwegian schools. Pupils and teachers express their opinion) Oslo, Universitetsforlaget.
SJOBERG, S. and IMSEN, G. (1988) 'Gender and Science Education' in Fensham, P. (Ed.) *Development and Dilemmas in Science Education*, Lewes, Falmer Press.

Discussion (Reporter: Joan Bliss)

It was agreed that many of the findings confirmed other studies carried out elewhere, including Britain. That point suggested that the results had considerable generalizibility value. Three particular issues raised in the chapter merited detailed comment.

The evidence that more girls than boys gave 'no response' to some questions should not simply be seen as evidence of indecisiveness. This finding can be equated with the evidence from Gilligan on moral development that females tend to think more holistically and resist the invitation to choose a simple answer to a complex question. The well recorded dislike of girls to multiple-choice type questions was quoted.

There was some discussion of the evidence that between the ages of 11 and 16 boys failed to shift in their attitudes and belief towards the position of girls. If we accepted as our goal a society in which the gender differences were minimized then this evidence reinforced the belief that it would prove the males who are most resistant to change. As our society is constituted there was little direct incentive for males to change, as they benefitted most, at least in the more obvious ways, from the present situation. It might be true, though, that males paid a hidden price, for example, an inability to express emotions freely.

The finding that pupils reacted to the immediate impression of a science topic in a gender specific way was confirmed by the British APU data. For example, any question about electricity received a poor response rate from girls, even when the question was elementary and in other contexts the girls had displayed considerable scientific ability.

9.4 Imagery, Cognition and Spatial Ability

Ann C. Howe

It is widely assumed that spatial ability is an aspect of intelligence on which males are superior to females and that there is a correlation between spatial ability and achievement in science (Finn, Dulberg and Reis, 1979; Maccoby and Jacklin, 1974; Witkin, Moore, Goodenough and Cox, 1977).

A number of tests have been developed to measure spatial ability. Factor analysis of the results have led to the identification of two subfactors, the ability to orient oneself, or an object, in space and the ability to manipulate visually presented information. A recent comprehensive review of research on spatial ability (Linn and Petersen, 1985) labeled these subfactors spatial perception and spatial visualization and added mental rotation as a third factor or category.

Our interest centers on the second factor, spatial visualization, and more specifically on performance on the Group Embedded Figures Test (GEFT). Although this is but one of the tests used to measure spatial visualization, it has come to have significance greater than the simple ability to identify figures that are embedded in a drawing. Performance on this test is used as an indicator of 'cognitive style', a trait first defined as field-dependence or independence but later defined as an indicator of the ability to solve problems analytically as opposed to globally. The lower GEFT scores of females reported by some workers have been cited as evidence that females are less analytical than males and, by inference, less competent in science (Witkin, *et al*, 1977).

The Embedded Figures Test is directly related to the puzzles with hidden figures that we were given as children. A line drawing of a country scene would have a bird, a rabbit and a squirrel 'hidden' somewhere among the foliage or the swirls in a tree trunk. The Embedded Figures Test was designed to measure the ability or skill required to find the simple figures hidden in a complex field. The test is composed of a series of increasingly complex figures that contain certain simpler figures embedded within. We used the form of the test that is administered to a group and is called, reasonably enough, the Group Embedded Figures Test (GEFT).

The question that interested us was whether performance on this test is a matter of perception and imagery or of cognition. In other words, is superior performance on the Group Embedded Figures Test associated with superior ability to form and retain mental images of the simple figures or is it related to cognitive operational processes? What are the processes underlying spatial visualization? To study this question we turned to a Piagetian model of mental functioning. This model distinguishes two modes of thought, the figurative which includes perception, imitation and imagery, and the operational which includes the cognitive processes needed to structure knowledge. We administered a series of tasks from *Mental Imagery in the Child* (Piaget and Inhelder, 1971) and one task from *Epistemology and Psychology of Functions* (Piaget, Grize, Szeminska and Bang, 1977). Multiple linear regression was used to analyze the data obtained from these tests.

Tasks

The Group Embedded Figures Test (GEFT)

This is a standardized test that requires the subject to locate and trace one of eight standard forms incorporated into a complex geometric pattern. Total testing time is twelve minutes. The range of test scores is 0 to 18. A correct response consists of a complete tracing of the appropriate standard form in exactly the same proportions and orientations as the given standard form.

Perceptual Fidelity

The subject is asked to draw a line equal in length to a given line, starting at the end of the original line and continuing it in one direction, without the aid of any measuring device. The length of the line is the score (Piaget and Inhelder, 1971, pp 16–26).

Simple Imagery

Starting at the same point as in the preceding task, the subject is asked to imagine that the line just completed is rotated ninety degrees until it is perpendicular to the original line and to draw the imagined line (*ibid*, pp 26–32). This and the preceding task focus on preoperational perception and imagery. In the simple imagery task, the subject has previously acted upon the initially given line and can be said to have internally imitated it and is now asked to reproduce the line in a position that has not been perceived but must be imagined.

Pseudo-Conservation 1 and 2

The subject is given a line and asked to draw two lines equal in length and parallel to the given line. One line to be drawn above and to the left of the given line, the other line to be drawn below and to the right of the given line. In each case a starting point is given. This task focuses on the interaction of preoperational thought and imagery *ibid*, pp 32–34.)

Complex Imagery 1

The subject is presented with a circle and asked to draw a straight line equal in length to the circumference of the circle, i.e., to transform a circle into a straight line. This task differs from the proceding tasks in that the required product is not among the perceptible forms supplied and cannot be produced by imagery alone but only by the interaction of cognitive processes and imagery (*ibid*, pp 190–7).

Cognitive Regulation

This problem set is based on a graphic representation of an apparatus consisting of a horizontal spring attached at one end to a wall and at the other end to a string. The string is stretched out horizontally until it reaches a pulley over which it is draped. A pan in which weights may be placed is attached to the end of the string. As weights are placed into the pan, the spring stretches and the string is pulled in a vertical direction so that some lengths are changed (the length of the spring, the length of string which is in a horizontal orientation, and the length of string which is vertical) while other lengths are conserved (the distance between the wheel and the wall, the overall length of the string) (Piaget, Grize, Szeminska and Bang, 1977, p 49–63). A series of questions regarding conservation of lengths calls upon cognitive operations involving seriation and reversibility. Although perception and pseudo-conservation may be involved in this task, assessment focuses on the cognitive operations. The score is the number of correct responses.

Reliabilities

Test-retest reliability was determined for each test prior to data collection, using a sample of tenth grade biology students drawn from a school district other than that used in the study. The following Pearson Product Moment correlations were obtained: Perception, $r = .67$; Simple Imagery, $r = .79$; Pseudo-conservation 1, $r = .89$; Complex Imagery 1, $r = .90$

Table 9.4.1   *Raw score means and standard deviations*

VAR.	Total sample		Males		Females	
	M	SD	M	SD	M	SD
GEFT	*11.21*	*4.72*	*11.57*	*4.55*	*10.86*	*4.93*
PR	8.83	.77	8.86	.81	8.81	.74
SI	8.07	.77	8.16	.72	7.99	.83
PC1	8.76	1.04	8.56	.61	8.97	1.32
PC2	9.17	.55	9.19	.55	9.16	.57
CI1	10.03	2.17	10.20	2.14	9.85	1.29
COR	4.22	1.55	4.54	1.33	3.91	1.17

Method

Sample

A sample of twenty-eight males and twenty-eight females was drawn randomly by sex from a pool of 168 students enrolled in a 10th grade academic biology course in a suburban school. The school population is mixed with respect to socioeconomic status, ethnic group, and parental education but is predominantly middle class. The range of subjects was 14 years 6 months to 16 years 8 months with a mean age of 15 years 5 months.

Procedure

Tests were given to small groups of subjects in a room equipped with testing cubicles. Oral directions were given for each item, followed by time for subjects to write responses. The order of administration, designed to minimize learning effects, was as follows: GEFT, Perception, Simple Imagery, Pseudo-conservation, Complex Imagery, Cognitive Regulation.

Results

Scores

Scores on all tests, broken down by sex, are shown in table 9.4.1. The sex difference in GEFT scores proved to be non-significant.

Data Analysis

As noted above, multiple linear regression was used to determine the variance in GEFT score accounted for by each of the Piaget tasks. The order of entry of variables into the regression, dictated by the theoretical model was as follows:

Table 9.4.2 *Multiple regression summary table*

	R^2	F	$(Partial\ C.)^2$	Overall
Perceptual Reg.	.003	.907	.018	F = 5.27*
Simple Imagery	.031	1.984	.040	DF = 6, 49
Pseudo-Con. 1	.032	.605	.013	
Pseudo-Con. 2	.039	1.192	.024	
Complex Imagery	.168	2.562*	.050	
Cognitive Reg.	.392	18.056*	.269	

* $p < .05$

Perceptual Fidelity, Simple Imagery, Pseudo-Conservation 1 and 2, Complex Imagery and Cognitive Regulation. The results of this analysis and the partial correlations, also calculated, are shown in table 9.4.2.

Only Complex Imagery and Cognitive Regulation contribute significantly to the variance in GEFT score. When it is recalled that Complex Imagery calls on cognitive processes combined with imagery, the results can be interpreted to support the hypothesis that the processes underlying performance on the GEFT are cognitive rather than perceptual or imagal alone.

Discussion

The finding of no significant sex difference in GEFT score is consistent with the results of the meta-analysis of Linn and Petersen (1985). They found that the sex difference in spatial visualization is either very small or non-existent. The much publicized difference in spatial ability is mainly in spatial orientation perception. The finding of little or no sex difference in spatial visualization is also reported by Caplan, MacPherson and Tobin (1985) and and was reported earlier by Sherman (1978).

In view of the consistency of this finding, it seems time to conclude that two decades of research have failed to show a sex difference in spatial visualization that is large enough to have educational significance.

The finding that performance on the GEFT is associated with cognitive processes rather than perception or imagery alone is also consistent with findings from a considerable body of research (Witkin, *et al*, 1977; Maccoby and Jacklin, 1974). A consensus is emerging that spatial visualization is not a part of spatial ability but that it is an integral part of general problem solving ability, which is to say, general intelligence.

This does not suggest that spatial visualization should be ignored. It is an important facet of intelligence, useful or even necessary in many human endeavors. The results suggest, rather, that spatial visualization problems be included along with other problems in science instruction but that such problems should be included for all pupils, not for girls only.

References

CAPLAN, P., MACPHERSON, G. and TOBIN, P. (1985) 'Do sex-related differences in spatial abilities exist?', *American Psychologist*, 40, pp 786–99.

FINN, J., DULBERG, L. and REIS, J. (1979) 'Sex differences in educational attainment: A cross-national perspective', *Harvard Educational Review*, 49.

LINN, M. and PETERSEN, A. (1985) 'Emergence and characterization of sex differences in spatial ability: A meta-analysis', *Child Development*, 56, pp 1479–98.

MACCOBY, E. and JACKLIN, C. (1974) *The Psychology of Sex Differences*, Stanford, CA, Stanford University Press.

NATIONAL ASSESSMENT OF EDUCATIONAL PROGRESS, *Three National Assessments of Science: Changes in Achievement*, Denver, CO, Science Report #08-s-00.

PIAGET, J. and INHELDER, B. (1971) *Mental Imagery in the Child*, New York, Basic Books.

PIAGET, J., GRIZE, J., SZEMINSKA, A. and BANG, V. (1977) *Epistemology and Psychology of Functions*, Hingham, D. Reidel Pub. Co.

SHERMAN, J. (1978) *Sex-related Cognitive Differences*, Springfield, I, Charles Thomas.

WITKIN, H., MOORE, C., GOODENOUGH, D. and Cox, P. (1977) 'Field-dependent and field-independent cognitive styles and their educational implications', *Review of Educational Research*, 47, 1, pp 1–64.

Ann C. Howe

Discussion (Reporter: Denise Whitelock)

There was widespread agreement that differences in learning styles are important but have been inadequately researched. Howe's findings confirm the need for a fresh look at the whole area.

There was some review of the evidence relating spatial abilities to academic success in a variety of areas, including geometry and reading, and usually a general cognitive ability seem to be a better predictor of success than measured spatial skills, although dyslexia is an exception.

It was also agreed that it was most unlikely that possible differences in spatial skills could account for the gender differences in the uptake of science. Not only was the evidence inconclusive, as Howe had pointed out, but that the one field in physical science where women were strongly represented was in crystallography, which is probably more dependent on spatial skill than any other field.

9.5 Piaget and Interest in Science Subjects

Fritz Kubli

1 Is it necessary to think about interests in scientific subjects in Switzerland?

A recent investigation (Häuselmann 1984) analyzed the attitude towards science and technology of students aged 19 before entering university. It exposed more than 1700 of these students to a questionnaire about their preferences for school subjects. (In Switzerland there is no specialization to that age, all of them have to study languages as well as mathematics and science.) They had to rate the different subjects according to their popularity. The results are shown in figure 9.5.1.

The schedule clearly shows that 'hard sciences' like physics and chemistry are not very popular in Switzerland. Their low ratings are mainly due to the girls' antipathy to these subjects. The lack of popularity of scientific subjects is rather disquieting considering the fact that the high standard of living in Switzerland is due not only to chocolate and the Swiss banking system, but also and to a great deal to its technical industry and skills. Efforts to improve the situation are therefore regarded with interest and sympathy by the authorities, among them the Swiss Counsel of Sciences, and some leaders of the Swiss economy. It is necessary, however, to continue thinking about interest, and I hope to gain some ideas from this symposium. The question if this topic should be investigated in Switzerland can be answered with 'yes', an answer which also applies to the next question.

2 Is it useful to consider interests in a Plagetian perspective?

My personal contribution to the subject consisted in an empirical inquiry (Kubli, 1987). More than 100 students from several Swiss high schools were questioned during an hour or longer. The interviews covered not only the students' expectations and their experiences with regard to their scientific education, but also their interests outside school, and gave them in addition an

Fritz Kubli

Figure 9.5.1   *Popularity of subjects and gender*

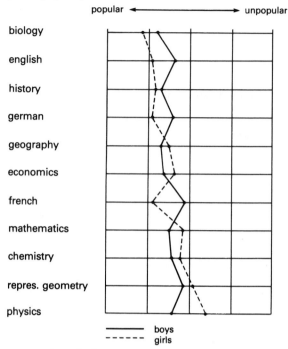

popular ◄———————► unpopular

biology
english
history
german
geography
economics
french
mathematics
chemistry
repres. geometry
physics

——— boys
- - - - girls

opportunity to express their feelings during the interview (whether they would appreciate more familiar contacts, similar to the interview situation, with their own teachers). The general communication behaviour of the students with familiar partners was also inquired.

A link between these interviews and a Piagetian view of science education can be seen in the definition of 'interests' the students gave. A science course is interesting, according to their definitions, if their spontaneous activity is stimulated and guided towards the goal of the lesson. In their words:

Interest is stimulated, if they

..... have no problems concentrating on the subject discussed during the lesson;
..... continue thinking about the subject when the lesson is over;
..... discuss the subject during the break with colleagues;
..... obtain answers to questions they had been asking themselves;
..... spend time and efforts on the subject in their spare time.

Obviously, the generation of interest is a question of resonance. The better the teaching fits the spontaneous reasoning of the students, the more interest can be expected. This is one of the major reasons for a thorough investigation of the spontaneous thinking of students, as undertaken by several attendants to this symposium. Jean Piaget was a pioneer in this area.

3 Does a Piagetian theory of science teaching need a complementation by an investigation of interests?

Piaget's theory needs to be supplemented by a theory of interests. His theory is often considered a mere description of the interaction between a subject and his material environment, without taking into account social intercourse. To this interpretation lead his well-known statements that a) all cognition goes back to actions and that b) the subject is autonomously constructing the tools to his own intellectual activity. This aspect of Piaget's view makes it hard to see how anybody else, a teacher for instance, can induce learning processes. His most important function seems to consist in the teacher's ability to trigger interest — the rest will be done by the learner himself![1]

But the concentration on an isolated subject with a completely independent development is not the only possible way of following Piaget. Another way, which goes back to the early Piaget (1926), shall be discussed now.

4 In which way shall the Piagetian theory of science teaching be interpreted in the light of an investigation of interests?

The observation of children in clinical experiments and epistemological arguments given by modern physicists, for example Max Born, Erwin Schrödinger, Herman Weyl, and Alfred N. Whitehead, both clearly show that cognitive development in the sense of Piaget, who focussed the attention on conceptual systems and structures, cannot be understood isolated from the social relations of the developing mind. Confronted with a problem in a clinical experiment, the child — as mentioned in an earlier paper (Kubli, 1983) — is guided by the expectation that the problem has a solution and that the observer of the experiment knows it. The child hopes to come to a generally accepted interpretation.

A generally accepted solution must evidently be a view of the subject which is intersubjectively transmittable. Before the child can find the right solution, he must generate ideas which can be communicated to somebody else and, in the case of inconsistencies, can be developed further on. Questions like 'Did my colleagues also find the right solution?' clearly show that the child is creating his ideas in an open mental space, to which others have access, at least potentially. This conception fits into Piaget's general ideas, because for him, equilibrated thinking always is an enlargement of the initially egocentric perspective through reciprocal assimilation or integrative fusion of different perspectives, which might be brought to his mind by somebody else. The cognitive competence of children develops not only by the growing number and generality of his concepts, but also by his ability to adopt somebody else's point of view (see Piaget's 'three-mountain experiment', Piaget, 1956).

The question: 'How is a subject conceived by others' is fundamental to any intellectual development. Operations, for instance, are essentially a means to an intersubjectively accessible approach to reality.[2] The construction starts from his immediate environment and his subjective sensuality, and it becomes more and more independent of the actual here-and-now without turning into pure fantasy. Evidence that the subjective construction develops in the direction of objectivity in the sense of a common reality, consistent with the constructions of other thinkers, can only follow from intellectual exchanges with others. Mental development as described by Piaget in his experiments is therefore primarily determined by the dualism of a subjective construction and a transmittable, objective structure.[3]

This gives us indications of a possibility to further the natural process of thinking, which is one of the most important means for the stimulation of interests. Interests can be stimulated by critically reflecting the personal views of children or students. This allows them to verify that their private constructions make sense to somebody else. Clinical interviews are generally well accepted by the children and students interviewed. In my opinion this is mainly due to their being given an opportunity to compare their private thinking with the reactions of an educated person. The eagerness with which children try to accomplish any task in a clinical interview stands in strange contrast to the stress and lack of interest experienced in school teaching. Piaget thought that this eagerness was due to the fact that children could execute actions during clinical interviews. In my opinion, it is mainly due to the looking-glass effect caused by the interviewer's attention to the children's thinking. The reactions of the interviewer give evidence that the 'private' thinking is understood and accepted by the listener, and therefore transmittable to others. This is a help often underestimated for the development of spontaneous ideas.[4]

This looking-glass effect also works in another direction. Many students would discuss the taught subjects at home, if some family members took an interest in their newly acquired knowledge. This would be the case if the acquired knowledge was considered part of daily life and not only to scientific areas. (It is evident that the same subject matter can be presented as an abstract 'scientific' insight or as something related our daily life.) Repeated demonstration that the taught subjects are related to everyday life is not only a momentary motivation but also an incentive invitation for the student to take advantage of his natural communication partners as reflectors of his private thinking. This followed clearly from the answers of our interview partners. Interest is increased if several partners pay attention to the subject.

It is therefore advisable to consider a student as intellectually integrated into a network of communication structures linking him with different partners. He develops his mind by exchanging information with them. This prevents us from isolating the school activity from more general social exchanges. It is essential to interesting teaching that advantage be taken of the 'social resonators' which can reinforce or nullify our efforts. This obviously asks for an adaptation of the 'official' language. Scientific precision must be combined with formulations that are as close as possible to everyday language, as we read it in newspapers. Interesting teaching has to be tuned to topical issues of a general purport as, for instance, the Tschernobyl catastrophe.

Notes

1 Piagetians might admit that some equilibration processes can be triggered by an argumentation that shows for instance inconsistencies in the intellectual comprehension of a subject. But the general dilemma consists in the fact that the teacher is either too early with his argumentation, because the schemata that should be equilibrated do not yet exist, and the inconsistencies cannot be seen, or he is too late, because the spontaneous equilibration has already worked without further help.

2 Concrete operations, for instance, are the bases to methods of measuring by creating unities (conservation of length, number, and so on). The famous question 'has the displaced stick changed its length, is essentially an invitation for a semantical interpretation of the signification of the term 'equal length'. It is useful to compare Piaget's definition of operations with the original considerations of P. Bridgman, the 'father' of modern operationalism. Piaget, to my knowledge, did not explicitly agree with Bridgman's operationalism, but even then, his structuralism was very much consistent with it.

3 The signification of the dualism between 'private' constructions and 'public' operations is underlined by many modern physicists. The physicist Max Born described the problem as follows: A naive thinker is convinced that his personal sensual impressions, his immediate information about reality must be shared by anybody. But there is no way of verifying that the impression a tree makes on the retina of a human being is identical with that made on another human being — if the word 'identical' makes any sense at all in this context (Born, 1964). Isolated sensual data are not objective, they are not transmittable and provable to other people. Only relations between two or more sensual impressions, which can be developed to more complex structures, can be compared and controlled by interpersonal judgments. The focus on intellectual structures is justified because they are the only objective (that means intersubjectively tranferable) epistemological elements.

4 In our investigation, students agreed that they appreciated the attention payed to their ideas about science teaching. The general atmosphere in science teaching could be improved if teachers increasingly took the students' experience of it into consideration. Many complaints about the science teaching experienced regarded the teachers' lack of sensibility for difficulties in understanding or for the momentary emotional needs of students. According to our interview partners, the ideal teacher would have intuitive knowledge of the students' intellectual and emotional conditions and he would fittingly tune his argumentation.

References

BORN, M. (1964) 'Symbol and reality' in BORN, M. (Ed.) *Natural Philosophy of Cause and Chance*, New York, Dover.

BRIDGMAN, P. (1927) *The Logic of Modern Physics*, New York, Macmillan.

BRIDGMAN, P. (1936) *Nature of Physical Theory*, Princeton, Princeton University Press.

HÄUSELMANN, E. (1984) *Maturanden und Technik*, (edited by the Swiss Academy of Technical Sciences SATW in Zurich), Zurich.

KUBLI, F. (1983) 'Piaget's clinical experiment: A critical analysis and study of their implications for science teaching', *European Journal of Science Education*, 5, 2.

KUBLI, F. (1987) *Interesse und Verstehen in Physik und Chemie*, Cologne, Aulis.

PIAGET, J. (1926) *The Language and the Thought of the Child.*, London, Kegan Paul. 1926.

PIAGET, J. (1956) *The Child's Conception of Space*, London, Routledge and Kegan Paul.

Fritz Kubli

WEYL, H. (1949) *Philosophy of Mathematics and Natural Science*, Princeton, Princeton University Press.
WHITEHEAD, A.N. (1911) *An Introduction to Mathematics*, Oxford, Oxford University Press.

10 The Social Constraints on Learning Science

John Head

The last paper included in chapter 9, that by Kubli, acts as a bridge into this chapter. Kubli ended his account on attitudes to science, a topic firmly located in the affective area, which was the brief for that chapter, with questions about the social climate of the classroom. We now explore the social influence on science learning in three widely differing contexts.

Solomon's paper is simultaneously a part and a critique of the mainstream constructivist school of science education. She shares with others a concern with the nature of individual pupil's understanding of science and how prior ideas might inhibit learning. She differs from many by placing the emphasis on the social world of the child, rather than personal development, in order to discover how children develop these ideas and influence each other. Knowledge construction is seen to be largely a social activity.

Kutnick develops a similar line of argument in his paper which reviews the curriculum development projects financed by the Nuffield Foundation in the 1960s. He argues that the implicit model guiding these projects, based on a particular tradition in British psychology, saw learning solely as an individual activity. Consequently the importance of group work, of pupil interactions, of cooperation in place of competition, was never adequately appreciated. Kutnick argues that we now know enough about the importance of social relationships in influencing learning and development to begin to plan learning experiences which make positive use of this social dynamic and the next phase of school science innovation should make use of this knowledge.

The paper by Domingos related underachievement in science to social factors. She distinguishes between the simple acquisition of knowledge and the ability to make use of knowledge and shows that it is the latter factor which appears to be most influenced by social constraints. She makes use of Bernstein's description of cultural reproduction to illustrate how disadvantaged children can become caught in situations which magnify the initial disadvantage and indicates how changes in pedagogic practice might break that cycle.

10.1 Social Influence or Cognitive Growth

Joan Solomon

Rational Personal Constructivism

It has always been clear that there are many different approaches to the study of children's ideas about scientific matters. In any early pre-paradigmatic field of social research the way to start, it seemed, was to listen attentively, with respect, and with as little in the way of preconceived ideas as possible, to the words of the subjects themselves.

But the very respect which is so essential for an ethnograpic study very soon begins to engender a cluster of theoretical perspectives. These used to show up in heated discussions concerning the use of labels such as 'misconceptions', 'preconceptions', and 'alternative frameworks'. The ethnographic methodology, because it documented the comments of individual students, and also because it was so often carried out by those trained in science, gave rise to a strong rational personal constructivist position. This attitude comes out strongly in a paper about conceptual change by Strike and Posner (1982) where the authors based their argument on pupil rationality — 'being rational has primarily to do with how we move from one view to another'.

There is a strong anecdotal tradition of thought, or 'gedanken', experiments in physics (Helm and Gilbert, 1985), which is popularly exemplified by the story of the young Einstein imagining what it might be like to chase after a beam of light at a speed approaching that of light itself. Perhaps these examples are even more famous than they deserve to be, and they encourage us to seek a comparable rationality in the fluid inventions of students. My own impression is that it is a rare phenomenon. Interviewers in the ethnographic tradition certainly met with plenty of homespun ideas but, as the talk continued, the students often moved from one to another.

Personal rationality was also thought to be applied to the pupils' motor experiences although how or when this modelling from observation or action had been made did not then seem to be an important part of the research programme. But we know that verbalized ideas are at a far remove from the sense data of raw experiences. They need to be reconstructed into mental models which can then be stored in the memory so that they are retrievable, and often they are also transmuted into verbal accounts and then talked over with others. Through their sheer familiarity such acts often become opaque, even to self-explanation. Thus craft or body knowledge may simply remain within the memory as non-verbal procedural 'tacit knowledge' (Polanyi, 1958) which is hard to relate to the personal construction of ideas.

Polanyi wrote of the 'focus of attention' of the user moving from the body to the contact point of the tool. This is not a conscious move but it makes a vital difference in the location at which the experiential construction of understanding takes place. Not all craft knowledge is either opaque or destined to remain opaque. That which can be used to comment on experience is of the greatest importance for science education and has been grossly ignored. It is one which was addressed in *Teaching Children in the Laboratory* (Solomon, 1980) and which the recent appearance of interactive experiences in science museums makes even more interesting.

Careful exploration of how students cope with problem solving (for example, Viennot, 1979; and Champagne and Klopfer, 1980) has also shown that they do not apply their ideas rationally and consistently, even when the scientific problems being discussed are very similar. In a theoretical paper based on South African data, Hewson (1981) accepted that taught scientific ideas could oust, be defeated by, or even live alongside, the childrens' own notions. If rationality does not govern the young students' subsequent learning of science is it right to assume that these persistent and widespread pre-instructional ideas have been severally formulated for the purpose of providing rational systems of explanation?

The Social Construction of Meaning

Children are great social communicators long before they learn about scientific ways of constructing theories. Social interactions are based on empathy rather than consistency because they depend on the shared understanding of meaning. Not just children but all of us strive hard to fit into the general scheme of what is being discussed, and we also rely very strongly on the messages of recognition, understanding and support which come back to us from others when we speak about our experiences. Back in 1934 Mead had written that social interactions are responsible for the appearance of new objects in the field of our experiences and indeed that 'objects of common sense' can only exist through this social communication. Both he and Schutz and Luckmann (1973) wrote of the 'interchangeability of perspectives' with others who have a social relationship with us. If the construction of the meaning of an experience takes place within a group — friends, family, club or nation — it is small wonder that students' notions are found to be common to many. If the art of changing perspectives in order to understand others is an essential skill in social circumstances it also explains why students' explanations can be so inconsistently applied without causing them any apparent cognitive discomfort. Perhaps the most glaring hole in modern educational knowledge is simply an understanding of that age-old amorphous epistemological system that we call 'common sense'.

The social need to reach consensus, and not to rock the conversational boat by demanding logical argument and definition at every turn, looks, at first sight, like an influence for stasis and non-growth rather than one we should encourage during education. However there are two substantial reasons why this is not so. In the first place the very fluidity of perspective on which social interaction depends is valuable for exploring new ideas, and is one which both the SISCON and the CLISP projects have used. Secondly social groupings themselves mature and allow individual children to be exposed to new consensual ideas and consensual media. This, as we shall see in the subsequent reports on research, is important for cognitive growth.

Personal Styles of Verbal Expression — Electricity

To these three perspectives — personal rationality, experiential actions, and social mediation — some more need to be added. What I have in mind are individual in character but not related so much to rationality and cognition as to other personal traits.

This area is so fluid and idiosyncratic that it is hard and perhaps even misleading even to try to discuss it in any theoretical way. Instead I want just to describe some data obtained by the British STIR (Science Teachers In Research) group in the field of electricity. These are to be found set out in greater detail in Solomon *et al* (1986 and 1987).

In the earlier paper (1986) the results of a network analysis of the free writing showed the similarity of the views and beliefs about electricity given by the two groups of children. We assumed from this that these were socially derived notions which had proved either resistant to or emotionally more salient than the teaching given at school. The main areas used in the analysis were USE, DANGER, SUPPLY and PHYSICS (this latter to be taken very loosely as being an early attempt at conceptual formulation). We were intrigued at the large category of first year responses in the DANGER category, which had diminished significantly two years later.

> What might have caused the fear of electricity which seemed to underly the DANGER statements?

> Was there any structural difference in the way the two year groups expressed themselves in their writing?

> Was the correct use of simile to describe electricity an equal problem to both year groups?

We sought an answer to the first question partly by group interviews of 'fearing' and 'non-fearing' students (as defined by the number of DANGER statements made), and partly by internal evidence within the questionnaire. We found that having had an electric shock was not a significant factor in being fearful, but that not having full parental licence to use electrical appliances was. We also found that these fearing children were much more likely than the others to place a ring around the picture of the plug of a disconnected table light as a place where there was electricity.

We deduced from this that familiarity with the use of electrical appliances had moved the locus of operation of electricity from the plug to the socket. Here were indications of a change in conceptual understanding very nicely related to Polanyi's discussion of motor learning.

Examining the sentences from a syntactical point of view proved interesting. This analysis showed a regular age progression similar to one found by Kempa and Hodgson (1976) in sentences written about the nature of acids, in which these authors had found an age progression which did not seem to be related to high and low scorers in an IQ test.

The nearest we had come to setting an intelligence test was the use of simile. The ability to find a quality through which to compare two objects also showed significant development from first to third year. However, it was interesting to find that, within any one year group, there was no significant correlation between ability in the use of a simile and the hierarchy of sentence construction.

This conclusion was intriguing: it could have been the effect of either social learning or personal style of verbal expression.

Personal Styles of Non-verbal Expressions — Light

A small separate study of third year pupils was carried out on classes just beginning their first course on optics. Before it began the students were given coloured pencils and asked to draw a picture of a sunset 'putting in all you can about light'. In their first lesson the same students used a ray box and a lens to trace beams of light across a piece of paper. Shortly afterwards they were asked to draw diagrams to show why a person's shadow was different in the morning when the sun was high in the sky, and in the evening when it was lower down. They were also asked, in the next lesson, to explain in words what a shadow was.

The collection of coloured pictures ranged from a lurid orange ball cut in half by the horizon, to more complicated sea or landscapes in which several other objects were sketched. These were simply categorized into ones where light effects were shown — lighter and darker shading on the sides of objects or clouds, shadows or paths of light across the sea — and others which showed no light effects at all apart from uniform sunset colours.

The diagrams of shadows were surprising. Some had drawn the shadow as a black shape completely separated from the person, while others had related it to both the person and the position of the sun. In the written explanation it was again possible to see two main categories of response: — 'where the sun's light was blocked out', 'an image, shape or reflection' (Solomon, 1986). These showed a high and significant association — $Q = 0.81 +/- 0.14$ (n = 36). Clearly an analytical approach could display itself in both words and simple diagrams.

However when the earlier coloured pictures were examined no significant association of any kind could be found. We might conclude from this that a personal trait for observing coloured effects, is not necessarily matched by an explanatory way of thinking about them. This difference of cognitive style might be typified perhaps by Leonardo da Vinci's minute exploration of the blueness of distant vistas, and Isaac Newton's preoccupation with explaining refraction and dispersion by the corpuscular theory.

Lifelong Education

So it seems that the task of understanding how school pupils' ideas grow and change may have to include personal rational constructivism, the trace material of motor experience, socially mediated ideas, and also personal traits of style. There can thus be no easy recipe for better classroom teaching. The potentiality for learning is quite staggering in its complexity.

Whether or not cognitive growth in some narrow rational sense continues after the end of formal education may be debatable, but we may be sure that the growth which depends on change of social context and personal need will go on throughout life. Layton *et al* (1986) have written of science learning by members of specialist clubs, environmental groups, and mothers of Down's syndrome children. Recent work (for example, Macgill, 1987) shows that changed social circumstances do indeed spur on groups of adults to expand their scientific knowledge. Centres for adult education, gardening clubs, museums and other informal sources for continuing learning in science (Lucas, 1983) bear witness to this need to learn. The new move for 'Universities of the Third Age' arise from the most daring claim of all for the life-long continuation of learning potential.

References

CHMAPAGNE, A. and KLOPFER, L. (1980) 'Cognitive research and the design of science instruction', *Educational Psychology* 17, 1, pp 31–53.

HELM, H. and GILBERT, J. (1985) 'Thought experiments and physics education', *Physics Education*, 20, 3, pp 124–33.

HEWSON, P. (1981) 'A conceptual approach to learning science', *European Journal of Science Education*, 3, 4, pp 383–96.

KEMPA, R. and HODGSON, G. (1976) 'Levels of concept acquisition and concept maturity'. *British Journal of Educational Psychology*, 46, pp 253–60.

LAYTON, D., DAVEY, A. and JENKINS, E. (1986) 'Science for specific social purposes' *Studies in Science Education*, 13, pp 27–52.

LUCAS, A. (1983) 'Scientific literacy and informal learning', *Studies in Science Education*, 10, pp 1–13.

MACGILL, S. (1987) *The Politics of Anxiety*, London, Pion.

MEAD, G.H. (1934) *Mind Self and Society* Chicago, 1L, University of Chicago Press.

POLANYI, M. (1958) *Personal Knowledge*, London, Routledge and Kegan Paul.

SCHUTZ, A. and LUCKMANN, T. (1973) *Structures of the Life World*, London, Heinemann.

SOLOMON, J. (1980) *Teaching Children in the Laboratory*, London, Croom Helm.

SOLOMON, J. (1986) 'Children's explanations', *Oxford Review of Education*, 12, 1, pp 41–51

SOLOMON, J., BLACK, P., OLDHAM, V. and STUART, H. (1986) 'The pupil's view of electricity', *European Journal of Science Education*, 7, pp 281–94.

SOLOMON, J., BLACK, P. and STUART, H. (1987) 'The pupil's view of electricity revisited: Social development or cognitive growth?', *European Journal of Science Education*, 9, 1, pp 13–22.

STRIKE, K. and POSNER, G. (1982) 'Conceptual change and science teaching', *Science Education*, 4, 3, pp 231–40.

VIENNOT, L. (1979) 'Spontaneous learning in elementary dynamics', *European Journal of Science Education*, 1, 2, pp 205–21.

Joan Solomon

Discussion (Reporter Peter Kutnick)

It was suggested that the title of the paper was misleading as Solomon did not really deny the reality of cognitive development, but raised questions about how this occurred in the real world. She accepted this point but thought that the title did draw attention to the points she wanted to make.

It was argued that recent studies in the history of science suggest that cognitive conflict may have been more common than previously realized. By refering to original papers by Newton and others one often finds that their advances in theory came after massive conflicts which lasted several years. Nevertheless, in the teaching of science the conventional ideas are presented as uncontroversial facts, and no hint of conflict is given. It was noted that in this conference we were using the word conflict freely without having an agreed meaning.

The role of parents in contributing to children's ideas was raised. Solomon could not report on this specific point as she did not have any relevant data, but it might be assumed that parental advice, for example, cautionary warnings about using electricity, would contribute to the total social effect. There was some debate whether the curriculum for electricity should and could take more account of historical and conceptual development.

10.2 A Social Critique of Cognitively Based Science Curricula: The Case of the Nuffield Schemes

P.J. Kutnick

Introduction

A social criticism of cognitively-based science curricula is a many-headed beast. At the head I shall assert that many modern curriculum planners do not have a full grasp of the cognitive theory which is said to underlie their work; hence the process of intellectual/scientific development has become overly individualized and does not account for the dynamics of cognitive development which should underlie curriculum planning. The rest of the animal acknowledges and seeks to explain how a developmental curriculum can be better implemented in the classroom. The paper emphasizes that there has been a divide between curriculum planning and classroom implementation; that this divide has all-too-often been described in terms of curriculum versus learning process. But cognitive development theory (as asserted by Piaget) involves the learning process as part of what is learnt. Curriculum planners as well as science educators should be aware that cognitive development and its schemes of learning in science are embedded in relationships between learners; one is forced into a concept of social development as the root of individual development. And, for the most part, the relationships between learners that are currently allowed to develop in classrooms may be just the relationships which hinder the development of learning.

I propose to identify one curricular approach and provide a brief overview of its planning and implementation. Next, an approach to enhance the effectiveness of this curriculum will be described. Both curriculum and enhancement models will be questioned for their understanding and implementation of the cognitive theory upon which they are substantially based. A number of classroom studies on the effectiveness of these models will be cited. The studies find that concepts of individualized and child-centred curriculum have not been effectively implemented, and a reappraisal of the underlying theory which informs the models is needed. From the reappraisal, alternative routes to effective implementation of curriculum (planning and classroom organization) can be cited.

Nuffield Chemistry Scheme

The movement in the 1960s and 1970s in England towards progressive education was also accompanied by the development of many new curricula. During this time there was a simultaneous resurgence of child-centredness in curriculum planning which drew upon current interpretations of developmental psychology of child learning. Amongst the groups which were very involved with curriculum planning, and drawing upon child development theory was the Nuffield Foundation.

The Nuffield Foundation drew up several new curricula for primary and secondary schools. Their curricula initially focused on the 'O' and later 'A' level courses in the sciences (physics, chemistry, biology), followed much later by a combined sciences introductory course for secondary pupils, and introductory science and mathematics courses for primary pupils.

The curriculum was designed with the developing pupil in mind; but was the Nuffield understanding of development enough to allow effective learning to take place? As a general introductory statement to the Nuffield science programmes let me cite a statement from the chemistry course:

(a) Pupils should gain an understanding that lasts throughout their lives of what it means to approach a problem scientifically.

(b) Which ideas are discussed, how they are presented, what materials and techniques are used to demonstrate them, depend on the level of development reached by pupils and should be chosen accordingly. (Nuffield Foundation, 1967, pp 2–3)

The curriculum description presents very laudable points in its introduction. But are these points (especially concerning development) designed and structured into the curriculum? In a chapter entitled 'Form and content of the syllabus' they state, 'Present chemistry syllabuses ... are predominantly lists of specific materials and of concepts. We replace them by a syllabus emphasizing manipulative and intellectual skills, and state our requirements in terms rather of prowess than of items of information that should be remembered.' (*ibid*, p 17).

Here we approach a first substantial problem. The problem is: for everyone to be actively engaged on practical and meaningful work to enhance individual development, there will be too many pupils and too little equipment in today's classrooms. Curriculum implementation must make use of classroom groups. Grouping may bring the 'hum of purposeful activity, but it does not mean that they abandon sensible behaviour' (Nuffield Foundation, 1970, p xii). Yes, the curriculum which brings about individual development is a group curriculum, and one which must be controlled by the teacher. In the 'School and classroom organization' chapter the sole statements that are made concerning pupils' development within the curiculum are those which emphasize 'order and discipline' (for understandable safety purposes) and 'collaboration between class and teacher' (Nuffield Foundation, 1967, p 113). The chapter continues by describing types and distribution of hardware, but nothing about classroom approach.

We are left with a contradiction: Individual teachers may be aware of the need and use of pairs and groupings for development within the science curriculum, but the teacher must impose and maintain order which potentially destroys the potential for learning. And as the curriculum was designed to promote development we should legitimately question how effective the Nuffield science curricula have been.

The overtly individualistic bias in science education has been a tradition in England — with the work on individual intelligence (Galton and others) followed by faculty psychology propounded by pundits such as Cyril Burt. Individuation is not new in British psychology or philosophy (for which we can turn back to Locke and others); but it is curious that it excludes the social philosophy of Rousseau, Marx and others (which was the educational background for Sputnick and inadvertently a major stimulus for Nuffield).

Thus the structure of Nuffield chemistry contained both a mismatch between student level and curriculum level and an overly individualistic basis. We are now in a position to frame some questions. Remember: (i) there is still a need for group work although the course is based on individualized development; (ii) the necessity of group work, especially in mixed ability classes, may mean that there is no clear level from which the curriculum may be approached; (iii) ineffective implementation of a curriculum as the Nuffield could be interpreted as a curriculum set at too high of a level for the pupil population; and (iv) pupils may not have a sound concrete basis upon which to approach formal operations. What these issues point to is a further consideration of: (a) the adequacy of implementing such a curriculum in real classrooms; and (b) was developmental theory of the 60s and 70s a sound basis for curriculum planning?

The Adequacy of Implementing the Curriculum in Real Classrooms: Case Studies from Primary Schools

While I have provided information on the science curriculum of the secondary school throughout this paper, why make a sudden change down to the primary level? The quick and simple answer is that there have been similar developmental curricula established in primary schools for a substantial period of time. And, unlike research at the secondary level, there have been a number of recent studies which explored curriculum effectiveness. Let me focus on three issues that have been mentioned so far in the developmental curriculum:

individualized instruction, group work and matching. All three issues are based on the concept of increased adequacy in development and that development is a 'child-centred' phenomenon — a move away from the teacher dominated classroom. While the curriculum may make these claims, are they effected in the classroom? Three studies which I shall cite give a resounding 'no' as the answer.

Primary Education in England; A Survey of a Representative Sample of Primary Schools Throughout England (HMSO, 1978) by HMI reported a large-scale investigation. Following an initial survey, randomly selected classes of 7, 9 and 11-year-olds were observed and tested on academic attainment. The survey attested to a move away from streaming to mixed ability classes in school. Also the Inspectorate identified 'teaching styles' of the teachers surveyed as either 'didactic' (traditional) or 'exploratory' (progressive). Seventy-five per cent of the teachers surveyed were rated as didactic. Only 5 per cent were exploratory. They found that schools spent a large amount of time on teaching the core basics (3 Rs); instead of using integrated and applied ideals. The survey found that primary schools, even in a liberal/progressive climate, were decidedly traditional. And the developmental curricula was taught in an overwhelmingly (95 per cent) non-progressive manner.

1980 saw the publication in the first of a series of studies by the ORACLE (Observational Research and Classroom Learning Evaluation) team at the University of Leicester (see Galton, Simon and Croll, 1980). ORACLE was interested in the process and product of teaching. They chose a representative sample of teachers and schools from three education authorities which closely matched national survey data. Classrooms of children age 8 to 10+ were selected to focus upon. Over a year in school, interactional data was accumulated and the following results were presented: Both teachers and pupils interacted, but there was an 'asymmetry' between the interactions. Teachers most often worked with individual pupils, and this took up most of their day. But the large number of pupils in any class meant that individual pupils had little opportunity to interact with their own teacher (about fifty-four seconds per hour was available). Most classrooms were divided into groups for teaching purposes, but the teacher had little time to interact with the groups. Within the groups most work was undertaken individually; little evidence of cooperation amongst pupils was found. Group work, supposedly used to alleviate pressures on the teacher, was present in name but not function. Plowden-like progressive ideals had not failed in schools; they had not been attempted.

A study by Bennett and colleagues (1984) sought to question whether the learning experiences offered to children matched their attainments and capacities in the primary school. They acknowledged that teachers were in control of their classrooms and the learning experiences of their pupils. But Bennett also noted that teachers were under time and other constraints which could hinder effective learning. To undertake this study, Bennett focused on sixteen teachers of 6 and 7-year-old pupils. Classrooms were structured to allow pupils at various ability levels to receive individualized curricula. But actual 'demand' made by teachers was overwhelmingly for practice (about 60 per cent of teaching time); not the expected cognitive enhancement at the base of individualized learning.

Because of individualization, extra responsibility was placed on the teacher to make proper diagnoses of pupil problems and apply appropriate curricula. Teachers appeared to be adept at recognizing tasks that were too difficult. But they had problems in recognizing tasks that were too easy. Children conspired with their teachers by showing typical cheerfulness and industry in their work, even if they were totally bored. Teachers' difficulties in diagnosing problems was further compounded by the apparent need to look at the 'product' of pupil work. Teachers were under pressure to answer a continuous stream of questions and corrections. Large queues built-up around the teachers' desks. Teachers' response to individual pupils became limited by the need to move on to the next pupil and still maintain classroom control. The study showed that classroom management conspired against the teacher in not allowing adequate time for full 'matching' of pupil need to curricula.

There are several conclusions that should be drawn from these studies. Minimally we find that, while developmental curricula may exist, teachers are not (on the whole) implementing them. We may ask why the curricula have not been effective. To this question, at least four answers may be provided:

(iii) the curricula have not caught the 'fancy' of teachers;
(ii)   pupils are not asserting their 'independent' learning skills and individualization becomes dependence learning;
(iii) groupwork may physically bring a number of children around a common work area, but it rarely means working together; and
(iv)   teachers do not have adequate time to match the demands of the curriculum to the needs of their pupils.

A Theoretical Critique

From studies of classroom implementation we are led to ask: why does individualization of the developmental curricula not lead to 'autonomous and independent' learning, and groupwork lead to individualistic anarchy? Whether they are structured into the developmental curriculum or simply perceived as implementational methods of the developmental curriculum, independent learning and groupwork should be working more successfully. The theoretical point to be made is that curriculum planners' concept of development is limited. Planners appear to base their curricula on a particular understanding of Piagetian/developmental theory; the understanding is most easily described as a stage identification or typification approach. But if one takes the time to return to the early work of Piaget and others, a greater appreciation of the 'whole' theory is gained. For example, in his early work

(1928, 1932 and 1936), Piaget arrived at the basic logical-mathematical stages which underlie all of his succeeding work. While undertaking these studies, Piaget also noted that development was firmly rooted in social relationships and schemes of action (both physical and social). Three points of relevance for curriculum planners (as well as implementers) are derived from these writings:

(i) In the child's quest for autonomy and independence s/he must experience archetypical relationships of constraint and cooperation; usually characterized as parent/teacher and peer relations respectively. Autonomy cannot be achieved with just one or the other type of relationship. A full understanding of both is necessary, along with the formal operational ability to balance between the two.

(ii) The peer group is particularly vital for the transition from pre-operations to concrete operations. Minimally the peer group provides cognitive conflict amongst its members in an atmosphere of mutuality and equality. This conflict (without the presence of hierarchy) forces the child to decentre, reflect upon action and explain individual perceptions to others. There are a few experimental studies which illuminate the importance of the peer group for cognitive development (see Doise, 1978; Perret-Clermont, 1980). Interaction with cognitive conflict between children working on conservation tasks helps all types of children, non-conservers as well as conservers; once they were ready for some advancement. Social/peer interaction is a necessary (perhaps not sufficient) component of cognitive development and is also effective in promoting the transition to formal operations (see Bearison, 1986).

(iii) A derived point from the two previous points reinforces that peer interaction leading to cooperation must take place in a situation which does not impose constraint on children. Constraint can be found in the dominance orientation of the teacher-pupil relationship, an assumed hierarchical view of knowledge, and even in an imposed leadership amongst peers. Peer relations which promote cooperation and cognitive development must be carefully structured so as to do just that.

We are left with a number of contradictions. The developmental curriculum needs to acknowledge and build in social/implementational criteria; more particularly, pupils need cooperation to promote learning but do not practice it in school. The developmental planning of many science curricula has been based on individual development; but pupils need to work with other pupils in an atmosphere of cooperation in order to attain the most basic level (of the concrete operational nature) of curriculum demand.

If we take Shayer and Adey's (1981) criticism that Nuffield science is not being learnt successfully in schools and move beyond matching demand and cognitive level to include social and cooperative relationships in curriculum planning, we are left with an approach which development theory warrants (and is supported in Piaget's sole writing on schools [1969]). Cooperation is the basis of the transition to concrete operations; which is the basis for an effective introduction to secondary science curricula. But we need to clarify models of cooperation which go beyond the simple recognition that cooperation cannot take place in a constraining context. We know that too much teacher direction will be a hindrance. Interesting models which have been experimentally and practicably applied to the classroom include:

(i)   A successful, behaviourist approach by Slavin (1983). To Slavin instructional systems of the school have two distinct components: the task structure of the presentation of the curriculum; and the incentive structure. To promote effective learning both structures must be accounted for in classroom organization. The individual learns in the context of the group, thus necessitating coordinated efforts amongst group members to allow effective functioning. Slavin has documented a wide range of improvements by the pupils who have participated in this model of cooperative learning. In comparison to control groups (who were given similar, but non-cooperative learning experiences), cooperative learning pupils showed consistent academic improvement, they also overcame barriers to 'within school' friendships (crossing racial and sex discriminative lines), and were able to work effectively in mixed ability groups (sometimes incorporating handicapped children). The range of positive intellectual and social results from Slavin's classroom research should, minimally, encourage more exploration into cooperative learning for the development of social relationships and for an effective classroom motivator in today's mixed ability, co-active classes in science.

(ii) Another model of classroom cooperation is based on research undertaken by the author (Kutnick and Brees, 1982). Instead of drawing upon the behavioural outcome and reward of Slavin's model, the focus of investigation was on the development of relationships (in natural and close social senses). This study structured experiences (sensitivity exercises) which have been used to promote a sense of trust and dependence into the classroom experience of primary school children. The 'experimental' children showed themselves: (a) more willing to express concern for and offer help to peers in distress (as opposed to withdrawing or seeking adult attention); (b) wishing to affiliate to a group if they, themselves, were in distress; (c) more likely to share and take turns (as opposed to taking from competitively) in play situations; although (d) cognitively no more or less advanced than all of the other children. These experimental children developed similarly in an academic sense, but were more socially aware and concerned about other children. The skills of social perception-taking (decentring) are at the base of the transition from pre-operations to concrete operations; and, thus, are an essential prerequisite for today's science curricula.

(iii)   A further cognitively applied, collaborative approach has focussed specifically on the transition between pre-operations and concrete operations; although there is evidence that collaboration also facilitates the transition from concrete to formal operations (see Bearison, 1986). The underlying mechanism promoting transition is cognitive conflict generated between peers; encountered when solving a conservation problem. The cognitive conflict forces peers to decentre, acknowledge and allow for other perspectives in their own thinking. Cognitive conflict is generated in the above studies only when there is a mutual (non-hierarchial), participatory, and non-individualized 'learning situation'; that is, equal peers must work together to solve a problem — not just observe one another or be told what to do.

The educational implications drawn from this cognitive and cooperative research are immediate and will have implications for curriculum planning, classroom organization and classroom interaction. More specifically, implications criticize the use of the individualized curriculum and traditional didactic methods of teaching. Pupils will need to achieve common resolutions to scientific problems in small groups, and come to their resolutions without the domination or specific control of teachers. If one wants a science curriculum that is truly based on developmental principles, then that curriculum must plan for social relationships. The most potent and least understood of the social relationships is cooperation. It should not be taken naively. It does not necessarily exist in grouped classrooms. It does not exist in 'developmental' curricula as they are presently written. Hopefully these experimental studies and criticism of curriculum design will be a useful starting point for the planning of curricula which can fully account for development.

References

ALEXANDER, R. (1984) *Primary Teaching*, Eastbourne, Holt, Rinehart and Winston.
ARONSON, E. (1978) 'The effect of a cooperative classroom structure on student behaviour and attitude' in BAR-TAL D. and SAX L. (Eds) *Social Psychology of Education*, New York, Wiley.
BEARISON, D. (1986) 'Transactional cognition in context: New models of social understanding' in BEARISON, D.J. and ZIMILES, H. (Eds) *Thought and Emotions*, Hillsdale, NJ, Erlbaum.
BENNETT, N., DESFORGES, C., COCKBURN, A. and WILKINSON, B. (1984) *The Quality of Pupil Learning Experiences*, London, Lawrence Erlbaum Associates.
DOISE, W. (1978) *Groups and Individuals*, Cambridge, Cambridge University Press.
EGGLESTON, J.F., GALTON, M.J. and JONES, M.E. (1976) *Processes and Products of Science Teaching*, London, Macmillan.

GALTON, M., SIMON, B. and CROLL, P. (1980) *Inside the Primary Classroom*, London, Routledge and Kegan Paul.

HMI (1978) *Primary Education in England*, London, HMSO.

KUTNICK, P. and BREES, P. (1982) 'The development of cooperation: Explorations in cognitive and moral competence and social authority', *British Journal of Educational Psychology*, 52, pp 361–5.

NUFFIELD FOUNDATION (1967) *Chemistry* London, Longman.

NUFFIELD FOUNDATION (1970) *Combined Science*, London, Longman.

PEPITONE, E. (1980) *Children in Cooperation and Competition*, Lexington, MA, Lexington Books.

PERRET-CLERMONT, A.N. (1980) *Social Interaction and Cognitive Development in Children*, London, Academic Press.

PIAGET, J. (1928) *Language and Thought of the Child*, London, Routledge and Kegan Paul.

PIAGET, J. (1932) *Moral Judgement of the Child*, New York, Free Press.

PIAGET, J. (1936) *Judgement and Reasoning*, London, Routledge & Kegan Paul.

PIAGET, J. (1969) *The Science of Education and Psychology of the Child*, London, Longman.

SHAYER, M. and ADEY, P. (1981) *Towards a Science of Science Teaching*, London, Heinemann.

SLAVIN, R. (1983) *Cooperative Learning*, New York, Longman.

WARING, R. (1979) *Social Pressures and Curriculum Innovation: A Study of the Nuffield Science Teaching Project*, London, Methuen.

Peter Kutnick

Discussion (Reporter: Guy Claxton)

It was agreed that we tended to underestimate the importance of interactions in small groups when investigating learning. Probably a mix of intense discussion within such groups and periods of quiet individual reflection are needed for optimal learning. Possibly our culture emphasized the individual component too much, but the evidence from cross-cultural studies was not clear cut, although group work was the norm in some countries. Concern was expressed that the proposed introduction of national attainment targets for British pupils will further emphasize the role of the individual pupil and ignore the potential for group work.

It was argued that Kutnick had been unfair in suggesting that the workers on the early Nuffield scheme were committed to a psychology of individualism. In fact, the thinking was essentially pragmatic, the combined intuition of a group of experienced teachers, with little basis in formal theories of learning.

It would be worthwhile for some empirical studies to be made of just what the interactions in school science groups are really like and how they contribute to learning.

10.3 Conceptual Demand of Science Courses and Social Class

Ana M. Domingos

Introduction and Objectives

The study[1] is within a line of research which aims at relating the underachievement in sciences with sociological factors. The central argument is that the new paradigm for science education emphasized the understanding and application of general scientific principles through the use of pedagogic theories emphasizing 'learning by discovery' and 'learning the structure of the subject'. Such new curricula and pedagogic theories, stressing the active involvement of the child in his/her acquisition, were expected to increase the understanding of all children at a *higher* level of scientific literacy.

Essentially, the new paradigms have their origin in psychology, more specifically in theories of child development (Piaget and Bruner) especially concerned with cognitive development and in theories of the ordering and teaching of subjects in school (Gagné). Both of these groups of theories abstract the child from his/her institutional and cultural context and the school/teacher from the social context regulating the processes of transmission and acquisition. My view is that the failure of the new paradigm to recognize the sociological context of learning in school may well have affected the success of this paradigm in improving the achievements of large numbers of pupils in school, more specifically of children of working-class backgrounds.

The study started with a broad problem arising out of the current underachievement in the science classrooms of secondary schools in Portugal. The questions addressed were related to the division between two groups of children with respect to achievement in sciences; a group constituted by those children who have high levels of success and another group constituted by those who show high levels of failure. Before I started my research I had been led to believe that the introduction of new methods and new contents in science education was at least partially accountable for this sharp division between two groups of children. Modern contents and methods in science teaching seemed to have pushed the 'brightest' children to a greater development of higher competencies and, although this kind of teaching fulfilled its goals, it appeared to do less for the 'less bright' children, who seemed to me to have fallen behind.

I initially believed that this failure was caused by the high level of conceptual demand entailed in the modern science teaching and based on Bernstein[2] I was led to believe that the working-class children who tended to be failures at school, failed within its present pedagogic regime because of the high level of abstraction entailed in modern science courses.

Based on Bernstein's theory and on the results of a pilot investigation[3], I devised a detailed empirical study in which I tried to unveil possible relations between social class and achievement in different types of competencies in the sciences. I aimed at understanding the complex of interrelations I felt existed behind children's underachievement in the sciences, and possibly in other school subjects. I extended the research to include the consideration of a number of other sociological factors besides the direct indicators of nominal social class (father and mother's educational qualifications and occupations). Thus, variables more associated with the family (gender, siblings, etc.) and more associated with the school (teacher, type and area of school, etc.) were introduced in the research.

The theoretical fundaments of the study are in Bernstein, his model of cultural reproduction through education having been used to interpret the results and to explore the possibilities of increasing the efficiency of pedagogic practice. The aim of this paper is to give a short account of *some* aspects of that study.

General Procedure and Sample

In essence, my research is composed of three interrelated investigations which I considered were essential if I was to obtain a globality in the results and their interpretation. In the main study I tried to find relations between the sociological variables and achievement in two types of competencies, those which require a low level of abstraction (A — Acquisition of Knowledge) and those which require a high level of abstraction (U — Use of Knowledge). This study was supplemented by two other studies, a second study in which I intended to characterize the pedagogic practice of the teacher and a third one which intended to establish patterns of achievement in A and U competencies.

The sample was constituted by 1300 pupils of middle and upper secondary school, eleven teachers and eight schools. The schools were located in big cities and in towns in the country, they were all comprehensive and had either a predominantly working-class population (referred as working-class schools) or a mixed class population (referred as middle-class schools). The teachers were all female.

For the main study the data were obtained through questionnaires to pupils and parents and through tests made by teachers[4] and in which A and U competencies were clearly distinguished.

The characterization of teachers' pedagogic practice was made in joint work with them, using materials developed by themselves and the researcher. It was mainly intended to determine their degree of conceptual demand and the ability to bring pupils to attain the level they had established to their courses. The measures I carried out were supplemented by more qualitative assessments.

For the establishment of patterns of achievement in different competencies, I started from the selection of a limited number of objectives to which a special attention was paid in the transmission-acquisition process. These patterns were used to appreciate the ability of the teacher to bring the pupils to achieve a given level, thus making the characterizing of the pedagogic practice more complete. They were also used to appreciate the results of a change in that practice.

Results and Interpretation

For the first search of predictive variables of pupils' achievement, the practice of using stepwise regression was followed.[5] The analyses showed the teacher as the most striking influence, followed by the parents' education and occupation, area and type of school, gender and repeating. It pointed out clearly the dominant influences of family and teacher/school. It also showed that the quantitative results for stepwise regression cannot be taken as definitely conclusive in a quantitative sense because of balancing influences among some variables. Using this form of analysis, the exact nature of the relationships between the different factors could not be pursued in the depth required. In order to obtain a more delicate understanding of the complexity of the interactions I proceeded with a different form of analyses[6] which entailed the use of both quantitative and qualitative forms of data study.

The results showed that the achievement in sciences is much lower in working-class pupils, both in middle and upper school, and that such difference is mainly due to a high differential achievement in U competencies. Thus, a course with a low level of conceptual demand will originate a reduced differential achievement and a course with a high level of conceptual demand will produce the opposite effect. This seems to confirm the initial hypothesis. However, the results also showed that the picture is much more complex.

Although I found a pattern of differential achievement related to social class for most teachers, such differential achievement is not equal to all of them and for some of them is even non-existent. On the other hand, I see that a teacher pedagogically very competent,[7] produces classes of pupils which exhibit a pattern of class regulated differential achievement. Thus, such differential achievement is difficult to attribute entirely to the lack of pedagogic competence of the teacher and may well be, in part, a function of the high level performances required by U competencies which perhaps working-class pupils are less likely to acquire under particular pedagogic regimes.

Ana M. Domingos

The conclusions I reached leaves some discrepant cases and differences between teachers' sub-samples of pupils to be explained. Many hypotheses can be put forward to explain the discrepancies and I am going to explore the likeliest ones on the basis of the date I possess. First I shall deal with each hypothesis separately, then I shall examine them together.

The Mediation of Gender

I was able to see[8] that differential achievement is related to gender: lower working-class girls attending working-class schools perform worse than boys of the same social class, especially in U competencies. I have also seen that when the sample is divided in two groups, boys and girls, the relationship between social class and differential achievement is much more marked and well defined for girls than boys. Thus, there are gender differences *within* social class position which affect girls' achievement within the working-class.

From this point of view I may think that that part of the comparative underachievement of the lowest social groups in working-class schools is more due to the underachievement of girls than to the underachievement of boys. If in such schools boys outnumber girls, differential achievement related to social class should be less evident. If girls outnumber boys differential achievement related to social class should be more evident, i.e., whenever the lower working-class is fundamentally represented by girls, differential achievement will tend to be greater. The more the lower working-class predominates in the school population the more that effect should be important.

The Mediation of Repetition

Trying to find whether or not the relation between repetition and achievement is influenced by a third variable, social class, I was able to see[9] that: (a) non-repeaters are in general better than repeaters especially in the case of U competencies; (b) for U competencies the pattern of differential achievement between different social groups is strongly marked for repeaters.

These findings are strong support for the hypothesis that there is a relation between social class, repetition and differential achievement.

The relative underachievement of the lowest social groups is more due to the underachievement of repeaters than to the underachievement of non-repeaters. If non-repeaters outnumber repeaters differential achievement related to social class will be less marked. However, if repeaters outnumber non-repeaters, differential achievement related to social class will be more marked, i.e., whenever the lowest social groups are mainly represented by repeaters differential achievement will tend to be the greatest. The more the lowest social groups predominate in the school population the more that effect will be evident.

In order for there to be an interrelation between social class, repetition and achievement then the school classes must contain representatives from both middle-class and working-class. Some teachers do not have the full social class range represented among their pupils and, as a consequence, although they have a high percentage of repeaters and a high proportion of low social class pupils, the social class/repetition/achievement relation does not hold for these teachers. On the basis of my argument I would expect the class/repetition/achievement effect to be most strongly marked for teachers who have a social hierarchy among their pupils and both a high percentage of repeaters and a high proportion of low social class pupils. The class/repetition/achievement effect should be least marked in the case of teachers who have a low percentage of repeaters and a high proportion of middle-class pupils.

The Mediation of the Teacher's Pedagogical Practice

I was able to see[10] that the teacher's pedagogical practice is strongly influenced by the social composition of the school: teachers in schools with a low social composition tend to lower their level of conceptual demand and therefore the level of abstraction elicited by their courses tends to be low.

From this, it can be deduced that the focus of transmission will be more directed to the pupils of the social class which predominates in the school. In such circumstances, where a relation exists between social class and achievement, a working-class child in a working-class school will tend to show higher achievement when compared to a middle-class child than if he/she were in a middle class school. Therefore, differential achievement between different social groups will tend to be greater in middle class schools.

The focus of transmission is likely to be more directed to the middle class pupil with teachers who have taught (or had usually taught) in middle class schools and more directed to the working-class pupil with teachers who have taught in working class schools.[11]

The above appears to indicate that part of the differential achievement in relation to social class can be due to the influence of this factor, in schools where a social class hierarchy exists among the pupils.

I must stress that the differential achievement between social groups due to the effect described above is directly related to the teacher's pedagogical practice but is indirectly related to the social class composition of the school.

The above appears to indicate that there is a complex interaction between social class, differential achievement, social composition of the school class and focus or orientation of the teacher's pedagogic practice.[12]

According to my conclusions, teachers with a high degree of conceptual demand will tend to sharpen the division between different groups of pupils. Thus, part of the differential achievement between social groups may be due to the influence of this factor, affecting teachers who were found to be in the category of high conceptual demand.

Ana M. Domingos

Differences in Differential Achievement

I have now considered a number of hypotheses and carried out a series of analyses to explore the reasons for the differences in achievement in the sub-samples of pupils.

Conclusion — Introduction of a Theoretical Model

The above shows that in accounting for social class effects upon differences in differential achievement, both the influences of family and teacher/school factors must be considered. Some variables are more closely associated with the influence of the family (gender, parents' occupation and education) some are more closely associated with the influence of the teacher/school (pedagogic practice, type of school, repetition) but all relate to both the family and the teacher/school. However, the crucial variable which produces differences in differential achievement appears to be, from this analysis of our data, the teacher.

The pedagogic practice of the teacher is strongly related to the school context where she teaches.[13] It is that social context which makes teachers develop courses with a low or a high level of abstraction to match what they consider (consciously or unconsciously) to be attributes of the school population they teach. A working-class school and/or a school in the country acts selectively on the conceptual level of the teaching so as to produce a reduced conceptual demand and focus of the pedagogic practice. This means that the achievement of some groups of pupils is dependent upon the context in which they are taught and/or the experience of the teacher. Although a superficial analysis may indicate that all pupils are equally affected by the lower level of teaching as all receive this kind of teaching, it is the working-class group of children which is most affected. They are the children who are less likely to develop competencies of a relatively high level of abstraction, because *both* sites of acquisition (family and school) are less likely to provide them with the opportunity to develop these kind of competencies. For middle-class children, the family will help them to a lesser or greater extent in the development of relatively high level abstract pedagogic competencies, whether or not the school carries out this function.

What was said above makes clear that when marked differential achievement between groups of children (social class, gender) does not exist at school in our study it is *not* because all children are achieving a high conceptual level of scientific understanding, but because they are *all* being provided with a low conceptual focus. I would argue that teachers who make a very low level of conceptual demand have failed to understand the sociological implications of the transmission-acquisition process they are promoting. Children who enter the school disadvantaged will leave it still more disadvantaged.

As has been seen, the causes which lie behind differential achievement in the sciences are of a very complex nature but the causes which we have explored are directly and indirectly related to social class, which acts directly in the family and indirectly in the school. To summarize I would say that between social class and achievement in the sciences lies the invisible regulation of the social context of the school class which acts selectively upon the conceptual focus of the teacher and upon the ability of the teacher to enable pupils to attain required levels.

Although teachers of higher competence and high conceptual demand increased, in general, the gap between two groups of children (in terms of social class, gender), both of them attained higher levels, including the most disadvantaged group. [14] On the other hand, the results of the study on patterns of achievement in different types of competencies,[15] and which correponded to an explicitness of sequencing rules and criteria and a weakening of pacing, suggested that differential achievement may decrease when there is a change in the pedagogic practice. It seems possible, therefore, that teachers with a good knowledge of psychology of education and methodology of the subject and who provide a structured teaching can introduce an improvement in learning, provided the teaching conditions allow for the use of such competencies and *provided* those teachers are aware of the implications of the sociological context of education in school.

I shall now try to develop a theoretical model, drawing on Bernstein, which allows, me to offer a more general interpretation of my findings. Figure 10.3.1 summarizes the main relations in this model.

Bernstein argues that the school requires an elaborated orientation to meanings where there is an indirect relation to a local material base, i.e. an orientation to universalistic meanings, independent of the context. However, the *realization* of these meanings is regulated by the classification and framing procedures of the school. Thus, from this point of view, the school requires of the pupil an orientation to its orders of meaning *and* an orientation to the contexts, contents and rhythms it creates for their realization in a given pedagogic practice.

Whereas the socialization of some children in the family allows them to acquire an elaborated orientation, some other children are limited to a restricted orientation, i.e. an orientation to context dependent particularistic meanings. Middle class children tend to be found in the first position and working class children, especially lower-working class children, are likely to be found in the second.

Bernstein argues that restricted orientations arise out of the forms of solidarity based upon a simple division of labour, whereas elaborated orientations are more likely to arise out of the forms of solidarity based upon a complex division of labour. From this point of view, class relations broadly distribute elaborated and restricted orientations, according to whether the conditions of work in which individuals find themselves approximate either to a simple or complex division of labour. Bernstein points out that restricted orientations may

Figure 10.3.1 Social class and pedagogic practice.

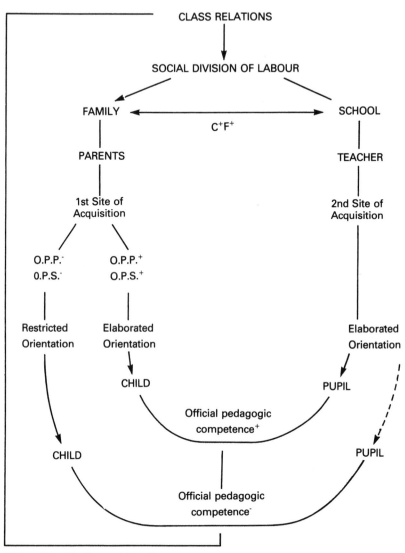

C F – Classification and Framing
O.P.P. – Official pedagogic practice
O.P.S. – Official pedagogic space
$^+$ strong; $^-$ weak
We have given only extreme positions; other variations are
likely to be found.

be transformed by work itself through the activity of agencies of defence, challenge, opposition, for example, trade unions, political parties.

It has been seen how there is little difference between the pupils with reference to the achievement of A competencies; the crucial differences arise out of differential acquisition of U competencies. The fact that working class children arrive at school without an elaborated orientation may explain their underachievement in the U competencies, because these are the competencies which require a high level of abstraction. It also explains why differential achievement is higher where the conceptual demand of the courses is higher. The fact that these pupils can be successful with teachers who make a low level of conceptual demand (teachers whose pedagogic practice is selectively focussed upon A competencies) does not mean that this kind of teaching requires a restricted orientation: the orientation of the school is always elaborated. Rather it means how *measured* achievement can give us a measure of memorised knowledge in A competencies and not necessarily an understanding of that knowledge, which would require and elaborated orientation.

How the school creates the contents, contexts and rhythms of elaborated orientations may well affect crucially those who acquire the modality of its elaborated codes.

If the school insulates itself strongly from the family, that is if there is a strong classification between the home and the school, then in the case of working-class families their practices, relations and orders of relevance and language variety are less likely to be seen as legitimate and encouraged by the school. In this case there is a double disadvantage entailed in the school's pedagogic practice. In the first place, the orientation to elaborated meanings required by the school may not be encouraged in the family and in the second place the contexts, contents and rhythms of the school are not related to the contexts, contents and rhythms of the family's local pedagogic practice.

It is true that a decontextualizing of knowledge and local practices acquired at home always, to some extent, occur at school to children of all social classes. The school selects, refocusses and abstracts from the knowledge and practices the child brings to it and this decontextualizing process is followed at the same time by a recontextualizing of the child into the official pedagogic practice of the school. Given that this practice is much nearer to the middle-class because the official pedagogic practice of the school is imbedded in, and perhaps dominates, their local pedagogic practice, then the twin processes of decontextualizing and recontextualizing will favour the middle-class child and place the working-class child under a crucial disadvantage. It is likely in Portugal, especially in the country, that working-class families are less likely to incorporate in their local pedagogic practice the official pedagogic practice and the specialized space it requires.

I saw that[16] pacing seems to be important for, when it is reduced, there is time available for explicating both the sequencing rules of learning and its criteria. This would seem to be necessary because the working-class children in my study, especially those in the country, are less prepared in their homes to meet the rules and orientation of the transmission regulating the teaching practice. A strongly paced transmission in the school requires a second site of pedagogic acquisition, i.e. the home.

That second site of acquisition, the home, must be capable of creating what I can call an official pedagogic space. The distinguishing features of this space depend upon the context of acquisition in the school. If this context requires silence, isolated learning, relatively context independent texts acquired in competitive relations with others there is good reason for believing that social class regulates the distribution of such contexts in the family.

I can distinguish families in terms of those who have imbedded in their practices an official pedagogic space from those families who do not create such a space. Such an official pedagogic space in the home creates the context of acquisition of the school's pedagogic performances. For example, if it is not possible to provide in the home a space for the child as *pupil*, that is a space where noise is excluded, which is isolated, where material conditions for learning exist, then acquisition is more difficult. In working-class homes such a space is less likely to be found. Indeed the presence of such an isolated space for solitary learning could well be antithetic to the more communal and supportive practices often found in such homes, especially in the country in Portugal. Furthermore, the independence of children often valued in these homes is not so much based upon the independence in the learning encouraged by the school but an independence of the parents so that the child can leave the parents free and assist both in the home and as a wage earner.

The school constitutes an individual called pupil; the family an individual called child. Pupil and child overlap in the middle-class. They are more likely to be sharply separated in the Portuguese working-class and a double-life, one at home and another different one at school may be created. There is in this case a strong classification between the two agencies of pedagogic transmission as boundaries and practices between them are sharp indeed. For the middle-class this classification is weaker.

The pedagogic competence of the individual is a result of a complex of interactions between the child who comes from the social institution called the family and the pupil who attends the social institution called school. Thus, for the working-class child, the official pedagogic competence will be less developed and for the middle-class child will be more developed. In fact, the school maintains and emphasizes the competencies brought into it by the middle-class children and *by omission* it also maintains and reinforces the competencies brought by working-class children. In other words, little is changed by the school; on contrary, differential reproduction is maintained and legitimised. In such conditions, each child follows separate ways under the same roof of the comprehensive mixed classes and mixed sex school.

This model is liable to be challenged because it appears to entail a deficit approach: working-class children lack the competencies middle-class children possess. In fact, according to this model, working-class children as we have defined this group in this study, relative to middle-class children, are more likely to lack the pedagogic competence to achieve *U* competencies *with respect to the pedagogic regime of the school*. However, because the working-class children in my sample perform differently than the middle-class children it does not mean they do not have the same potential to acquire the modality of the elaborated code demanded by the school. Indeed, it may well be that, if the modality of the school's elaborated code was changed (its classification and framing strengths) so that the contexts, contents and rhythms of the school's pedagogic practice had greater relevance to the contexts, contents and rhythms of the children's family and community culture, the acquisition of crucial *U* competencies would be facilitated. The pedagogic practice shown by the most competent teachers in this study and also the change in pedagogic practice occurred in the sub-study, on patterns of achievement in different types of competencies, support this suggestion. In fact, such practices correspond, in some aspects, to a new modality of code. To seek new forms of institutionalizing the elaborated code of the school, i.e. to develop a new modality of code seems to be a promising direction for future research.

Whilst it is indisputable that working-class children possess a valid competence and this competence should be respected and incorporated into the pedagogic practice of the school, it appears from our findings that working-class children do not have the same facility in acquiring the *U* competencies of science. The acquisition of these competencies, however, would not necessarily make the children middle-class in their cultural practice. Neither should the understanding of scientific concepts and principles, and the competence to use this knowledge in solving new problems and in understanding and criticizing the world, be a preserve of a socially selected few. Scientific literacy is a necessary condition for equal access to the discourse and decisions of power. To defend the culture of the working-class does not entail that the children should be deprived of scientific literacy nor that such literacy entails the adoption of what are considered to be middle-class values and practices and the loss of their own values and practices.

We can use the general form of our model to analyze differential gender achievement in the acquisition of *U* competencies. We suggest that, as in the total school population working-class pupils are disadvantaged as compared to middle-class pupils, so *some* girls are disadvantaged compared to boys. These are the girls from families where different patterns of male and female behaviour are expected and which, in Portugal, occur mainly in working-class families in the country. In Portugal, the school, its ethos and teachers do not have a bias against girls. I argued[17] that the difference in achievement arises from gender differences in the upbringing of the children so that boys and girls are socialized into different values, aspirations, practices and competencies. In Portugal, this occurs mainly in the working-class in the country, where very strong patriarchal values and practices dominate the family, and it is in the country that differential gender achievements are to be found in my research. Clearly in societies where the school holds different expectations, attitudes for boys and for girls and where the curriculum offers the possibility of gender

Ana M. Domingos

differentiated subjects, then we would expect a compounding of school and family influences to produce differential achievement in science.

If I had to sum up and point to the major issue raised by my argument, it would be the following. At the moment, the curriculum and padagogic practice in science education in Portuguese secondary schools through the direct and indirect effect of social class is producing a stratification of knowledge broadly parallel to the hierarchy of social class. On the whole, working-class children particularly lower-working class are restricted to a level of understanding of science which denies to these pupils what is available to the middle-class children: the ability to understand, develop and apply the principles of science. We could consider that A competencies represent the vocabulary of science, whereas U competencies represent the syntax. From this point of view, working-class children are acquiring the vocabulary without the syntax. In a sense, it may even be the case that working-class pupils are over-socialized into A competencies and under-socialized into U competencies by the school. And this has many implications. Working-class pupils are confined within a very limited conception of science, science as definitions, elementary procedural rules, rather the science as an imaginative exploration and explanation of the physical world. From this point of view they are likely to be cut off from the power of its discourse. I can say that, from this perspective, the school is institutionalizing inequalities in the acquisition of the power of discourse. However, from another point of view, particularly in developing societies such as Portugal, working-class pupils have unequal access not only to the power of discourse but also unequal access to the discourses of power and their dominant agencies and practices in society.

Notes

1   See Domingos (1984) for a complete description of the study.
2   For Bernstein's theory see, for example, Bernstein (1977, 1981 and 1985); and Domingos *et al*, (1986).
3   Domingos (1984) *op. cit.*, p 55.
4   *Ibid*, see sample of tests in appendix IV.
5   *Ibid*, see a full description of the stepwise regression treatment in chapter 5 on 'Quantitative analysis of sociological variables and achievement'.
6   *Ibid*, see chapters 6 and 7 on 'Gender and achievement' and 'Social class and achievement'.
7   *Ibid*, see chapter 4 on 'Teacher's pedagogic practice.'
8   *Ibid*, see chapter 6 'Gender and achievement'.
9   *Ibid*, see chapter 7 on 'Social class and achievement'.
10 *Ibid*, see chapter 4 on 'Teacher's pedagogic practice'.
11 *Ibid*.
12 *Ibid*, see chapters 4, 6 and 7, on 'Teacher's pedagogic practice,' 'Gender and achievement' and 'Social class and achievement'.
13 *Ibid*, see chapter 4 on 'Teacher's pedagogic practice'.
14 *Ibid*, see chapters 4, 6 and 7 on 'Teacher's pedagogic practice', 'Gender and achievement' and 'Social class and achievement'.

15   *Ibid*, see chapter 3.
16   *Ibid*, see chapters 6 and 7.
17   *Ibid*, see chapter 6.

References

BERNSTEIN, B. (1977) *Class, Codes and Control, Vol. 3 — Towards a Theory of Educational Transmissions*, London, Routledge and Kegan Paul.

BERNSTEIN, B. (1981) 'Codes, modalities and the process of cultural reproduction: A model', *Language in Society*, 10.

BERNSTEIN, B. (1985) 'On pedagogic discourse' in RICHARDSON, J. (Ed.) *Handbook of Theory and Research in the Sociology of Education*, New York, Greenwood Press.

DOMINGOS, A.M. (1984) 'Social class, pedagogic practice and a achievement in science: A study of secondary schools in Portugal', PhD Thesis, University of London, published in CORE (1987) *Collected Original Resources in Education*, 11, 2, Birmingham, Carfax Publishing Co.

DOMINGOS, A.M., BARRADAS, H., RAINHA, H. and NEVES, I. (1986) *A Teoria de Bernstein em Sociologia da Educacao*, Lisbon, Fundacao Gulbenkian.

11   *Models in Action*

Philip Adey

Three papers are presented in this chapter in which particular ideas about the way that children's cognition develops are used as the bases for teaching strategies. The application of learning theories derived from psychological models to teaching in schools may seem, at first sight, to offer the chance of two important outcomes: the validation of the learning theory (and by extension support for the psychological model) and, simply, more effective learning in schools. In the opinion of some, including some contributors to the present work, such studies are based naively on a model of science which even physical scientists do not, in practice, follow — namely the building of theoretical models based on experience and observation, the use of these models to make predictions ('*if this* is how children's thinking develops, then *this* technique should promote such thinking') and the testing of those predictions in the classroom. For those who consider such approaches to the improvement of learning to be fundamentally flawed, the fact that the outcomes of such studies are often less than clear-cut or seem to offer a variety of distinct (and sometimes mutually contradictory) True Paths to learning is not surprising.

But those who do believe that there is something to be gained from measuring cognitive outcomes, from valuing those measurements, and from investigating and tinkering with classroom variables antecedent to the measurement, should not be too disappointed that no single True Path emerges. Even the most fervent and hard-nosed 'scientific' investigator of education is well aware of the multiplicity of variables that cannot be controlled and whose values therefore must be assumed to be randomly distributed in experimental and control groups. Although the quality of personal interactions between teacher and pupils must rank high on any list of imponderables, none of the authors in this chapter consider that such personality efffects could be so important that the development of certain teaching techniques becomes redundant. Put crudely, both a naturally charismatic teacher and a naturally pedestrian teacher may improve the learning of their own pupils by employing techniques based on an understanding of how children learn, most especially if the teacher herself has some appreciation of that learning theory and applies it with comprehension.

Novak's 'techniques' are based on developing children's metacognitive strategies. Those of Adey *et al* include metacognition but place greater emphasis on cognitive conflict. Psillos *et al* focus on exposing pupils to the same general concepts in a variety of contexts and at different levels of complexity. All claim that their techniques lead to significant improvements in learning, and Novak and Adey at least believe that the improvement is to general thinking skills. Only the years ahead will provide evidence of what parts and combinations of parts of these and many other techniques can be developed to improve learning reliably (and humanly).

11.1 The Use of Metacognitive Tools to Facilitate Meaningful Learning

Joseph D. Novak

Two key ideas are discussed in this paper: (i) metacognitive tools, i.e., tools to help students learn about learning and learn about knowledge; and (ii) facilitation of meaningful learning, i.e., helping students to move from rote, limited learning approaches to approaches that build on experience and prior knowledge and *change the meaning* of experience.

In our work we have drawn heavily on Ausubel's (1963, 1968 and 1978) assimilation theory of meaningful cognitive learning, but also considered the important work of Jean Piaget, George Kelly (1955) and more recent work in cognitive psychology. We have also used ideas from contemporary philosophy including the work of Kuhn (1962), Toulmin (1972), Brown (1979) and Gowin (1981). An early effort was made to synthesize ideas from cognitive learning theory, philosophy and curriculum into a comprehensive theory of education (Novak, 1977). Currently I am working on a major revision of this book, including more emphasis on metacognitive tools and the role that feelings play in learning. The learning theories we have been using all emphasize the idea that each person *constructs* his/her own representations of the world and these representations collectively determine the meaning of events or objects the person deals with. Language codes much of this representation in the form of concept labels and propositions and this acquired concept/propositional structure is the cognitive organization that determines the meaning of experience for the person. We define a concept as a *perceived regularity* in events or objects designated by a label (usually a word). Two or more concepts linked together semantically form statements about how some piece of world appears or behaves. The philosophies and epistemologies we have been using all emphasize that knowledge is a human construction and that knowledge evolves across cultures and over time in an endless succession of conceptual change. These *constructivist* views of both learning and epistemology are necessary and highly complementary ideas to understand how humans construct and change their meanings of experiences, or the perceived regularities and relationships they experience.

Feelings also play an important role in both choice of experiences and in the meanings of experiences. In our view, humans usually seek a positive, constructive interaction between thinking, feeling and action. We prefer to use the label act or action, rather than behaviour, since most humans use thought and feeling to guide their actions most of the time. They rarely behave 'instinctively' or passively, as is the case for much other animal behaviour studied by ethologists or psychologists.

Our early research studies on children's learning relied heavily on the use of modified Piagetian clinical interviews. We used this methodology to try to identify what relevant concept meanings children held before instruction and how these meanings changed during and after instruction. The challenge of trying to interpret changes in the learner's concept/propositional frameworks from interviews led us in time to evolve a tool we call a concept map. This is a hierarchical representation of the concepts and propositions a learner has as they relate to the events or objects discussed in the interview. Figure 11.1.1 shows two concept maps drawn from interviews with Phil in grade two and ten years later. Figure 11.2.2 shows a concept map constructed on a computer to show the key concepts and propositions that underlie what I label as 'human constructivism'. These ideas are central to our current work on the refinement of procedures to use metacognitive tools to facilitate meaningful learning.

Concept maps help teachers to organize subject matter for instruction and they help students to see the concept/propositional framework of a unit of study. My colleague, Bob Gowin, invented in 1977 another metacognitive tool that we have found useful, especially as regards epistemology and our efforts to help students understand the structure of knowledge and the process of knowledge construction. Figure 11.1.3 shows the Vee diagram and the 'epistemic elements' that all function together to form new knowledge or to characterize the *structure* of knowledge dealing with some piece of the world. Figure 11.1.4 shows an example of a Vee diagram constructed by a seventh grade (12-year-old) student in one of our projects.

We have now completed about two dozen studies using concept mapping and/or Vee diagrams as metacognitive tools. A brief discussion of key findings from some of these studies follows.

Using concept maps with college students in a remedial math course for college freshman, Cardemone (1975) and later Minemier (1983) found that students using concept maps not only performed better on problem solving tests but also gained increased confidence in their ability to do mathematics. Futai'a (1986) found that secondary school students in American Samoa not only performed better on typical math achievement test, but they were also highly superior on their ability to do novel math problems, after instruction with concept maps and Vee diagrams. Mathematics is one of the most 'conceptually opaque' subjects taught in schools (dance and music are similar), and from our perspective it is not surprising that many students find maths distasteful and remember almost nothing functional a few months after a course. Most students see no alternative to rote learning of theorems or

Figure 11.1.1   *Two concept maps drawn from interviews with a student (Phil) in grade 2 (top) and grade 12 (bottom). Note that even after junior high school science, biology, physics and chemistry, Phil has not integrated concepts of atoms and molecules with states of matter nor corrected his misconception that sugar or smell molecules are 'in' water molecules.*

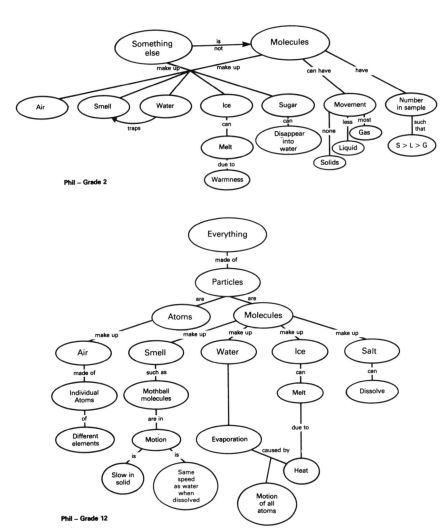

*Figure 11.1.2   A concept map showing the key concepts and propositions that I see
as underlying human constructivism (see Novak, 1987). Over time my
concepts and concept relationship will modify and my views on
constructivism will change — at least to some extent.*

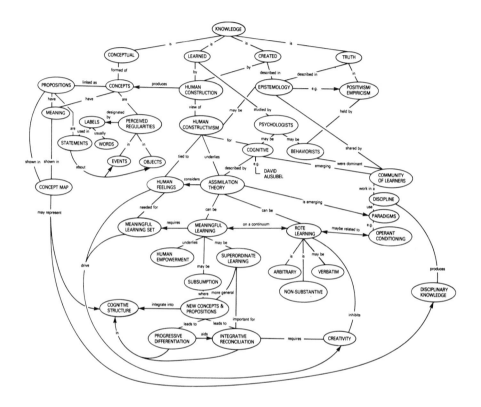

Figure 11.1.3   The Vee diagram showing epistemic elements as used in our computer programs with college biology students

FOCUS QUESTIONS

DEFINITION: The focus question asks specifically what you want to determine.
It guides the inquiry. A focus question emphasizes a particular aspect concerning the events or objects in the investigation.
CONSIDER: What do you want to determine by conducting this study?
TUTORIAL EXAMPLES: A) What is the relationship between the angles before and after the bounce? B) Is there a fixed change in speed after each bounce?

PHILOSOPHY

DEFINITION: Philosophy is a statement that reflects a world view. It is larger in scope than a theory.
CONSIDER: How does this study fit into a world view?
TUTORIAL EXAMPLES: A) and B) knowledge construction

THEORIES

DEFINITION: A theory is an explanation of the relationships between concepts. It also organizes concepts and principles to describe events and make claims about them. A theory is broader and more inclusive than principles.
CONSIDER: WHY do the events and objects appear and behave in the way they do? Is there a relationship between the principles?
TUTORIAL EXAMPLES: A) conservation of momentum
B) conservation of energy

PRINCIPLES

DEFINITION: A principle is a conceptual rule that indicates significant relationships between two or more concepts. It answers how events or objects appear or behave. A principle comes from knowledge claims produced over time.
CONSIDER: HOW do the events and objects appear or behave? What is the relationship between the concepts?
TUTORIAL EXAMPLES: A) and B) Newtonian Mechanics

CONCEPTS

DEFINITION: A concept is a word or a symbol which stands for regularities in an event or an object. It may also bring to mind specific characteristics of the object or event. Concepts are neither right or wrong, but are intended to be useful as a guide in the investigation.
CONSIDER: What are some characteristics of the objects and events? What terminology do you need to understand?
TUTORIAL EXAMPLES: A) angle, change, equal, reflection, incidence, path, incoming, outgoing, normal
B) motion, energy, conservation, velocity, speed, collision, incoming, compression, outgoing, bounce, momentum

VALUE CLAIMS

DEFINITION: A value claim states the worth of the knowledge claims produced during the investigation.
CONSIDER: Does the investigation make sense? Does it have worth to your understanding of the field?
TUTORIAL EXAMPLES: A) Relationships between angles is important to billiard players. B) Knowledge of the momentum lost during a collision is important to a shuffle board player.

KNOWLEDGE CLAIMS

DEFINITION: A knowledge claim is a conclusion derived from the study. It is based on the transformations of the observations and linked to the concepts, principles, and theory guiding the investigation.
CONSIDER: What is your interpretation of the results of this study? What is your answer to the focus question?
TUTORIAL EXAMPLES: A) angle in = angle out
B) speed in = .9 x speed out

TRANSFORMATIONS

DEFINITION: A transformation is the organization of observations made in the record. This can be done by various techniques such as summarizing, creating tables, calculating, graphing, and doing statistical tests.
CONSIDER: How can you organize and/or analyze the observations made in the records?
TUTORIAL EXAMPLES: A) and B) table and graph

RECORDS

DEFINITION: A record is a compilation of raw data, which can be descriptive or quantitative. It is an account of the events and objects – the results of testing and sampling.
CONSIDER: What observations can you make that may lead to an answer to the focus question?
TUTORIAL EXAMPLES: A) measure the angles of the bounces
B) determine the speed of the ball

EVENTS & OBJECTS

DEFINITION: An event is a thing that happens or can be made to happen. An object is a thing that exists and can be observed.
CONSIDER: What equipment, organisms or other objects do you need to answer the focus question? What can you do with these objects to facilitate an answer?
TUTORIAL EXAMPLES: A) and B) ball bouncing against a wall

Joseph D. Novak

Figure 11.1.4 An example of a Vee diagram prepared in a class discussion with seventh grade biology students. The Vee heuristic can help students to understand the constructed nature of knowledge and to take charge of their own meaning making in science or math activities.

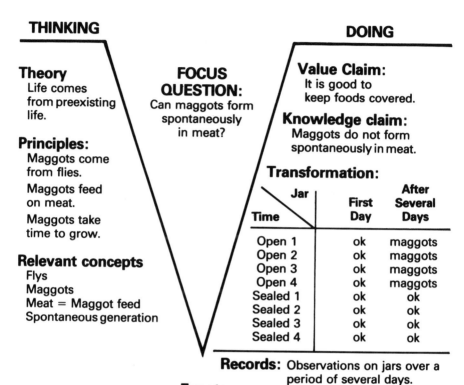

THINKING   **DOING**

Theory
Life comes
from preexisting
life.

FOCUS QUESTION:
Can maggots form
spontaneously
in meat?

Value Claim:
It is good to
keep foods covered.

Knowledge claim:
Maggots do not form
spontaneously in meat.

Principles:
Maggots come
from flies.
Maggots feed
on meat.
Maggots take
time to grow.

Transformation:

Time	Jar	First Day	After Several Days
Open 1		ok	maggots
Open 2		ok	maggots
Open 3		ok	maggots
Open 4		ok	maggots
Sealed 1		ok	ok
Sealed 2		ok	ok
Sealed 3		ok	ok
Sealed 4		ok	ok

Relevant concepts
Flys
Maggots
Meat = Maggot feed
Spontaneous generation

Records: Observations on jars over a
period of several days.

Events:
8 jars prepared –
4 with meat – sealed
4 with meat – open
All exposed to flies

algorithmic procedures, with no associated conceptual understanding. In fact, most school maths teachers (and many university maths professors) see mathematics as 'meaningless' and aconceptual; to them, maths is only procedures for solving problems that lead to *the* correct answer. They are neither psychological nor epistemological constructivists (Volmink, 1983).

In the sciences, our early studies were with college students using concept mapping and later, Vee diagramming. Bogen (1977) found that instructor-prepared concept maps for college genetics were of little value (and vociferously disliked by many students), but those students who tried to use the maps, and made some of their own modifications found them helpful. The maps proved to be useful to the instructors for planning exam questions. The maps prepared by Bogen did not show 'linking words' on the lines joining concepts, and this proved to be confusing to students (and to other geneticists). We learned in this study that to be helpful, students must construct their own concept maps. They must also be careful and explicit in 'labelling the lines' between concepts. Furthermore, we recognized the importance of seeking maps with good 'conceptual hierarchy', and avoiding the tendency to construct 'flow charts' that showed sequences of events rather than superordinate-subordinate relationships between concepts (see Novak and Gowin, 1984.)

Most of my Cornell University class teaching has used concept maps and Vee diagrams both for instruction and for evaluation from 1976 to date. My students have remarked repeatedly that they wished they had learned to use these tools earlier, so we began experimental work with elementary and junior high school students in the late 1970s. We found that there was almost an inverse correlation between years of school and ease of learning how to construct good concept maps. Most junior high school students (age 12–16) seemed to gain facility in concept mapping and Vee diagramming in a matter of weeks.

In a study with seventh and eighth grade students (ages 12–15), we found (i) seventh grade students were as good or better than eighth grade students in acquiring competence in the use of the strategies; (ii) most student found Vee diagram construction 'easier' than concept mapping, partly because a scaffold-like structure was already present; (iii) there was little correlation between concept map scores and ordinary class test performance, but significant ($r = .53$) correlation with the latter and Vee map scores; (iv) zero correlation with concept map scores and Scholastic Aptitude Test score ($r = \pm 0.02$); (v) concept map and Vee diagramming performance continued to improve over the school year; (vi) highly significant differences favouring concept mapping students on novel problem solving task (Novak, Gowin and Johnson, 1983.)

'Laine Gurley (1982) working with high school biology students using concept maps and Vee diagrams found that students were 90–95 per cent 'on task' in laboratory work, compared with 40–45 per cent 'on task' for students not using these strategies. Moreover, students reported being very conscious of their own responsibility for learning, and also of the long-term value of meaningful learning over rote learning which was their ordinary pattern. One of the common complaints of students asked to concept map text chapters was that 'you have to *read* the chapter carefully, sometimes two or three times' whereas ordinary instruction answering end-of-chapter questions seldom required more than copying down definitions of bold-faced words in the chapter or referring to listed details.

Our most recent research at the Environmental High School at Sede Boker, Israel, has shown very positive results using concept mapping and Vee diagramming techniques with sixty-three grade 11 students (16–18 years) in conjunction with a short course on 'learning how to learn' (Bar-Lavie, 1987). The eight lesson (45 minutes each) instructional unit on 'learning how to learn' emphasized the differences between rote and meaningful learning and the necessity for the learner to take responsibility for his/her own learning. All students at Sede Boker participate in Eco-Field-Shop courses that included one week of study while living in twelve selected environments. All subject matter areas coordinate instruction with the forthcoming Eco-Field-Shop and do follow-up studies as well. Bar-Lavie compared performance on achievement tests for a class taking the course in 1985 (N = 55) with a class taking the course in 1986 (N = 63). The latter group received instruction in Learning How to Learn (LHTL). In general, the 1985 class had performed better on classroom tests and in field work than the 1986 class. This was also true at the beginning of the Eilat study and is shown in figure 11.1.5 where the non LHTL group had significantly lower achievement scores on class exams prior to and after the study unit. However, on the basis of other evaluation criteria, the reverse difference was observed, with the largest difference favoring the LHTL group on the staff evaluation of group project reports after the Eilat field study.

Bar-Lavie also compared performance of a group classified as 'meaningful learners' (N = 4) with a group classified as 'rote learners' (N = 11) in the 1986 group all of whom received the LHTL course. This points up the fact that a short (eight-lesson) LHTL course will not result in changing the learning approach of all students who have been using predominately rote learning for ten years of schooling. Figure 11.1.6 shows that there was little difference between rote and meaningful learners on class exam scores, but significant differences in the quality of their concept maps prepared just before the Eilat study. Using data from interviews and video tapes of class activities, Bar-Lavie also rated each student on the extent of their positive or negative feelings prior to, just after and one year follwing the Eilat Eco-Field-Shop. Figure 11.1.7 shows that meaningful learners were significantly more positive in their attitudes prior to and one year after the Eilat study than were rote mode learners. On the basis of both the quality of their concept maps and the extent of their postive feelings toward study, meaningful learners clearly were better demonstrating achievement of truly important educational objectives.

Over the past decade using concept maps and Vee diagrams with my graduate students and undergraduates enrolled in a Learning to Learn course, I have observed the excitement and empowerment that comes to students who move from predominantly rote learning patterns to highly meaningful learning

Figure 11.1.5   Differences in 'Objective' Exam Scores and· staff ratings among the Learning How to Learn Group and the Non-LHTL·Groups before, during and after study of the Eilat-Eco-Field-Shop

Source: Bar-Lavie (1987).

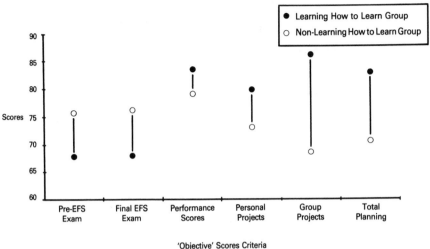

patterns. I have also seen that this transition may take one to four years and requires a very explicit desire on the part of the student to achieve this transition. Metacognitive tools are helpful, but they are neither a 'sure cure' nor a 'quick fix'.

Probably the most difficult learning task any human faces is the acquisition of language (English, Hebrew or any other). All non-brain damaged children are highly successful at this by age 3! Why then do we see much learning failure in school? In my view, this is due primarily to maleducative practices that rely on and reward rote memorization, and often penalize more creative meaningful learning manifestations. By grade six or seven, we already face a formidable task as educators to help students return to the more powerful, ego-enhancing meaningful learning strategies they used to acquire spoken language. The best solution would be to change school practices so that these problems would not arise in the first place. Metacognitive tools could be helpful. Concept mapping and Vee diagramming has been used successfully with primary grade children (Alvarez and Risco, 1987). I find that teaching six year olds how to make concept maps is far easier than teaching college students or professors to map. And young children enjoy making maps much more than most of the drill and practice activities required in schools. Use of metacognitive tools should (and I predict will) become a standard practice in schooling. Children also need early instruction in learning how better to learn meaningfully.

The problems adolescents face in their rapid hormonal and body changes,

Joseph D. Novak

Figure 11.1.6   Differences of 'Objective' Exam Scores Between Meaningful and
            Rote Learners at Sede Boker.
Source: Bar-Lavie (1987).

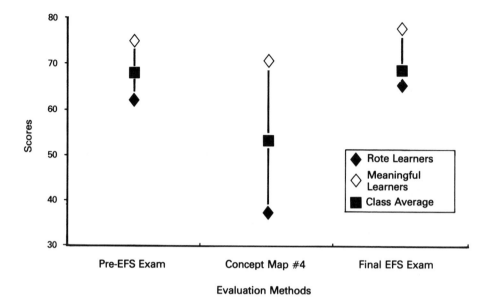

peer pressures, and their search for personal identity and emancipation from their parents are not only exacerbated by drugs, divorce and other social factors but also by school practices that emphasize or require disempowering rote learning approaches. In sciences and especially mathematics, the result is that too many students, expecially females, move away from studies in these areas. As educators there is very little we can do to change the negative social forces impacting on adolescent students, and even less to mollify the effects of physiological changes. We can, however, help them to understand better how their minds work and the positive feelings and empowerment that can come with successful meaningful learning. At Sede Boker, Bar-Lavie and his colleagues are moving to establish the only school I know of where commitment to meaningful learning practices and instruction in learning will characterize all classes for the entire grade 9–12 school experience. It should be interesting to observe the results.

*Figure 11.1.7   Percentages of Positive Thinking-Feeling-Acting Among Meaningful
and Rote Learners During the Study.*
Source: Bar-Lavie (1987).

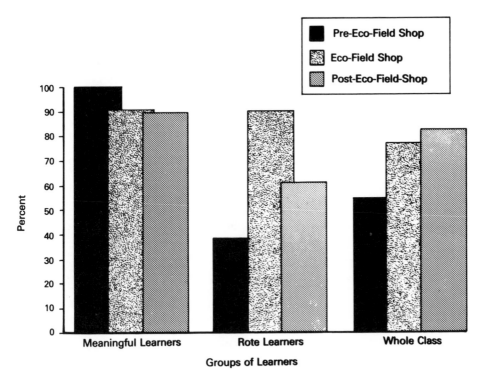

References

ALVAREZ, M.C. and RISKO, V.J. (1987) 'Concept maps and vee diagrams: A visual
representation of children's thinking', paper presented at the annual meeting of the
American Educational Research Association, Washington, DC, April.

AUSUBEL, D.P. (1963) *The Psychology of Meaningful Verbal Learning*, New York, Grune
and Stratton.

AUSUBEL, D.P. (1968) *Educational Psychology: A Cognitive View*, New York, Holt,
Rinehart and Winston.

AUSUBEL, D.P., NOVAK J.D. and HANESIAN H. (1978) *Educational Psychology: A
Cognitive View* (2nd ed.), New York, Holt, Rinehart and Winston, reprinted in 1986
by Warbel and Peck.

BAR-LAVIE, B. (1987) 'Enhancing meaningful learning in an environmental education
program: A case study of a class empowered through the use of Novak's and
Gowin's *Principles of Learning How to Learn, Concept Mapping, Interviewing,
and Educating*', unpublished PhD thesis, Ithaca, NY, Cornell University.

Joseph D. Novak

Bogen, C.A. (1977) 'The use of concept mapping as a possible strategy for instructional design and evaluation in college genetics', unpublished Master's thesis, Ithaca, NY, Cornell University.

Brown, H.I. (1979) *Perception, Theory and Commitment: The New Philosophy of Science.* Chicago, 1L, University of Chicago Press.

Cardemone, P.F. (1975) 'Concept mapping: A technique of analyzing a discipline and its use in the curriculum and instruction in a portion of a college level mathematics skills course', unpublished Master's thesis, Ithaca, NY, Cornell University.

Futai'a, K. (1986) 'Use of vee maps and concept maps in the learning of form five mathematics in Samoa College, Western Samoa', unpublished Master's thesis, Ithaca, NY, Cornell University.

Gowin, D. (1981) *Educating*, Ithaca, NY, Cornell University Press.

Gurley, L.I. (1982) 'Use of Gowin's vee and concept mapping strategies to teach responsibility for learning in high school biological sciences', unpublished PhD thesis, Ithaca, NY, Cornell University.

Kelly, G. (1955) *The Psychology of Personal Constructs*, New York, Norton and Company.

Kuhn, T.S. (1962) 'The Structure of Scientific Revolutions', *International Encyclopedia of Unified Sciences* (2nd ed.) Chicago, 1L, University of Chicago Press.

Minemier, L. (1983) 'Concept mapping: An educational tool and its use in a college level mathematics skills course', unpublished Master's thesis, Ithaca, NY, Cornell University.

Novak, J.D. (1977) *A Theory of Education*, Ithaca, NY, Cornell University Press.

Novak, J.D. (1987) 'Human constructivism: Toward a unity of psychological and epistemological meaning making' in Novak, J.D. (Ed.), *Proceedings of the Second International Seminar on Misconceptions and Educational Strategies in Science and Mathematics Education*, Ithaca, NY, Department of Education, Cornell University.

Novak, J.D. and Gowin, D.B. (1984) *Learning How to Learn*, New York, Cambridge University Press.

Novak, J.D., Gowin, D.B. and Johnsen, G.T. (1983) 'The use of concept mapping and knowledge vee mapping with junior high school science students', *Science Education*, 67, 5.

Toulmin, S. (1972) *Human Understanding, Vol. I: The Collective Use and Evolution of Concepts*, Princeton, NJ, Princeton University Press.

Volmink, J. (1983) 'Meaning in mathematics: On integrating thinking, feeling and acting in a first-year calculus course', unpublished Master's thesis, Ithaca, NY, Cornell University.

Discussion (Reporter: Charles Ryan)

The definition of 'concept' presented in the paper was questioned. Novak considered that the important word for him in the definition was 'perceived', rather than the relationship of observation to concept.

The differential performance of tasks by boys and girls and the relationship to rote and meaningful learning was discussed. Novak showed data indicating that girls performed better on metacognitive tasks, but he argued that they were unable to convert this into better science ability scores. School testing, after all, tests only about 15 per cent of human aptitudes.

Had a way been found to investigate the affective dimension, which had been claimed as an important part of the procedure? Initially, test scores often went down, and this hurt the pupils and persuaded some teachers to abandon the strategy. Where rote learning is the norm, some peer pressure is inevitable. The majority who persevered found scores following a J curve, and there was evidence of increased motivation although no strategies were yet articulated for harnessing this motivation. In Novak's reworking of his education theory, the basis would be that humans seek to integrate thinking, feeling, and acting. Rote learning leads to disintegration and disempowering whereas meaningful learning leads to integration.

11.2 Cognitive Acceleration: The Effects of Two Years of Intervention in Science Classes

Philip Adey, Michael Shayer and Carolyn Yates

Introduction

Our intention was to investigating the extent to which the development of thinking in average secondary school children could be accelerated. Only a limited amount of special treatment was to be delivered, by the classes' normal science teachers in the context of the science curriculum. Specifically, we were concerned to investigate possible conditions under which the onset of formal operational thinking could be brought forward as compared with the known norms of the English school population (Shayer and Adey 1981).

Subjects

Three types of school were included in the experiment:

I *The Laboratory School.*
An ordinary secondary school in which the project staff taught the intervention lessons to two classes over a period of eighteen months. The purposes were (a) to try out new material; and (b) to investigate what effect could be achieved by teachers who fully comprehended the model underlying the interventions.

II *The Main Experiment Schools.*
Nine schools were selected to participate in the project. Although the headteachers and heads of science agreed to participate, they were not volunteers. The schools included inner city, suburban, and rural schools. All were mixed-sex. Experimental and control groups were chosen from 12 + and 11 + age groups.

III *Third Year Schools.*
Another six schools used intervention lessons for one year only. The

teachers were volunteers, who had heard of the project and asked to
be allowed to participate.

Controls

In each school control classes were chosen that were supposed to be parallel in
ability to the experimental classes, and who normally received the same science
curriculum. Two types of control class were identified. *Control 1* classes were
taught science by the same teacher who was using the CASE material with the
experimental classes. *Control 2* classes were taught by a different teacher.

The Interventions

Intervention lessons were designed around the following schema of formal
operations: Control and exclusion of variables, ratio and proportionality,
equilibrium, compensation, combinatorial thinking, correlation, probability,
compound variables, and conservation involving formal modelling. However,
no attempt was made to teach the use of these schema in a direct way.

The strategy of the intervention lessons was based on the experience of
many workers in the field of cognitive acceleration. In particular, Kuhn and
Angelev (1976) and Rosenthal (1979) have shown that it is possible to obtain
general transfer from the schema involved in training tasks to the development
of schema which have not been part of the training schedule. Their methodology has in common the initial concentration on the terminology required, used
in entirely concrete contexts. Once familiar with terms such as *variables, values
of variables*, and *relationships between variables*, pupils are given practical
problems which require the use of the formal schema for their solution. There is
no attempt to teach, for instance, 'rules for controlling variables'. Rather, the
pupil is put in the position where she has to construct the schema for herself in
order to solve a practical problem. For example, a set of tubes of different
length, thickness, and material are provided, and the pupil has to decide which
variables effect the note produced when they blow across the tube. Feedback
from the problem, organized by the teacher, shows the pupil the extent to
which she is being successful in reaching a solution. In this example, a pupil
who says 'the note depends on length' is asked to show how he knows. He may
demonstrate with two tubes of different length and different thickness. The
teacher probes what this says about thickness. Even if the pupil does not see
that variables have been confounded, he does see that there is some problem
with his conclusion. This is the cognitive conflict with which he may be left, but
which it is supposed 'loosens' an existing cognitive structure, making it more
amenable to restructuring at a higher level on another occasion.

Another aspect of the intervention strategy is that each schema is related
to examples from the regular science curriculum. In the science curriculum,
reference is made to experiences from the intervention lessons. This 'bridging'
back and forth is hypothesized to be necessary for the generalization of the
development of formal schema.

Philip Adey, Michael Shayer and Carolyn Yates

Materials and In-service

Project teachers received the intervention lessons in the form of teachers' notes and pupils' worksheets and problems. Once per term all teachers would come to a meeting at the project centre where they were introduced to the activities and to some of the underlying theory. Teachers provided feedback on their experiences so far. As the project progressed teachers played an increasingly participatory role, providing their own suggestions for new activities and for bridging from the interventions to the regular science curriculum.

Each school was visited by project staff at least once per term, when lessons were observed and discussed with the teacher.

Tests

Testing occasions for experimental and control groups were planned as follows:

Pretests, before any intervention lessons were given;
Midtests after approximately one year of intervention with the experimental group;
Post tests after approximately two years of intervention with the experimental group;
Delayed post tests, one year after the post tests and one year after intervention lessons with the experimental group had ceased.

Third year schools had no mid-test and received the post-test after one year.

The main test instruments used were Piagetian Reasoning Tasks (PRT). These are demonstrated group tests of cognitive development whose development and validation have been reported elsewhere (Shayer, Adey and Wylam, 1981). PRTs yield a score which may be interpreted in terms of levels of development, from early concrete (2A) = 3 to late formal (3B) = 9.

In addition to the PRTs, post test batteries in main experiment and third year schools included a common science achievement test designed in co-operation with the project teachers. Wherever available, results of whatever science tests were given in each school were collected for experimental and control groups.

Results

At this stage (September 1987), results are available only from the Piagetian Reasoning Tasks, from the laboratory school (including delayed post tests) and from the main experiment schools (not including delayed post tests).

Laboratory School

Mean scores for experimental and control groups on pretests, mid tests, post tests and delayed post tests in the lab school are shown in table 11.2.1 and figure 11.2.1.

242

Table 11.2.1 Piagetian Reasoning Task pretest, mid-test, post-test, and delayed post-test scores and gains in lab school

Test	Date	Experimental				Control			
		N	mean	σ	gain	N	mean	σ	gain
Pre	12/84	29	5.89	0.55		19	6.46	0.36	
Mid	7/85	19	6.46	0.72	0.61**	18	6.72	0.56	0.23
Post	7/86	29	6.35	1.00	0.46*	19	6.26	0.87	−0.20
Del	7/87	29	7.01	1.20	1.13***	19	7.01	1.09	0.54*

signficance levels: * .05, ** .01, *** .001.
Gains of exp group pre-pos and pre-del > those of control at <.02 and <.05 significance levels respectively.

Figure 11.2.1

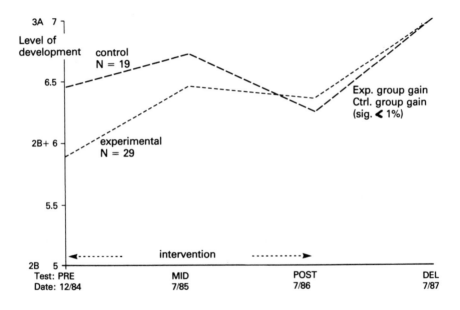

By the end of the intervention period the experimental group had experienced a significantly greater gain in levels of cognitive development than had the control group. What is more, in the subsequent year when there was no further intervention, the experimental group continued to develop at the same rate as the control group, so that their overall pretest to delayed post test gains were significantly greater than those of the control group. It appears that having being moved on to a faster developmental track, the experimental group continued on this track without further special treatment.

Main Experiment

There was no significant difference in scores or gains made by the two control groups, and in the discussion that follows they are merged as one control group.

Mean scores of experimental and control groups at pre, mid, and post-tests are shown in table 11.2.2 and figure 11.2.2.

The question may arise whether the effect observed is one of training — that the interventions in some sense 'taught' the subject matter of the tests. As mentioned already, the interventions specifically did not make any attempt to teach the strategies of formal operations in a direct way, since much previous experience (see for example, Lawson and Wollman, 1976) has shown this is unlikely to lead to general transfer to untaught schema. Furthermore, the PRTs yield results which are independent of the content of the science curriculum. Some evidence for this argument is provided by one school which specifically did *not* use any of the intervention lessons concerned with the probability schema. Table 11.2.3 shows the gains made by control and experimental groups in this school separately from pretest to pendulum post-test, and from pretest to probability post-test.

Although with the small sample and wide variance neither differences between experimental and control group gains reaches significance, it does appear that the gain made by the experimental group to the PRT which is concerned with schema not covered in the interventions (probability) is as high as that made to the PRT concerned with schema that were covered in the intervention programme (pendulum — control and exclusion of variables). This is suggestive of general transfer, and indicates that the gains made are not the result of direct teaching of the subject of the tests, but reflect deeper changes in cognitive structures.

Class/school Differences

The overall results shown above hide a great variety of results from individual schools. The overall effect appears to be the accretion of many small gains (and some setbacks) in the individual schools. The relationship of individual school gains to teacher variables and school variables will be the subject of an immediate follow-up study.

Table 11.2.2   Piagetian Reasoning Task pretest, mid-test, and post-test scores and gains in main experiment schools

Test	Date	Experimental				Control			
		N	mean	σ	gain	N	mean	σ	gain
Pre	9/85		6.09	0.82			6.06	0.98	
Mid	7/86	222	6.37	1.02	0.28	259	6.29	0.93	0.23
Post	7/87	208	6.94	1.19	0.85	235	6.73	1.22	0.66

The pre-post gain made by the experimental group is significantly greater than that made by the control group at the .05 level.

Figure 11.2.2

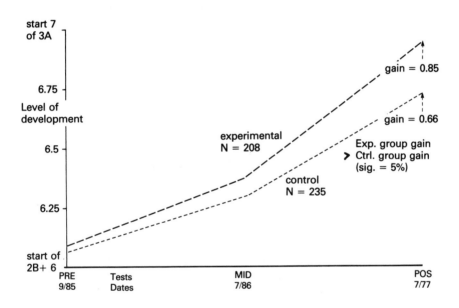

Table 11.2.3 *Gains made by experimental and control groups in one school from pretest means to probability post-test and to pendulum post-test*

		Experimental	Control
Gains	N:	39	61
pre to	mean:	1.07	0.81
pendulum	σ :	1.28	1.12
Gains	N:	35	66
pre to	mean:	1.01	0.76
probability	σ :	1.31	1.19

Table 11.2.4 *Gains made over two years by boys and girls separately*

	Experimental			Control		
	N	gain	σ	N	gain	σ
Boys	106	0.97	1.00	127	0.61	1.09
Girls	109	0.66	1.04	108	0.72	0.99

Sex Differences

Gains made by boys and girls in experimental and control groups are shown in table 11.2.4.

The mean gain made by boys in the experimental group is significantly greater than that made by boys in the control group ($p < .01$). There is no significant difference between the gains made by girls in experimental and control groups, indeed the gain made by the control group girls is numerically greater than that made by the experimental group girls.

How is this to be explained? We cannot be at all certain at this stage, but we do have some post-hoc hypotheses and some different forms of analyses which we will be happy to discuss.

Age Group

If one looks separately at the gains made by pupils who started the intervention programme when they were in the 11 + age group, and those who started in the 12 + age group, a sharp difference emerges: (table 11.2.5)

It appears that the younger age group has not benefitted at all from the intervention lessons, but that the effect is concentrated in the group starting at about 12 + — the second year of secondary school in Britain. Does this suggest an optimum time at which interventions designed to accelerate cognitive development will be effective? It might seem plausible to suppose that a more pertinent factor than chronological age would be the level of development of

Table 11.2.5 Gains made over two years by 11+ and 12+ (starting) age groups

Pupils at age ~	Experimental			Control		
	N	gain	σ	N	gain	σ
11 −	86	0.79	1.09	100	0.87	0.98
12 +	122	0.90	0.99	135	0.50	1.18

the pupils at which the intervention starts. And yet a further look at the data in terms of the starting levels of the subjects shows no clear distinction between those whose pretests indicate them to be mid-concrete or below, and those whose starting level is concrete generalization or above. The evidence suggests that chronological age is a better predictor of the effectiveness of the intervention programme than is initial developmental level.

Delayed post-tests will be given in July 1988. Possibilities to be looked for are (i) a withering away of any greater gains made at post-test by experimental groups; (ii) a maintenance of gains at a similar level to those found at post-test; or (iii) the emergence of increased gains of ex-experimental groups over control groups. This last possibility may occur if the interventions had only just started to take effect at the end of the two-year programme, and if newly improved cognitive strategies (including metacognition) provide a springboard for further development without further interventions.

Conclusion

We have some tantalizing evidence here, encouraging to those who would like to believe that general intelligence can be raised in ordinary school settings. We have seen that some teachers can do it, and the most urgent need now is to investigate the teacher variables that seem to be related to the ability to promote cognitive development, and then to devise in-service programmes designed to help teachers develop the necessary understandings and skills.

References

Kuhn, D. and Angelev, J. (1976) 'An experimental study of the development of formal operational thought', *Child Development*, 47, pp 607–706.

Lawson, A.E. and Wollman, W.T. (1976) 'Encouraging the transition from concrete to formal cognitive functioning — an experiment', *Journal of Research in Science Teaching*, 13, 5, pp 413–30.

Rosenthal, D.A. (1979) 'The acquisition of formal operations — the effect of two training procedures', *Journal of Genetic Psychology*, 134, pp 125–40.

Shayer, M. and Adey, P. (1981) *Towards a Science of Science Teaching*, London, Heinemann.

Shayer, M., Adey, P., and Wylam, H. (1981), 'Group tests of cognitive development — ideals and a realization', *Journal of Research in Science Teaching*, 18, 2, pp 157–68.

Discussion (Reporter: Ruth Stavy)

One focus of the discussion was on the nature of teacher or school variables which could account for the observed differences between schools. Adey explained that a follow-up questionnaire plus interview was planned to elucidate these further, although it was accepted that in-depth classroom observations at the time would have been better, had the resources been available.

The importance of delayed post-test results and of transfer to science achievement scores was emphasized. Adey thought that the latter may well not show up this year, since it was likely that any significant cognitive effect on pupils would only start to bear on their ability to learn science *after* the intervention programme.

The difference between boys and girls was commented on. Shayer and Yates proposed hypotheses based on possible differences in the age of relevant maturation, and the tendency of the intervention lessons to be convergent towards a 'correct' answer, and thus not girl-friendly.

11.3 Didactical Transposition and Pupils' Learning

P. Koumaras, D. Psillos and A. Tiberghien

Introduction

Research on the teaching and learning of electricity points out that pupils' views affect the way that they understand the teaching content (Psillos *et al*, 1987). In this paper we analyze the content of the teaching, its structure and presentation, from the point of view of learning conditions. We make the hypothesis that the following aspects are conditions for learning at this age (13–15 years).

— the introduction of new concepts by properties of objects or events;
— the establishment of links both between properties and between concepts through the introduction of mechanisms which may be interpreted at different levels;
— the use of the same concepts or the same relationships between concepts in different frameworks, namely here electrostatic and electrokinetic, and at the two levels — macroscopic and microscopic.

Such conditions might establish a learning environment more likely to keep the pupils' interest and in which the tasks presented are 'intelligible, plausible, and fruitful' (Hewson, 1981; Posner *et al*, 1982).

The Context

This study has been carried out in Greece where electrostatic and electrokinetic phenomena are taught at the end of compulsory schooling (14–15-year old). In this context we decided that in its main lines, the project should follow the model of electrical phenomena implied in the curriculum. Further, we opted that among our foci, one would be the development by the pupils of an independant voltage concept to describe, interpret and predict electrical phenomena such as:

— the bulb brightness in circuits containing several batteries and bulbs;
— the duration of the battery.

The Conditions for Conceptual Understanding: Teaching

Pupils' conceptions concerning electrokinetics have been extensively studied, researchers proposing models in terms of a 'source-consumer' causality.

Therefore, we consider that the features and the power of pupils' models of electrical phenomena presented above imply the construction of conditions for effecting conceptual change, at least in terms of:

— the content of teaching;
— the method of hierarchically structuring the content;
— the method of actually presenting this content to the pupils.

The Content

This includes five concepts: voltage, current, energy, charge, and resistance which are related together in a framework of mechanisms and functional relationships mainly in a qualitative way. New concepts are introduced from properties of objects, events and from mechanisms of functioning at the macro level and at the micro level. Properties and concepts are used in two domains: electostatic and electrokinetic. The different steps of the content have been presented elsewhere (Psillos *et al*, 1987).

In our teaching the links between electrostatic and electrokinetic are:

— at the level of the property: tendency or potentiality of two poles that have different charge accumulations to establish a current (macro), a flow of charge (micro) or to attract or repel one another. In both electrostatics and electrokinetics, it is this potential that is the condition to establish something: functioning of the circuit (bulb lights) or attraction or repulsion of charged objects.
— at the level of concepts: voltage and charge differences.

Main Differences Between Pupils' Prior Knowledge and the Desired Knowledge

Essential differences between the pupils' knowledge and the desired knowledge are presented here.

Desired knowledge	Prior knowledge
— What is transferred i.e. energy, is differentiated from how the transfer occurs i.e. current	one concept which has some properties of energy and current ('current')

Desired knowledge	Prior knowledge
— Two conditions make possible transfer of energy in the electrical circuit: non zero voltage and closed circuit.	some quantity of 'current' has to be stored in the battery in order to get it to work
— The potentiality for the battery to function is related to the tendency of electrical objects to interact.	no link at all
— charge separation and charge movement are the underlying microscopic processes in the model.	pupils know names such as electrons and charge which are elements of a microworld

Structure

The different steps in the process of providing structure to the content have been presented elsewhere. We just mention here that:

— differentiation between current and energy is related to two different aspects: conservation of current along the circuit and variation of energy which is used up in the circuit. At this point, the pupils try to reconcile their new knowledge i.e. current conservation with the question that appeals to them: how does the battery wear out? During this sequence, questions about the nature of current spontaneously arise amongst the pupils and accordingly the idea of microscopic charges are presented.

— electrostatic phenomena are treated afterwards and serve to elaborate the properties of charge which are utilized as an interpretive microscopic entity. Voltage here indicates the tendency of differential charge distribution in space to interact.

Aspects of the Teaching

In the process of carrying out the teaching, one aim is to develop tasks in which the pupils have to make use of previously taught knowledge. In other words the meaning of the concepts should be within the desired knowledge framework and not in the pupils' alternative framework.

In this paragraph we present, as an example, the part of the teaching which is dealing with the establishment of links between the electrostatic and electrokinetic classes of phenomena in terms of the underlying microscopic process. This was done in the unit on the function of the battery (see elsewhere for the presentation of voltage as a property, Psillos *et al*, 1987). This presentation is in terms of the task in figure 11.3.1.

Figure 11.3.1

In the figures the batteries are identical.
Which battery will be used up first? Please justify.

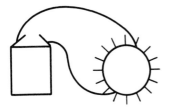 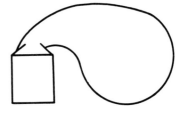

In the figures the batteries are identical. Which battery will be used up first? Please justify.

This task was also presented in a written test before teaching. Here is one representative pupil's reply:

> Certainly the battery with bulb. The short circuit battery has no bulb that consumes current. It goes back to the battery so the current remains the same. The short circuit battery will never finish.

It appears from this answer that pupils' initial model provided for them a satisfactory yet not scientifically correct prediction.

In the unit where this experiment was carried out the pupils had to face the task in terms of their new knowledge. At the beginning of the unit, the teacher asked:

> Initially you said that the current goes to the bulb where it is consumed to light it. Now you say that the current is not consumed. Then, how does the bulb light?

The pupils had to construct a new interpretation of the short circuit task in order to accommodate their newly acquired conceptions with the new experiment. It appears that at this level the use of a microscopic mechanism, though not elaborated, is a help for the pupils.

Discussion of the Conditions that Affected Conceptual Change

In the research reported here, the teaching was carried out in two classes comprising a wide ability range (N = 44). Immediate and middle term understanding of the knowledge acquired by the pupils was evaluated by a series of tasks given during the teaching and several times after the teaching.

Results showed that the majority of the pupils were not so far from the desired knowledge. These results allow us to analyze further the conditions developed so far in terms of learning conditions related to pupil behavior following Posner *er al* (1982).

As an example, we apply these conditions to analyze the teaching on the battery function.

Dissatisfaction: the short circuit task (figure 11.3.1) cannot be interpreted in terms of pupils' prior knowledge. Further, at the stage it was introduced, the pupils were able to ask questions and wonder about this task in terms of conservation of current which was new knowledge to them.

Intelligible: voltage and charge were presented as unifying concepts of electrostatic and electrokinetic phenomena both at the micro and macro level. Further crucial aspects of the microscopic mechanisms for the battery operation were illustrated by a multitude of analogies, for example:

— the charge separation and accumulation in the arms of the Winshurst machine was related to the charge separation and accumulation in the battery terminals;

— the measurement of voltage between the arms of the Winshurst machine was related to the measurement of voltage between the battery terminals;

Plausible: the use of properties and the establishment of links between properties and concepts through mechanisms made it possible to organize the desired knowledge in terms of causally transmitted chains of events. For example, when somebody turns the Winshurst machine crank, one can observe the deviation of the voltmeter needle; the faster you turn the more volts are indicated.

In this way, we consider that it was possible not to be far away from the pupils' intuitive patterns of reasoning such as simple causal reasoning. At the same time we could elaborate gradually the level of modelling of the phenomena.

Fruitful: the desired knowledge provided a means to interpret the short circuit task which could not be solved in terms of the pupils' prior knowledge.

Further on, most of the tasks like the short circuit one were situated in the context of three questions which appeal to the pupils. Thus these tasks possibly provided the pupils with the motivation to construct new meanings for familiar phenomena.

References

HENSON, P.W. (1981) 'A conceptual change approach to learning science', *European Journal of Science Education*, 3, 4, pp 383–96.

P. Koumaras, D. Psillos and A. Tiberghien

POSNER, G.J., STRIKE, K.A., HEWSON, P.W. and GERTZOG, W.A. (1982), 'Accomodation of scientific conception: toward a theory of conceptual change', *Science Education*, 66, pp 211–27.

PSILLOS, D., KOUMARAS, P. and TIBERGHIEN, A. (1987) 'Voltage presented as a primary concept in an introductory teaching on D.C. circuit', *International Journal of Science Education*, 10, 1, pp 29–43.

HEWSON, P.W. (1981) 'A conceptual change approach to learning Science', *European Journal of Science Education*, 3, 3, 4, pp 383–96.

Discussion (Reporter: Ehud Jungwirth)

The problem of differentiation between current and energy, and conservation of both, was emphasized. Psillos pointed out that only certain aspects, not a global definition of energy, were presented to pupils.

It was suggested that the size of the gap between pupils' prior and the desired knowledge was too wide to be bridged. Psillos pointed out that the relevant terms were already known, and only had to be given meaning. The 'push-pull' analogy of current was found to be useful.

Regarding 'potentiality' and 'charge', it was suggested that this approach *increased* the difficulty for pupils, especially since the notion of 'containing energy' presupposes the notion of conservation of energy. Psillos explained how such prior formation of problems could be avoided.

12   Children's Conceptions of Science

Joan Bliss

The chapters in this section are concerned with children's informal ideas about science. The first paper (Duit) gives an overview of how this type of research has developed in Germany, while the other two papers (Bliss, then Stavy) examine two particular domains, dynamics and matter, and show how children's ideas are different from those of the science teacher.

Research into how children make sense of the world is not new, Piaget being perhaps one of the more important forerunners of work in this area. Duit, in his chapter, also shows how, from a pedagogical point of view, science educators in Germany have considered it important to start instruction from the students' point of view, and this work dates back to the German educator, Diesterweg in the early nineteenth century but has been followed by many, such as Wagenschein, much more recently. The last decade or so has, however, seen a tremendous growth of research into children's ideas about physical phenomena, more particularly focussed on the secondary pupil, with the reasons for this sudden growth varying from author to author. Among these reasons are: the dissatisfaction with curriculum development in the sixties and seventies; an absence of descriptions of children's ideas about science at the secondary level, with the work of people such as Piaget and Bruner tending to focus on the primary level; and an expressed desire to match the science to be taught more closely to learners' ideas about science.

The research in this field has yielded a rich set of particular results, but reseachers differ as to whether pupils' conceptions represent systematic mental structures or ad hoc and temporary constructions. Proposed sources include language, kinaesthetic and sensory experience, socialized forms of explanation, even simple confusion. Some take a constructivist position, whether derived from Piaget or Kelly; others view pupils' conceptions as misconceptions arising from defective learning.

Bliss (together with Ogborn) propose a common sense theory of children's ideas about motion. Her paper describes how they set out to test the theory, and how the initial results would tend to confirm that children's conceptions of motion derive from schemes which are systematic and which are developed very early in the experience of the child. Stavy draws out some crucial teaching implications as a result of her research on matter and its properties during changes of state. More particularly, she indicates that some ideas are so basic that they seem self-evident to the science educators but this is not the case for the pupils. While such ideas may have their origins in everyday life (common with ideas in Bliss' paper), their meanings are very different from the scientific ones. Duit's wide-ranging paper about research in science education in West Germany is very welcome since it shows that there are developments in Germany which are parallel to if not precursors of much of what has been happening in England. It is a great pity that there has not been cooperation earlier and Duit's request in his paper for colleagues to exchange ideas about what is happening in their country should be taken seriously.

12.1 Research on Students' Conceptions in Science — Perspectives from the Federal Republic of Germany

Reinders Duit

Remarks on the Attention Students' Conceptions have been given in the History of Science Education in the Federal Republic of Germany

Research on students' conceptions in Germany does not deal with totally new problems and does not develop totally new ideas of teaching and learning science. The belief that learning is an active construction process on the basis of the already existing conceptions has a long-standing tradition. The German educator Diesterweg (1790–1866) pointed out that it is of utmost importance to start instruction from the students' point of view and that it is necessary for the teacher to investigate students' preconceptions. Diesterweg's ideas have not been forgotten over the last 150 years — at least not by educators, particularly leading science educators. This is true, for instance, of Martin Wagenschein (see Wagenschein, 1965) who is the outstanding science educator (especially physics educator) in our country.

There is not only a tradition in Germany to start science instruction from 'where the students are' but there is also something of a tradition of empirical studies on students' conceptions of natural phenomena within the psychology of child development. This dates from the middle of the thirties and was influenced by the work of Jean Piaget. The basic ideas of this research and results concerning specific and general conceptions as well as problems of conceptual change are very much in accordance with research in our field now (see Banholzer, 1936; Zietz, 1936). The Second World War interrupted studies on students' conceptions until the fifties. But since then several studies have been carried out.

Why Did the 'Students' Conceptions Movement' Start and Grow so Rapidly

Some ten to fifteen years ago the 'students' conceptions movement' started and grew so rapidly that it is no overstatement to speak of a research boom in this area. It would be interesting to get to know the reasons for this rapid development, and perhaps obtain thereby a deeper insight of what is going on and where research should aim. As no comprehensive analysis of this kind has been made so far I would like to venture a preliminary contribution. It would be interesting to have similar sketches from other countries (for example, France, Great Britain, the United States) in order to get to know the main aspects which led to research of students' conceptions. Hopefully, colleagues will feel encouraged to work out such sketches.

General Remarks on the Growth of the 'Students' Conceptions Movement'

There appear to be two main reasons for the start and the rapid growth of research in the field of students' conceptions (see Duit, 1987). First, there was dissatisfaction among science educators with curriculum development through the sixties and the early seventies. An orientation to basic science concepts and processes, as well as careful planning of content and process set-up, appeared inadequate, not guaranteeing students' success.

Second, there was a turn in psychology to 'cognitive science'. It happened that there was a considerable overlap of interest between the two groups. Science educators were looking for some theoretical foundation for learning science. The ideas of cognitive science seemed promising. Cognitive psychologists were in search of learning domains which were not too narrow and came across the topic of science, especially physics. Since the middle of the seventies there has been a fruitful cooperation between the two groups within our field of research.

The above-mentioned two reasons were responsible for setting research to work. But for the continuous growth of research until now another aspect has to be taken into consideration, namely the constructivistic view (see for example, Pope, 1985; Driver, 1986). The ideas within the 'students' conceptions movement' run into a mainstream of contemporary philosophical thinking. This 'constructivistic mainstream' comprises ideas of philosophy of science as developed by Hanson, Kuhn, Feyerabend and others, ideas stemming from information processing theories, especially ideas of artificial intelligence research and new trends in science which run under such headings as 'self-organization'.

A Brief Sketch of the Growth of Research on Students' Conceptions in the Federal Republic of Germany

Throughout the sixties there was a rather vehement discussion on aims and organization structures of education in the Federal Republic of Germany. Concerning science education, there was quite a considerable change. On the one hand there was a general tendency to a scientific orientation of education in all types of school. On the other hand there was a strong tendency to student orientation of instruction, i.e. to orient instruction to the abilities, interests etc. of students.

As a result of both these tendencies science instruction in all three types of school (gymnasium, realschule, hauptschule) became a little more similar. The gymnasium oriented instruction a little more to the everyday life of students, to application of science in technology and to implications of science in society. The volksschule and realschule, which had so far been oriented rather closely to 'natural studies' ('Naturlehre') and 'technology' respectively, changed orientation more to the sciences. This change of viewpoints in the different types of schools appears to have been of considerable importance for the interest of science educators in the role of students' conceptions. Whereas so far investigations (see above) had mainly been carried out in the context of Volksschule, research now was done in all types of school.

As part of the 'reform movement' in education there was a boom of curriculum development through the end of the sixties to the early seventies, when several studies on students' conceptions were also carried out. But research on students' conceptions on a broader scale started only in the middle of the seventies when the boom of curriculum development was over. It was dissatisfaction with the success of the new curricula which led to concentration on the role of students' conceptions in the process of learning science (comparable with the start of research in other countries). Research was carried out mainly by science educators who wanted to investigate possibilities of guiding students to science conceptions. Cognitive science also played a certain role. On the one hand it was used as one source of theoretical foundation for research. On the other, research work was not exclusively oriented to investigating conceptions of specific science topics (such as the simple electric circuit, the energy concept, the particle model) but was also investigating general features of the learning process.

An Overview of Research on Students' Conceptions in the Federal Republic of Germany

Topics of Science Investigated

Research in Germany and outside Germany mainly concentrates on the same topics (see Pfundt and Duit, 1987). Most of the available studies are in the area of physics (some 70 per cent). The number of studies on chemistry topics may total around 30 per cent. Biology topics appear to be given less attention in Germany than outside, only a small number of them are available in our country.

Theoretical Frameworks of Research Work

The outstanding researcher in the field of students' conceptions in the Federal Republic of Germany is the physics educator Walter Jung. He enlarged the above-mentioned tradition of research on students' conceptions in our country especially by introducing aspects of recent philosophy of science (which may be briefly characterized by philosophers like Hanson, Kuhn and Feyerabend). Jung is not so much interested in investigating specific conceptions of science domains but is in search of more general conceptions he calls frames (Rahmen). The ultimate aim of science instruction is — according to Jung — not to simply replace 'everyday frames' (students' frames) by science frames but to enable students to switch between the frames (Jung, 1983). Research on students' conceptions in Germany is very much influenced by Jung's position (see, for example, the following studies: Pfundt, 1981; Duit, 1981; Kircher, 1981; Rhöneck, 1981; Nachtigall, 1986; Spreckelsen, 1986).

Whereas Jung's research concentrates on cognitive aspects, Niedderer and the members of his group at Bremen University (see Niedderer, 1987) try to take into consideration not only students' conceptions of science topics but also students' interests in the topics and students' conceptions of the nature and range of science conceptions.

A major idea of our research area is that students themselves have to be active when learning. To a certain extent Aufschnaiter and Schwedes at Bremen University give students not only the possibilty to be active themselves but also a choice of what to learn. These ideas are embedded into a 'play-oriented' approach ('spielorientierter' Ansatz) which does not mean that students are allowed simply 'to play around' but that learning is given some of the major aspects of a play (for a study carried out in this spirit see Schwedes, 1983).

Schaefer's research work in the area of biology is quite compatible with the theoretical positions mentioned so far. It is based on what he calls the 'burr model' of concept formation. In this model relations between the 'logic core' and the 'associative framework' play an important role. The 'burr model' leads to the idea of 'inclusive thinking' (Schaefer, 1980). This type of thinking does not restrict concept learning to the logic core but includes the manifold associations of the logic core with other concepts.

Redeker (1982) has introduced a standpoint into our research area which rests on very different theoretical foundations from the ones close to Jung's position. Redeker follows a phenomenological tradition of philosophy which may be briefly characterized by the names of Husserl and Heidegger. It may be interesting that there is quite an intense discussion on the nature of conceptual change, especially among researchers concentrating on primary education (see for example, Löffler and Köhnlein, 1985). Some take Redeker's position that between students' conceptions and science conceptions there is no continuous passage but a principal of discontinuity. Jung (1987) does not agree with this point of view. He is of the opinion that a discussion of conceptual change in terms of continuity and discontinuity is misleading and that there are possibilities to bridge the gap between students' and science conceptions.

From an international point of view it may be surprising that an explicit constructivistic position has not been developed or adopted in our country. So far there appears to be only one major adoption. Dierks (1986), a chemistry educator at the IPN, has adopted Kelly's (1955) theory of constructive alternativism to analyse learning in chemistry.

A brief remark on Piagetian research may be necessary. There has been and still is some Piagetian type research in the area of science instruction (see, for example, Bormann, 1978; Gräber and Stork, 1984). But most research does not explicitly follow Piaget's lines of thinking.

Concluding Remarks

It is difficult to foresee which path research will take in the Federal Republic of Germany. There are some hints that the theoretical foundation may be enlarged by recent 'new trends of thinking', for example, by aspects of evolutionary epistemology, theories of self-organizing systems and activity theory. Further enlargement may be expected from phenomenological approaches.

References

BANHOLZER, A. (1936) 'Die Auffassung physikalischer Sachverhalte im Schulalter, dissertation, Universität Tübingen.

BORMANN, M. (1978) 'Die Piagetsche Entwicklungspsychologie und der Physikunterricht', *Der Physikunterricht*, 12, Heft 4.

DIERKS, W. (1986) 'Ein ungewöhnlicher Vorschlag für den Chemieanfangs-unterricht. Die Konsequenz aus grundsätzlichen Überlegungen zum Lernverhalten', Kolloquiumsvortrag vor der Sektion Chemiedidaktik der Universität Rostock, April.

DRIVER, R. (1986) 'Reconstructing the science curriculum: The approach of the children's learning in science project', paper presented at the annual meeting of the American Educational Research Association, San Francisco.

DUIT, R. (1981) 'Students' notions about the energy concept — before and after physics instruction' in JUNG, W., PFUNDT, H., RHÖNECK, Ch. v. (Eds.) *Proceedings of an International Workshop*, pp 268–319.

DUIT, R. (1987) 'Research on students' alternative frameworks in science — topics, theoretical frameworks, consequences for science teaching', paper presented at the Second International Seminar 'Misconceptions and Educational Strategies in Science and Mathematics', Cornell University, Ithaca, July.

GRÄBER, W. and STORK, H. (1984) 'Die Entwicklungspsychologie Jean Piaget's als Mahnerin und Helferin des Lehrers im naturwissenschaftlichen Unterricht', *MNU* 37, pp 257–69.

JUNG, W. (1983) *Anstöße. Ein Essay über die Didaktik der Physik und ihre Probleme*, Frankfurt/M., Diesterweg.

JUNG, W. (1987) 'Verständnisse und Mißverständnisse', *Physica Didactica*, 14, pp 23–30.

JUNG, W., PFUNDT, H. and RHÖNECK, Ch. v. (Eds) (1981) 'Problems concerning students' representation of physics and chemistry knowledge', *Proceedings of an International Workshop*, Ludwigsburg, Pädagogische Hochschule.

KELLY, G.A. (1955) *The Psychology of Personal Constructs*, Vol. 1, 2. New York, W.W. Norton.

KIRCHER, E. (1981) 'Research in the classroom about the particle nature of matter (grades 4–6)' in JUNG, W., PFUNDT, H., RHÖNECK, Ch. v. (Ed.) *Proceedings of an International Workshop*, pp 342–64.

LÖFFLER, G. and KÖHNLEIN, W. (1985) 'Weg in die Naturwissenschaften — ein bruchloser Weg?', *Physica Didactica*, 12, Heft 4, pp 39–50.

NACHTIGALL, D. (1986) 'Die Rolle von Präkonzepten beim Lernen und Lehren von Physik', in BLEICHROTH, W. *Aufsätze zur Didaktik der Physik. Festschrift zum 60. Geburtstag von W. Jung. physica didactica*, 13, Sonderheft, pp 97–101.

NIEDDERER, H. (1987) 'A teaching strategy based on students' alternative frameworks — theoretical concept and examples', paper presented at the Second International Seminar 'Misconceptions and Educational Strategies in Science and Mathematics', Cornell University, Ithaca, July.

PFUNDT, H. (1981) 'Das Atom — letztes Teilungsstück oder erster Aufbaustein? Zu den Vorstellungen, die sich Schüler vom Aufbau der Materie machen', *Chimica Didactica*, 7, pp 75–94.

PFUNDT, H. and DUIT, R. (1987) *Bibliography: Students' Alternative Frameworks and Science Education* (2nd ed.), Kiel, IPN.

POPE, M. (1985) 'Constructivist goggles: Implications for process in teaching and learning', paper presented at the annual meeting of the British Educational Research Association, Sheffield.

REDEKER, B. (1982) *Zur Sache des Lernens — am Beispiel des Physiklernens*, Braunschweig, Westermann.

RHÖNECK, Ch. v. (1981) 'Students' conceptions of the electric circuit before physics instruction' in JUNG, W., PFUNDT, H., RHÖNECK, Ch. v. (Eds) *Proceedings of an International Workshop*, pp 194–213.

SCHAEFER, G. (1980) 'Inclusive thinking with inclusive concepts' in ARCHENHOLD et al. (Eds) *Cognitive Development — Research in Science and Mathematics, Proceedings of an International Seminar*, Leeds, University of Leeds, pp 382–96.

SCHWEDES, H. (1983) 'Zur Kontinuitätsvorstellung bei Wasserstromkreisen und elektrischen Schaltungen' in DPG — Fachausschuß Didaktik der Physik (Hrg.) *Vorträge der Frühjahrstagung*, Gießen, 1, Physikalisches Institut, pp 264–9.

SPRECKELSEN, K. (1986) 'Schülervorstellungen im Grundschulater' in Bleichroth, W. (Hrg.) *Aufsätze zur Didaktik der Physik. Festschrift zum 60. Geburtstag von W. Jung. physica didactica*, 13, Sonderheft pp 103–8.

WAGENSCHEIN, M. (1965) *Ursprüngliches Verstehen und exaktes Denken*, Stuttgart, Klett.

ZIETZ, K. (1936) *Die Physik des Kindes. Die Deutsche Schule* 40, pp 263–9.

Discussion (Reporter: Guy Claxton)

The perennial issue of what exactly is meant by 'constructivism' was raised. The use of the term by philosophers of science, such as Kuhn, seems a different one from that subjected to Bereiter's critique to which Duit has referred. This was accepted in part, but Duit suggested that overlap existed in the belief that knowledge was relational.

The question was raised of why interest in constuctivism mushroomed in Britain in the 1960s. It was suggested that this was in part to do with the thrust towards comprehensive education. Another speaker thought we should see children's alternative frameworks as real alternatives that should coexist, providing a basis for choice, and not be seen as 'misconceptions'. It was agreed that it might be unwise to see children's intuitive ideas as in need of extinction and replacement.

The issue of how best to promote change in teachers was raised. One area considered was whether researchers should 'train' teachers into an understanding of their findings, or encourage teachers to see themselves as researchers in the classroom. Another was concerned with what to do about teachers, perhaps the majority, who did not voluntarily seek to take on a researcher role. Another speaker defended the value of informing teachers about children's alternative conceptions since it helps to validate and crystallize many teachers' semi-conscious apprenticeship of childrens' 'funny ideas'. It was noted that there were additional problems in reaching primary school teachers, many of whom themselves would have 'misconceptions' about science.

It was noted that in general the problem of promoting teacher change is a difficult one since such change is often slow and involves a radical shift in underlying values and attitudes towards education. It follows that research to evaluate programmes for teacher change have to be long-term. There is an additional danger of premature dissemination of research 'findings' and 'implications', when these are still under debate by the research community.

12.2 A Common-Sense Theory of Motion: A Theoretical and Empirical Approach

Joan Bliss

Introduction

This research is carried out in cooperation with Professor Jon Ogborn and Denise Whitelock of the University of London Institute of Education. Educational research over the past fifteen years into various scientific concept areas such as light, heat, electricity, etc has shown that children's ideas about such phenomena are often very different from those of the scientist. Because of the importance of dynamics to the teaching of physics, research in this area has been particularly prolific, revealing a variety of findings, some more puzzling than others.

Researchers differ as to how they view pupils' conceptions but a constructivist position whether derived from Piaget or Kelly often lies behind a great deal of the work (Driver, Erickson 1983; Andersson, 1985). It is not easy, however, to examine empirically the merits of these different approaches.

Ogborn (1985) proposed an outline of a common-sense theory of motion (summarized briefly below), derived from Hayes' (1979) *Naive Physics Manifesto*, which attempts a formalization of ordinary everyday knowledge of the physical world. The present research sets out to develop a methodology which will allow the proposed theory to be tested, and, in the light of the findings, to refine and develop the theory. An earlier paper (1989) looked at the results of a similar study with primary children; in this paper we shall describe the results of an interview study with secondary school children.

Outline of a Common-sense Theory of Motion

Two basic and related terms of the theory are 'support' and 'falling'. If an object is not supported it falls until it is once more supported. There is an initial cause for falling — lack of support — but one does not need to look for any further cause for this motion to continue. Everything needs support, except the ground which gives support but is not itself supported. 'Strength' or 'effort' (or both) is needed to support things. If the strength of a support is not enough it may break or yield. Air and water can also support things but this is partial support only.

Movement is considered as taking place on the ground, (or on something supported by the ground), or as taking place in the air, above the ground. Two more basic concepts are needed to describe motion: 'place' and 'path'.

A first type of motion consists of changing the place of something, for example, pushing or pulling something. Another type of motion is that in which — once initiated — the object is moving by itself such as a football or tennis ball. The object is located by the path it is following, not the place it happens to be at any specific moment.

Apart from falling, all motions require some type of effort either to change the place or path of an object or to sustain the motion along a path. There are three possible sources of effort:

- effort of another agent ON the object;
- effort generated BY the object;
- effort OF the object (effort preserved within an object, once given by an agent, which sustains its independent motion until the effort is used up.)

The theory does not mention forces, including gravity, though the general term 'effort' covers some of their possible uses. Such terms could be added later to the basic natural scheme, gaining properties from the scheme rather than giving properties to the scheme.

Methodology

Many recent studies have used situations which have been very similar to or derived from school science. We felt it crucial to avoid tasks which might suggest 'scientific' responses and so set out to find ordinary natural situations such that any response given by subjects would be in common-sense terms. The fundamental difficulty with eliciting people's common-sense ideas about dynamics is that such knowledge would be tacit. Thus in the experimental situation we would be asking subjects to make explicit things which are so obvious that they would normally remain unsaid. It was important, therefore, to find a world which was 'normal' where the rules of the real world could be suspended so that it would be reasonable to ask if such rules did apply — comics seemed to us to fit many of these requirements. Comics are a smaller and more amusing version of our world, with events ranging from the ordinary to fantastic.

Materials

Beano, Dandy, Topper and *Beezer* were the four comics used, with the pilot work showing that they were still read by many children of all ages. The stories chosen contained a large number of movements which were very diverse and a number of unusual or unexpected situations. After preliminary trials, the comic strips chosen were: Ginger, Plug, Fred and Beryl, with fifteen episodes being selected for the interview as follows:

GINGER
G1 Ginger imagines himself hit on head by hockey puck.
G2 Cool scuttle and rubbish falling from shelf.
G3 Walking stick hanging from nail.
G4 Ginger swings stick, knocking collander from shelf.
G5 Woman knocks Ginger over and he slides backwards downhill.
G6 Ginger takes off over bump and falls, landing on ice.
G7 Children throw hockey sticks and snowballs at Ginger.

FRED, the burglar
F1/2 Fred slides down drainpipe which breaks. He falls onto the ground.
F3 Fred runs with pole as battering ram to force open locked door.
F4/5 Fred uses vaulting pole which snaps. He falls on pile of pipes.

PLUG
P1/2 Plug jumps out of window with umbrella, falling with inside-out umbrella.
P3/4 Plug lands on wheelbarrow, ejecting rubbish which flies over the house.
P5 Plug jumps from roof with parachute made from curtain.
P7 Plug lands on his father.

BERYL
B3 Beryl heads ball which bounces, knocking over objects in room.

Procedure and Sample

Each child was interviewed on all fifteen episodes in the four stories (data on 386 episodes). Children were first asked to describe what was happening in a sequence of pictures. They were then asked: 'Do you think this could really happen, or that it could not really happen?', and to explain why. Twenty-six secondary school pupils, girls and boys, were interviewed: first and second year: 5; third year: 5; fourth year: 5; fifth year: 5; sixth form: 6.

Results: Frequency of Different Types of Explanations

A set of categories derived from the theory was applied to the data. These were: Support and Falling, Effort (sub-categories: Effort needed to initiate motion, to maintain motion, or as an exchange of effort), Gravity and Impact. Each pupil's interview was divided into the fifteen episodes, with each episode being analyzed in terms of the presence or absence of one or more of the above categories (repeated explanations of the same type were counted only once).

Only about 5 per cent of the responses were school-science type explanations, these appearing mainly with the older children. Of the 292 explanations given, 212 or 79 per cent were interpretable as Support and Effort which is a quite surprising result. The number of explanations given for the four main categories is as follows: Support: 126 (43 per cent); Effort (all three categories): 106 (36 per cent), Gravity: 44 (15 per cent) and Impact: 16 (6 per cent).

Support: Frequency of Use

Analysis of Variance (repeated measures) shows that there is no significant variation between subjects, nor between incidence of explanations and school year. There is significant variation between situations, with only five of the twelve situations eliciting a substantial number of Support explanations. Overall, notions about Support were used in twelve of the fifteen episodes, F1/2, P5, P1/2, F4/5 and G2 being the five most popular (88 per cent, 76 per cent, 72 per cent, 72 per cent and 68 per cent response per episode respectively). The other seven episodes received only a total of thirty-two explanations of a possible 175. Those episodes where Support does not get mentioned are G1, F3, and B3.

Effort: Frequency of Use

As with the Support category, there was no significant relationship between the year of schooling and incidence of explanations. The significant differences were again between situations, with only five eliciting a substantial number of explanations about Effort. Again overall, notions of Effort were mentioned in ten of the fifteen episodes, F3, P3/4, G5, G6, and G7 being the five most popular (88 per cent, 72 per cent, 72 per cent, 64 per cent and 56 per cent response per episode respectively). The other five episodes received a total of eighteen explanations of a possible 125 responses. Those episodes where Effort does not get mentioned are F1/2, G3 and P1/2, P5 and P7.

Some Correlational Evidence for Support and Effort

In the above sections the frequency of the different categories of explanation in relation to the range episodes has been analyzed. It could further be argued that we would expect certain situations to be interpreted similarly by the pupils. The present data is too restricted in number of subjects and range of situations to go too far in this direction. Factor analysis would be relevant, but probably not in this case valid. However some correlational evidence has been examined and some patterns appear to emerge.

With the Support category G6 and P7 correlate positively and tend to correlate negatively with P1 and P5. The first two episodes are both concerned with falling onto a doubtful support whereas the last two are about being partially supported by the air. Another pair, G2 and G4, correlate and are both about objects being knocked off a support.

With the Effort responses, there are similarities between G7, B3 and P3 which are seen as unlike G2 and F4/5. What would seem to be common to the first three is idea of the agent's effort causing the motion which could be contrasted to the other two episodes where the motion is happening without effort, that is, falling.

Gravity and Impact

The forty-four explanations about Gravity appear in eight episodes with only two eliciting a substantial number of responses G7 (thirteen explanations), and P5 (eleven explanations). Gravity explanations are used mainly by the older children, fourth to sixth year with only eight of the forty-four explanations being given by children in the first to third year of school. Sixteen explanations are given in terms of Impact and six of these appear in G1, Ginger imagining himself hit on head by hockey pucks. There are two other situations which elicit a few Impact responses F3 and F1/F2, (four and three responses respectively).

Conclusions

The present research has its limitations with, for example, the selection of situations not being systematic enough to cover all aspects of the theory. Also the numbers involved were somewhat small. However, the use of comics proved to be very worthwhile since some of the children would spend up to an hour with the interviewer, and they also enjoyed the task. There are also areas where the theory is incomplete or too inexplicit, for example, the interaction of a moving and a static object as in impacts.

The common sense theory of motion does provide a reasonably simple framework of concepts within which the data from children could readily be interpreted, in particular, Support and Effort conceptualized as two essential components of common sense reasoning about motion. It is interesting to note these explanations appeared in a way which did not distinguish between pupils over a considerable age range, as predicted by the theory.

References

ANDERSSON, B. (1985) 'A framework for discussing approaches and methods in science education', paper given at the Educational Research Workshop on Science in Primary Education, Council for Cultural Cooperation, Strasbourg.

BLISS, J. and OGBORN, J. (1989) 'A commonsense theory of motion: Issues of theory and methodology examined through a pilot study' in BLACK, P. and LUCAS, A. (Eds) *Children's Informal Ideas about Science*, London, Croom Helm.

DRIVER, R. and ERICKSON, G. (1983) 'Theories in action: Some theoretical and empirical issues in the study of students' conceptual frameworks in science', *Studies in Science Education*, 10, pp 37–60.

HAYES, P. (1979) 'The naive physics manifesto' in MITCHIE, D. (Ed.), *Expert Systems in the Microelectronic Age*, Edinburgh, Edinburgh University Press.

OGBORN, J. (1985) 'Understanding students' understandings: an example from dynamics', *European Journal of Science Education*, 7, pp 141–50.

Discussion (Reporter: Charles Ryan)

Two main threads ran through the discussion, one about the nature of the analysis of pupils' response the other on the implications of the findings for future research and for classroom practice.

It was pointed out that only between about 5 per cent and 10 per cent of the pupils' answers corresponded to typical school science responses. The other responses could be classified according to the categories either derived from the theory, support and effort, or determined by the data, for example, impact and gravity.

Participants wanted to know the types of language actually used by pupils in their responses. Examples of the different categories were read from the transcripts. Participants expressed their surprise at the directness and simplicity of the children's language.

The discussion of the implications for further work revealed that a replication study by questionnaire based on the results of the work so far was in progress. The questionnaire used simplified comic drawings and asked children to compare two motions and say how similar or how different they were. It was hoped that this study would show the stability and/or rigidity of the pupils' common sense theory. If the findings reveal a stability in the children's ideas then the implications for teaching and production of class material could be considered.

It was pointed out that one approach to teaching might be to show pupils the gulf between their views and those of Newtonian mechanics. It was mentioned that in addition a computer simulation involving a model of the common sense theory was nearing completion. It was hoped later to embed the simulation into a type of game situation so that pupils could examine and compare predictions made by the computer for a number of different movements.

12.3 Students' Conceptions of Matter

Ruth Stavy

The science curriculum for junior high school students in Israel deals with the states of matter and with the particulate theory of matter. The curriculum was developed with the underlying assumption that students know what matter means. Thus, there is no attempt to explain or define the term as it is being used in science. This underlying assumption is best illustrated in the way students are being taught that gases are material: students are shown that gases have weight and volume, assuming that this is enough to make them believe that gases are material.

Previous studies on students' understanding of change of state from liquid to gas (Stavy, in preparation) indicated that children might have alternative ideas about matter. The purpose of this study is to investigate students' conceptions of matter. Students' ideas about matter where examined in two ways: (a) directly, by asking students (grades 1–8) to explain what matter means and to classify items into matter and non-matter; and (b) indirectly, by analyzing students' (grades 4–9) responses to different questions regarding changes of state (conservation of matter, of weight, of qualitative properties and reversibility). Educational implications will then be discussed. Before describing the results of this study I would like to make a comment about the meaning of the word matter in the Hebrew language. The meaning of the word matter in Hebrew is: clay, material, matter, substance, and in a more literary context also pile or severity. Of course, this ambiguity of the term may affect students' conception of matter.

Direct Approach

Students Explanations of 'Matter'

Students from grade 1–8 (twenty students in each age group) were directly asked if they knew what 'matter' means and if they could explain what it is.

Table 12.3.1 Students explanations of 'matter' (percent in each grade)

Grade		1	2	3	4	5	6	7	8
Explanation									
1	by example: clay, plasticine	40	42	45	25	20	17	20	—
2	by function: something that one uses, or, works with, or creates something else with.	45	53	20	30	25	40	15	—
3	by structure: (a) made from components	—	—	15	15	25	10	15	20
	(b) made from compounds mixtures, elements, atoms, etc.								25
4	by properties (a) hardness, colour, tangibility etc.	—	—	—	5	—	17	10	25
	(b) state (solid, liquid, gas, powder, crystals)	—	—	—	—	35	7	35	55
	(c) weight and/or volume	—	—	—	—	—	—	10	10
5	other kinds of 'matter' learning, reading etc.	—	37	35	5	5	10	—	—

Most of the students in all the age groups could do so. Students responses could be divided into several types (see table 12.3.1):

1 Explanation by means of example: This type of response appeared in most of the groups but was more popular in the lower grades (1–3). The characteristic examples given were: plasticine, clay, glue, cleaning materials, building materials, sugar, wood, iron.

2 Explanation by means of function: This type of response also appeared in all grades except eighth grade. Students explained matter as something you work with or use. For example, 'something that one uses' or, 'a thing that you work with'.

3 Explanation by means of structure: This type of response appeared from grade 3 onwards. It could be divided into two sub-groups: (a) as something which is 'made (or built, or composed) of things'; and (b) as something which is made out of compounds, mixtures, elements, atoms etc. These explanations are probably the result of schooling and appear only in the eighth grade.

4 Explanation by means of properties: This type of response appeared in the upper grades (sixth grade onwards). It could be divided into three

sub-groups: (a) specific properties such as hardness, tangibility, colour, etc; (b) state of matter such as, solid, powder, etc., (c) properties of weight and/or volume — these appeared only in 10 per cent of the seventh and eighth graders (usually only with one of the properties).

5 The last type of response refers to other kinds of matter usually learning materials, reading materials, etc.

These results indicate that the intuitive mental model young children have with regard to matter is associated very strongly with mouldable, useful materials such as plasticine, clay or cement. This intuitive model persists until the seventh grade. From third grade on children start to think of matter in terms of structure and properties, but only 10 per cent of the seventh and eighth grades relate their model to the properties of weight and volume which are relevant in the scientific context. Children's model of matter can lead them to misclassify liquids or gases.

Classification of Different Items into Matter and Non-matter

Children were presented with a series of items (matter and non-matter) and were asked to judge whether they thought of them as matter or not.

The items were: (a) solids: rigid solids (iron cube, piece of wood, ice cube), non-rigid solids (cotton wool and metal spring), powders (sugar, flour, potasium per manganate, and soil); (b) liquids (mercury, milk, water); (c) biological materials (flower, human body, meat); (d) gas (air); (e) phonomena associated with matter (fire, electricity, wind, smell); (f) non-matter (light, heat and shadow).

Figure 12.3.1 shows how children in the different age groups relate to the different groups of items. It seems that the different groups of items can be ordered according to their being regarded as matter in the following ways: solids, liquids, biological materials, phenomena associated with matter, gas, non-matter. Figure 12.3.1 also shows that children's classification of items into matter and non-matter improves with age and by the seventh and eighth grades the majority of children regard solids liquids and biological materials as matter and do not include in the matter group non-matter, items. At these ages children still have some problems with classifying gases and phenomena associated with matter (see figure 12.3.2).

The results from the classification experiment, suggest that young childrens' intuitive core concept of matter is on the one hand underextended, not including some solids, most liquids and biological materials and all gases and, on the other hand, overextended including some phenomena associated with matter and non-matter items.

During development there is a gradual shift in the classification pattern toward a more scientific mode of classification. But it seems that this shift is not a consequence of a parallel shift in the nature of explanation or definition of the

Figure 12.3.1 Classification of different groups of items into matter and non-matter (in percent)

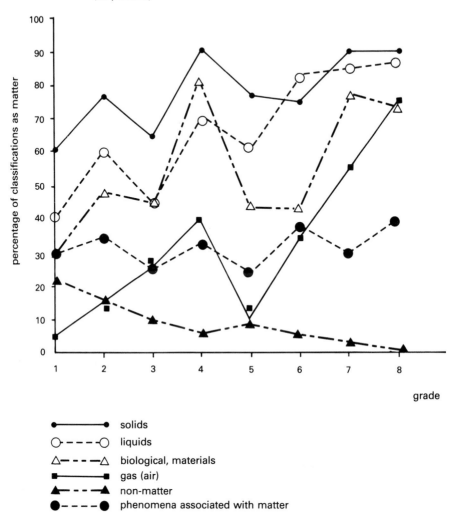

term 'matter'. The improvement of explanation of the term 'matter' lags behind the ability to classify items into matter and non-matter and even in the seventh and eighth grades only 10 per cent of the students defined matter in terms of the properties of weight or volume.

Indirect Approach

In the previous section children's conception of matter was discussed in terms of definition of matter and classification of items into matter and non-matter. In

Figure 12.3.2   Classification of different items into matter and non-matter

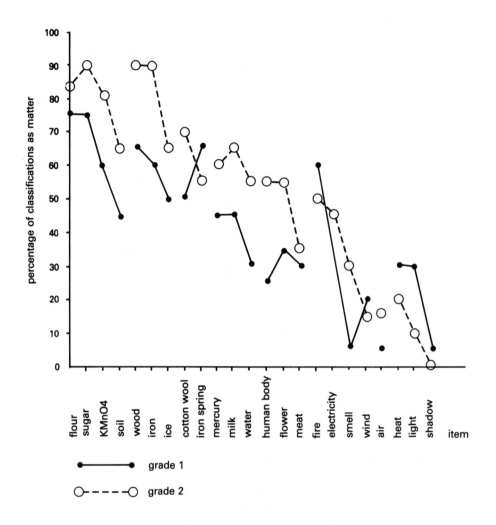

the present section children's conception of matter will be derived from their responses to problems related to change of state from liquid (or solid) to gas.

Each student from grades 4–9 (twenty in each age group) was presented with two identical closed test tubes, each containing an equal amount of acetone (one drop). The acetone in one of the test tubes was heated until it completely evaporated. The student was asked about the conservation of matter ('Is there matter in the heated test tube?') and about the conservation of properties of matter ('If we open the test tube will there be a smell of acetone?'). The student was also asked about conservation of weight ('Is the weight of both test tubes the same or different, and if different, which is heavier?'), as well as the reversibility of the process ('Can we retrieve liquid acetone and if so, how?'). With each question the student was asked to explain his answers and to state what had happened to the acetone.

Then the student was presented with two identical closed test tubes, each containing an iodine crystal of identical size to that in the other tube. The iodine in one of the test tubes was heated, turning completely to a purple gas and filling the entire volume of the test tube. The student was asked about conservation of matter ('Is there matter in the heated test tube?'); about conservation of properties of matter ('If alcohol is added to the iodine crystal, brown medicinal iodine is formed. If alcohol were to be added to the heated tube would such an iodine solution be formed?'); about conservation of weight ('Is the weight of the test tubes equal or different. If different which is heavier?'); about the reversibility of the process ('Can solid iodine be reobtained? If so, how?'). With each question the student was asked to explain his answer and to state what had happened to the iodine. A qualitative analysis of the students' explanations for their different judgments follows. Five main ideas related to matter and its properties were found:

1   *Matter is grasped as a concrete, solid object*: Children in the fourth and fifth grades, i.e. ages 9–11 would appear to conceive of matter as something concrete and solid. Gas and liquid are not perceived as matter. The explanations of a number of children of the iodine sublimation task support this view: 'the colour in the test tube is from the *matter* that was in it before' or 'the iodine *matter* is not there — the crystal is not there'. The purple gas which filled the test tube is not seen as matter by these children, though the solid crystal of iodine which was in the test tube before heating is considered as matter. The children's reaction to the evaporation of acetone was similar to that regarding gas — 'the water of the acetone disappeared, the material and even the smell remain stuck to the walls of the test tube and the cap'. Liquid or water are presented as non-matter. This narrow conception of matter is seen mainly in children younger than ten years of age.

2   *Children conceive of matter as being made up of a material core and non-material properties such as colour, smell, flammability or weight (heaviness)*: These properties can be disassociated from the material especially

when the material undergoes a change. Smell can escape from the material, leaving it without smell, or the material can disappear, leaving its properties of colour, smell, sweetness, etc. This can be seen from the explanation of students for the evaporation of acetone: 'the acetone disappeared but the smell remained'. This view of the world is characteristic of children between the ages of 9 and 12. Piaget and Inhelder (1974) found a similar conception, at a younger age, for the dissolution of sugar in water.

3   *Children believe matter exists only when there is evidence of its existence*: According to this idea, matter does not have to be solid or liquid to be conceived of as matter but there must be perceptual evidence of its existence. It ceases to exist when the evidence disappears. As a result its existence is not conceived of as permanent. The coloured iodine gas, for instance, is perceived as matter whereas the colourless gas of acetone is not, due to the lack of perceptual evidence of its existence. Responses to the question whether there was iodine in the test tube which had the purple gas were that 'there is matter because there is colour'. On the other hand, when the drop of acetone evaporated in the closed test tube the children explained that the acetone was not in the test tube, since 'the drop disappeared or dissolved'. The visual property of colour provides for children between 9–12 much stronger evidence of the existence of matter than does smell.

This is similar to the findings of Piaget (1969) regarding the existence of air, where air exists only when it moves. Similarily, Sere (1985) found that students (ages 11–12) believed that gas exists when it moves, or when the pressure it exerts can be felt.

4   *Weight is not seen as an intrinsic property of matter*: Weightless matter can exist, or weight can change with the state of matter. Children construct a set of intuitive rules regarding the correlation between the weight or heaviness, of matter and its state.

The perceived rules found in this research are as follows:
— Rule I (common among the youngest children): gas has no weight
— Rule II: gas always weighs less than liquid (or solid).
— Rule III: the weight of a gas is equal to that of the liquid or solid from which it is derived.

The weight of matter (and not necessarily its quantity) is grasped as a function of an undefined property related to its state, density (the specific 'heaviness' that characterizes a particular material, rather than the mass/volume relationship), and hardness or strength. A dense solid whose weight can be felt is considered heavy by the young child, but the gas obtained from it is conceived of as weightless. At a later age it is thought of as having less weight than the solid from which it is derived. The following perceived rules were found in the case of a candle melting:
— Rule I: the liquid weighs more than the solid. This rule is most common among five-year-old children, probably because liquids fall downward.
— Rule II: liquids have no weight since their heaviness cannot be felt.

— Rule III: liquids weigh less than solids.
— Rule IV: the weight of a liquid is equal to that of the solid from which it was formed.

These rules are found among children younger than in the case of the acetone tasks. Similar rules were also found regarding the dissolution of sugar in water (Andersson, 1984).

The intuitive feeling that children have regarding 'lightness' and 'heaviness' of matter (or groups of materials) are related to intensive 'quantities' or properties of matter. The child refers to the intensive quantity instead of the extensive or absolute quantity, weight, about which he was asked. Can it be assumed that the child does not properly understand the meaning of the term weight and thinks that weight refers to the relative weight of the material? This is almost definitely not the case. It is clear that from a very young age children understand the idea of the weight or heaviness of an object and know that a large body of a certain material is heavier than a smaller body of the same material. Reference to the extensive rather than the intensive property was observed by Piaget and Inhelder (1974), and Megged (1978), all of whom studied the development of children's concept of density.

5   *Matter is composed of particles and the state of matter is explained according to the arrangement of these particles*: Although this concept is taught in the seventh and eighth grades, it appears in only 15 per cent of the eighth and ninth grade students' explanations. There were rare cases in which the students mentioned particles, although they claimed that dense particles are heavier than rare particles. The children had in fact adapted the particulate theory to their own conception according to which solids weigh more than gases. In other words, the particulate theory is not internalized and does not become useful for most of the students even though they have learned it in school.

Educational Implications

The results presented in this paper indicate two major difficulties students have with regard to the concept of matter. One is related to their ability to define matter and to classify items into matter and non-matter and the second to their understanding of the relationship between matter and its properties during change of state.

It seems that there is no point in teaching the particulate theory of matter when students do not know what matter is, and do not believe, for example, that gas is material (Stavy, in preparation). There is also no point in teaching photosynthesis, breathing, nutrition, etc. when student do not regard biological objects to be material.

It is therefore suggested that prior to teaching the particulate theory of matter there should be discussion and clarification of the meaning of the concept of matter with students. The course should start with items which are regarded as matter and extend to items not regarded as matter by searching for criteria. Non-material items regarded by students as matter should be discussed in order to reveal how they do not match the established criteria.

With regard to the relationship between matter and its properties during change of state it is suggested that students are actively engaged in tasks involving changes of state, reversibility of processes, and invariance of weight and chemical properties (such as solubility and inflammability).

Many times in the course of science teaching we tend not to pay enough attention to the very basic and fundamental concepts and ideas. Being so basic they seem to us to be self-evident, but this apparently is not the case. It is true that many of these basic concepts are notions which are used in everyday life and language and develop spontaneously but their meaning is not exactly the same as the scientific one. Since they are so very fundamental, not paying attention to them may result in difficulties in understanding of other advanced concepts, principals or theory.

References

ANDERSSON, B. (1984) *Chemical Reactions*, EKNA report no. 12, Goteborg University, Sweden.

MEGGED, H. (1978) 'The development of the concept density among children aged 6 to 16', MA thesis, Tel-Aviv University.

PIAGET, J. (1969) *The Child's Conception of Physical Causality*, Towoa, NJ, Littlefield, Adams & Co. (original 1927).

PIAGET, J. and INHELDER, B. (1974) *The Child's Construction of Quantity*, London, Routledge and Kegan Paul (original 1940).

SERE, M.G. (1985) '*The gaseous state*', in DRIVER, R., GUESNE, E. and TIBERGHIEN, A. (Eds) *Children's Ideas in Science*, Milton Keynes, Open University Press.

STAVY, R. and STACHEL, D. (1985a) 'Children's ideas about 'solid' and 'liquid'. *European Journal of Science Education*, 7, pp 407–21.

STAVY, R. and STACHEL, D. (1985b) 'Children's conception of changes in the state of matter: From solid to liquid', *Archives de Psychologie*, 53, pp 331–44.

STAVY, R. (in preparation) *Children's Conception of Changes in the State of Matter: From Liquid (or Solid) to Gas.*

STAVY, R. (in preparation). *Children's Conception of Gas.*

Discussion (Reporter: Ehud Jongwirth)

It was pointed out, and generally agreed by the participants, that pupils find it easier to classify elements than to define them. It was also mentioned that some pupils might and possibly do see 'simple' substances as composed of 'stuff' plus 'water' and that this might explain some of their ideas about changes of state.

A point of clarification was raised as to whether the term 'matter' was used throughout the study. It was pointed out that this term was not used in the changes of state phase of the research.

One participant queried whether pupils had been given a wrong definition of 'matter'. It was indicated that Israeli texts (elementary and junior high) only deal with the 'true nature of matter' and do not define the term. The point was made that the 'metaphysics', i.e. the 'nature of things' had been taken for granted by curriculum developers and teachers. This is an assumption which needs to be critically examined. Participants began a discussion about other sorts of assumptions that are made concerning pupils' taken-for-granted knowledge, for example, about how many of the concepts necessary for a deeper understanding of science are thought to be automatically part of the pupils' knowledge. Such assumptions all need questioning.

It was suggested that the notion of 'pure' substance should be introduced into school curricula at as early a stage as possible. Time ran out before there could be a deeper discussion of this point.

13   Some Detail

Philip Adey

The four papers in this chapter offer a variety of detailed descriptions of some difficulties encountered by students in learning science, as well as some of their successes. Two are concerned with specific domains in the curriculum — photosynthesis and stoichiometry — and two address broader issues of concern to science educators — causality and practical skills. Together, they exemplify the kind of information gathering and analysis essential to provide the data on which theories may be elaborated. This is not to say that the studies in this chapter are atheoretical, only that their theoretical assumptions remain, for the most part, implicit. The primary aim of this chapter is not the furtherance or refutation of theory, but the provision of description and analysis which will both serve science educators in a direct and practical manner, and at the same time provide those who are trying to piece together the big picture of learning in science with some important pieces of detail in the jigsaw.

Jungwirth shows that all too often students fail to use acceptable criteria of logical reasoning in assessing evidence or in trying to draw conclusions from inadequate evidence. Even student teachers and teachers do not perform flawlessly in this area, in spite of the recognition by teachers of 'logical thinking' as an important goal of science education. This paper adds to a considerable body of evidence (cited by Jungwirth) that many teachers in training are not yet capable of the level of abstract reasoning which might be supposed to be necessary for them to develop effective enquiry approaches in their pupils. What, if anything, can be done about this rather serious deficiency in the teacher populations of many, if not all, countries remains a matter for speculation. On the face of it the consequences are serious both for the way in which new science curricula are actually delivered, and for the way that the community assesses the blandishments of unscrupulous politicians and advertisers. The possibility of social pressure as an influence in the answering of such tests is taken seriously.

Eisen and Stavy analyze the causes of difficulties which arose with a unit for teaching photosynthesis in the eighth grade. Drawing some principles from constructivist notions of learning, but recognizing at the same time the difficulty of treating each concept individually with the exposure-plus-conflict method, they describe a revised curriculum which streamlines unnecessary detail and highlights centrally important concepts. It will be interesting to see whether the method proposed proves to be more successful than the old in leading students to a deeper understanding of the process and importance of photosynthesis.

Schmidt also provides a detailed analysis of students' 'errors' — this time in the field of stoichiometry. What emerges is that sometimes those who choose the wrong answer do so because they have thought about the chemistry, but have failed to take all variables into account or to reason through accurately. On the other hand, some of those who make the correct choice may do so by applying algorithms without regard to the chemistry. There is a lesson to be learnt here: teachers and students have much to gain from asking how a particular error arose.

From a detailed analysis of the results of the process skill tests from the second IIE study, and some international comparison, Tamir is able to identify variables which contribute to the development of practical process skills. It is reassuring to read the evidence that an emphasis on practical laboratory work in school does help in the development of process skills. In times when the effectiveness of schools is being called into question in many parts of the world, it is even more encouraging to note that school variables account for such a large proportion of the variation in student achievement. Insofar as we can ascribe a causal link in this correlation (*pace* Jungwirth), it holds out the hope that student achievement may be improved by the manipulation of variables over which we, as educators, do have some control.

13.1 Secondary School Pupils' and Biology (Student) Teachers' Attributions of Cause-and-Effect Relationships in Situations Requiring Suspension of Judgment.

Ehud Jungwirth

Background

There appears to be a global consensus (for example Queensland 1981; BSCS, 1978; CME 1981; RP, 1980; Demielova *et al* 1986) that it is one of science education's main objectives to inculcate skills in the domain of critical/logical/analytical thinking with special emphasis on judgment processes, cause and effect relationships, the evaluation of evidence and the validity of conclusions. Studies in Israel suggest that teachers share this consensus (Jungwirth, 1971; Tamir and Jungwirth, 1972). In a more recent study (Dreyfus, Jungwirth and Tamir, 1985) 71 per cent (N = 110) of experienced biology teachers strongly supported the emphasis of the curriculum on 'the methodology of scientific enquiry'. It would appear that the majority of these teachers identify with the view of the establishment. However, Arons (1984) contends that 'teachers rarely consciously articulate or point out to their students the necessity to ask "what is the evidence for?" when approaching a problem in order to be explicitly aware of the gaps in available information, and recognizing when firm inferences ... regarding cause and effect *cannot* be drawn'.

What have teachers to say in this respect? In the first of the above-quoted Israeli studies the majority had allotted highest priority to critical thinking skills, but, when asked about the feasability of achieving this objective, it came eighth out of fourteen. In the second study only 24 per cent expected top achievement while 61 per cent had it given it top priority. So we have the curriculum demands on the one hand and a certain amount of skepticism about the feasability and the actual development of the skills demanded.

Ehud Jungwirth

Diagnosis

The data presented here are part of a parallel study at the tenth grade level (16-year-olds) of Israeli (N = 143) and Philippine (N = 193) pupils, as well as of two small comparison groups, one of postgraduate biology student teachers and another of a mixed group of secondary biology techers voluntarily attending an in-service course at university (both N = 20) in Israel. The test used was a version of one fully described in Jungwirth (1987). The present study was undertaken in 1986/87. This version consists of twenty-eight items, half of them with biological content (BIO-items) and the other half relating to (school-)life, sports, etc. (LIFE-items). The first half of the test contains both BIO and LIFE items having the logically sound response (logsound) specifically spelt out, the second half comprises both BIO and LIFE items lacking such options, and respondents are expected to choose 'I don't agree with any of these' *and* state their reasons for doing so. The test contains eight categories of logical fallacies, six of which are connected to attribution of causality:

(a) Assuming that events which follow others are caused by them (post-hoc reasoning).
(b) Attributing causality on the basis of an insufficient number of instances (sample too small, in the extreme case a 'sample of one').
(c) Attributing causality to a factor or phenomenon on the basis of a non-representative sample.
(d) Imputing causal significance to correlations.
(e) Attributing causal significance to a factor, when there are only very small differences which might have arisen fortuitously.
(f) Attributing explanatory power to mere tautologies. Only two of these (a) and (b) will be dealt with here in detail.

Two items are given below as examples:

Item 4 (LIFE with logsound option — 'b')
Two schools (A and B) arranged a mathematics contest. Two ninth grade pupils from each school took part. School B won. School B's pupils were happy that their school was better in mathematics than school A. What is *your* opinion?

(a) The pupils' conclusion is wrong, since one has to think not only about the pupils in a school, but also about the teachers.
(b) Two pupils from a school are not enough for such a contest.
(c) The pupils' conclusion is right, since school B won.
(d) I don't agree with any of these choices.

Item 18 (BIO without logsound option)
A tenth grade class performed the following exercise: They grew one bean-plant at 10°C and another one at 25°C. All other conditions were the same. After several weeks the plant grown at 25°C was much better developed than the one grown at 10°C. What is *your* opinion?

Table 13.1.1   (rounded %)

Item	High school pupils						Student teachers Israel (N = 20)	Teachers Philipp. (N = 20)
	Israel (N = 143)			Philippines (N = 193)				
	top 25%	bot 25%	total	top 25%	bot 25%	total		
A. 'No sample' items								
4 (LIFE)	100	96	96	87	50	68	100	100
18 (BIO)	2	2	1	14	—	5	39	13
B. 'Post hoc' items								
3 (BIO)	75	52	64	25	1	12	100	93
17 (LIFE)	18	9	15	12	—	6	46	27
C. Total test results with								
logsound	69	48	59	53	20	45	68	69
without								
logsound	31	8	14	17	3	10	38	18

  (a)   The results show that a temperature of 25°C is much better for beans than one of 10°C.

  (b)   It is well known that warmth is needed for plant-development so the results could have been expected.

  (c)   There are different kinds of beans, some grow better in higher and some in lower temperatures. This explains the result.

  (d)   I don't agree with any of these choices.

The first item's logical structure is a 'sample of two', and that of the second item a 'sample of one' situation. Obviously the 'gaps in the evidence' in such cases are so large as to leave only one possible response — no decision is possible.

Whenever respondents did not choose the logsound option, but gave a different valid logical reason (in 'd') their response was scored as 'correct'.

From results for these items ('No sample' item, table 13.1.1) we can see that:

  (a)   *Pupils* — Scores for the item *containing* the logsound response were very much higher than for the second item i.e. spelling out the desired response had *not* automatically elicited a reasoned rejection of unjustified options later on. This was generally true for *both* BIO and LIFE items in *both* populations.

  (b)   *(Student-) teachers.* — A similar pattern, especially on the first item, with higher (but still unreasonably low) scores on the second item.

Let us now look at another pair of items:

Item 3 (BIO with logsound response)
Pupils grew tomatoes in the school laboratory. One day there was a gas

leakage, which was soon repaired. Soon afterwards purple spots appeared on the leaves. What is your opinion?

(a)   One cannot draw any conslusions from this report.
(b)   Gas leakages have happened before, but purple spots did not appear, so that cannot be the reason for the spots.
(c)   The gas caused the appearance of the spots since none had been there before.
(d)   I don't agree with any of these choices.

Item 17 (LIFE without logsound option)
A new coach prepared the school's athletic team for the annual sports competition. The team *lost* in almost all contests. In previous years the school had won in almost all contests. A group of pupils saw the director and demanded that the former coach be invited to train the school team again next year. What is *your* opinion?

(a)   The pupils probably did not take the training as seriously as in former years, so the new coach was not to blame.
(b)   If the school team succeeded in all the previous years, then the new coach must be held responsible for the failures.
(c)   The pupils were wrong. The team may have lost because this year's paticipants in the other schools were much better trained than before.
(d)   I don't agree with any of these choices.

The structure common to these items is that they report a temporal sequence. A (for example, gas leakage) and — later — B (for example, purple spots). An A — and later B sequence *without additional data* does *not* permit attribution of causality to A. People doing so would commit the 'post hoc ergo propter hoc' fallacy. Results are shown as 'post hoc' items in table 13.1.1.

Again — the 'prompting effect' (Dreyfus and Jungwirth, 1980a) of the first item had not been very substantial on responses to the second item, pupils and adults showing a similar pattern, with the latter scoring relatively higher on the second item.

This phenomenon occurred in all the test categories. The overall data (BIO and LIFE combined) are shown in part C of table 13.1.1.

Responses to the item without a logsound option represent a *refusal to suspend judgment* by the majority of these respondents — pupils *and* (student-) teachers. There were *no* significant differences between the genders in any of the pupil-samples (over-all and within classes) in either Israel or the Philippines, within and across these test categories.

What do people actually do when they do *not* choose the logsound response (where it *is* given), or refuse to suspend judgment (where *that* is called for by the logical structure of the item)? There are three possibilities: They may either commit a logical fallacy (logfal) by accepting a logically *un*sound option, they may ignore the logical structure of the situation altogether by accepting a

Table 13.1.2 Breakdown of total test data

	10 th grade		Adults	
N =	Isreal 143	Philippines 193	Students 20	Teachers 20
A. Overall response patterns (rounded %)				
logsound	38	24	55	40
logfal	28	33	11	25
context	34	43	33	36
B. Logsound responses, BIO vs. LIFE				
BIO — mean	5.02	2.83	7.92	6.14
LIFE — mean	5.54	3.94	7.00	6.00
t =	2.32	5.41	0.74	0.00
p <	0.05	0.01	n.s.	n.s.
C. Logfal responses, BIO vs. LIFE				
BIO — mean	4.57	5.56	1.38	3.80
LIFE — mean	3.16	3.82	1.77	2.93
t =	8.17	8.70	0.76	1.53
p <	0.001	0.001	n.s.	n.s.
D. Context responses, BIO vs. LIFE				
BIO — mean	4.23	4.95	4.73	4.61
LIFE — mean	4.95	6.23	5.20	4.61
t =	3.17	6.15	0.62	0.00
p <	0.01	0.001	n.s.	n.s.

context-related option, or they may indeed choose the expected 'don't agree' option, but given non-logical reasons for doing so. Again — since response-patterns across test categories were very similar — total test data will be given from here on. Table 13.1.2 will show the response-pattern.

Boys in the Israeli group committed significantly more logfals than girls ($t = 2.73$), while there were no gender differrences in the Philippine group. On the other hand there was no gender difference in the Israeli group as regards context-options while girls in the Philippines selected such options more frequently ($t = 2.20$). *All* groups — pupils *and* (student-)teachers chose more context- than logfal options.

Did pupil-responses differ when confronted with BIO-items as compared with LIFE-items? The following relate to logsound responses on the total test (Part B of table 13.1.2).

The same trend appeared in both pupil-groups, stronger in the Philippines i.e. more logsound responses on LIFE-items, but no significant differences in the adult groups. Note that the LIFE-items *preceded* the BIO-items! Looking at the top and bottom groups (upper and lower 25 per cent) in both pupil-groups we found that there was no significant difference in the top Israeli group (similar to the adult Israeli groups), but significant differences in favour of

LIFE-items in the bottom Israeli group and *both* Philippine groups, but smaller in the top-group. It appears that the trend towards higher LIFE scores stems mainly from the weaker sections of the pupil-populations. How do the BIO and LIFE items compare as regards the logfal and the context-responses? First — the logically *unsound* (logfal) response (part C of table 13.1.2).

There were significantly more logfal responses on BIO-items than on LIFE-items, in both the Israeli and the Philippine groups. Looking at the top and bottom quarters revealed the same trend in all four sub-groups.

Second — the context-centred responses (ignoring the logical structure of the situations) (part D of table 13.1.2).

There were significantly more context-responses in LIFE-items than in BIO-items (the opposite of logfal responses). Looking at the top and bottom quarters, chi-squared analyses showed *no* differences for *both* top-groups, but *both* bottom-groups chose significantly more context-options in the LIFE-items. And finally — 'don't agree' responses for *non*-logical reasons came to approximately 20 per cent of such responses in *both* the Israeli and Philippine groups, varying widely across classes. If reasons-for-choice (for 'd') had not been asked for, these responses would have been counted as 'correct', thereby elevating the scores considerably, and hampering the diagnostic potential of the test. With reasons-for-choice, however, these responses could be added to regular context-responses, giving a better portrayal of the situation.

Analysis

General

What can be said about the absolute level of the test-results (recall that six of the eight test categories relate in some way to causal analyses), and the two categories illustrated here in particular? Recall further, that in most places compulsory (science) education terminates with the tenth grade, and only a minority of such pupils will have a chance to benefit from further (science) education.

Moreover, postgraduate student-teachers and graduate-teachers are a highly selective population. Bearing all that in mind — the test-results are in sharp contrast to the curricular expectations outlined above, as well as the quoted teachers' own priorities (but not with these same teachers' expectations of feasibility of achieving these objectives). The overall phenomenon represents a strong tendency to either accept (others') attribution of causality in contravention of 'the laws of scientific evidence', or to identify with options which do not relate (are irrelevant) to the logical structure of the situation but to its contextual (specific) aspects in which the logical structure is embedded. The response-*patterns* — as distinct from the absolute quantitative level of achievement — of pupils and adults were in most cases very similar.

Attributions of Cause-and Effect Relationships in Biological Situations

Responses as a Function of Item-format

In the adult and the top pupil groups acceptance of a logsound option was high to very high (depending on the specific situation) BUT the 'prompting effect' of these items on the measure of respondents' rejection of logfal and context-option by suspending judgment where there was no logsound option was weak to very weak. It would appear that the selection of logsound responses (where given) did *not* stem from a developed *generalized* thought-habit i.e. application of the 'rules of evidence or enquiry', but rather from ad hoc behaviour in specific situations.

Responses as a Function of Item Content (BIO vs. LIFE)

The overall response-trend of the adult samples and the top Israeli quarter resulted in a no-difference situation, with the other sub-groups significantly higher on LIFE-items, but specific item-content still had a role to play. However, correlations of individual scores (BIO vs. LIFE) showed very moderate to very weak common variances, again pointing to a lack of consistency i.e. a non-generalized approach. Inter-category correlations were also uniformly low, reinforcing the other data.

The Two Main Types of Incorrect Responses and Their Sources

Acceptance of the logfal — in all groups — was lower to much lower than acceptance of context-options, which were the preferred type of *undesirable* response. The overall tendency was to explain *why* something happened/might have happened, even in situations where such an explanation lacked any *logical* basis whatsoever. This trend was reinforced by respondents' offering of such explanations even in items where the logically sound response had been explicitly spelt-out, or by rejecting logfal responses by offering another logfal instead, or indeed rejecting all offered options, but giving non-logical (context-related) reasons for doing so. The feeling by respondents 'that they had to remember, at any price, some bits of information, some rules, that could justify their choice of one of the offered conclusions' (Dreyfus and Jungwirth, 1980b) is apparently behind such behaviour. The cause of such behaviour has also been termed a 'social imperative' (McClelland, 1984) or 'a coercive class-room situation' (Dreyfus and Jungwirth, 1987). Driver, Guesne and Tiberghien (1985) also talk about pupil-reactions 'in an ad hoc way in response to the social pressure to produce an answer...', resulting in respondents' tendency to invent ad hoc theories — 'instant inventions' (McClelland, 1984) — not as a basis *for* choice, but as a post-factum justification of their acceptance of one of the *invalid* conclusions. This social pressure (perceived rather than real in the test situation, but probably carried over from the classroom), coupled with many respondents' misinterpretation of the logical structure of the test-situation and/or many respondents' obliviousness of the fact that there *is* a logical structure demanding attention, resulted in the unsatisfactory state of affairs reported here.

Some Educational Implications

People committing a logfal accept or formulate a plausible conclusion instead of testing its validity. Such behaviour patently transcends the boundaries of science-education, and would constitute a serious handicap in any decision-making process. For example: the prevalence of the post-hoc logfal would make unscrupulous propaganda, clever electioneering, or commercial advertising a much easier task. The tendency to accept 'a sample of one' as representative of a population is the basis for stereotyping (all A's are B's based on ONE A is a B).

Implications for Teacher Education

The level of (student) teachers' achievement on this test — and others' performance on the former test-versions — (Jungwirth, 1987) left much to be desired. It seems indeed that 'many teachers do not possess the reasoning patterns which activity-centred science curricula seek to develop' (Garnett and Tobin, 1984). Arons (1984) states that 'we force a large fraction of students into blind memorization by imposing upon them ... materials requiring abstract reasoning capacities they have not yet obtained, and of which many of their teachers are themselves incapable'. Judging from discussions with both postgraduate student teachers and practicing teachers in Australia, South Africa, the US and Israel, I do not share the view that they are indeed 'incapable'. It has become quite clear to me that low teacher-performance — let alone pupil-performance — is attributable to lack of awareness of the existence of certain simple rules of causal analysis and similar processes. Holford (1985) says that 'teachers expect that their training should equip them with a better understanding of the quality of argument put in support of truth-claims in situations where science is used'. Hall's *et al* (1983) warning that these skills should not be taken for granted (referring to pupil-populations) should be seen as applicable to (student) teacher populations as well. Teacher-educators should pay explicit attention to the development of such skills if — to paraphrase Black (1962) — the arguments of the market-place and the classroom are to become sounder, and correct reasoning is *not* to remain as rare as perfect health.

References

ARONS, A.B. (1984) 'Education through science', *Journal of College Science Teaching*, 13, pp 210–20.

BLACK, M. (1962) *Critical Thinking*, Englewood Cliffs, N.J., Prentice Hall.

BIOLOGICAL SCIENCES CURRICULUM STUDY (1978) *Biology Teachers' Handbook* (3rd edn.), (edited by W.V. Mayer), New York, Wiley.

COUNCIL OF MINISTERS OF EDUCATION, CANADA (1981) *Science — A Survey of Provincial Curricula at the Elementary and Secondary Levels*, Ottawa, CME.

CRONBACH, L.J. (1963) *Educational Psychology*, New York, Harcourt, Brace and World.

DEMIELOVA, S.I., RAZUMOVSKI, V.G., TSUETKOV, L.A. and MYAGHKOVA, A.N. (1986) *Science and Mathematics Education in the General Secondary School in the Soviet Union*, Document Series No. 21, Paris Division of Science, Technical and Environmental Education, UNESCO.

DREYFUS, A. and JUNGWIRTH, E. (1980a) 'A comparison of the "prompting effect" of out-of-school with that of in-school contexts on certain aspects of critical thinking', *European Journal of Science Education*, 2, 3, pp 301–10.

DREYFUS, A. and JUNGWIRTH, E. (1980b) 'Students' perception of the logical structure of curricular as compared with everyday contexts — A study of critical thinking skills', *Science Education*, 64, 3, pp 309–21.

DREYFUS, A. and JUNGWIRTH, E. (1987) 'The pupil and the living cell: A taxonomy of dysfunctional ideas about an abstract topic', paper presented at the Second International Seminar on Misconceptions and Educational Strategies in Science and Mathematics, Cornell University, July.

DREYFUS, A., JUNGWIRTH, E. and TAMIR, P. (1985) 'Biology education in Israel as viewed by the teachers', *Science Education*, 69, 1, pp 83–93.

DRIVER, R., GUESNE, E. and TIBERGHIEN, A. (1985) *Children's Ideas in Science*, Milton Keynes, Open University Press.

GARNETT, J.P. and TOBIN, R. (1984) 'Reasoning patterns of preservice elementary and middle school teachers of science', *Science Education*, 68, 5, pp 621–31.

HALL, D., LOWE, I, MCKAVANAGH, C., McKENZIE, S. and MARTIN, H. (1983) *Teaching Science, Technology and Society in the Junior High School*, Brisbane, Brisbane College of Advanced Education.

HOLFORD, D. (1985) 'Training science teachers for science — technology-society roles' in HARRISON, G.B. (Ed.) *World Trends in Science and Technology Education*, Nottingham Trent Polytechnic.

JUNGWIRTH, E. (1971) 'The pupil — the teacher — and the teacher's image', *Journal of Biological Education*, 5, 4, pp 165–71.

JUNGWIRTH, E. (1987) 'Avoidance of logical fallacies: A neglected aspect of science-education and science-teacher education', *Research in Science and Technological Education*, 5, 1, pp 43–58.

JUNGWIRTH, E. and DREYFUS, A. (1980) 'Secondary school biology students' reactions to logical fallacies in scientific as compared with every-day contexts' in: ARCHENHOLD, W.F., DRIVER, R.H., ORTON, A. and WOOD. ROBINSON, C. (Eds) *Cognitive Development Research in Science and Mathematics*, Leeds, University of Leeds.

McCLELLAND, J.A.G. (1984) 'Alternative frameworks: Interpretation of evidence', *European Journal of Science Education*, 6, 1, pp 1–6.

QUEENSLAND BOARD OF SECONDARY SCHOOL STUDIES (1981) *Draft Junior Syllabus in Science*, Brisbane, Queensland Board of Secondary School Studies.

REPUBLIC OF THE PHILIPPINES, NATIONAL SCIENCE AND TECHNOLOGY AUTHORITY, *Philippine Science High School Special Curriculum in the Sciences — Philosophy and Objectives*, Quezon City, Manila, Philippines.

TAMIR, P. and JUNGWIRTH, E. (1972) 'Teaching Objectives in biology: Priorities and expectations', *Science Education*, 56, pp 31–9.

Discussion (Reporter: Carolyn Yates)

In response to a question, Jungwirth made it clear that responses to the items were accepted as correct if they related to the problem in way that was logically sound, even if it was not a response that had been anticipated by the researchers. Responses that were purely contextual, but not logical were counted as incorrect. The students were not told that the test was about logical structure.

One participant noted that even students who were formal thinkers would not necessarily use a logical approach to the test. Jungwirth noted that discussions with students during the test suggested that incorrect responses were not always the result of inability to respond correctly, but could be a failure to identify that the test was about causality, and could be interpreted using simple rules of logic. Many students see a tautological answer as correct (and so do some university professors!). Jungwirth emphasized his belief that logical reasoning could be taught, but it would not happen automatically, it must be built into the curriculum. Reference was made to Lawson's paper which also suggested that reasoning patterns were teachable. The notion that logical thinking and reasoning patterns had nothing to do with science education was one that needed to be changed.

13.2 Development of a New Science Study Unit Following Research on Students' Ideas about Photosynthesis: A Case Study

Yehudit Eisen and Ruth Stavy

Teachers and science curriculum developers can no longer ignore the notion that even very young children possess ideas about various scientific concepts and processes before starting their formal science studies. Nor can they ignore that children's ideas in science are not necessarily consistent with scientists' ideas, and that very often children hold their ideas even after they complete their studies at school (Gilbert, Osborne and Fensham, 1982; Eisen and Stavy, in press).

Conclusions with implications for science teaching have been drawn by all of the researchers concerned with children's alternative frameworks. Most of the implications are of relevance to teachers, and suggest that they be aware of children's ideas; that they alter teaching strategies in order to encourage children to discuss their ideas; that they use socratic questioning techiques; that they change the sequence of teaching; that they introduce discrepant techniques; and that they deal specifically with misconceptions (Driver, Guesne and Tiberghien, 1985; Osborne and Freyberg, 1985; Posner *et al.*, 1982). Some of the authors suggest the development of learning materials to deal with specific misconceptions.

The implications stated above relate mostly to specific concepts: heat, light, matter, earth, etc. Less attention has been given by most of these authors to the choice of, and approach to content. The content of science curricula in secondary schools all over the world was developed according to the structure of the specific domains without considering children's existing alternative framworks. It is suggested here that the choice of content and approach taking in to account children's misconceptions may improve children's under-standing.

In the present paper the development of a new science study unit following research on students' ideas about photosynthesis will be presented and discussed (Eisen and Stavy, in press; Stavy, Eisen and Yaakobi, 1987).

Photosynthesis in the Current Israeli Junior High School Curriculum

The Israeli junior high school science curriculum contains a study unit dealing with the topic of photosynthesis, 'The plant and light'. This unit is taught in the eighth grade (age 14–15).

There are two main ideas in 'The plant and light'. The first is the general ecological concept of an ecosystem consisting of physical and biotic environments operating in mutual relationship. Understanding of mutual dependency in the ecosystem is essential for understanding the role and place of man in nature. The second main idea is that of the correlation between structure and function, a biological principle repeated in many study units. Development of process skills and understanding of the scientific method are also claimed to be objectives of this unit (Israeli Education and Culture Department, 1979).

A list of topics and some suggestions for simple experiments are provided. In addition, various teaching sequences are suggested, including short and long sequences. The topics are:

1 An introduction to plants and light — do plants need light?
2 From where do plants take the materials they need to grow?
3 What sort of materials are plants built of? — organic materials, starch and sugar.
4 What do plants need for producing organic materials? — cholorophyll, light and carbon dioxide.
5 The photosynthesis process including: what is photosynthesis?, oxygen release, the source of oxygen, analysis and synthesis of compounds using light energy, the function of light, the function of chlorophyll, chloroplastids.
6 What happens to the products of photosynthesis in the plant? — storing materials in plants and bulbs, transfer of organic materials in the plant.
7 Leaves and their function in photosynthesis — shapes of leaves, stomata, transpiration and antitranspiration; the cactus plant 'Sabra'.
8 Green plants and their importance to the animal world — carbon dioxide balance in the atmosphere, plant respiration, Priestley's explanation of the purification of the air, respiration and photosynthesis, producers and consumers in nature, parasitic plants, material cycles in nature, man's intervention in material cycles, energy transfer in the animal world, food and energy pyramids.
9 The influence of light on plants' development.

Difficulties Children have in Understanding Photosynthesis

In our previous study (Stavy, Eisen and Yaakobi, 1987) we identified several difficulties that students experience in understanding photosynthesis. The difficulties can be grouped into those of psychological origin and those of instructional origin.

Difficulties of Psychological Origin

1   Understanding photosynthesis requires a conceptual change from a conception that differentiates qualitatively between the living and non-living realities (vitalistic), which most probably characterizes students' thought, to one that does not make such a distinction (naturalistic). This was manifested in our study in the difficulties students had in treating the living body as a chemical entity, their difficulty in describing biological phenomena in chemical terms and their resistance to such a treatment.

2   There is a need for conceptual change in considering the status and importance of 'man' in the world around him. Apparently children at this age tend to consider man as the 'centre of creation' and assume that man has full control over his environment. It is difficult for them to accept that human (and animal) life depends on the existence of plants. Usually children tend to think of plants as dependent on man, and not the other way around. This was seen in our study in the difficulty students had in understanding autotrophic feeding.

3   Students knew many separate items of information related to photosynthesis ('information overload'), but they lacked a meaningful and general view.

Difficulties of Instructional Origin

This group of difficulties originates from inadequate prerequisite knowledge in specific domains. For example, students lack basic knowledge in chemistry; they have incorrect preconceptions about respiration; and it is probable also that problems exist in relation to the subject of energy.

Basic Assumptions Underlying the Development of the New Study Unit

In developing our unit on photosynthesis we took into account the following points (Stavy and Eisen, in press).

1   The unit should contain and emphasize ideas which match with children's existing intuitive knowledge (Osborne and Freyberg, 1985). For example, children believe that there is order in the world. They know that people cannot live without oxygen, so they intuitively believe that there is a mechanism which renews the oxygen in the used air. They understand the fact that animals cannot live without plants, because that is the way the world is ordered. Bearing this in mind, we chose to deal with the issue of photosynthesis via the material cycles in Nature. These cycles represent a form of natural order.

2   Children tend to look at the world in an egocentric way. We therefore

decided to motivate them by starting the unit with the child's body as an object of examination.

3   Misconceptions that were revealed in our previous study were treated:

(a)   Children's difficulty in grasping the human body as a chemical entity led us to emphasize the material aspects: the chemical composition of living organisms and the changes that these substances undergo in their cycle within living organisms and in the surroundings.

(b)   The tendency of children to notice differences between plants and animals rather than similarities led us to emphasize their similarities. However, we do stress the difference between animal and plant nutrition, because we observed that in spite of their tendency to notice differences, they did not consider this particular difference between plants and animals to be important.

(c)   It was found that children confuse respiration and photosynthesis: they perceive photosynthesis as a sort of respiration. This finding prompted us to deal with the two concepts separately and to emphasize the relationship between these two very important life processes.

(d)   In our study as well as in others (Driver *et al*, 1985) it was noticed that children sometimes have ideas reminiscent of scientific theories that were favoured in the past. Some children think, as Aristotle did, that plants are fed from the soil; others think, like Van Helmont, that water is plants' food. We dealt with such misconceptions by introducing stories from the history of science.

4   It was found that children do not relate knowledge acquired in chemistry lessons with that learnt in biology, and that their knowledge seems to be compartmentalized according to the subject taught. Therefore in the new unit we tried to integrate issues which are regularly dealt with in chemistry lessons with those from biology lessons. We also integrated some technological issues in this unit.

5   Children do know quite a lot about photosynthesis. Their knowledge consists of unrelated pieces of information, but their general overview of the ecosystem is deficient. In the new study unit we intentionally ignore many facts that we consider inessential for the general understanding of the ecosystem, and for the same reason we also avoided using an excess of concepts. We refer, for example, to the chemical composition of organisms only on the level of elements, and not of compounds. We use the same principle with regard to photosynthesis — we do not refer to chlorophyll or chloroplasts, nor do we use the concepts of producers and consumers which are widely used in other curricula, and which children use without understanding. Instead, we concentrate on the general view of the ecosystem as a whole.

6   In order to arouse children's motivation and to gain significant learning we deal in this study unit with issues that are relevant to people's lives in modern society, related to fuel resources and to the disturbance of the ecological equilibrium by modern technology.

Study Unit Content: 'On and On ... Material Cycles in Nature'

Chapter 1: *What are the elements your body is built of?*
The chemical composition of the human body, emphasizing the chemical elements carbon, hydrogen and oxygen.

Chapter 2: *The balance of materials entering and leaving the body*
The quantity of materials entering the body is larger than the quantity leaving it.

Chapter 3: *What happens to the body materials?*
The synthesis of body compounds from food materials and their break-down by oxygen during the respiration process. During respiration oxygen is being used and carbon dioxide is being released.

Chapter 4: *Why is it that the oxygen in the air is not used up?*
Plants release oxygen and improve the atmosphere which is degraded by respiration. The story of Priestley.

Chapter 5: *What elements are plants built of?*
Plants are built of carbon, oxygen and hydrogen — the same elements from which animals are built.

Chapter 6: *What happens to the materials in the plant?*
The origin of plant materials in carbon dioxide and water. The materials are built during photosynthesis and are broken down during respiration. Aristotle's and Van Helmont's ideas of the origin of plant materials are presented as examples of ancient scientific theories.

Chapter 7: *On and on ... material cycles in Nature*
The carbon-oxygen cycle, the water cycle and the nitrogen cycle.

Chapter 8: *Carbon resources in Nature*
Fuel reservoirs (coal and oil) and their origin in living organisms — plants and animals.

Chapter 9: *Man's influence on the carbon cycle*
The influence of technology on the carbon cycle in nature, especially its probable influence on the future world climate.

The ideas which are introduced in this unit are based on facts which are either presented to the learner, or discovered by the learner himself from experiments suggested in the course of study.

Conclusion

The existing study unit, 'The plant and light', and the proposed unit 'On and on ...', both deal with the same basic ideas. The older unit was developed prior to studies on students' alternative frameworks. The developers did not have any information about children's ideas or about their difficulties in understanding photosynthesis. The content and the sequence of the curriculum were developed according to the requirements of the structure of the subject matter. The unit includes many aspects of photosynthesis, all of which are presented at the same level of importance. No focus on the general principle is given and the learners are expected to generate for themselves the overall picture of the ecosystem from the abundant information presented to them.

Our research on the difficulties that children experience in understanding photosynthesis in the old study unit reveals that children did acquire knowledge of a considerable number of factual details, but they seemed to lose their way with them and did not succeed in building a general picture as was expected.

In the new unit we therefore decided to omit as many details as possible that are inessential for the understanding of the general principles, and instead to concentrate on the main ideas: the existence of an ecosystem consisting of both physical and biotic environments operating in mutual relationship, with materials cycling from the atmosphere to plants, to animals, back to the atmosphere, and so on. We also tried to correlate the learning sequence to children's intuitive ideas and so to avoid the development of misconceptions.

Other research studies have recommended that each of the misconceptions be treated specifically by classroom discussions or creating a conflict in order to weaken pupils' confidence in their ideas and in addition to introduce an acceptable alternative (Driver, Guesne and Tiberghien, 1985; Posner *et al.*, 1982). Sometimes this approach has succeeded and has been found to be efficient (Stavy and Berkowitz, 1980), but when dealing with a complex issue like the ecosystem we thought that it would be too complicated and inefficient to deal specifically with each of the problems and we tried to choose a different content and approach to the teaching of photosynthesis dealing simultaneously with all the difficulties children have in understanding that topic.

Will our approach succeed in bringing children to a better understanding of photosynthesis and the ecosystem? We will have to study the effect of the new study unit on children's understanding of photosynthesis in the future.

References

Driver, R., Guesne, E. and Tiberghien, A. (Eds) (1985) *Children's Ideas in Science*, Milton Keynes, Open University Press.

Eisen, Y. and Stavy, R. (in press) *Who Remembers Their School Biology?*

Gilbert, J.K., Osborne, R. and Fensham, P. (1982) 'Children's science and its consequences for teaching', *Science Education*, 66, 4, pp 623–33.

Israeli Education and Culture Department (1979) *The Plant and the Light*, Maalot, Curriculum Development Center.

Israeli Education and Culture Department (1982) *Basic Contents Abilities and Skills in Teaching Biology in 7th and 8th Grades*, Jerusalem, Supervision of Science Teaching Curriculum Development Center.

Osborne, R. and Freyberg, P. (1985) *Learning in Science, the Implications of Children's Science*, London, Heinemann.

Posner, G.J., Strike, K.A., Hewson, P.W. and Gertzog, W.A. (1982) 'Accommodation of a scientific conception: toward a theory of conceptual change', *Science Education*, 66, 2, pp 211–27.

STAVY R. and BERKOWITZ, B. (1980) 'Cognitive conflict as a basis for teaching quantitative aspects of temperature', *Science Education*, 64, pp 678–92.

STAVY, R., EISEN, Y. and YAAKOBI, O. (1987) 'How students aged 13–15 understand photosynthesis', *International Journal of Science Education*.

Discussion (Reporter: David Squires)

The first question in the discussion asked how long each unit in the course was planned to last. It was stated that there were no fixed times for the units.

The course consists of eight units, the central unit being of critical significance. The first three units are concerned with the human body and the last four units are concerned with plant metabolism. The central unit is concerned with 'Why is oxygen in the air not used up?' The question was asked as to how this central unit would be introduced and how would the link between the early and late chapters be made. In reply it was stated that it was intended to stress the similarities between the operation of humans and plants.

Some discussion centred on the wisdom of using the concept of an element which some people thought was too difficult for use in this context (as a non-observable entity). It was stated in response to a question that practical examples that implied the fundamental nature of elements were given — burning foods, meats, hair to get carbon. In discussion it was stated that the conservation of matter was a central idea in the course. There is a problem associated with using the word 'substance' as a replacement for the word 'element' in the Hebrew language. It was asked why is the assumption made that the concept of an element is easier than the concept of energy.

In response to a question about plans to monitor the course, it was stated that there are no plans to monitor the course at the moment.

13.3 A Study of Students' Alternative Frameworks in Stoichiometry

Hans-Jürgen Schmidt

Introduction

This paper deals with difficulties experienced by secondary school students and undergraduates studying chemistry when attempting stoichiometric calculations. A large sample of students was asked to work through specific multiple choice questions. We were particularly interested to find out how the students obtained the answer.

Our hypothesis is a follows: when students make errors, they follow a certain strategy to reach a given result. These strategies may be investigated by the use of empirically designed multiple choice questions. By studying the answer profile of a given multiple choice question, and using notes made by students while they were answering the question, it is possible to throw some light on these strategies. In order to highlight possible strategies, a number of multiple choice questions and the analysis of the answers given will be presented.

The students came from all parts of the Federal Republic of Germany. Their ages ranged from 16 to 19 years and they came from the tenth to thirteenth grade, i.e. from the last four years of the gymnasium. They had either studied a basic course of two hours per week chemistry or a more advanced course of five hours per week. The sample consisted of 6262 students. We had an additional 650 first year undergraduates from six different universities within the Federal Republic. Every eighth pupil and every third university student was given one of the following questions i.e. the results are based on a sample of 800 school pupils and 200 university students.

Relationship Between Mass and Number of Particles

Students' Understanding of Chemicals Symbols

Let us first of all look at question 16.341 and the answer profile figure 13.3.1):

Figure 13.3.1   *Answer profile for question 16.341. This question was given to students in grade 10 (striped column), to students in grade 11 (black column) and also to students in grades 12 and 13 who had followed the basic and more advanced chemistry courses (two black columns).*

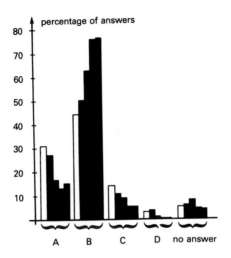

Question 16.341

The formula for sulphur dioxide is SO_2. How many grams of sulphur are contained in 6 grams of sulphur dioxide?

4 g (A) / 3g (B) / 2.5g (C) / 2 g (D)

The most important distractor is D, and A must also be taken into account. An analysis of the pupil records shows what thoughts led to their obtaining these results:

SO_2 contains 3 atoms, one of which is sulphur. So sulphur must be 1/3 of the weight: 2g.

Here it is assumed — deliberately or not — that the ratio of masses is directly proportional to the ratio of atoms:

(1) $n(S) : n(O) = m(S) : m(O)$

Other pupil records point to the fact, that the ratio of molar masses is often equated with the ratio of masses:

"... $32/16 = 2$, ratio $S : O = 2 : 1$,
$2/3 \times 6 = 4(S)$
$1/3 \times 6 = 2(O)$

A Study of Students' Alternative Frameworks in Stoichiometry

Figure 13.3.2 *Answer profile for question 91.000. The striped column refers to students from grade 10, the first black column to students from grade 11, the next two black columns refer to students in grades 12 and 13 having followed the basic and more advanced chemistry courses respectively and the final column refers to students following the chemistry diploma and chemical technology courses at university.*

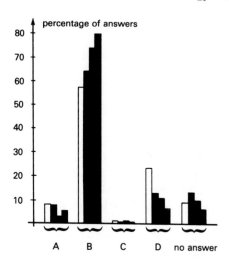

In this case the pupil has divided the 6g of sulphur dioxide into three parts and allocated two-thirds to sulphur and one-third to oxygen. This is based on the wrong assumption:

$$(2) \qquad M(S) : M(O) = m(S) : m(O)$$

This explains why distractor A was chosen.

In question 91.000 the chemical formula is not given but has to be deduced.

Question 91.000

2g of a compound contains 1g copper, the rest is sulphur. Which of the following formulae satisfies this condition?

$$CuS \ (A) \ / \ CuS_2 \ (B) \ / \ Cu_2S \ (C) \ / \ Cu_2S_2 \ (D)$$

Here also two distractors are in particular evidence (figure 13.3.2)

The same mistake is made here as in the SO_2 question 16.341. Pupils do not distinguish between the ratio of atoms and the ratio of masses:

$$(3) \qquad m(Cu) : m(S) = n(Cu) : n(S)$$

Here is an example of a commentary provided by one chemistry student in the first semester:

Hans-Jurgen Schmidt

As the proportion of Cu to S is $1:1$, this must show itself in the chemical formula ... hence solution A.

Again it is evident that the ratio of molar masses is regarded as the same as the ratio of number of atoms:

$$(4) \qquad M(Cu):M(S) = n(Cu):n(S)$$

Here is a typical student commentary:

Cu has 64g, S has 32g, so the proportion is $2:1$, so $Cu_2 S$.

The Generalizability of the Results

I would now like to add an additional dimension to the issue. The students who took part in the research did not get there by chance and in no sense can they be regarded as a representative sample of all pupils in the statistical sense. It would therefore be wrong to generalize the results and hypotheses that have been obtained. If one wants to discover whether the hypotheses are valid for other samples, then the same research must be repeated with these other samples. We therefore obtained multiple choice questions, with answer profiles, from a number of examination boards in other countries in order to check (i) whether the multiple choice questions contain the type of distractor which we would expect according to our hypotheses to be chosen by students, and (ii) whether the students actually choose these distractors.

It is of course possible in a study of this kind to use multiple choice questions that have been previously set and to check whether the same answer profile is obtained as in Germany. With the next question we did precisely this.

> The formula of an oxide of sulphur is SO_2. What mass of oxygen combines with 16g of sulphur in this oxide? (Relative atomic mass: O 16, S 32)
>
> 2g (A) / 4g (B) / 8g (C) / 16g (D) / 32g (E)

It was first set in England and is our question number 16.341. It was sent to us by the Oxford and Cambridge Schools Examination Board. The question was set in an 'O' level examination in 1983 and was attempted by 4641 pupils. The percentage of pupils choosing each option was as follows:

(A) 1% / (B) 4% / (C) 15% / (D) 66% / (E) 13%

The most important distractors are C and E. These are selected either if the candidate compares molar masses:

$$(5) \qquad M(S):M(O) = 32:16 = 16:8$$

or compares the number of atoms:

(6) $$n(S):n(O) = 1:2 = 16:32$$

Question 91.000 is very similar to one set by the Scottish Examination Board:

An analysis of a sulphide of copper gives the following results:

mass of copper = 1.0g (relative atomic mass 64)

mass of sulphur = 1.0g (relative atomic mass 32)

Which formula correctly represents this sulphide?

CuS (A) / CuS_2 (B) / Cu_2S (C) / Cu_2S_2 (D)

The above question was set in the 'O' grade examination in 1983 and the percentage of pupils choosing each option was as follows:

(A) 15% / (B) 57% / (C) 27% / (D) 1%

the most important distractors were A and C. These are obtained by using the ratio of masses

(7) $$m(Cu):m(S) = 1:1$$

or by considering the ratio of molar masses

(8) $$M(Cu):M(S) = 64:32 = 2:1$$

The following question was also obtained from the Scottish Examination Board:

An analysis of an oxide of tellurium (Te) gave the following result:

mass of tellurium = 8g

mass of oxygen = 1 g

Which of the following formulae correctly represents this oxide? (Take the relative atomic mass of tellurium as 128, oxygen as 16

TeO (A) / TeO_2 (B) / TeO_3 (C) / TeO_4 (D)

This question was set in the 'O' grade examination in 1979 and the percentage of candidates choosing each option was as follows:

(A) 76% / (B) 7% / (C) 6% / (D) 11%

If the strategy of proportion of number of atoms or the proportion of molar masses is used, the formula Te_8O is obtained. This solution is not contained in the question and in any case it would be a somewhat strange formula.

It should be noted that the students had greater success with the tellurium oxide question than with the copper oxide question. Although the above two questions were set four years apart, the Scottish Examination Board monitors the performance of pupils and it is possible to say that there was no change in standards in this relatively short time interval. It is also possible to say that the candidates came from the same catchment areas and that chance determined which particular set of questions they were given in examination.

As part of this study we gave pairs of questions to the same student sample. With one pair it is possible to obtain the same answer if the mass ratio is assumed to be equivalent to the ratio of atoms, but by using another pair, this is not the case. The questions are more difficult if the above mistake is recognized by the candidate. This particular aspect of the research will be reported in the *Journal of Research in Science Teaching* and I will not elaborate it here.

The above finding is very interesting. One sees, for instance, that two questions that look completely alike nevertheless are different. On the other hand the result leads one to be able to say something about the stability of misconceptions.

First assumption: The pupils keep to the same strategy (wrong or right) in tackling both questions. In the case of the copper sulphide question, their answer is one of the distractors whereas in the tellurium oxide question, there is no appropriate answer and they are unclear what to do. They do not attempt the question again. In this case both questions should be equally difficult.

Second assumption: Pupils who obtained one of the preferred distractors in the copper sulphide question, find no appropriate answer in the case of the tellurium oxide question. They realize that they have used a wrong strategy and try another one. The tellurium oxide question must therefore appear to be easier and this is shown to be so in the analysis.

Implications of the Findings

I will now attempt to interpret the two types of mistakes identified in (1) to (4). Students who obtain the correct answer to questions 16.341 and 91.000 must relate three variables correctly: the mass (m), the molar mass (M) and the number of moles (n). Many pupils simplify their calculations by only considering two variables and forgetting about the third. This is in line with the findings of Piagetians who state: 'Younger and less able pupils will be limited to the use of concrete operational thinking, while older and more able pupils will have available a facility to handle abstractions and many-variable problems which is a characteristic of formal operations' Questions 16.341 and 91.000 should therefore divide the sample into formal operational and non-formal operational thinkers. However, if question 16.341 is used then it would appear there are more formal operational thinkers than if question 91.000 is considered. It would seem that the criteria 'able to use three variables' is not sufficient to explain our empirical findings.

Let us now consider a more practical aspect of our research. The two test items differ in a certain way. The problem stated in the stem of test item 91.000 is to find the chemical formula of a compound, whereas in test item 16.341 the chemical formula has already been given. Compared with test item 16.341 students have been less successful with test item 91.000. We have tried out quite a number of similar pairs of test items and in each case arrived at the same result:

— it is an easier problem to solve if the chemical formula is given,
— it is more difficult, if the chemical formula is asked for.

One principle in arranging a teaching sequence might be to begin with an easy example. If one does practical work with students, one has to develop the chemical formula from experimental data. This means it is necessary to calculate chemical formulae from masses. According to the result of our research, this is not the easiest way to introduce stoichiometric calculations. Does this mean that the ideas of practitioners do not correspond to the results of our work?

In the revised version of Nuffield chemistry a method has been described that fits our findings. It says, present students with samples of copper oxide and encourage them to suggest possible formulae for this material. Plot a graph on the blackboard in which the mass of copper is plotted against that of oxygen. Use this graph for comparison of experimental results (figure 13.3.3).

Conclusion

Our research has shown that many pupils, who do not get the correct result, have nevertheless had useful thoughts about chemical combinations, even if these do not coincide with the basic principles used by chemists. Many errors occur because a wrong strategy is used. It might even be postulated that some pupils have obtained the correct result because they have thought less about the chemistry and only applied learnt algorithms. Many errors made by pupils might even be regarded as 'honest' and pupils should not be ashamed of them.

Acknowledgements

I wish to acknowledge the cooperation of the Oxford and Cambridge Schools Examination Board and the Scottish Examination Board who made multiple choice tests and the results available and agreed to their publication.

We are grateful to Frau Dipl. Volksw. M. S. Schach for statistical advice at all stages of the investigation. A friend of mine, Fred Archenhold of the University of Leeds in England, kindly translated part of the text into English.

Hans-Jurgen Schmidt

Figure 13.3.3   Determining the chemical formula of copper oxide. The reacting masses can be plotted on this graph and will be found to correspond with the line for the formula CuO.

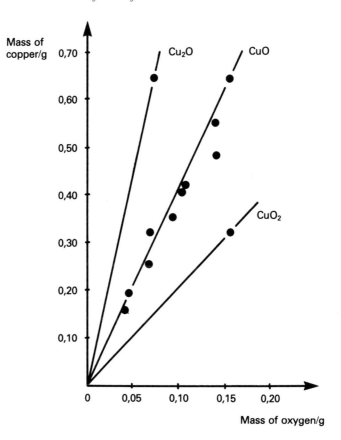

I would like to express my thanks to all above and also to the Minister für Wissenschaft und Forschung des Landes Nordrhein-Westfalen, who supported the research in 1985/86 with a financial grant (No. IV A 2-7000 2285).

References

SCHMIDT, H.J. (1984) 'How pupils think — empirical studies on pupils' understanding of simple quantitative relationships in chemistry', *School Science Review*, 66, 234, pp 156–60.

SCHMIDT, H.J. (in press) 'Secondary school students' strategies and errors in stoichiometry, *Journal of Research in Science Teaching*.

SHAYER, M. and ADEY, P. (1981) *Towards a Science of Science Teaching*, London, Heinemann.

A Study of Students' Alternative Frameworks in Stoichiometry

Discussion (Report: Ruth Stavy)

The discussion centered around three main points:

1   The multiple choice format does favour certain pupils. For instance, boys generally do better at such items than do girls. It would be worth investigating characteristics of pupils who do, and do not, respond better to the multiple choice format than to more open-ended question types.

2   Perhaps more information could be obtained about the nature of students' misunderstandings if a different type of research instrument were to be used. For instance, open-ended questions or interviews about the responses given to multiple choice questions would reveal something of the students' thinking underlying the answers given.

3   It seems that the information obtained from this study about (a) the type of misconceptions that students have in stoichiometry; and (b) the type of plausible answer to which such misconceptions lead, could become the basis of new multiple choice items. Distractors based on such information would give the teacher or researcher a richer idea of the origins of students' erroneous ideas.

13.4 Science Practical Process Skills of Ninth Grade Students in Israel

Pinchas Tamir

Practical examinations were included in the Second International Science Study (SISS) and designated as process skills tests. The present study reports the results of the SISS practical test of ninth grade (15-year-old) students in Israel and compares them with those obtained in Japan (Matsubara, 1986).

Method

Instruments

The following instruments were designed specifically for the second IEA study: a student background questionnaire, a thirty item multiple choice science test, an attitude inventory focussing on attitudes towards school as well as attitudes towards science, an understanding of science measure, and a classroom activity inventory in which the students reported on the frequency of various instructional experiences. These instruments are described in detail elsewhere. Process skills tests, which serve as the focus of the present study, were chosen on the basis of the following criteria:

1 the tasks are assessing important skills;
2 the tasks do not require elaborate or expensive equipment;
3 the tasks have no national or any other bias;
4 the tasks represent different science disciplines, namely biology, chemistry, and physics;
5 the difficulty and reasoning level are appropriate for the target population;
6 the tasks can be administered as group tests;
7 assessment can be done later, based on written answers;
8 the task problems are interesting.

Task 2A₂ asks the examinee to hold a strip of cobalt chloride paper between the fingertips for two minutes. Then the examinee holds the same strip with tongs 10cm above a flame. Based on the observations s/he should conclude that the cobalt chloride paper is blue under dry conditons and pink under moist conditions. Now the examinee compares the behaviour of the cobalt chloride paper when attached to the upper and lower sides of a leaf. From the results a conclusion is made about the relative rate of transpiration from each side of the leaf.

In *Task 2A₃* the student is required to etermine whether given samples of sour cream contain flour, using iodine solution.

In *Tasks 2B₁* asks the student to find out the mass and volume of a given rock and calculate the density.

In *Task 2B₂* the student has to identify which of three given test tubes contains ammonia, which vinegar, and which water, given phenolphthalein, litmus paper, and a reminder of the colours these indicators have in basic and acidic solutions.

The tasks involve a variety of process skills, presented in table 13.4.1. They also represent the three science disciplines: biology (task 2A₂), chemistry (tasks 2A₃, 2B₂), and physics (task 2B₁).

Sample

The sample consisted of 534 students from nineteen schools spread all over the country and was representative of Israeli ninth grade students.

Test Administration

The tests were administered to whole classes by the local science teachers according to detailed instructions provided by SISS. The tasks were grouped into two sets each representing physics, chemistry, biology respectively as follows:

Set one: 2B₁, 2A₂, 2A₃
Set two: 2B₁, 2A₂, 2B₂

Each student performed one set. Administration time was sixty minutes. The tests were collected and scored at the National Centre by two independent evaluators following a scoring key designed by SISS. Inter-rater agreement was high and ranged between 82 per cent in task 2A₂ and 92 per cent in task 2A₃. Since the same tests and same procedures were used in other countries participating in SISS, valid comparisons can be made.

Table 13.4.1   Results of the practical test of Israeli ninth grade.

Problem	Item	N	Process skill	$\bar{x}$	S.D.
2A$_2$	total score	534		53.0	28.3
	1		Observing	99.0	12.0
	2		Observing	98.0	14.0
	3		Concluding	38.0	47.0
	4		Observing	41.3	28.0
	5		Concluding	26.7	40.3
2A$_3$	total score	314		92.6	21.9
	1		Planning	95.5	19.0
	2		Reporting	89.5	29.0
2B$_1$	total score	534		73.2	25.0
	1		Planning	86.5	31.0
	2		Concluding	78.0	31.0
	3		Calculating	50.5	31.5
2B$_2$	total score	220		66.2	32.5
	1		Observing	70.0	23.0
	2		Concluding	64.6	43.3
	3		Planning	78.0	38.0
	4		Reporting	62.6	45.0
	5		Concluding	50.0	46.7
Whole test		534		65.7	20.6

Table 13.4.2   Achievement in different process skills across problems of the practical test (N = 534)

Skill	No. of items	x	S.D.
Observing	4	81.9	21.0
Calculating	1	55.8	31.2
Planning	2	86.2	24.0
Concluding	5	55.4	29.2
Reporting	2	80.6	26.8

Results

Performance of Israeli Students

Results are shown in tables 13.4.1 and 13.4.2.

Table 13.4.1 shows that the easiest task for Israeli students was 2A$_3$ (chemistry, identification of starch) and the most difficult was 2A$_2$ (biology, transpiration). 2B$_1$ (physics, density) and 2B$_2$ (chemistry, acids and bases) were intermediate. The list of skills involved in each task offers some clues as to the sources of difficulty. Apparently the demand on the skills of observation, planning and reporting were quite modest for most students. On the other hand

Table 13.4.3   Achievement of boys and girls in the practical test

Problem or skill	Boys			Girls			
	N	x	S.D.	N	x	S.D.	t
Whole test	210	72.9	18.6	323	61.2	20.4	6.65***
2A$_2$	210	63.4	28.6	323	46.3	25.9	7.12***
2A$_3$	116	95.3	17.4	197	91.0	24.1	1.81
2B$_1$	210	81.4	20.1	323	68.1	27.6	6.44***
2B$_2$	94	68.4	29.4	126	64.5	34.7	0.88
Observing	210	86.5	18.0	323	78.3	22.8	4.65***
Concluding	210	57.4	29.6	323	39.4	27.2	7.09***
Planning	210	92.0	18.7	323	83.8	26.5	4.16***
Reporting	210	77.2	39.8	323	79.3	37.9	0.58
Calculating	210	65.0	29.8	323	49.2	30.6	5.91***

***$p < 0.001$

the level of reasoning required for inferring and drawing conclusions as well as the relatively simple calculation required, raised serious difficulties for about half of the students. One may also note that observations are not always so easy. For example, in task 2A$_2$ the students had no difficulty in observing the colour change of the cobalt paper when held between their finger tips, but 60 per cent failed to observe the colour changes when the same paper was attached to the upper and lower sides of a leaf. No wonder that only one-quarter of the students were able to draw reasonable conclusions based on these observations.

Similarly inferring and drawing conclusions may be more or less difficult. For example, in task 2B$_2$ 65 per cent were able to conclude which test tube contained ammonia. However, only 50 per cent were able to identify correctly which of the remaining test tubes contained vinegar and which contained water.

The reasons for these substantial differences in levels of performance in the same skills even within the same task are not clear. Perhaps there is an effect of the context or more specifically, the task becomes more difficult with the need to process simultaneously more bits of information.

Gender Differences

Table 13.4.3 shows that in general boys perform better than girls and that the differences are statistically significant in two of the four tasks, one in biology and the other in physics. There were no statistically significant differences in the two chemistry tasks, perhaps because of their contextual closeness to the everyday experience of girls (for example, yogurt, starch, vinegar). One may speculate that the higher achievement of boys in the physics task (2B$_1$) is a result of the general superiority of boys in physics (for example, Johnson and Murphy,

Table 13.4.4 Intercorrelations among scores of different tasks in Israel and in Japan

	$2A_2$	$2A_3$	$2B_1$
ISRAEL (N = 220–390)			
$2A_3$	.18**		
$2B_1$	.32**	.19**	
$2B_2$	.42**	NA	.39**
JAPAN (N = 588)			
$2A_3$	.19**		
$2B_1$	.30**	NA	
$2B_2$	.39	NA	.39**

** $<p\ 0.01$ NA = not available
The Japanese data were taken from Matsubara (1986)

Table 13.4.5 Intercorrelations among practical process skills (N = 310–390)

	Observing	Concluding	Planning	Reporting
Concluding	.52**			
Planning	.16**	.28**		
Reporting	.13**	.06	.23**	
Calculating	.24**	.36**	.19**	.05

** $<p\ 0.01$

1986). The higher achievement of boys on task $2A_2$ may be result of their higher facility in handling difficult practical investigations which involve higher levels of inference. This assertion is supported by the comparative data pertaining to the particular process skills.

Thus, table 13.4.3 shows that boys outscore girls in all skills except reporting. However, the magnitude of the difference is very small regarding observation (one-quarter of the standard deviation) medium in planning and calculating (about one-half of the standard deviation), and rather large in drawing conclusions (about three-quarters of the standard deviation).

Interrelationships Among Tasks and Skills

As may be seen in table 13.4.4 the intercorrelations among the scores in the different tasks are all positive and statistically significant.

The similarity between the Israeli and Japanese results is striking. For most tasks the correlations range between 0.3 and 0.4. However, correlations with task $2A_3$ are lower indicating that this task requires somewhat different skills. Indeed, when process skills are considered across tasks one finds a wide range of relationships.

The data in table 13.4.5 reveal a relatively high correlation between observing and concluding. This could be expected since most inferences and conclusions were based on the observations. The medium correlation between concluding and calculating indicates that both require somewhat similar reasoning skills, which are totally unrelated to reporting skills. All other correlations are low but positive and statistically significant.

The Relationship of the Practical to the Paper and Pencil Test (Table 13.4.6)

The highest correlation was found between the total scores of the two tests. Thus achievement in the paper and pencil test accounts for close to one-third of the total variance of achievement in the practical test (r = 0.56). This result is quite close to that obtained in Japan in the present study: r = 0.51 for one set and r = 0.59 for the second set (Matsubara, 1986) as well as to that obtained in Japan in the First IEA Science Study (r = 0.63, Kojima, 1974). The correlations between particular tasks and the subtests representing different science disciplines reveal no consistent effect of specific subject matter knowledge. Thus, for example the correlation of task $2A_2$, which deals with biological contents, with subtest physics are higher than with subtest biology. Similarly, the correlation of task $2B_2$ (chemistry content) with subtests biology and physics is higher than with subtest chemistry. Obviously subject matter knowledge does *not* contribute much to performance on these tasks. This conclusion is supported by the fact that, with the exception of task $2A_3$, the correlations with sub-test knowledge are lower than with sub-tests comprehension and application.

As to the different process skills, the highest correlations with the performance in the paper and pencil test are between drawing conclusions and application, indicating that where higher cognitive skills are involved the weight of the common variance is greater than in cases which involve lower cognitive skills. Another finding which may have some generalizable quality is that performance in subtest Physics has the highest correlations with two process skills namely drawing conclusions and calculating, which in turn have the highest correlations with application.

Table 13.4.7 show that when the correlations between achievement in the paper and pencil test with that in the practical test are calculated at the school level (rather than the individual student level as in table 13.4.6), the values are consistently higher. On the average the difference amounts to 10 per cent of the explained variance (r = 0.56 as compared with r = 0.65). However, when each of the four tasks is considered separately, the difference in explained variance ranges from 7 per cent in task $2A_2$, through 18 per cent in tasks $2B_1$, 21% in task $2A_3$ and up 46 per cent in task $2B_2$. It may be inferred that the school environment exerts substantial influence and that this influence is not uniform for all tasks.

Table 13.4.6 Correlations between achievement in the paper and pencil test and the practical process skills test (N = 366)

Practical	Earth Science	Biology	Chemistry	Physics	Knowledge	Compre-hension	Application	Whole test
Problem 2A$_2$ (B)	29	39	34	43	35	43	42	48
Problem 2A$_3$ (C)	16	17	26	23	30	20	20	26
Problem 2B$_1$ (P)	33	30	31	35	31	34	38	41
Problem 2B$_2$ (C)	27	40	32	41	24	38	50	48
Observing	13	36	25	33	26	32	32	36
Concluding	36	37	37	45	36	42	46	50
Planning	26	27	27	28	26	28	32	34
Reporting	04	04	09	07	06	06	07	07
Calculating	22	25	29	32	25	28	33	35
Whole test	38	44	42	48	40	48	51	56

Decimal points omitted
if r = 0.10, p = 0.01
(B) = biological contents; (C) = chemistry contents; (P) = physics contents

Table 13.4.7 Correlations between achievement in the paper and pencil tests and the practical process skills test at the school level (N = 17)

Practical	Earth Science	Biology	Chemistry	Physics	Knowledge	Comprehension	Application	Whole test
Problem 2A$_2$	39	58	29	61	36	50	60	56
Problem 2A$_3$	90	40	44	46	80	36	46	52
Problem 2B$_1$	76	48	44	57	64	47	57	59
Problem 2B$_2$	72	84	68	63	59	63	84	83
Observing	62	60	42	62	51	52	66	63
Concluding	50	62	42	65	49	54	65	62
Planning	62	36	40	37	47	32	44	44
Reporting	49	19	33	12	41	19	18	24
Calculating	71	61	50	68	65	62	66	68
Whole test	66	60	48	61	57	54	64	64

Decimal points omitted
if r = 0.42, p = 0.05

Table 13.4.8 *Correlations between achievement in the practical process skills test and background variables (N = 366)*

Background Practical	SES	Interest and motivation	Times devoted to practical work	Science ability	Maths science	Liking school, maths	Liking school
Problem A$_2$	21	35	08	23	22	29	22
Problem A$_3$	20	10	11	03	04	14	08
Problem B$_1$	10	24	13	12	18	24	15
Problem B$_2$	42	30	24	06	17	09	06
Observing	23	24	08	13	16	18	08
Concluding	25	36	08	21	21	29	25
Planning	24	22	13	07	15	16	08
Reporting	09	10	06	01	02	00	00
Calculating	20	27	19	08	18	20	24
Whole test	29	38	14	20	22	30	21

Decimal points omitted
if r = 0.10, p = 0.05

Relationships With Background Variables

Correlations between background variables and performance in the practical test were calculated both at the individual student's level (table 13.4.8) and at the school level (table 13.4.9).

Here again the values obtained at the school level are consistently larger. The data in both tables reveal some interesting findings:

1 Interest in and motivation to study science appears to have the highest correlation at the individual level, and the same correlation at the school level. It may be inferred that the contribution of the school to this relationship is nil.

2 While time devoted to practical work has very low correlation for individual students it exhibits a very high correlation (r = 0.68) at the school level. Somewhat lower correlation was found for opportunities to experiential learning (r = 0.47). Hence, classes which devote more time to practical work and experiential learning achieve better. This conclusion is supported by the high correlation (r = 0.71) between opportunity to learn various science concepts and skills as reported by the teacher and performance in the practical. It may be concluded that one way to improve practical process skills is to devote more time to experiential learning and to practical work as well as to the study of science in general.

3 SES (socioeconomic status) exerts significant impact both at the student and the school level. The difference between r = 0.29 and r = 0.52

Table 13.4.9   Correlations between achievement in the practical process skills test and certain background variables at the school level (N = 17)

Background Practical	SES	Interest and motivation	Attitude toward school	Time devoted to practical work	Opportunity to learn	Liking school, science	Experiential learning	Understanding the nature of science	Attitude toward science
Problem A$_1$	39	26	03	69	58	36	39	37	35
Problem A$_3$	75	27	65	25	46	01	83	74	18
Problem B$_1$	48	299	28	59	60	38	48	73	41
Problem B$_2$	42	36	39	48	69	53	37	83	67
Observing	49	37	15	69	51	39	55	57	40
Concluding	48	42	09	68	63	43	38	47	38
Planning	43	30	54	52	56	22	42	76	42
Reporting	24	07	43	17	44	16	24	56	42
Explaining	50	31	16	51	59	51	37	55	45
Whole test	52	38	31	68	71	42	47	68	50

Decimal points omitted
if r = 0.41, p = 0.05

Table 13.4.10 Differences in achievement in the practical test among schools

Process skill	Best School			Lowest school			F df = 18, 515	R^2 (ETA)
	N	x	S.D.	N	x	S.D.		
Observation	32	95.0	8.8	31	64.5	28.7	5.7***	.17
Concluding	11	80.4	21.6	26	18.0	21.4	10.7***	.27
Planning	23	98.9	5.2	26	48.5	33.5	7.9***	.22
Reporting	23	100.0	0.0	26	29.5	44.5	9.3***	.25
Computing	11	77.3	34.4	29	36.2	29.6	6.4***	.18
Total Score	28	83.1	13.6	26	34.3	21.2	12.4	.30

***$p < 0.001$

implies that a student of low SES has a better chance to achieve better in a school in which the average SES is higher.

4 Science ability and maths ability as estimated by the school marks equally predict performance in the practical test for individual students: $r = 0.20$ and 0.22 respectively. The equivalent correlations in Japan were 0.27 and 0.19 respectively. These data support an earlier conclusion that achievement in this practical test depends on general cognitive abilities more than on specific subject matter knowledge.

5 Certain information was available only at the school level. For these variables the following picture has emerged: performance in the practical test is strongly correlated with the understanding of the nature of science (as assessed by the understanding of science measure), has medium correlation with attitudes toward science and low correlation with attitudes toward school. Here, as in other studies (for example, Kojima, 1974), performance in the practical is related to cognitive measures more strongly than to affective measures and attitudes toward science are better predictors of achievement in science than attitudes toward school.

The Contribution of the Schools

It seems clear that the school environment exerts a substantial impact on the performance of students. Table 13.4.10 reveals the range of scores obtained by the nineteen schools which participated in the study. The difference between the best and the worst school amounted to forty-nine percentage points! Thus the school environment accounts for close to one third of the explained variance.

Israel Compared with Japan

We have already seen that many of the correlations between the performance in the practical test and other measures found in Israel are similar to those

Table 13.4.11 Results of Israel and Japan in the practical process skills test

Task	Japan			Israel		
	N	$\bar{x}$	S.D.	N	$\bar{x}$	S.D.
$2A_2$ (biology)	587	53.0	23.8	534	53.0	28.3
$2A_3$ (chemistry)	588	33.0	26.8	314	92.6	21.9
$2B_1$ (physics)	588	27.0	22.0	534	73.2	25.9
$2B_2$ (chemistry)	588	43.0	22.3	220	66.2	18.4

found in Japan. However, substantial differences exist in actual performance (table 13.4.11)

It may be seen that only on task $2A_2$ were the Japanese and Israeli scores similar. In all other tasks the Japanese performance was much lower than that of the Israeli sample. Since in the paper and pencil test the Japanese results were relatively high, it may be concluded that Japanese schools fail to develop practical process skills. On the other hand, performance of Israeli students on the practical was, on the average, substantially better than their performance on the paper and pencil test. This reflects the strong emphasis on laboratory work in most Israeli lower secondary schools.

Discussion and Implications

Firstly, our results provide further evidence regarding the uniqueness of the practical mode in science learning and science performance.

Secondly, we would like to stress the benefit of international comparison. For example, conclusions from intercorrelations among scores in the different tasks carry a higher level of generalizability when similar results are obtained in different countries. Consider also the problem of determining success or failure on the basis of test scores: the relatively low performance of Japanese students in the practical test could have been interpreted as indicating that the practical test is inherently more difficult than the paper and pencil test. However, comparison with the results from Israel show that the tasks in the practical are not inherently more difficult, so other reasons must account for the relatively low performance in Japan. Similarly, Israel may regard the performance of its students as success rather than as an artifact of the ease of the tasks.

Thirdly, the results highlight the effects of the school compared with the home environment. It is reassuring to see that the school accounts for 30 per cent of the variation in achievement and that factors such as opportunities to learn, time devoted to laboratory work, emphasis on experiential learning, and efforts invested in learning do indeed make a significant difference.

Fourthly, the underachievement of girls in practical process skills raises serious questions. What is it in the nature and/or background of girls that causes this underachievement? The context hypothesis put forward by Johnson and Murphy (1986) may partially account for this as evidenced by the relatively high achievement of girls in the two chemistry tasks which involve materials and manipulations encountered by many girls in their everyday life.

Lastly, the importance of using practical tests for regular student assessment in school should be emphasized. Many science teachers in Israeli secondary schools use such tests in their classrooms, to a large extent as a result of the fact that practical tests constitute an important component of the external matriculation exams in biology (Tamir, 1974) and in physics. Countries that wish to improve practical process skills might encourage their science teachers to incorporate practical tests in their regular assessment scheme

Referrences

JOHNSON, S. and MURPHY, P. (1986) *Girls and Physics*, APU occasional paper No. 4, London, Department of Education and Science.

KOJIMA, S. (1974) 'On the measurement of practical abilities in science in Japan'. *Comparative Educational Review*, 18 pp 263–7.

MATSUBARA, S. (1986) *Summary of Practical Results in Japan*, SISS document S86–01, Hawthorn, Australian Council for Educational Research.

TAMIR, P. (1974) 'An inquiry oriented laboratory examination', *Journal of Education Measurement*, 11, pp 25–33.

Discussion (Reporter: Yehudit Eisen)

Some doubt was expressed about the validity of the practical tests, since it was known that Japanese students performed better in formal operational tasks than American students, and so it was surprising that they performed less well in the tasks described here. Tamir reminded the questioner that Japanese students did perform as well as Israeli students on the biology task, which probably was more intellectually demanding than the others. The evidence indicates that the practical process skill tests do indeed measure practical skills as distinct from knowledge or higher level cognitive skills.

14 Formal Operations: Its Validity and Application to Science Learning

Michael Shayer

In these four papers the interaction of science context and developmental level of pupil is touched on in different ways. Leslie Smith is at the furthest remove from context, yet his distinction between concrete and formal operations sets up a tool for analysis in terms of the differences in abstraction involved. Concrete models can *describe* the presence or absence of concepts or characteristics A and B applied to real objects as four possible combinations. But, from an exhaustive inspection of a set of objects to note that A never occurs without B, and to realize that this means there is an asymmetric relation between A and B (given the other three combinations), is a qualitatively different and higher step in thinking. It requires both generalization and abstraction. This would be the kind of question to address to science learning tasks: Which of these qualitative types is required? As to development, '... nothing will come of nothing', so one needs an aspect of *potential* in the model, and Smith argues that Piaget's treatment of *possibility* and *necessity* allows in principle a description of how the logical model gets applied in particular instances, and develops from very early beginnings. Smith is not disturbed by a gradual and 'spotty' evolution of competence in logical operations in any individual, and although not offering to gather it himself, calls for fresh empirical data on modal understanding (Is it necessary, or is it only possible?) to allow a better test of the validity of Piaget's work.

It is therefore of some interest that Trevor Bond has in fact constructed a multiple choice test embodying in combinatorial form all the sixteen binary operations distinguished in the use of formal thought [BLOT]. This means that an empirical test can be carried out of Piaget's logical model against the Inhelder/Piaget behavioural description model of formal tasks. Rasch analysis of the BLOT items is then compared with discrimination-level analysis of the same items against the criterion of performance on the pendulum task. The analyses give a linear relation. Affirmation, negation and incompatibility then appear as *concrete* relations in the data; equivalence, conjunction and disjunction appear at the concrete generalization level; implication and its relatives scale at the early formal level, and only non-implication (the crucial step in deduction) scales nearer the mature formal level. Inasmuch as Piaget ever comitted himself in writing, these combinatorial operations do appear at the stages he showed them operative in his analyses of behaviour.

It should be impossible for an inconsistent model to give *consistent* accounts of different behaviours. Jarkko Hautamäki has replicated the CSMS developmental survey work on Finnish adolescents, using Finnish versions of the pendulum and volume and heaviness tasks. The agreement is striking. In addition, the application of Rasch analysis to the test-item data confirms the quantitative attribution of stage to peformance, originally described in Geneva and built into group-test form in Britain. But perhaps the most interesting test of a model is its ability to reveal aspects of reality hitheto unperceived. Peter Matthews has used the taxonomy, derived from the Genevan work by Shayer and Adey (1981), to shed light on the detail of pupils' understanding of chemistry. He used a necessary-condition model of cognitive development, and then looks at the specifics of the chemical concepts pupils develop in relation to instruction and their own biases. He asks the question: Does GCSE examining do what it claims; that is, if different pupils get the same mark, does this have the same meaning? He shows in some detail that the same mark neither has the same meaning for the chemical concepts the pupils have, nor for the way they relate the same cognate set of concepts, nor for the (Piagetian) level of processing at which they take the same concepts. The notion of *Piaget-Specific Levels* would seem to have some mileage ahead.

Reference

SHAYER, M. and ADEY, P. (1981) *Towards a Science of Science Teaching*, London, Heinemann.

14.1 Constructing Formal Operations

Leslie Smith

There is some dispute about Piaget's theory of formal operational understanding. It is claimed both that the theory is acceptable in being the only one available (Neimark, 1982) and that it should be set aside since untestable (Johnson-Laird, 1983). The argument in this paper is that Piaget's theory requires interpretation as a preliminary to its adequate evaluation. The discussion is in four steps.

Developmental Process

Piaget's theory is an empirical account of the growth of understanding. The developmental process has an invariant functional form with variable structural manifestations (Smith, 1986a and 1987a). There are two interpretations of this process. On the absence-to-presence interpretation (Donaldson *et al.*, 1983), understanding which is present later is absent at earlier developmental points. A decisive objection however is that this interpretation leads straight to the 'learning paradox' (Bereiter, 1985): it is impossible for something to emerge from nothing, for knowledge to emerge from ignorance. An alternative interpretation is that the process is one of indifferentiation-to-differentiation (Smith, 1985a and 1987b). This position has the explicit support of Piaget (1983, p 7) It is also implicit in the title of Inhelder and Piaget's (1955/1958) work, *From Childhood Logic to Adolescent Logic*.

Modal Model

Three criteria need to be met in an acceptable model of this developmental process. The model should (i) identify an invariant feature of development (functioning); (ii) specify a variable feature of development (structure); and (iii) capture the differentiation of understanding. The first two criteria are discussed in this section and the third one in the next.

In his constructivist works (Smith, 1987c), Piaget makes use of a modal model of development. The modal (Hughes and Cresswell, 1972) conepts of possibility and necessity are central to human understanding. Piaget (1986) contends that modal understanding is a pervasive feature of development (criterion 1) which is manifest in different ways in that modal error leads to developmental differences in understanding (criterion 2). Two main types of model error may be noticed (Smith, 1985b and 1986b). A false-positive modal error occurs when someone judges to be possible (necessary) that which is not so. Examples occur in performance on the flexible rods task, when it is believed that a causal attribution can be made even when two variables are un-controlled, as well as in children's measurement of length (Piaget, 1983). A false-negative modal error occurs when someone judges to be not possible (necessary) that which is so. Examples arise in the chemicals combination task, when there is denial that other combinations can be made, as well as in tasks of spatial thinking (Piaget, 1981). Significantly, the claim is made that 'formal thought brings about from the outset a synthesis of possibility and necessity' (Inhelder and Piaget, 1955, p 220/1958, p 251 — my trans.)

Logical Model

Piaget's (1972) logical model is here taken to be compatible with his modal model. Doubts have however been expressed as to whether Piaget's use of propositional logic is acceptable. In a recent review (Braine and Rumain, 1983), the options available seem bleak. Either Piaget's logical model lacks an interpretation and so amounts to nonsense; or, no adequate interpretation has so far been given.

A fuller attempt to outline an acceptable interpretation is made elsewhere (Smith, 1987d), one that addresses the differentiation of formal from concrete operations (criterion 3). Multiplicative thinking during concrete operations allows an individual to understand the four possible ways in which two concepts can be instantiated. Specifically, an individual who uses two concepts can make observations corresponding to: (a) instances of both concepts, (b) instances of the first concept but not the second; (c) instances of the second concept but not the first; (d) instances of neither concept. Formal operations is a generalization of, and an abstraction from, concrete operations. Generaliz-ation occurs in the realisation that there are sixteen ways in which observations can be patterned in conformity with (a)–(d). For example, observations (a) and (b) and (c) and (d) together are different from observations (a) and (d) alone, whilst both are different from observations (b) and (c) alone; and so on. Abstraction occurs in the realization that each pattern has a unique identity. Thus the first case amounts to complete affirmation or independence; the second case amounts to equivalence; the third case amounts to reciprocal exclusion. During concrete operations, individuals have the ability to make any of these four base types of observation; during formal operations, its generalization and abstraction leads to new forms of understanding. Crucially, each of (a)–(d) is compatible with eight different operations. The mere observation corresponding to (a) alone is inconclusive: does the individual realise that complete affirmation, implication, converse implication and equivalence are each compatible with (a)? Piaget uses propositional logic for epistemological purposes in which the distinction between propositional operator and formal operation is central.

Minimal-Maximal Competence

The definition of any one operation requires reference to the complete system of formal operations. It is however possible for any one operation to be used without a display of the complete system. The full (maximal) display of competence is an ideal towards which actual development progresses. Conversely, an individual's development proceeds from incomplete (minimal) displays of formal operations, culminating in full competence (Smith, 1985b).

Four reasons can be given in support of this position. Firstly, no case has been documented of one individual who displays all sixteen formal operations across all fifteen tasks. At best, Inhelder and Piaget cite one subject who displays full competence on only one task; at worst, since that one case is open to divergent challenge, no one subject displays full competence on even one task. Secondly, low inter-task correlations are frequently reported, even when subjects are presented with Genevan tasks (Smith, 1986c). This finding is to be expected by those who accept the proposed position. Thirdly, recent attempts to design a numerical scale for the measurement of operational understanding have led to the discovery of heterogeneity in the demands of formal operational tasks (Shayer, 1987). Individuals who succeed (maximal competence) on one formal operational task may perform differently on another (minimal competence). Finally, Piaget now accepts that precursors of adolescent understanding are present during early childhood. (During the semiotic function we are witness to) 'the precocious formation, at the level of actions, of operations each of which — considered separately and relative to its meaning-context — is ismorphous with each of the sixteen binary operations of the logic of propositions' (Piaget and Garcia, 1987, p 15; my trans.).

Conclusion

When a theory is negatively evaluated, there are two options. One option is to devise a better theory. A second is to devise a better alternative of the existing theory. The latter option is commended here, one that invites further elaboration. Firstly, the compatibility of Piaget's modal and logical models has yet to be demonstrated. Secondly, new empirical research is required in the investigation of modal (mis)understanding. Thirdly, the systematic application of Piaget's theory to school learning has yet to take place. Questions about the validity and utility of Piaget's theory remain open (Smith, 1987e).

References

BEREITER, C. (1985) 'Toward a solution of the learning paradox', *Review of Educational Research* 55, pp 201–26.

BRAINE, M. and RUMAIN, B. (1983) 'Logical reasoning' in FLAVELL, J. and MARKMAN, E. (Eds) *Handbook of Child Development*, Vol. III, New York, Wiley.

DONALDSON, M., GRIEVE, R. and PRATT, C. (1983) *Early Childhood Development and Education*, Oxford, Blackwell.

HUGHES, G. and CRESSWELL, M. (1972) *An Introduction to Modal Logic*, London, Methuen.

INHELDER, B. and PIAGET, J. (1955/1958) *De la Logique de l'Enfant à la Logique de l'Adolescent*, Paris, Presses Universitaires de France/*The Growth of Logical Thinking*, London, Routledge and Kegan Paul.

JOHNSON-LAIRD, P. (1983) *Mental Models*, Cambridge, Cambridge University Press.

NEIMARK, E. (1982) 'Adolescent thought' in WOLMAN B. (Ed.) *Handbook of Developmental Psychology*, Engelwood Cliffs, NJ, Prentice Hall.

PIAGET, J. (1972) *Essai de Logique Opératoire*, Paris, Dunod.

PIAGET, J. (1981) *Le Possible et le Nécessaire*, Vol. I, Paris, Presses Universitaires de France.

PIAGET, J. (1983) *Le Possible et le Nécessaire*, Vol. II, Paris, Presses Universitaires de France.

PIAGET, J. (1986) 'Essay on necessity', *Human Development*, 29, pp 301–14.

PIAGET, J. and GARCIA. R. (1987) *Vers Une Logique des Significations*, Geneva, Murionde.

SHAYER, M. (1987) 'The scaling of formal operations', article submitted for publication.

SMITH, L. (1985a) 'Making educational sense of Piaget's psychology', *Oxford Review of Education*, 11, pp 181–91.

SMITH, L. (1985b) *Ability Learning*, York, Longmans Resources Unit.

SMITH, L. (1986a) 'Children's knowledge', *Human Development*, 29, pp 195–208.

SMITH, L. (1986b) 'Common core curriculum', *British Educational Research Journal*, 12, pp 55–71.

SMITH, L. (1986c) 'General transferable ability', *British Journal of Developmental Psychology*, 4, pp 377–87.

SMITH, L. (1987a) 'The infant's Copernican revolution', *Human Development*, 30, pp 210–24.

SMITH, L. (1987b) 'On Piaget on necessity' in RUSSELL J. (Ed.) *Philosophical Perspectives on Developmental Psychology*, Oxford, Blackwell.

SMITH, L. (1987c) 'Jean Piaget' in CHAPMAN A. and SHEEHY N. (Eds) *Who's who in Psychology*, Brighton, Harvester.

SMITH. L. (1987d) 'A constructivist interpretation of formal operations', *Human Development*, 30.

SMITH, L. (1987e) 'Developmental theory in the classroom', *Instructional Science*.

Discussion (Reporter: David Squires)

Smith had maintained that it was possible to detect examples of some of the sixteen formal operations identified by Piaget in pre-operational children. However, formal operations in a comprehensive sense are not observed. Smith was asked what was it that promotes development in this context? He replied that he was offering a descriptive model, not necessarily a causal one. The point was also made that if the sixteen operations are not displayed, it could be (a) a problem with the Piagetian model; (b) a problem with devising tests to discover evidence for each operation; or (c) because a person does not necessarily display all of the operations even if they have internalised them.

14.2 An Investigation of the Scaling of Piagetian formal operations

Trevor G. Bond

The English language translation of Inhelder and Piaget's *De La Logique De L'Enfant A La Logique De L'Adolescent* (GLT) in 1958 was welcomed with reserved praise from psychologists (for example Bruner, 1959) — directed, in the main, at the behavioural descriptions of formal operational thought. The reception from logicians who set about to interpret the descriptions of the underlying model of thinking at this level (for example Parsons, 1960) was rather scathing, to say the least. Now, some thirty years later, those early reviews remain uncannily prophetic of the acceptance of the Genevan description of the ultimate stage of cognitive development. Some researchers with long term research interest in the area — of whom Shayer in the UK and Lawson in the US are particularly productive and useful examples — have documented a wealth of evidence in support of the Piagetian descriptions of the behaviours characteristic of formal operational thought. On the other hand, there remains, as influential as ever, a body of argument and evidence — take, as an example, the work of Ennis — which denies the value or appropriateness of the underlying logico-mathematical model. Yet the complete dismissal of the Piagetian logico-mathematical model may be premature. The work of Leiser (1982) and Smith (1987) at the logico-mathematical level, as well as that of the present author (Bond, 1978 and 1980) indicates that the debate should not yet be concluded. In this paper a test of the logical model is compared with performance on a traditional Genevan fomal task.

Sample

One hundred and forty third-year secondary school pupils in a country school in England took part in this segment of the project. All children were in the 15.0–15.11 years age group. Class groups of pupils were assessed on *Piagetian Reasoning Task III — Pendulum and Bond's Logical Operations Test* during the school's end-of-year exam period.

334

Tests

(i) Piagetian Reasoning Task — Pendulum (PRT III) is one of a well-known and widely-used Piagetian based group of tasks of formal operational thinking devised by the CSMS team (NFER, 1979). Their use has provided a thorough substantiation of Piaget's behavioural descriptions from GLT. The application of the Rasch model to these tests in Australia and in Finland (for example Hautamäki 1987,) further emphasizes their utility. In this project PRT III was adopted as the reliable measure of formal operational thinking for this group.

(ii) Bond's Logical Operations Test (BLOT) is an item-by-item operationalization of the schema of the formal operations stage including the sixteen binary operations and the INRC four-group (from GLT) in multiple-choice, common language forms. The more-than-adequate statistical qualities of the test have been reported elsewhere (Bond, 1980; Christianson 1983). Whilst it is necessary to be aware of the limitations of multiple-choice testing in this domain and the difficulties inherent in expressing logical operations in suitable language forms, it is suggested that these problems (if admitted) should detract from, not enhance, the quality of the results.

Results

(i) Correlation: Past experience shows that where there is only partial (not complete) overlap in the range of abilities assessed by pairs of tests or where the age or ability range of the subjects is restricted, the correlation between raw scores on the tests will provide a very conservative estimate of the relationship between the variables. All three of these conditions apply in this case yet the Pearson correlation coefficient between raw scores on Pendulum and Blot was $r = .75$

(ii) Discrimation analysis is a technique that has been used for scaling formal and post-formal thinking (Demetriou and Efklides, 1985). It can utilize the stage assumptions inherent in Piagetian data (Shayer, 1981) and provides scale values which can be directly related to the Genevan stage levels (IIB, IIIA etc.). In this instance, the stage allocations for pupils from the pendulum PRT are used as a measuring stick for the BLOT abilities shown by those students. For each BLOT item, successful students are designated as belonging to a particular Piagetian stage according to their performances on the PRT. In the example of BLOT item 5 (p $\subset$ q) it is calculated that 100 per cent of IIIB students, 69.2 per cent of IIIA students and 33.3 per cent of IIB students were successful in using the reciprocal implication operation — see figure 14.2.1.

Fine scaling of the item is then estimated by linear interpolation for the 67 per cent sucess level — corrected by $+0.5$ level (as with Yate's correction for chi-squared). The discrimination level of the BLOT item is then indicated as the point on the Piagetian concrete-formal continuum at which BLOT item I5 (p $\subset$ q) discriminates, estimated as $7.8 + 0.5 = 8.3$ (above IIIA).

Figure 14.2.1 Discrimination analysis graph based on data from item 15

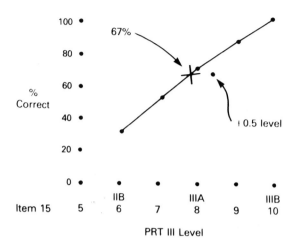

Discrimination levels for selected BLOT items (representing the sixteen binary operations) are shown in figure 14.2.2.

(iii) Rasch analysis: Although the application of the Rasch model to these data is not yet complete, previous analysis of BLOT results (with N = 899) shows that the vast majority of items fit the Rasch model. At this point, the Rasch measure used for further investigation here, is the logit of p (item facility). The relative difficulty of those selected BLOT items referred to above is shown in figure 14.2.3. BLOT item 15 (reciprocal implication, $p \subset q$) is one of the more difficult items with a log p value of $+0.42$.

When the Rasch scale values (logit p) for BLOT items are entered on one axis and plotted against the levels derived from discrimination analysis, the items lay along a plot which is substantially linear (see figure 14.2.4). The apparent mathematical congruence of these two formulations is consistent with that described by Shayer (1987) for items from five PRT's including the pendulum task. Not only does this allow for the item by item scaling of BLOT against Pendulum in this instance but, by use of other Rasch analytical techniques, will allow at a later date the scaling of the sixteen binary operations and INRC four-group items to be extrapolated against the larger set of Piagetian formal-operations tasks. The notable exception to the substantial linearity of the plot is BLOT item I2 (aff p). As expected this item is one of the easiest of the schemata measured by the BLOT. However the inappropriateness of PRT III to measure at the lower concrete level and the lack of adequate numbers of students below that level caused its discrimination level to be overestimated.

Figure 14.2.2   Discrimination levels for selected BLOT items

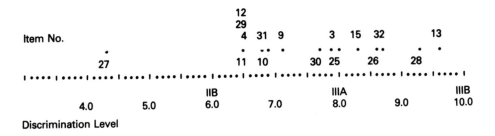

Figure 14.2.3   Relative difficulty of selected BLOT items

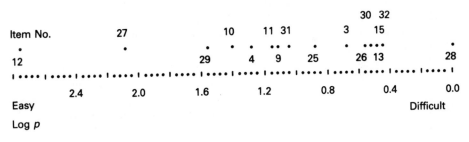

Figure 14.2.4   Piagetian stage level v. item difficulty.

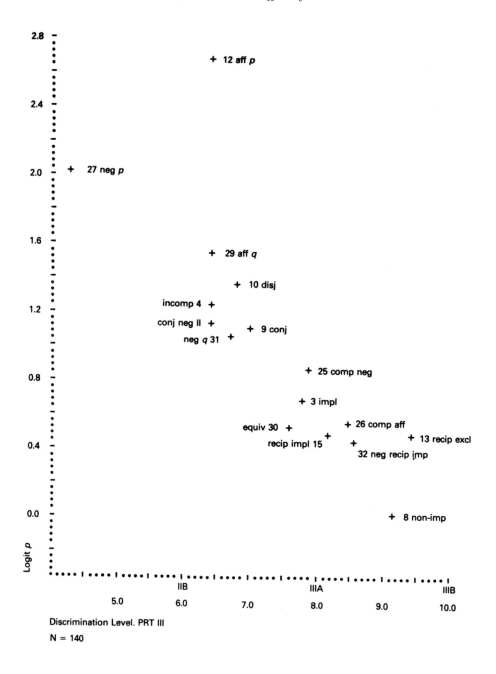

Discrimination Level. PRT III

N = 140

Discussion

Until the wider, underlying issues are more thoroughly addressed it would be premature to make strong claims for the impact of these results for the more general problem of the validity of the Piagetian logico-mathematical model of the formal operations stage. However an inspection of the results does indicate a number of interesting aspects of the research that are worthy of further investigation/amplification. The conservative estimation of the relationship between PRT III pendulum and BLOT of $r = .75$ is admittedly modest but better than many researchers have achieved with other pairs of formal operations tests where the dissimilarity between test content/format is considerably less marked (for example, Lawson, 1979; Douglas and Wong, 1977). The similarities between the psychometric properties of the BLOT and the results reported by Shayer (1987) support the likelihood that the BLOT is associated with other measures of traditional Piagetian formal-operational competencies — the PRT's for Chemicals, Balance, Inclined Plane and Flexible Rods as well as the Pendulum task used here. The more thorough investigation of the Rasch analysis and its consequent conditional probabilities is obviously warranted.

It is interesting to look at the discrimination levels of the items representing the sixteen binary operations (in particular) as they are represented in relation to the Piagetian stages. Two broad groups of skills from within the sixteen binary operations are immediately obvious — a group of eight operations at the IIIA and IIIB formal levels and a group of the remaining eight binary operations which apparently occur during the later part of the concrete operations stage. This latter group of four pairs of complementary operations are those which might reasonably be expected by their function (as outlined in GLT *pp* 293*ff*) to be the precursors of the later operations. They deal with the presence or absence of either of two variables or their joint presence or absence. This is consonant with the position expounded in GLT (p 298) that these skills form an important part of the 'concrete structuring of the data (*which*) is an indispensable prerequisite of the propositional structure'.

In GLT Piaget goes to great lengths to argue the co-requisite nature of the operational skills and task performance; he rarely expounds on the timing or ordering of the onset of operations. It is interesting that one of the few claims he makes is that *implications* will be possible at the IIIA level and that the *denial of implication* occurs after that. The results of the present analysis are consistent with that aspect of the Genevan work. While this paper will not make a strong claim for the validity of the underlying logico-mathematical model to the formal operations stage, it is suggested that if the model were valid then the consequences of that validity would be data of the sort that is outlined here.

For the more pragmatic needs of the educator, the implications of this research are somewhat different. Of course, the data here represent merely a cross-sectional look at the relationship between these logical abilities and

Trevor B. Bond

performance on Piagetian tasks. Will longitudinal study confirm that the former are merely temporal precursors of the latter, or will it be shown that competence on each group of the sixteen binary operations are prerequisites to the solution of the traditional formal tasks? The ease of administration and marking of the BLOT facilitate its use in educational settings.

References

Bond, T.G. (1978) 'Propositional logic as a model for adolescent intlligence-additional consideration', *Interchange*, 9, 2, pp 93–8.

Bond, T.G. (1976) *Bond's Logical Operations Test*, Townsville, Townsville College of Advanced Education.

Bond, T.G (1980) 'The psychological link across formal operations', *Science Education*, 64, I, pp 113–7

Bruner, J. (1959) 'Inhelder and Piaget's *The Growth of Logical Thinking*', *British Journal of Psychology*, 50, pp 363–70.

Christianson, D.J. (1983) 'An investigation of the relationships between cognitive developmental stage and quantitative skills in college students', doctoral dissertation, Stockton, CA, University of the Pacific.

Demetriou, A. and Efklides, A. (1985) 'Structure and sequence of formal and post-formal thought', *Child Development*, 56, pp 1062–91.

Douglas, J.D. and Wong, A.C. (1977) 'Formal operations: Age and sex differences in Chinese and American children', *Child Development*, 48, pp 689–92.

Hautamäki, J. (1987) 'The application of a Rasch model on Piagetian measures of stages and thinking', paper presented at Adolescent Development and School Science Seminar, King's College London (KQC).

Inhelder, B. and Piaget, J. (1958) *The Growth of Logical Thinking from Childhood to Adolescence*, London, Routledge and Kegan Paul.

Lawson, A.E. (1979) 'The developmental learning paradigm', *Journal of Research in Science Teaching*, 16, 6, pp 501–5.

Leiser, D. (1982) 'Piaget's logical formalism for formal operations: An interpretation in context', *Developmental Review*, 2, pp 87–99.

NFER (1979) *Science Reasoning Tasks*, Windsor, NFER.

Parsons, C. (1960) 'Inhelder and Piaget's *The Growth of Logical Thinking*', *British Journal of Psychology*, 51, pp 75–84.

Shayer, M. (1981) 'A new approach to data-analysis for the onstruction of Piagetian test', paper presented at annual meeting of the American Educational Research Association, Los Angeles, April.

Shayer, M. (1987) 'The scaling of the formal operations stage', article submitted for publication.

Smith, L. (1987) 'A constructivist interpretation of formal operations', *Human Development*.

Discussion (Reporter: Peter Matthews)

The first question was to check that results equivalent to figure 14.2.1 in the paper existed for all items of the BLOT test, as well as item 15. The author answered that they did. It was then asked about the meaning of the graph: how could any pupils assessed at the 2B level possibly get item 15 right? Should there not be a graph going up in discrete steps? A related question was to do with the linearity of this figure: would not an ogive shape be expected? Here the issue of test 'noise' was relevant, particularly where multiple choice questions were used. The author was also asked to explain the continuity correction of 0.5 level, and the use of a 67 per cent success criterion.

Discussion then shifted to figure 14.2.4: some listeners had to be persuaded that it did not merely mean the more difficult items were more difficult! It did indeed mean this, but the graph was needed to check on the equivalence of the two different ways of modelling the data. Items 27 and 12 were in an anomalous positions because the items in PRT III (Pendulum) were unreliable around and below the 2B level.

There was general agreement that his attempt to falsify Piagetian theory *could* have falsified it, and did not. Thus the theory remained alive and well after this analysis.

14.3 The Application of a Rasch Model on Piagetian Measures of Stages of Thinking

Jarkko Hautamäki

Introduction

The study of the Piagetian developmental model requires both conceptual and methodological approaches. It is possible to apply psychometric methods on Piagetian measures. The crucial issue has been the lack of reliable Piagetian tests (Shayer, 1978 and 1979). However, it is known that the traditional psychometric methods have a number of limitations (Hambleton *et al*, 1978; Elliot 1982 and 1983): the item parameters (difficulty and discrimination), the person parameters (ability) and also the reliability coefficients are sample-dependent.

Attention has been directed toward latent trait theories, i.e., item response theories or item characteristic curve theory (Baker, 1977; Elliot, 1982 and 1983; Whitely, 1979; Lord and Novick, 1968). The Rasch model can be viewed as a latent trait model in which the item characteristic curve is a one-parameter logistic function (Hambleton *et al*, 1978 p 474). All items are assumed to have equal discriminating power and vary only according to difficulty. The Rasch model has some special advantages for the Piagetian research.

The main advantage, in this context, is related to the first of the three central notions of latent trait models: dimensionality, local independence and item characteristic curves. The dimensionality means an assumption that a single latent ability is sufficient to account for individual differences in performance. This assumption defines also a class of unidimensional models (Hambleton, 1983, p 60). When items are measuring one dimension, test data will fit the Rasch model (Lumsden, 1978). The Rasch model can be character-ized as the only fully unidimensional model (Elliot, 1983). Fit to the Rasch model is a necessary, but not sufficient, criterion of the unidimensionality of test.

The Rasch model states that when a person is given a test item only two things determine the probability of a person getting the item right — the ability of the person and the difficulty of the item. For the estimation of the abilities

Table 14.3.1   The reliabilities of the tasks II
                and III

Task	Hautamäki	Shayer
II	.78	.79
III	.83	.83
II + III	.77	

and difficulties we need the total number of items in the test which a person gets right (estimation of the ability) and the total number of people in a sample, who get the item right (estimation of the difficulty). That means that the total test score contains all the information needed to estimate a person's ability and the difficulty of the item (Wright and Mead, 1975).

The Rasch model is therefore a method for analyzing the unidimensionality of tests and the theoretical assumptions of the test items. There are few attempts to apply the Rasch model on Piagetian type of measures (see for example Elliot, 1982 and 1983). The Piagetian measures are, however, based on the analysis of items according to their estimated stage. The items in a Piagetian test would be classifiable according to their difficulty, i.e., their stage. It will be assumed that the items of Piagetian test differ only according to their stage. The validity of Piagetian concepts can be approached as an unidimensionality question.

Methods

The Science Reasoning Tasks (Shayer, 1978 and 1979; Shayer and Adey, 1981; Shayer, Adey and Wylam, 1981) are based on original Piagetian tasks. The SRT-tests are group tasks, dichotomously scored, containing items with a theoretical criterion. The reliabilities are estimated with internal consistency models; the item analyses are careful and supported with factor analyses (as recommended by psychometricians like Lumsden, 1976).

Task II (Volume and Heaviness) and Task III (Pendulum) of The Science Reasoning Tasks were selected for the study. The tasks have been translated into Finnish (Hautamäki, 1984).

The reliabilities of the tasks, first assessed in different age-groups with KR-20 with Horst modification and then averaged, are presented in the table 14.3.1 with comparison to Shayer's results.

The Rasch model demands the estimation of person abilities, item difficulties, and describes their discrimination and also yields some goodness of fit testing procedure. There is available a program CALFIT (Wright and Mead, 1975) for calibrating dichotomously scorable test items and evaluating their statistical fit according to the linear log-odds Rasch measurement model. The program performs the data input and description, the data editing, the estimation of parameters and the analysis of fit.

There are two estimation procedures: PROX and UCON. PROX, an approximation method, is quicker and adequate for most applications. The UCON is a unconditional maximum likelihood procedure for badly skewed distribution of subjects. The distributions of raw scores in this study were normal for task II and combined task II + III, and somewhat skewed in task III. UCON was used for task III, but the results were in close agreement with the PROX estimations. Therefore PROX estimations are presented.

Subjects

The subjects were boys (493) and girls (467) from grades 2 to 9 of the Finnish comprehensive school. Their ages varied from 8 years to 16.5 years. There were together forty classes from the Metropolitan area and from the densely populated rural area with no statistically significant area differences (one-way ANOVA). The data were collected by four examiners with no examiner-effect (one-way ANOVA).

In the RASCH application there were 531 subjects for task II (Volume and Heaviness), 596 subjects for task III (Pendulum) and 240 subjects for the combined tasks II and III (both of the tasks given to same subjects).

Results

Distribution of Stages of Thinking in Finland

Distributions of stages of thinking in Finland and 14.3.1 in England (Shayer et al, 1976; and Shayer, 1978) can be seen in the figure 14.3.1. The Finnish results are combined with weighted averages from the tasks I, II and III. Only the resuls of those, who are at least at stage 2B (late concrete-operational) or 3A (early formal), are given (for these and others see Hautamäki, 1984).

The Goodness of Fit of the Tasks

All of the tasks (II, III and II + III) were found to fit the Rasch model (table 14.3.2).

The Item Analysis of Task II and Task III

The program provides for each item its difficulty estimate (with standard error) scaled with zero as the average. Also raw scores with respective scale abilities are given.

344

Figure 14.3.1

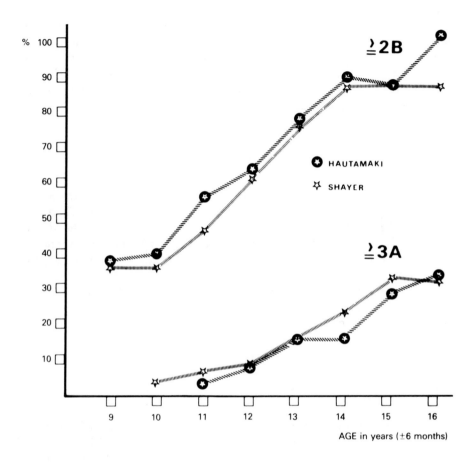

Table 14.3.2   The goodness of fit of the tasks to the Rasch model

task	chi²	df	signf.	interpretation
II	45.18	70	ns	fits
III	45.61	70	ns	fits
II + III	60.45	140	ns	fits

Table 14.3.3   The classification of task items according to difficulties

Task	Item	Difficulty	Shayer	Present
			classification	
II	2	−3.4	2A	2A
	1	−2.5	2A	2A
	8	−1.7	2B	2A/2B
	9	−1.3	2B	2A/2B
	3A	−0.99	2A	2A/2B
	6	−0.89	2B	2B
	11	−0.6	2B	2B
	10	−0.15	2B/3A	2B
	5	0.02	2B	2B
	3B	0.13	2B	2B
	7	0.45	2B	2B
	13A	1.82	2B/3A	2B/3A
	14	2.7	3A	3A
	12	3.0	3A	3A
	13B	3.4	3A	3A
III	1	−3.7	2B	2B
	8	−2.6	2B	2B
	5	−2.6	3A	2B/3A
	4	−2.2	3A	2B/3A
	10	−0.5	3A	3A
	6	−0.3	3A	3A
	12	−0.1	3A	3A
	11	0.3	3A	3A
	3	0.4	3A	3A
	9	0.6	3B	3A/3B
	7	0.9	3B	3B
	14	2.3	3B	3B
	13	3.1	3B	3B
	2	4.4	3B	3B

These data make it possible to compare the Shayer classification of the items with the results of this study. The results are presented in table 14.3.3.

The main differences are that some of the items seem to demand less that expected by Piaget and Shayer. Otherwise the classifications are alike.

It is possible to estimate the optimal area of task II and task III by combining the information from the raw score, from the item difficulty and

Table 14.3.4   Stages of thinking, ability scores and scale abilities of tasks II and III

	Stage of thinking			
	2A	2B	3A	3B
Task II				
ability score	2–5	7–11	13–14	
scale ability	−2.8−−1.2	−0.3–1.7	3.1–4.1	
Task III				
ability score		2	6–9	12–14
scale ability		−3.1	−0.5–1.0	3.1–4.3

from the theoretical classification of the items. The assumption is made that the ideal subjects solve the items in their difficulty order and a stage is reached when at least two thirds of the respective stage items are solved. The results are in table 14.3.4.

The optimal area area is 2B (concrete-operational) for task II and 3A (early formal operational) for task III.

The Item Analysis of the Combined Task II + III

The combined task II + III is analyzed using data from difficulty estimations and Shayerian item classifications. The results are presented in table 14.3.5.

Items II/1 and III/4 have been omitted from the estimation process. Items II/3A, II/13A and III/1, III/3 and III/11 have the poorest fit.

The reason for the misfit for items II/3A and II/13A is due to the lowest ability group, which solved the items better than expected. The misfits of the items III/1, 3 and 11 are due to the highest ability group, which solved the items worse than expected. The program, however, formed the ability groups in an untheoretical way so that included in the highest ability group were pupils with ability scores from 15 to 26 (27 was the maximum score).

Discussion

The comparison of the results of SRTs in the UK and Finland pointed to high internal consistency reliabilities and to almost identical distributions of the stages of thinking.

The application of the Rasch model illuminated the SRT-tasks, but did not provide any radical changes in the interpretation of the tasks or the items.

The Rasch model was found to support the unidimensionality hypothesis. In discussions of the unidimensionality it is, however, of interest to note that some kind of circularity is present. There is no single method which would

Table 14.3.5 *The combined task II + III: item difficulties, theoretical and empirical classifications and the emergence of stages of thinking*

Item	Item difficulty	Shayer	Present	2A	2B	3A	3B
		classification					
II/2	−5.23	2A	2A	+			
II/3A	−3.83	2A	2A	+			
II/8	−3.47	2B	2A/2B		+		
II/9	−2.84	2B	2A/2B		+		
II/6	−2.22	2B	2A/2B		+		
II/3B	−2.06	2B	2B		+		
II/11	−2.06	2B	2B		+		
II/10	−1.75	2B/3A	2B		+		
II/5	−1.50	2B	2B		+		
III/1	−1.50	2B	2B		+		
II/7	−1.13	2B	2B		+		
III/5	−0.89	3A	2B/3A			+	
III/8	−0.79	2B	2B		+		
III/4	−0.70	3A	2B/3A			+	
II/13A	0.81	2B/3A	3A			+	
III/10	1.11	3A	3A			+	
II/14	1.22	3A	3A			+	
III/6	1.38	3A	3A			+	
III/12	1.55	3A	3A			+	
II/12	1.96	3A	3A			+	
II/13B	2.02	3A	3A			+	
III/11	2.08	3A	3A			+	
III/9	2.15	3B	3B				+
III/7	2.15	3B	3B				+
III/13	4.70	3B	3B				+
III/2	5.22	3B	3B				+
III/14	5.22	3B	3B				+

provide a solid basis for determining the possible unidimensionality structure of tests. There are cross-references between internal consistency measures, factor analyses and latent trait models.

The main advantages of the Rasch model are not, however, in the traditional domain. The Rasch model allows banks of items to be formed and yields good measures for testing the effects of educational interventions and teaching of scientific thinking.

References

BAKER, F.B. (1977) 'Advances in item analysis', *Review of Educational Research*, 47, pp 151–78.

ELLIOT, C. (1982) 'The measurement characteristics of developmental tests' in MODGIL, S. and MODGIL, C. (Eds) *Jean Piaget. Consensus and Controversy*, London, Holt, Rinehart & Winston.

ELLIOT, C. (1983) *British Ability Scale. Manual 1: Introductory Handbook*, Windsor, NFER-Nelson.

HAMBLETON, R.K., SWAMINATHAN, H., COOK, L.L., EIGNOR, D.R. and GIFORD, J.A. (1978) 'Developments in latent trait theory: Models, technical issues, and applications, *Review of Educational Research*, 48, pp 467–510.

HAUTAMÄKI, J. (1984) *The Measurement and Distribution of Piagetian Stages of Thinking in Finnish Comprehensive School*, University of Joensuu, Publications in Social Sciences 1/1984.

INHELDER, B. and PIAGET, J. (1958) *The Growth of Logical Thinking from Childhood to Adolescent*, New York, Basic Books.

LORD, F.M. and NOVICK, M.R. (1969) *Statistical Theories of Mental Test Scores*, Reading, Addison-Wesley.

LUMSDEN, J. (1976) 'Test theory', *Annual Review of Psychology*, 27, pp 251–80.

LUMSOEN, J. (1978) 'Tests are perfectly reliable', *British Journal of Mathematical and Statistical Psychology*, 31, pp 19–26.

SHAYER, M. (1978) 'A test of the validity of Piaget's construct of formal operational thinking', unpublished Ph.D. thesis, London, Chelsea College, University of London.

SHAYER, M. (1979) 'Has Piaget's construct of formal operational thinking any utility?', *British Journal of Educational Psychology*, 49, pp 265–76.

SHAYER, M. and ADEY, P. (1981) *Towards a Science of Science Teaching*. London, Heinemann. Books.

SHAYER, M. ADEY, P. and WYLAM, H. (1981) 'Group tests of cognitive development: Ideals and a realization; *Journal of Research in Science Education*, 18, pp 157–68.

SHAYER, M., KÜCHEMANN, D.E. and WYLAM, H. (1976) 'The distribution of Piagetian stages of thinking in British middle and secondary school children', *British Journal of Educational Psychology*, 46, 164–73.

WHITELY, S.E. (1979) 'Latent trait models in the study of intelligence', *Intelligence*, 3, pp 97–132.

WRIGHT, B.D. and MEAD, R.J. (1975) *CALFIT: Sample Free Item Calibration with a Rasch Measurement Model*, Research memorandum 18, Statistical Laboratory, Department of Education, University of Chicago.

Discussion (Reporter: Peter Matthews)

Firstly, the author's reclassification of the levels of some items in SRTs II and III was acknowledged as agreeing with reanalyses done on British data by Michael Shayer.

In an animated discussion which followed, it was thought remarkable that a theory originating in Geneva, modified by Shayer in Britain and then translated into the Finnish enironment should still show unidimensionality, as shown in the striking agreement shown in figure 14.3.1. In addition, it was noted that Rasch modelling showed equal differences between stages 2B and 3A, and between stages 3A and 3B. Such robustness and consistency of test with theory is unusual among psychological models, it was argued: so why do so many people consider it invalid?

To some, the absence of discontinuities is a scandal; it disturbs them that there are persons with intermediate scores on tests like 2B/3A, implying continuous development. It was also argued that the very success of Piaget's work has led to many simplistic versions of his theories, and many group tests being too far removed from the original Genevan research. Those who understand Piaget's work see how compatible it is with, for example, Ausubel's (who was the first educational psychologist, in 1962, to digest and use Piaget's account of operational thinking).

The final part of the discussion addressed the problem of task-to-task variability of performance, and whether application of Piaget's theory to older pupils is valid. Prior knowledge is a necessary condition for much further learning in secondary schools; thus it is difficult to acknowledge that an adequate Piagetian level is *also* a necessary condition. A related issue was that a too great emphasis on content can result in some pupils not using the thinking they were capable of.

14.4 Cognitive Structure Mapping as a Tool in Science Teaching

G.P. Matthews

Over the last four years, a novel method of testing has been developed which is based on the work of Piaget, Ausubel, Shavelson and Shayer. The testing method gives insights into the ways in which pupils learn chemical concepts in secondary schools [1–3]. In this paper we present an extension of the method to the analysis of the new GCSE examinations being introduced in this country for pupils aged 15 + .

Method

In the first part of our testing procedure we obtain concept maps by the so-called graph construction method. Pupils are given an alphabetical list of about ten concept labels, and are told to link them, in order of decreasing similarity, and that they must link all the labels. The pupil who drew the graph shown in figure 14.4.1(a), for example, thinks that acid and alkali are the two most alike concept labels in the list, and pH and neutralization the least alike. Other examples are shown in figures 14.4.1(b) and 14.4.1(c). We then construct a proximity matrix, and by some moderately complicated algebra, an extension of a method known as the Guttman-Lingoes algorithm, we calculate a two-dimensional map where the distances between each point correspond, to a best fit approximation, to the distances in the half-matrix.

Figure 14.4.2 shows the map corresponding to the tree-graph in figure 14.4.1(a). The most-linked concept label is placed centrally, and a scaling circle is drawn. The circle has no significance other than scaling, and there is no significance in the angle of presention of the diagram — it can be rotated if necessary.

Next we come to the Piagetian part of our test. We are chiefly interested in stages 2A to 3B, and have concentrated on the 13–15 year age range. The test described here uses part of Shayer and Adey's acids and alkalis taxonomy, shown in Figure 14.4.3.

Peter Matthews

Figure 14.4.1   (a) to (c). Examples of raw tree graphs

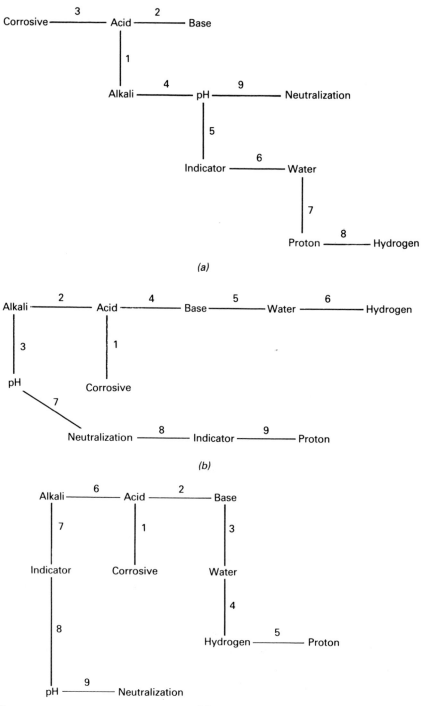

(a)

(b)

(c)

Figure 14.4.2   *Two-dimensional graph corresponding to tree-graph given in figure*
14.4.1(a)

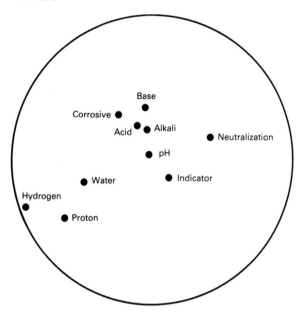

As we know, it is very dangerous to generalize these Piagetian stages —
to say that a pupil who is capable of learning up to stage 2B on one particular
topic will also attain the same level on all other topics. Indeed, it is such
generalization which has led to unreliable results and has contributed to recent
accusations of Piaget's theories being outdated. In our work we have allowed
for the fact that Piagetian stages measured in the classroom are highly specific
— indeed we have called them *Piaget-Specific Levels*. The three major causes
of this specificity are:

(iii)   that the stages depend on a particular pupil;
(ii)   that they depend on the particular concept taught; and
(iii)   that they depend on the type of instruction that the pupil has
undergone.

This specificity is carefully allowed for in the design of the test. It is also
important to realize, both in current examinations and the new GCSE
examinations, that we are testing Piaget-Specific levels, *not* Piagetian stages.

Testing Procedure

The tests are designed in three parts — first the graph construction test, which
we described earlier, and which takes the pupils about ten minutes. Secondly,
we demonstrate experiments in front of the class. The demonstrations take

Figure 14.4.3   Piagetian terms and concepts of acids and bases

	Topic	2A early concrete	2B late concrete
C.6	Acids and Alkalis	'Acid' as name of substances with certain properties— litmus, attacks metals, sour taste, but only one at a time, the properties are not seen as defining characteristics.	Acids and bases as opposing factions. The pH scale as an interval scale of degrees of acidity. Neutralisation by equal quantities of acid and alkali, if teacher has set up equivalent solutions. If you double quantity of acid, *or* if you double its concentration you need twice as much alkali. Metal oxides are basic (alkaline), non-metal oxides are acidic.

3A early formal	3B late formal
Reaction of acid with alkali is $$H^+ + OH^- \rightarrow H_2O$$ Limits to change of pH by dilution alone. Acids are solutions; without water they are not acidic. Conservations during neutralisation: nothing lost, and new product in principle recoverable. $N_1V_1 = N_2V_2$ problems, with practice.	The reaction between an acid and an alkali, understood in terms of the disturbance of the equilibrium between H^+ and OH^- ions in water. Use of molar quantities for finding equation of reaction between an acid and an alkali. Can appreciate that there are H^+ ions even in 1.0M sodium hydroxide, and hence has rational understanding of pH scale.

about fifty minutes, and thus take up the rest of a double period. Finally, we set a range of examination questions on the topic which we have chosen. The teacher supervises the children doing these in a subsequent lesson.

To date we have tested 340 pupils on the topics of acids and bases, oxidation and reduction, moles and reactivity, at five different schools in Oxfordshire and Cornwall.

Specimen Result

Figure 14.4.4 shows the cognitive structure map of a fifth year pupil tested on the subject of acids and bases. This map is constructed from the first two parts of the test by adding the Piaget-Specific levels associated with particular concept-labels as a third dimension above the two-dimensional maps described earlier.

We see that the most crowded concept-label, positioned in the centre of the circle, is base. Closely linked to this are alkali and acid. Neutralization is close to acid, base and alkali, and corrosive is quite closely linked to acid.

Figure 14.4.4   Acids and bases cognitive structure map of aa 5th-year high-flier.
Abbreviations:

acd   acid
alk   alkali
bse   base
cor   corrosive
hyd   hydrogen
ind   indicator
neu   neutralization
pH   pH
pro   proton
wat   water

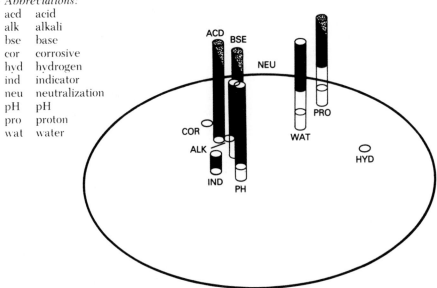

Indicator and pH form a fairly loose group near neutralization, and water, proton and hydrogen form a very loose, moderately peripheral group. At this stage we have to make a subjective judgment, with which we would hope any knowledgeable chemist would agree, namely that the arrangement of the concept labels on the graph is a fairly logical one. The cylinders above each concept label in the map indicate the corresponding Piaget-Specific levels. Working upwards from the bottom of each cylinder, the circles represent levels 2A, 2B, 3A and 3B respectively. The light shading indicates the zones tested, and the dark shading the levels achieved by the pupil. We see, for example, that neutralization is not tested below Piaget-Specific level 2B, in this case because it cannot be understood below this level. The pupil scored well on nearly all the concepts, but for acid, base, and proton, not all questions were answered correctly at the 3B level, as indicated by the diagonal lines. Thus both the proximities of the concept-labels, and the Piaget-Specific levels achieved, indicate that this 15-year-old has a well-ordered and well-understood cognitive structure with regard to acids and bases. By contrast, cognitive structure maps of other types of learner have a very different appearance, some being more tightly constructed, others being disjointed and widely spaced.

Location Graphs

We have discussed one cognitive structure map in detail, but in all we have 340 of them. To rationalize this large body of information, we have plotted the position of the pupils on 'location graphs'. These are formed by plotting the sum of the correct answers on the Piaget-Specific test against the score on the particular examination questions which form the third part of the test.

Applications

The main application which I wish to discuss is an analysis of the new GCSE examinations in chemistry. The GCSE assessment scheme is based on domains, which can be summarized as shown here:

A   Knowledge with understanding
B   Handling information and solving problems
C   Experimental skills and investigations

We can see that domain A involves testing mainly of Piaget-Specific levels 2A and 2B, whereas domain B is more concerned with Piaget-Specific levels 3A and 3B. Domain C is not covered in our tests. The three domains are then subdivided into descriptors. One particular descriptor is shown here:

> The ability, using oral, written, symbolic, graphical and numerical material to present reasoned explanations for phenomena, patterns and relationships.

We have applied these methods to small groups of fourth and fifth year (14-to-16-year-old) pupils studying chemistry this year in a Cornish comprehensive school. These pupils worked very hard and most willingly for us, carrying out not only the standard battery of tests which I have described but also answering a set of GCSE questions, all on the subject of acids and bases. All the questions are from general papers, incidentally — for the simple reason that we could find no questions on acids and bases on the advanced papers.

We identified interesting pupils by plotting location graphs of Piaget-Specific score against GCSE score (figure 14.4.5). The cognitive structure maps for these pupils have been plotted to demonstrate the different types of learner, and we shall examine them in a moment.

The other information which we have about the pupils is in the form of an objective analysis. Look at figure 14.4.6. The three domains we cover are summarized: Recall, Understand and Apply. Then both the GCSE and Piaget-Specific questions are analyzed according to the objectives which they test. These are marked as a bold square.

We see, for example, that the fifth question which we set on the GCSE paper tested the understanding of principles and concepts, and an understanding of their presentation and use. If the pupil answered those questions correctly, as in this case, then those descriptors are shaded in. For GCSE criterion referencing to be easily applicable, we would hope that horizontal rows in the table were either completely shaded or completely unshaded. However, even though we are testing only a tiny fraction of the syllabus — acids and bases —

Figure 14.4.5 Fourth year location graph

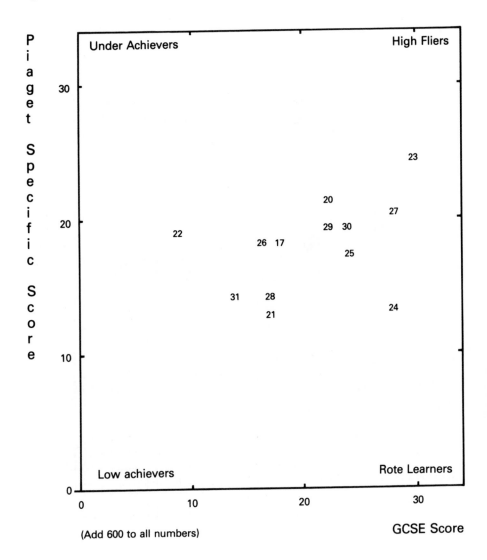

(Add 600 to all numbers)

Figure 14.4.6   GCSE objective analysis

Pupil no: 621

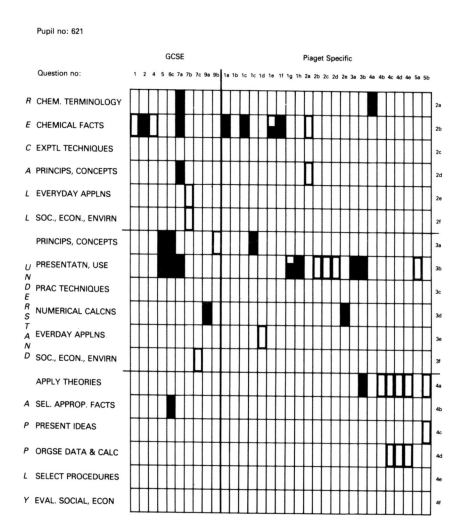

we nevertheless see a gradation. This pupil can neither recall nor understand everyday applications and the social, economic and environmental aspects, and is unable to present ideas and organize data.

The pupil we have considered, reference number 621, is shown simply as 21 on the location graph (figure 14.4.5). From this location graph we can see that pupil 626 obtained a significantly higher Piaget-Specific score, but a GCSE score of only 1 less than pupil 621. If we compare the objective analyses, figures 14.4.6 and 14.4.7, we see that these pupils are fairly similar learners and achievers. Their cognitive structure maps are also very similar.

On the same location graph, figure 14.4.5, we now compare pupils 623, and 624, who had almost identical GCSE scores. First let us compare the objective analyses of pupils 623 and 624, figures 14.4.8 and 14.4.9. We can see that the GCSE objective analysis for each is identical. However, the Piaget-Specific objective analyses of these three pupils, are very different. The three pupils also have very different cognitive sturcture maps, (Figures 14.4.10 and 14.4.11). So here we have an example of very different types of learner scoring the same GCSE mark.

Similar effects were observed in the fifth-year pupils we studied.

Conclusions

So what do we conclude?

First, that our method is once again showing up very clearly similar and different types of learning.

Secondly, that if we take a very small fraction of the chemistry syllabus, we see gradations of ability within the objectives. Acids and bases form a sufficiently small part of the syllabus as to yield 'unambiguous' information in terms of Piaget-Specific levels, as explained in Shayer and Adey (1981). It follows from the definition of unambiguity in this reference that if we do not see clear-cut responses to particular descriptors (i.e. all right or all wrong) in an unambiguous syllabus area, then we will never see it in any fraction of the syllabus, and certainly not over an entire GCSE subject. Thus we conclude that although criterion referencing might in theory be expected to work, we have shown that in practice it does not work, and indeed will never work.

Thirdly, we find that although there are similarities between extreme pupils obtaining similar GCSE marks, i.e. low achieving fourth years and some high achieving fifth years, in the middle range slight or even wild discrepancies are not reflected in the GCSE mark. In the GCSE, of course, there is an emphasis on in-course assessment, and this, if done carefully — more carefully indeed than it seems teachers will have time for — can make up the deficiencies of the final examination. But certainly it seems as if criterion referenced assessment in terms of the final examination is acting merely as a recipe for examiners as to the type of questions they should set, and that after

Figure 14.4.7 GCSE objective analysis

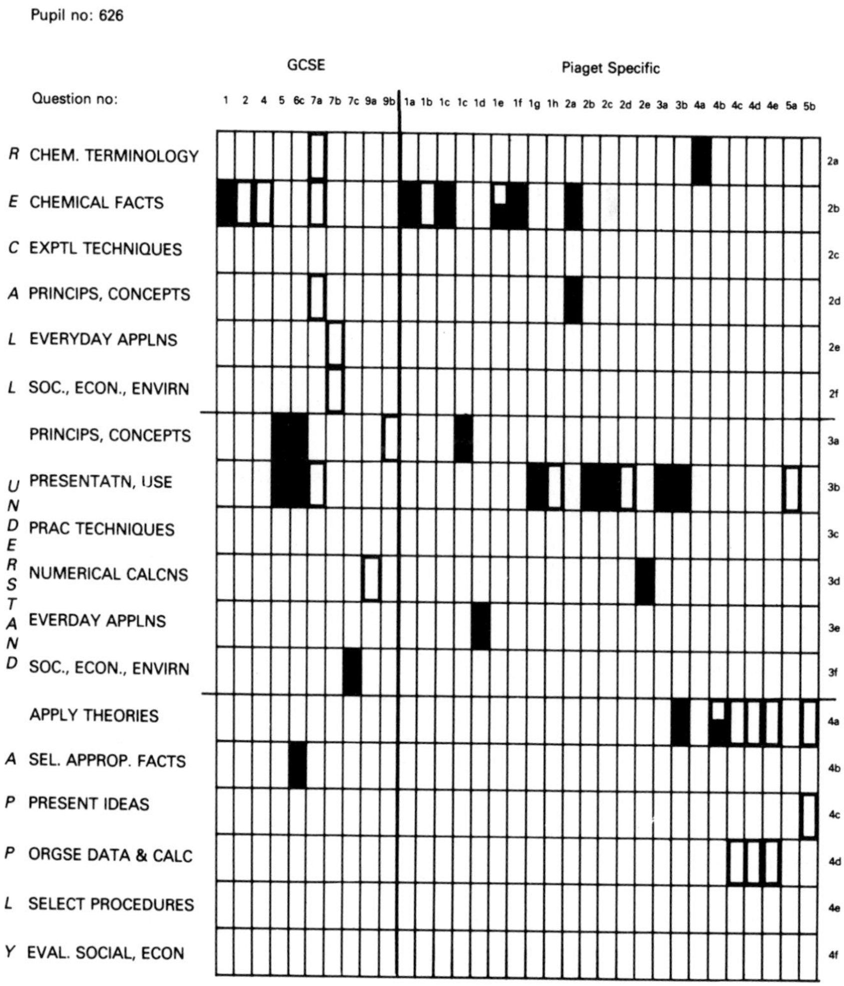

Figure 14.4.8   GCSE objective analysis

Pupil no: 623

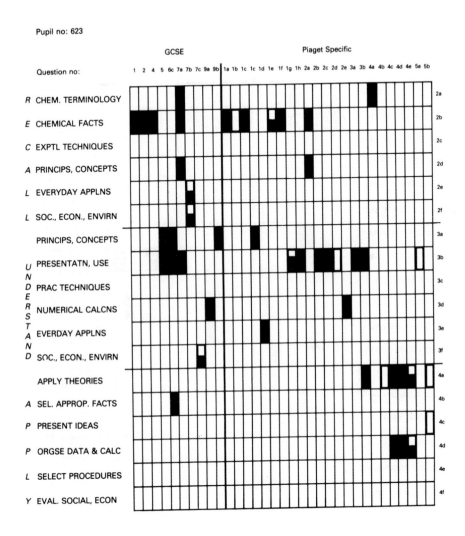

Figure 14.4.9   GCSE objective analysis

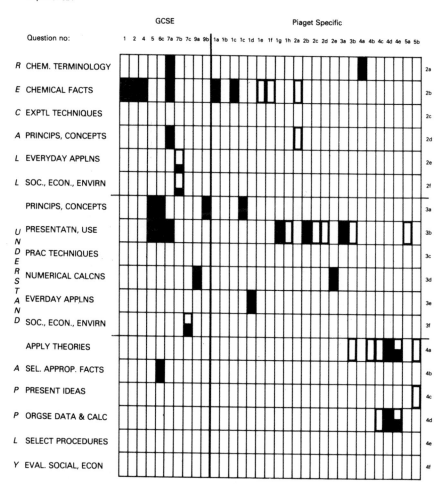

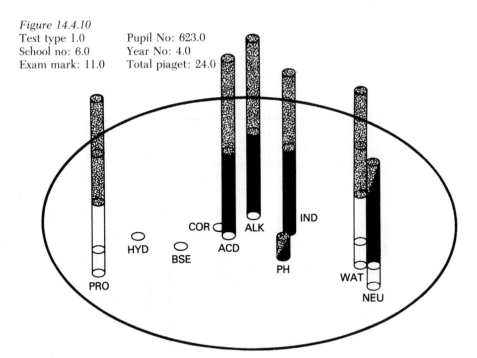

Figure 14.4.10
Test type 1.0   Pupil No: 623.0
School no: 6.0   Year No: 4.0
Exam mark: 11.0   Total piaget: 24.0

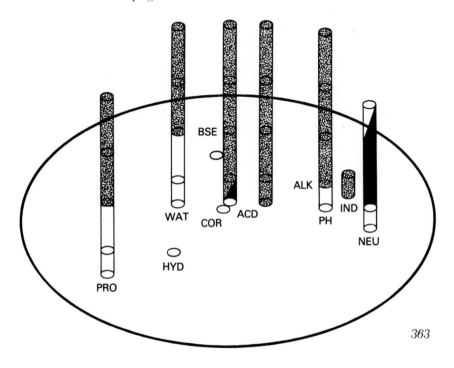

Figure 14.4.11
Test type 1.0   Pupil No: 624.0
School no: 6.0   Year No: 4.0
Exam mark: 5.5   Total piaget: 13.0

their sterling efforts we seem to be getting just as little information as with the previous CSE and 'O' level examinations.

One and a half centuries ago, Charles Colton warned that

> Examinations are formidable even to the best prepared, for the greatest fool can ask more than the wisest man can answer.

We must be careful in this country that we are not so foolish as to ask more in the way of assessment information than the wisest pupil can ever supply us with, and then scrabble this formidable demand into a single grade which gives less information than even the least curious pupil, parent or employer could wish for.

References

MATTHEWS, G.P., BROOK, V.G., ELIOT, G.P. and KHAN-GABDAOYR, T. (1985) 'Cognitive structure determinations as a tool in science teaching: Part 3 — Results', *European Journal of Science Education*, 7, 3, pp 263–79.

MATTHEWS, G.P., BROOK, V.G. and KHAN-GANDAPUR, T. (1984) 'Cognitive structure determinations as a tool in sceince teaching: Part 1 — A new method of creating concept maps', *European Journal of Science Education*, 6, 2, pp 169–77.

MATTHEWS, G.P., BROOK, V.G. and KHAN-GANDAPUR, T. (1984) 'Cognitive structure determinations as a tool in science teaching: Part 2–The measurement of Piaget-Specific levels', *European Journal of Science Education*, 6, 3, pp 289–97.

SHAYER, M. and ADEY, P. (1981) *Towards a Science of Science Teaching*, London, Heinemann.

Discussion (Reporter: Yehudit Eisen)

The audience was somewhat stunned by the complexity of detail presented. Nevertheless, the light this method showed on the issue of GCSE examining was acknowledged, and the questions asked were mainly for elucidation of detail, so that the relationship between pupil performances on Piagetian tasks and the GCSE test could be understood. The validity of the GCSE examination of chemistry studied was left quite in doubt.

Appendix: List of Particpants

Dr. Philip Adey,
Centre for Educational Studies,
Kings College London (KQC),
552 Kings Road,
London, SW10 OAU,
ENGLAND.

Professor Paul Black,
Centre for Educational Studies,
Kings College Lonon (KQC),
552 Kings Road,
London, SW10 OAU,
ENGLAND.

Dr. Joan Bliss,
Centre for Educational Studies,
Kings College London (KQC),
552 Kings Road,
London, SW10 OAU,
ENGLAND.

Trevor Bond,
Department of Pedagogics and
    Scientific Studies in Education,
James Cook University of North
    Queensland,
P.O. J.C.U.N.Q. Q 4811
    AUSTRALIA.

Ms. Angela Brook,
Centre for Studies in Science and
    Mathematics Education,
University of Leeds,
Leeds, LS2 9JT,
ENGLAND.

Professor Robbie Case,
CACS-OISE,
252 Bloor St. West,
Toronto,
CANADA, M5S IV6.

Dr. Guy Claxton,
Centre for Educational Studies,
Kings College London (KQC),
552 Kings Road,
London, SW10 QAU,
ENGLAND.

Dr. Ana Domingos,
Departamento de Educação de
    Ciêncis,
Univesidade de Lisboa,
R. Ernesto Vasconcelos,
Edificio C 1–3 Piso,
1700 Lisboa, PORTUGAL.

Dr. Rosalind Driver,
Centre for Studies in Science and
    Mathematics Education,
University of Leeds,
Leeds, LS2 9JT,
ENGLAND.

Dr. Reinders Duit,
IPN — Gebaude,
Olshausenstrasse 62,
D-2300 Kiel 1,
FEDERAL REPUBLIC OF
    GERMANY.

Dr. Yehudit Eisen,
c/o Room 2.208,
Centre for Educational Studies,
Kings College London (KQC),
552 Kings Rd,
London, SW10 OAU,
ENGLAND.

Professor Peter Fensham,
Faculty of Education,
Monash University,
Clayton, Victoria 3168,
AUSTRALIA.

Ms. Rufina Gutierrez,
I.E.P.S.
Velazquez, 114,
28006 Madrid,
SPAIN.

Dr. Jarkko Hautämaki,
Finnish Science Centre,
Department of Education,
Kielotic 7A 1300 Vantaa,
FINLAND.

Dr. John Head,
Centre for Educational Studies,
Kings College London (KQC),
552 Kings Road,
London, SW10 OAU,
ENGLAND

Dr. Ann C. Howe,
Department of Mathematics and
    Science Education,
326 Poe Hall, North Carolina State
    University,
Raleigh,
NC 27695–7801,
USA.

Professor Ehud Jungwirth,
Department of Agricultural
    Education
Hebrew University of Jerusalem,
P O Box 12, Rehovot 76–100,
ISRAEL.

Dr. A. I. Kamara,
Njala University College,
University of Sierre Leone,
PMB Freetown,
SIERRA LEONE.

Ms. Valda Kirkwood,
Science Education Research Unit,
University of Waikato,
Private Bag, Hamilton,
NEW ZEALAND.

Dr. Fritz Kubli,
Bäulistrasse 26,
CH-8049,
Zürich,
SWITZERLAND.

Dr. Peter Kutnick,
Education Development Building,
University of Sussex,
Falmer, Brighton, BNI 9RG,
ENGLAND.

Professor Anton E. Lawson,
Department of Zoology,
Arizona State University,
Tempe, Arizona 85287,
USA.

Dr. Pieter Licht,
Vakgroep Didaktiek Natuurkunde,
Boelelaan 1081,
1081 MV Amsterdam,
THE NETHERLANDS.

Dr. Piet Lÿnse,
Fysisch Laboratorium, Didaktick,
Postbus 80.000,
3508 TA Utrecht,
THE NETHERLANDS

Dr. G. Peter Matthews,
Deptartment of Environmental
    Sciences,
Plymouth Polytechnic,
Drake Circus,
Plymouth, PL4 8AA,
ENGLAND.

Professor J.D. Novak,
    Department of Education,
404 Roberts Hall,
Cornell University,
Ithaca, NY 14853,
USA.

Professor Jon Ogborn,
University of London Institute of
    Education,
20 Bedford Way,
London, WC1H OAL,
ENGLAND.

Ms. Anne O'Sullivan,
15 Shalimar Lodge,
Horn Lane,
Acton,
London, W3 6PR,
ENGLAND.

Dr. Dimitris Psillos,
Solid State Section 313–1,
Physics Department,
University of Thessaloniki,
Thessaloniki 54006,
GREECE.

Dr. Charles Ryan,
King Alfred's College,
Winchester, SO22 4NR,
ENGLAND.

Professor Hans-Jürgen Schmidt,
Universität Dortmund,
Abt. Chemie/Didaktik der Chemie,
Otto Hahn Strasse,
D-4600 Dortmund 50,
FEDERAL REPUBLIC OF
    GERMANY.

Dr. Marie-Geneviève Séré,
L.I.R.E.S.P.T,
Université Paris VII,
2 Place Jussieu,
75221 Paris CEDEX O5,
FRANCE.

Dr. Michael Shayer,
Centre for Educational Studies,
Kings College London (KQC),
552 Kings Road,
London, SW10 OAU,
ENGLAND.

Dr. Mary Simpson,
Northern College,
Hilton Place,
Aberdeen,
Scotland, AB9 1FA.

Dr. Svein Sjøberg,
Centre for Science Education,
Oslo University,
PB 1124, Blindern,
0317 Oslo 3,
NORWAY.

Dr. Leslie Smith,
Department of Educational
    Research,
University of Lancaster,
Lancaster, LA1 4YL,
ENGLAND.

Dr. Joan Solomon,
University of Oxford,
Department of Educational Studies,
15 Norham Gardens,
Oxford, OX2 6PY,
ENGLAND.

David Squires,
Centre for Educational Studies,
Kings College London (KQC),
552 Kings Road,
London, SW10 OAU,
ENGLAND.

Dr. Ruth Stavy,
School of Education,
Tel-Aviv University,
Tel-Aviv 66978,
ISRAEL.

Professor Pinchas Tamir,
The Amos de Shalit Science
    Teaching Centre,
Hebrew University of Jerusalem,
ISRAEL.

Dr. Poul Thomsen,
Centre for Studies in Physics
    Education,
Institute of Physics,
University of Aarhus,
DK-8000 Aarhus C,
DENMARK.

Mr. M. Vanderlocht,
Tiensestraat 115,
3000 Leuven,
BELGIUM.

Mrs. M. Vandermeulen,
Tiensestreat 115,
3000 Leuven,
BELGIUM.

Drs. Anthonius van der Valk,
Physics Education Department,
Ryks Universiteit Utrecht,
P.O. Box 80.008,
3508TA Utrecht,
FEDERAL REPUBLIC OF
    GERMANY.

Dr. Michael Watts,
Department Science Education,
Whitelands College,
Roehampton Institute of Higher
    Education,
West Hill,
London, SW15 3SN,
ENGLAND.

Mme. Annick Weil-Barais,
L.I.R.E.S.P.T.
Université Paris VII,
2 Place Jussieu,
75221 Pairs CEDEX O5,
FRANCE.

Mrs. Denise Whitelock,
Deptartment of Science Education,
University of London Institute of
    Education,
20 Bedford Way,
London, WC1H OAL,
ENGLAND.

Ms. Carolyn Yates,
3 Copthurst Cottage,
Birchin Lane,
Whittle-Le-Woods,
Chorley, Lancashire,
ENGLAND.

Name Index

Subject Index